M000239472

John Dee's Occultism

SUNY series in Western Esoteric Traditions
David Appelbaum, editor

John Dee's Occultism

Magical Exaltation through Powerful Signs

György E. Szőnyi

STATE UNIVERSITY OF NEW YORK PRESS

Published by
State University of New York Press, Albany

© 2004 State University of New York

For information, contact State University of New York Press, Albany, NY
www.sunypress.edu

Production by Michael Haggett
Marketing by Anne M. Valentine

Library of Congress Cataloging-in-Publication Data

Szőnyi, György Endre.
    John Dee's occultism : magical exaltation through powerful signs / György
Endre Szőnyi.
        p. cm.—(SUNY series in Western esoteric traditions)   .
    ISBN 0-7914-6223-4 (alk. paper)
    1. Dee, John, 1527–1608. 2. Symbolism. 3. Magic—History. 4. Occultism—
History. 5. Renaissance. I. Title. II. Series.

BF1598.D5S98 2004
133.'092—dc22   2003069327

10 9 8 7 6 5 4 3 2 1

Contents

Illustrations

Preface

My attention was drawn to the fascinating topic of Renaissance magic and occult symbolism by the books of Frances Yates, more than twenty-five years ago. Her *Giordano Bruno and the Hermetic Tradition* (1964) and other works belonging to the intellectual tradition of the Warburg school introduced me to those aspects of Renaissance cultural history, which were almost *terra incognita* in contemporary Hungarian scholarship. I must emphasize "almost" because—in spite of all ideological pressure and limitations—I had professors, Bálint Keserű and Tibor Klaniczay, who were aware of the trends of intellectual history and called my attention to these works. It was they—and two other teachers, László Vekerdi and Bálint Rozsnyai—who encouraged me to summarize this excitingly new image of the Renaissance in a small book which was published in Hungarian under the title *Secret Sciences and Superstitions: Questions of Fifteenth through Seventeenth Century Cultural History* (Szőnyi 1978). The topic has been haunting me ever since.

My early studies were stimulated by the question: how had it been possible that the so-called man-centered Renaissance also witnessed the golden age of magic? I was surprised to see how closely magic intertwined with the early modern scientific ideas on the one hand and with the premodern world picture on the other. I became even more surprised, however, to realize that magic did not disappear with the collapse of its foundation, the organic world picture. Magical approaches and magical symbolisation are present even in our contemporary world, and it is a challenging task to trace the roots of this tradition with the methodological equipment of the modern intellectual historian. As I see them today, these questions cannot be fully answered on the basis of the objective or positivistic techniques of traditional approaches to the history of science. We also need help from religious studies and historical anthropology. The concept of self-fashioning also seems useful, leading us, to some extent, to the territory of psychology as well.

The primary subject matter of this book is the magic of John Dee, of whom I also became aware through the works of Frances Yates. His character seems a suitable focus for researching Renaissance occultism because his career and works clearly demonstrate the various sides of this complex phenomenon. His connections with Central Europe, at the same time, justify why I, a scholar from Hungary, choose him as an anchor for my presentation of early modern magical symbolism.

A number of heterogeneous topics meet in my book, but there is a connecting link which, according to my intention, provides coherence to my treatment. This is, the ideology of *exaltatio*, that is, the deification of man, which I see as the intellectual foundation of magic, a foundation that even today validates magical aspiration and its scholarly research. I also argue that it was the desire for *exaltatio* which framed and tied together the otherwise amazingly heterogeneous thoughts and activities of John Dee. I give a definition of *exaltatio* in relation to magic in the chapters under the heading "Definitions." The following two parts of my book operate with different methodologies. After the Introduction, in the chapters of the second part entitled "Input 'In many bokes and sundry languages . . . ,' " I analyse a selection of eminent magical texts—all in the possession of Dee according to his library catalogue. Although these texts were all known to Dee, my aim is not simply to offer a review of his sources. As new historicism and related recent trends angrily rejected the positivistic ideals of source-hunting, I also think that what needs to be grasped here is the complex and often paradoxical interdependence of cultural and ideological inclinations and appropriations. In this section I disregard the chronology of Dee's intellectual development, and instead present the ingredients of the ideology of magic according to the chronology of European cultural history. The fact that Dee absorbed ancient, medieval, and Renaissance lores in a particular order and that his thought became composed of different layers of high and popular culture will become meaningful in the last part of the book, entitled "Output 'Glyms or Beame of Radicall Truthes.' " There I revisit Dee's works, following the order in which he wrote them, from his early scientific treatises to his most voluminous body of writings, the spiritual diaries or, as he called them, the *Libri mysteriorum*.

As for my intended methodology, textual interpretation will be complemented by historical approaches that touch upon various subtexts and contexts, including the history of mentality, historical anthropology, and comparative religion. I hope my chapters dealing with "Dee and the Interpretive Community" will highlight a little explored aspect of Dee studies. Here I connect the magical program to its psycho-sociological and politico-ideological contexts, using concepts such as patronage, self-fashioning, and techniques of identifying the Other. Some of these chap-

ters will deal with East-Central Europe, since this is the territory where
I might offer unique information to Western readers.

My approach is markedly hermeneutical, so I cannot neglect historiography, the trends of interpretation that preceded mine. The often
heated debates of the last decades (over hermeticism or over the "Yates
theses") did not always concentrate solely on the historical questions.
Quite understandably, they also served as exercise fields for the transition
from modern to postmodern historical and cultural theory. One of my
objectives is to juxtapose the results of classical (that is the Warburgian-
Yatesian) intellectual history with the newer approaches and see what is
still useful in the classical material, which, in the controversy related to
the history of science, has almost entirely been discarded. We certainly
cannot overlook two lessons of the post-structuralist philosophy of history: 1) We have to accept that historicist reconstruction is nothing else
than an ideological fiction, so whatever conclusion we arrive at, we cannot present it outside the *hic et nunc* position of us, the interpreters.
2) It also appears today that the efforts of the great intellectual historians
to boil down each epoch or period to a single great leitmotif of ideas or
social structure has been a failure and has led to (self)deception. Although it is a natural drive of any researcher to operate with abstractions
and categories suitable for generalizations, one must be extremely careful
not to blur the distinction among often contrary tendencies and the
variety of opinions, desires, and ideologies—the evidence of otherness in
the process of explanation and abstraction.

This book incorporates the material presented in two of my previous
books on Dee, one written in Hungarian (Szőnyi 1998), the other in
Italian (Szőnyi 2004). It should not be thought, though, that the three
books are identical, related to each other through mechanical translation.
I wrote the present book directly in English, having in mind the interests
and needs of English or American readers, which differ from those of the
Hungarians or Italians. I should also add that since the completion of the
three books, a lot of things have happened in Dee scholarship. In fact,
since the 1988 publication of Nicholas Clulee's monograph on Dee's
natural philosophy, Dee studies have been booming, producing new
evidence, new editions, new approaches, and new monographs almost
every year. My present book is intended to represent Dee research as it
stands in around 2000, and I am also aware of the fact that parallel with
my work, other books are also being written or have just appeared.

Acknowledgments

I have already mentioned some of my Hungarian masters but here I should also acknowledge the tremendous inspiration which the personal acquaintance of Dame Frances Yates meant to me. I met her for the first time as a young university student, coming from the East, thanks to a three-week British Council study trip, and naively ringing the doorbell of the Warburg Institute. She was most ready to meet me downstairs at the reception and then lead me into that "Temple of Renaissance Scholarship," as I emotionally fancied it. Later on, I was privileged to be her personal guide during her last lecture tour abroad, which led to Hungary in the summer of 1981. Today I look at these experiences with a more sober eye but I think one should never entirely recover from these rites of initiation. Next to her, among English scholars, I owe most to Robert J. W. Evans (the exemplary historian and philologist, in many ways the opposite of Frances Yates) who encouraged and helped me since the beginning of my studies.

My academic worldview was significantly formed during those occasions I spent on various scholarships near the historical sources and in the inspiring communities of colleagues. I would like to mention among the following institutions, whose staff always offered cordial assistance Biblioteka Jagiellońska (Cracow), Biblioteka na Piasku (Wrocław), Bodleian Library (Oxford), British Library (London), Collegium Budapest, Folger Library (Washington, D.C.), Herzog-August Bibliothek (Wolfenbüttel), Huntington Library (San Marino, California), Library of Congress (Washington, D.C.), Nationalbibliothek (Vienna), Statný Archiv (Třeboň), Somogyi Library (Szeged), and University Library (Hull). Among the many colleagues whom I met in these libraries and other research institutions I particularly thank the following: Michael J. B. Allen, Frank Baron, Enikő Basa-Molnár, Marianna D. Birnbaum, Audrey and Clifford Davidson, Joscelyn Godwin, George Gomori, Werner Gundersheimer, Richard Helgerson, Michael H. Keefer, Gábor Klaniczay, Nati H. Krivatsy,

Stanton J. Linden, Wolf-Dieter Müller-Jahncke, Michael O'Connell, David A. Richardson, Lech Szczucki. The completion of this book was made possible by generous grants of the U.S. Fulbright Fellowship Program, the IREX and Mellon Foundations, the TEMPUS Program of the European Union and, most recently, an Alfried Krupp fellowship of Collegium Budapest.

Among Hungarian friends and colleagues who were willing to read my writings and discuss my ideas with me, I would name only my wife, Ildikó Kristóf, herself a historian, who not only gave good ideas but also excercised a benevolent control on my style and expression.

One of the most difficult moments when one finishes the manuscript of a book is to find cordial and attentive readers to look through the text. This help is especially important when one has written the book in a language other than his/her native tongue. I am especially grateful for those who have read parts or the whole of my manuscript and were ready to polish my English as well as suggest possible improvements in my argumentation: first and foremost Urszula Szulakowska, then Håkan Håkansson, Stanton J. Linden, Michal Pober, and Marvin J. Overby who kindly helped with copyediting.

Special thanks to my sister, Etelka, who designed the Hungarian version of my book and who for many years provided important support for my work. I offer this book to the memory of my mother and father.

Part 1

Definitions

1

Principles and Demarcations

THE CHALLENGE OF THE ESOTERIC

The Magus (or as some might call him, the Magician) is entering his laboratory. His retorts are full of boiling, bubbling liquids; his mind is on the boil too, nursing dreams, noble or mad ambitions of omniscience, omnipotence, eternal life, and the ability to create gold or synthetic life—the famous homunculus. As the Great Work comes to a halt, some supernatural help is needed. The Magus now turns to God, praying for more strength, or, resorting to illicit assistance, calls on Satan. Often he is confronted with other men, friends or adversaries, dilettante antiquarians or greedy princes, who look at him with expectation or awe, who try to stop him or urge him to further efforts—but certainly cannot follow him on his dangerous path towards the unknown and forbidden. Almost invariably the end is failure. The Magus is punished for his arrogant self-conceit, or the Opus Magnum is disturbed by intruding bores—the retort blows up or the Adept cannot endure the presence of the Devil—until finally the Magus is paradigmatically killed among the flames of his laboratory.

The above narrative has roots as old as literature; the archetypal story of the magician gained cosmic significance in the Renaissance and has been popular ever since. Is this a story taken from life or merely derived from the pressure of literary conventions and the demands of the reading public? Does it follow the logic of scientific investigation, mixing experimentation with the supernatural? Is this all allegory and parable, or does it have a more direct relevance? One might be surprised that this literary framework has even passed into twentieth-century fiction, virtually un-shaken by the development of the natural sciences and the disqualification of magic as a scientific discipline. Should we then see this literary phe-nomenon as a reaction against the self-assuredness of the sciences? Is there any way of reconciling the rational-scientific way of thinking and the magical-occult worldview?

Questions like the above may bother the reader who finds himself in the web of modern fiction focusing on the theme of the magus, such as Thomas Mann's *Doctor Faustus*, Marguerite Yourcenar's *The Abyss*, Robertson Davies's *What's Bred in the Bone*, Umberto Eco's *Foucault's Pendulum*. The list could be extended ad infinitum. Looking at these novels of esoterica, we can clearly see the fascination of modern writers with the culture and world picture of the Renaissance, even if they place their plot in a contemporary setting. Due to the appeal of the sixteenth century, these magus figures paradigmatically seem to be variations either on the character of the historical, legendary Faust, perhaps the most famous black magician who ever lived, or his contemporary, the white magus-scientist Paracelsus. In fact, the hero of this book, the English magus-mathematician John Dee also offers himself as a suitable model for such characters. What is more, there is a growing set of modern novels in which Dee features as the main or secondary but nevertheless key character. One could start with Gustav Meyrink's *The Angel of the West Window* (1928) and more recently with Eco's *Foucault's Pendulum* (1987) or Peter Ackroyd's *The House of Dr. Dee* (1993).[1]

This increasing interest in Dee as a magus—and one should take into consideration the whole spectrum of publications between the above mentioned fictional works and the newly published scholarly monographs (such as Sherman 1995 and Harkness 1999), the manuals on Dee's Enochian magic (e.g., Laycock 1994), or the interest in his angelic con-ferences (cf. Fenton's edition, Dee 1998)—should hopefully justify yet another book on Dee's magic, this time focusing on his occultism as a self-contained discipline, although nevertheless situated, as Nicholas Clulee (1988) suggested, "between science and religion."

The word *magic* makes one associate a variety of things which may have little in common, except perhaps the atmosphere of secrecy, some mysterious elements, and, above all, the human will to control and manipulate the rationally incomprehensible sphere of life. Intervening in the supernatural world may happen in different ways and with different intentions: with pious or wicked purposes, with religious zeal or with a scientific interest, a philosophical or a folkloric foundation with guidance from theory or from rituals. There was a time when enlightened scholars would speak about the disappearance of magical superstitions as a desired result of the accumulation of knowledge and the development of sciences. Even nineteenth-century anthropologists, such as Edward B. Tylor and James Frazer, would create a scholarly paradigm assuming a linear development from magic through religion to science.[2] These expectations, in fact, have not been fulfilled so far, and by now cultural theory and the social sciences have virtually given up the hope. One should add that it has also become unusual to mechanically identify magic and the occult with scanty superstitions.

Trying to map the place of magic in the complex of human culture, E. M. Butler claimed that she did not want to define it in any restrictive way as "pseudo-science," or "pretended art," or "debased religion" (1980, 2). Instead, she approached magic as an independent, self-contained discipline that naturally connects to other areas of human intellectual activity. This standpoint locates Butler among those intellectual historians who in this century step by step broke with the views of patronizing positivist anthropology that labeled magic as outdated irrational misapprehension. The seriously focused scientific interest in magic, however, was only the first step of a new understanding. It did not question the notion originating in the seventeenth-century paradigm shift of the Scientific Revolution, according to which human thinking had two irreconcilable and separate tracks, the discursive-rationalistic way of science and the mystical-irrational way of magic.

It was especially the opposing movements of Romanticism and positivism around the middle of the last century that emphasized this fatal antagonism. The scientists interpreted esoteric attitudes as a kind of primitive phase in the development of mankind, which, in the course of intellectual progress, necessarily had to give way to logical thinking and the experimental sciences. The adepts of the spiritual approach, on the other hand, excluded discursive logic and historical thinking from their field. Let us compare, for example, two opposing early nineteenth-century opinions:

> The improvements that have been effected in natural philosophy have by degrees convinced the enlightened part of mankind that the material universe is every where subject to laws, fixed in their weight, measure, and duration, capable of the most exact calculation, and which in no case admit of variation and exception. Beside this, mind, as well as matter, is subject to fixed laws; and thus every phenomenon and occurrence around us is rendered a topic for the speculation of sagacity and

foresight. Such is the creed which science has universally prescribed to the judicious and reflecting among us.

It was otherwise in the infancy and less mature state of human knowledge. The chain of causes and consequences was yet unrecognized; and events perpetually occurred, for which no sagacity that was then in being was able to assign an original. Hence men felt themselves habitually disposed to refer many of the appearances with which they were conversant to the agency of invisible intelligences. (Godwin 1834, 1–2)

At about the same time as William Godwin's proclamation of scientism, Mary Atwood was already working on her voluminous summary of esoteric philosophy, which was finally anonymously published in 1850. Due to a religious revelation and a moral panic, she later considered her book too dangerous for the general public and took great pains to suppress the edition. The text has, however, survived and provides us with an interesting insight into that mode of thinking that seems to have changed so remarkably little from Hermes Trismegistus through Paracelsus, Jakob Boehme, and Swedenborg to Atwood herself, Rudolf Steiner, Madame Blavatsky, and indeed to many of our own contemporaries. Speaking about alchemy, Atwood asserted its reality as follows: "But many things have in like manner been considered impossible which increasing knowledge has proved true. . . ." This may sound nearly like scientism but the second part of the sentence touches upon the theme which is common in all esoteric thinking:

> . . . and others which still to common sense appear fictitious were believed in former times, when faith was more enlightened and the sphere of vision open to surpassing effects. Daily observation even now warns us against setting limits to nature. [. . .] The philosophy of modern times, more especially that of the present day, consists in experiment and such scientific researches as may tend to ameliorate our social condition, or be otherwise useful in contributing to the ease and indulgences of life; whereas in the original acceptation, philosophy had quite another sense: it signified the Love of Wisdom. (Atwood 1918, v–vii)

Clinging to her counterscientific and irrational principle, she did not see much use in employing a systematic historical approach when studying and explaining the hermetic philosophy. Her following statement clearly shows the romantic disgust with the then also fashionable piecemeal positivism:

> Nothing, perhaps, is less worthy or more calculated to distract the mind from points of real importance than this very question of temporal ori-

gin, which, when we have taken all pains to satisfy and remember, leaves us no wiser in reality than we were before. (Atwood 1918, 3)

Looking back to the nineteenth century, we can observe that the more the positivist enthusiasts of the scientific and industrial revolutions asserted the notion of linear progress and heralded man's victory over nature, the more the adepts and mystics became imbued with the search for forgotten, hermetic knowledge.

From Science History to Cultural Anthropology

I want to make clear from the outset that unlike Mary Atwood, I do think is vital to situate our discourse in history. Consequently, when writing a book on the intellectual patterns of Renaissance magic and its representative, John Dee, I find it important to reflect on the historiography of the subject by looking at the intertextually connected chain of interpretations offered in the nineteenth and twentieth centuries.

Modern metadisciplines, in the humanities but even in the natural sciences, have been expressing a growing suspicion of claims for absolute validity. In cultural theory, weighty arguments have been put forward to subvert the earlier scholarly self-assurance. To begin with, post-structuralism on the whole (from hermeneutics through deconstructivism, reader-response theory, and new historicism, whether idealist or Marxist) has rejected the basic assumption of old historicism that the past can and should be faithfully reconstructed. These trends have also increasingly considered the interpretation of historical "facts" as a kind of fictionalized narrative, a discourse, that is constructed in the field between the traditions in the possession of the narrator on the one hand, and by the often antagonistic individual and community interests at work on the other. In the light of Thomas Kuhn's propositions, it becomes particularly interesting to see the consequences of the above mentioned interpretive strategies in the history of science. The current propositions of social science theory have taught us to follow the principle: each fact or phenomenon has multiple sides and aspects and the same subject examined from different angles will produce different profiles. The problem is that our theory, even if we have one, will not be helpful in finding the ultimate correct interpretation. Thus, instead of enforcing selection and hierarchy over our subject, it seems desirable to introduce a polarity of viewpoints that will consider the *polyvalent* and *polysemic* character of each historical "fact."[3]

The historiography of Dee research faithfully mirrors the paradigm shift of historical and cultural theory. In his time John Dee was a respected scholar and although sometimes he was accused of being a "conjuror," even half a century after his death he was still remembered as "the wise doctor." The publication of his spiritual diaries by Meric Casaubon in 1659, however, especially in the light of the distrustful preface of the editor, gradually undermined his reputation and by the time of the Enlightenment he became considered, if at all, as a poor, credulous, and deluded philosopher who got stuck among the manipulations of his charlatan alchemist, Edward Kelly.[4]

Dee was not much mentioned then until the nineteenth century, when some historians unearthed his diaries and letters and, as part of a positivistic historical reconstruction of the Elizabethan age, published those (cf. Dee 1841, 1842, 1843, 1851, 1854, and 1880). While these papers were treated as important documents of their time, the evaluation of their author did not change, and the expressions "superstition," "delusion," and "obscure magic" were often used to describe him. Also the factual accounts of his life were mixed with anecdotes of dubious origin. It was not until 1909 that the first biography of Dee appeared by Charlotte Fell Smith. It gave a general picture about the Doctor, but since she was not a professional historian, much less a historian of science, Dee's scholarly activities were not treated in detail and his magic was interpreted hardly at all.

At that time the history of science had a teleological approach and only those achievements that pointed toward future developments of science were acknowledged. Everything else was dismissed as a failure or a dead end. With such a mentality the safest field from which to assess Dee's scholarship was that of geography and thus he earned an important place in E. G. R. Taylor's *Tudor Geography* (1930) and some generous mentions in F. R. Johnson's *Astronomical Thought in Renaissance England* (1937), especially as someone who, in his *Mathematicall Praeface,* usefully contributed to the creation of a mathematical vocabulary in the vernacular.

The situation had greatly changed by the middle of the century when, especially due to the research of the Warburg school (Franz Saxl, Paul Oskar Kristeller, Erwin Panofsky, Edgar Wind, and others), a radical reassessment of the intellectual climate of the Renaissance was undertaken. This new approach acknowledged the importance of the magical world picture in the "antechamber of the Enlightenment." The scholars working on this interpretation focused primarily on the neoplatonic revival of Ficino's Florentine Academy and its influence all over Europe in the first half of the sixteenth century. A typical fruit of this approach was D. P. Walker's monograph *Spiritual and Demonic Magic from Ficino to Campanella* (1958), which traced the development of neoplatonic magic in the works of Ficino, Pico della Mirandola, Agrippa, Giordano Bruno, and others. Walker belonged to the Warburg school; in fact, he was a member of the Warburg Institute of London, as was his famous colleague Dame Frances Yates. The latter was an extremely imaginative and erudite scholar who became receptive to the new interpretation of the Renaissance and developed it into an attractive and arresting vision that was soon to be known as the "Yates thesis." If one tries to summarize her thesis in a few sentences, the following model emerges. As Ernst Cassirer had already stated in his groundbreaking study on the Renaissance (*The Individual and the Cosmos*, 1963 [1927]), the most important philosophical innovation of that period had been the redefinition of man's place in the universe. The basic framework—the Great Chain of Being—remained more or less the same until the late seventeenth century when man's place was no longer seen as being fixed anymore. Instead he was imagined as capable of moving along the Chain of Being, either ennobling and elevating himself to the level of God, or degrading and associating with the brute beasts. Following the footsteps of Cassirer, Kristeller, and others, Yates came to the conclusion that the neoplatonic philosophers of the Renaissance developed the idea of man's elevation not only from the works of Plato and the Hellenistic neoplatonists, but also, in fact primarily, from the hermetic texts, attributed to the "thrice great" Hermes Trismegistus. The Yates thesis also implied that the Renaissance magus was a direct predecessor of the modern natural scientist because, as the *Corpus hermeticum* suggested, the magus could regain the ability to rule over nature that the first man had lost with the Fall. While the magi of the fifteenth and sixteenth centuries were mostly individual researchers, their seventeenth-century followers, as Yates proposed, came to the idea of collective work and formed secret societies, such as the Rosicrucians. For a while these ideas seemed to revolutionize our understanding of the early modern age and the birth of modern science. In such a context the magical ideas that had previously been discarded by intellectual historians now appeared to be important ingredients of human ambitions to understand and conquer nature.

The changing concepts of the Renaissance influenced the appreciation of John Dee, too. Already in 1952 historian I. R. F. Calder had written a Ph.D. dissertation in which he had contextualized Dee's magic as a neoplatonist theory. Although this thesis remained unpublished (today,

however, it is available on the internet), it inspired Frances Yates to include
Dee as a key figure in her narrative of the neoplatonic-hermetic Renaissance, and in fact Dee featured as a favorite character in all of her later
books (1964, 1972, 1979). As a climax of this trend, in 1972, Peter French,
a student of Frances Yates, wrote a full-size monograph devoted entirely to
Dee in which he characterized the English doctor as a prototype of the
Renaissance magus.

No matter how convincing the Yates thesis appeared and how eloquently it was presented by its author, by the mid-1970s critical refusals
could also be heard. The debate included questions of philological accuracy; for example, scholars could not agree to what extent the hermetic
texts influenced the magi of the sixteenth century, or to what extent
Frances Yates' conjectures on humanist and secret political links between
certain English intellectuals and the German Rosicrucians could be vali-
dated. One should remember that just in those years post-structuralism
started proposing serious revisions in the theoretical framework of the
study of intellectual history, and perhaps this turn of conceptualization
did the most for a new interpretation of John Dee.[5]

The post-structuralist historians started reproving intellectual historians for attempting to simplify history into great, overall patterns in
which differences and contradictions were neglected and overlooked for
the sake of the coherence of the "grand narratives." Yates was also suspected of having reduced those Renaissance magi to unproblematic cham-
pions of hermetic neoplatonism, when in fact more complicated, often
contradictory intellectual patterns should have been detected. In relation
to Dee, it was Nicholas Clulee who in 1988 ventured into writing with
the aim of displaying the wide spectrum of influences and programs at
work in the course of the career of the Doctor. Clulee rebuked the shared
concept of the Warburg/Yates school as follows:

> what is common to these works is that all approach Dee as a problem
> of finding the correct intellectual tradition into which he appears to fit,
> both as a way of making sense of his disparate and often difficult to
> understand works and activities and as a way of establishing his impor-
> tance by associating him with an intellectual context of recognized
> importance for sixteenth-century and later intellectual developments.
> (1988, 3)

In his own presentation Clulee has managed to establish a dynamic
picture as opposed to the more static previous image of the hermetic

magus. He also differentiated among various periods in Dee's career during which his intellectual outlook as well as the direction of his attention changed. Clulee particularly emphasized the medieval origins, such as al-Kindi and Roger Bacon, at the foundations of Dee's magical experiments.

The importance of the Yates/French interpretations lay in the recognition of magic as worthy of history of science investigations. They thus legitimized a preoccupation that had previously been considered mere obscurantism. Building on this legitimation of magic as a focus of inquiry, Clulee highlighted the diachronic reorientation during Dee's career and brought into the discussion the medieval roots of sixteenth century magic and science that had been overshadowed by the Yatesian enthusiasm for neoplatonic hermeticism.[6] The next phase in the course of Dee studies was heralded by William Sherman's monograph of 1995, *The Politics of Reading and Writing in the English Renaissance*, in which the author revealed a synchronic multiplicity in Dee's diverse interests and activities. If one contrasts the last three important opinions on Dee in modern scholarship—that of Yates/French, Clulee, and Sherman—one sees that each of them has contributed at least one important proposal to our understanding of Renaissance magic and its famous English practicioner. While looking at this historiographical line, we see a direction of scholarship moving from a somewhat static and simplistic interpretation of "Dee as an English magus" toward a more complex contextualization in intellectual history, in which elements of discontinuity have become emphasized and in which the originally proposed "master narrative" has become subverted by more and more—often conflicting and contradictory—subtexts.

It is interesting to notice to what extent the different orientations of scholarship determined even the possible range of questions and subject areas which a work on Dee could examine. As is well known, in his early career the Doctor had a humanistic orientation and concentrated on mathematics, but from the 1580s he gave up these endeavors and almost entirely involved himself with angel magic, or in his own terminology "angelic conversations." Researchers have been perplexed by the apparently sudden turn which transformed the venerable scientist into an eccentric enthusiast. Approaches from the viewpoint of the history of science—which, until recently constituted the majority of Dee scholarship—found this phenomenon difficult to come to terms with, and at best a superficial explanation was advanced, according to which the humanist became disappointed with the rational principles and logic of science and—not unlike Doctor Faustus, although avoiding the direct contact with Satan—could only imagine achieving his intellectual goals with the help of supernatural powers.[7] Very few efforts have been made to embrace both Dee's scientific experiments and his angel magic in their entirety and interconnectedness, especially given that such an examination would seem to promise little benefit for historians of science. Until recently, interpreters of Dee's magic have tried to underline the importance of magic as a vital precondition to the scientific revolution, and with this consideration in mind, Frances Yates invented the term "Rosicrucian Enlightenment" (cf. Yates 1968 and 1972).

As I have mentioned, the Yates thesis was challenged by historians of science, and although Clulee (1988) and Sherman (1995) have to some extent successfully restored Dee's place in the distinguished portrait gallery of science history, this restoration hardly includes his magic. My suggestion is to shift the focus of interest from the history of science to cultural anthropology and the history of mentality, inverting the usual question—"which elements of Dee's complex and largely unscientific ideas contributed to the development of modern science?"—by asking "in what way Dee's scientific activity inspired his visionary and occult program?" Seeking the company of angels may seem an eccentric monomania for the enlightened researcher; indeed, some historians have even suggested that Dee had become mentally ill (cf. Heilbronn, in Dee 1978, 15 and 43). By contrast, anthropologists and historians of mentality have learned how deep the roots of occult thinking were in the world picture of the sixteenth century.[8] Among the most recent contributions to Dee scholarship, it is Debora Harkness whose approach seems to combine the historical and the anthropological concerns and thus her interpretation runs quite close to my own. Although I became acquainted with her book of 1999 only at the stage when I had nearly completed my monograph, I shall reflect on her suggestions in the following discussion.

Looking at the relationship between magic and science in the early modern age, it would be a simplification to claim, as Frances Yates did, that Renaissance neoplatonist magic, let alone hermeticism, fostered the scientific revolution of the sixteenth and seventeenth centuries in a direct way. On the other hand, it is possible to say that in the works (as well as in the minds) of Dee and his fellow scientists/magi, layers of discursive logic and irrationalism, scientific thinking and occultism, happily coexisted in a variety of ways that would be dangerous to generalize. Each case should be approached individually: some of them entertained magical concepts that complemented their scientific thinking (Giordano Bruno, Francis Bacon); in others the two orientations showed an almost total discontinuity (Johannes Kepler, Isaac Newton); in still other cases science and magic were intermixed in a somewhat disorderly concoction (Paracelsus), and in Dee's case it seems that his magical ideas totally absorbed his scientific orientation, although in his middle career one can still see independently functioning subsystems in his thought (e.g., his interest in geography or his ideas about the publicity of science). To handle such a complexity of ideology and ideas, one needs to analyze the intellectual and the psychological constitution of the investigated subject as well as the philosophical and social contexts in which he was situated. At present, it seems to me, historical anthropology and post-structuralist iconology can offer the most fruitful methodologies to cope with this task.

THE POST-COMMUNIST PERSPECTIVE

In the year 2000, what can a scholar coming from Eastern Europe offer? Perhaps a few sentences about the background of my Dee research may be appropriate here. As I have already pointed out, I consider the historiographical aspect of great importance, especially to monitor the transitions that led from the negative attitude of the last century's positivists to the understanding of today's historians. For East-Central Europeans this process is particularly significant, since the establishment of officially enforced Marxist theory after World War II has made us particularly sensitive to nuances of theoretical grounding. Since state-promoted Marxism was almost exclusively interested in economic and social history with an emphasis on class struggle and a typological prefiguration of future revolutions, historical research in several fields became cut off from the main trends of Western scholarship during the 1950s and 1960s. It happened particularly in intellectual history, but also in the history of mentality and historical anthropology. The examination of areas that would testify to the inherent role of a "superstitious" misconception such as magic in a "progressive" age like the Renaissance was at best not encouraged in the centers of historical research and the syllabi of higher education listed more important issues on the agenda—such as the fight of the repressed for a better life and for liberation from ideological manipulation—than the investigation of the stubborn persistence of premodern ideas. Interestingly, this homophonic Marxism suppressed even the reception of alternative Marxist concepts. Thus, not only intellectual history and the analysis of cultural symbolization remained beyond the horizon of our historians, but so did the works of radical writers such as the early Foucault, whose works otherwise would have been available from the 1960s.

Although Renaissance research in Hungary was less affected by the official party ideology than other, more contemporary fields of history, the elimination of the mentioned white spots could only start in the mid-1970s, and only with small steps. Scholars such as the late Tibor Klaniczay did a lot to disassociate period styles from the labels "progressive" or "reactionary," thus enabling, for example, a balance within Baroque research in general, or an examination of the shadowy side of the Renaissance under the banner of Mannerism (cf. Klaniczay 1977). In this engagement the propositions of the Yates school came in more than handy and greatly refreshed the research topics as well as the vocabulary of our Renaissance scholarship. It should be noted here that the newly discovered intellectual history in East-Central Europe became not only a research tool and a theoretical orientation but also a means of ideological resistance against the grim, official party line. I set about examining John Dee and Renaissance occultism with this motivation in mind.

From the early 1980s, as a young scholar, I was applying for scholarships to the West with the intention of learning more not only about the facts, which were not readily available in Hungary, but also about the methods and theories that seemed so balanced, objective, and wide in spectrum compared with what was practiced at home. Without a party membership, of course, it was not easy to get such a stipend. After a brief visit in 1984, I finally received a Fulbright grant which in 1986 enabled me to get to the sources in the Folger and the Huntington Libraries.

One can imagine my enthusiasm arriving at those shrines of learning I had heard so much about, and also how stunned I was in realizing that the approach I wanted to follow was just going out of fashion. It was enough to buy Raman Selden's *The Reader's Guide to Contemporary Literary Theory* and see that as opposed to twenty-eight pages on Marxist theories (the book has 149 pages) no (sub)chapter was devoted to any form of intellectual history. The preface explained: "I have not tried to give a comprehensive picture of modern critical theory. I have omitted, for example, myth criticism, which has a long and various history, and includes the work of such writers as Gilbert Murray, James Frazer, Carl Jung, and Northrop Frye. It seemed to me that myth criticism has not entered the main stream of academic or popular culture, and has not challenged received ideas."[9] A look at the programs of talks and seminars at the libraries where I spent my time warned me that with new historicism and feminism on the offensive, I could hardly hope for sympathetic support towards my interests. I witnessed an enormous divergence between the nature of the bulk of the books available at those libraries and the scholarly discourse I came across in the lobbies or during coffee breaks.[10]

This abrupt paradigm shift in literary scholarship can be well illustrated by Norman Rabkin's words, which, although they refer to Shakespeare criticism, can easily be extrapolated to most researched authors and literary periods:

> Only yesterday it was widely assumed that the critic's job was to expound the meaning of literary works. Today, under an extraordinarily swift and many fronted attack, that consensus is in ruins. The reader-response theories argued in various ways by such critics as Stanley Fish and Norman Holland call into question the power of an imaginative work to elicit a uniform response from its audience; Jacques Derrida and his deconstructive allies see language and art so intractably self-reflexive as to be incapable of analyzable significance; Harold Bloom argues that all reading is misreading, that one reads well only to find oneself in the mirror.[11]

Since the time of its publication, Rabkin's examples have become outdated in the context of the present post-structuralist vogue, but his diagnosis still has the same startling validity. The problem is still not "why there is so much bad criticism," but "much more importantly: why is much of the best criticism vulnerable to attacks of the new critical trends, so that the kinds of theoretical rejection of critical study I mentioned at the outset have been able to find so ready an audience?" (Rabkin 1981, 4).

From 1986 onward I have developed an understanding of a great many of the concerns post-structuralists raised against traditional criticism, especially against close reading and the history of ideas. I myself have become aware of the reductionist dangers of explaining cultural phenomena from a set ideological framework, although I (and other Eastern European scholars) had suffered more from Marxist reductionism than the so-called "bourgeois idealist" or "humanist" approaches. In fact, I did find that new historicism could be suitably used as a weapon against the stalemate approaches that were to be changed in the East Bloc around 1990. And I have also learned that one of the strengths of post-structuralist approaches is that they can successfully reveal the politics of interpretation. Capitalizing on this insight, as an outsider, I would like to propose to revisit some of the fields of the historiographical battles.

It may seem surprising, but at this point, after the above historiographical and theoretical excursus, I would like to advocate a kind of cautious return to the Yatesian "master narrative," albeit with some modifications. While the above described diversification of the historical understanding of Dee has made me sensitive to the subtleties of our researched subject, alongside these I have become convinced that nonetheless there was little or no changes in the central concern of Dee's philosophical investigations. In spite of the various activities and diverse theoretical approaches he applied, I see a permanent and invariable feature that characterized all his works and actions. This was a fervent desire for omniscience in order to understand the divine plan of creation and God's intentions with the cosmos and man. His ambition was to use his knowledge for elevating himself to the level of God, thus realizing the potential granted in the Genesis: "And God said, let us make man in our image, after our likeness: and let them have dominion [. . .] over all the earth. So God created Man in his own image, in the image of God created he him" (Genesis 1:26–27). To describe this ambition I use the concept of *exaltatio* as I shall explain it in the following introductory chapters. Parallel to my view, Deborah Harkness used another, similar metaphor, found also in the Bible: she compared Dee's natural philosophical orientation to building Jacob's ladder. This mytho-icon supported the ideology that communication between heaven and earth was possible, and as Harkness notes, "Dee, along with many of his contemporaries, searched a variety of authoritative treatises for information on how to ascend 'Jacob's ladder' to learn the secrets of the cosmos, and then descend to share that information with the waiting world" (1999, 60).

In the followings I am thus going to approach Dee as a "magus" who had an amazingly wide range of interests but who also increasingly had a focused obsession, a magical program, not necessarily to improve the sciences in order to prepare for the scientific revolution, but rather to find an alternative system of knowledge. Since Dee clearly distinguished between science after the Fall and that of the primordial wisdom (the "radicall truthes" as he called it), we have to take seriously the fact that here we are really talking about *alternative* systems of knowledge. His aim was to restore the Adamic or Enochian wisdom of the Golden Age that had been lost with the Fall and which would not be compatible with the methods and means of the fallen science relying on discursive logic. Dee's program was by no means exceptional in the intellectual spectrum of the late Renaissance but in its compactness—together with its variety—it remains certainly outstanding.

The examination of magic is pertinent in our age, too. It is a challenging but also disturbing task to assess how our frustrated civilization with its relativistic views looks at a system of knowledge that, since the advent of rationalism, has been professing a declared alternative to analytical thinking. It is notable, at the same time, to what extent this alternative system has had a fundamental and orthodox nature, remaining practically unchanged for long centuries. In spite of its rigid doctrines, however, it invests the world with a multiplicity of meanings that for its believers and researchers seems inexhaustible. I am going to examine the paradoxical relationship of literature, culture, science, and the occult, concentrating on the epoch of the Renaissance, which witnessed the crystalization of the esoteric philosophy, parallel to the birth of Cartesian logic and modern experimentation.

It is intriguing to examine the parallel rise of two such contrary world pictures between which we can still observe intricate cross-fertilization. I am suggesting that occult philosophy and magic to some extent have catalyzed the development of experimental sciences—by now this has become a commonplace in science history—at the same time they have fostered a subversive approach that in fact prevented the ultimate conquest by the logical-rational world picture. Thus it contributed to the survival of a symbolic language, with some pathos one might say, and to the continuous rebirth of poetry. It is because of this effect that I propose an investigation into the ideology and iconography of occult philosophy.

2

Mysticism, Occultism, Magic Exaltation

FALL AND REBIRTH

In my introductory sentences I referred to the many fields and aspects of magic that in their entirety cannot be addressed in the present book. I am interested in that particular ambition of magic that aimed at producing a complete explanatory system of the world and since the early modern era has offered itself as an alternative to what we nowadays call the scientific way of interpretation. I am looking for the intertextualized documents of this primarily theological-philosophical program with its roots reaching back to Antiquity and with its various manifestations in Renaissance art, science, and also in diverse social practices. I shall concentrate on those elements that from the classical and Judeo-Christian sources became absorbed in European high culture, although—as we shall see—from time to time I will have to touch upon aspects of popular cultural programs as well as black magic and witchcraft.

Since the forthcoming investigations will try to analyze the occult philosophy and its manifestations in various symbolic systems—religion, magic, and art—it seems natural and necessary to start with some explanations of how I understand the key terms: mysticism, occultism, and magic. I relate all of these to the ambition and desire of man to reach exaltation and union with the Deity. A suitable start might be to recall the ancient, archetypal experience of mankind concerning the Fall, precipitated by some original sin, the loss of Eden, or the Golden Age. This theme can invariably be found in all religions and mythologies (cf. for example Barr

1992; Delumeau 1995; Eliade 1968 and 1992). This negative experience, however, has always been counterbalanced by the age-old ambition of man to regain the lost harmony, eventually to deify himself and regain his position at the side of God. The Hungarian cultural historian and sociologist Elemér Hankiss has named these experiences and the efforts to handle them the Promethean and the Apollonian strategies of humankind. The former comprises the technical side of civilization aiming primarily at the demarcation of human *Lebensraum* from the uncontrolled and chaotic universe by means of fences, walls, electronic rays, and innumerable other devices that provide the boundaries of those spheres within which the human being is the commanding master. The Apollonian strategy means a spiritual demarcation or fence-building: symbolization—the creation of a sphere of myths, illusions, images, and artworks.[1] The agenda of *exaltatio* can be connected with this latter strategy.

As an attentive reader of the Bible, Dee was, naturally, well aware of those pieces of information in the sacred book that intrigued many Renaissance philosophers. Primarily among such topics was the doctrine asserting the dignity of Adam in Paradise and, related to this, the omniscient intellectual capacity given to man prior to the Fall. Particular signs of this exceptional power and knowledge were Adam's linguistic qualities, namely, that he could directly converse with God and that he was entrusted to name the creatures of the world in Paradise. As we can read in *Genesis*:

> And out of the ground the Lord God formed every beast of the field, and every fowl of the air; and brought them unto Adam to see what he would call them: and whatsoever Adam called every living creature, that was the name thereof. (2:19)

The basis for this privilege was, of course, God's original intention in the creation of man:

> And God said, Let us make man in our image, after our likeness: and let them have dominion over the fish of the sea, and over the fowl of the air, and over the cattle, and over all the earth. . . . So God created man in his own image. (Gen., 1:26–27)

This happy state and high status, then, as we know, was ended by our forefather's disobedience. Even so, whole generations of Renaissance thinkers were enthralled by these words, which encouraged them to try the impossible: to regain the lost dignity and reinstate themselves in the bosom of God.[2] They were searching for other hopeful instances in the Bible that would testify to the possibility of occasional magical exaltations. So some verses of the Psalms suggested that man had (almost) the same all-powerful privileges as the angels:

> What is man, that thou art mindful of him?
> For thou hast made him a little lower than the angels
> and hast crowned him with glory and honor.
> Thou madest him to have dominion over the works of thy hands:
> thou hast put all things under his feet. . . . (Psalm 8:4–6)

And in the *Wisdom of Solomon* one could read that the mighty king directly received omniscience from the Creator:

> God hath granted me to speak as I would, and to conceive as is meet for the things that are given me: because it is he that leadeth unto wisdom, and directeth the wise. [. . .]
> For he hath given me certain knowledge of the things that are, namely, to know how the world was made, and the operation of the elements.
> The beginning, ending, and midst of the times: the alterations of the turning of the sun, and the change of seasons. [. . .]
> And all such things as are either secret or manifest, them I know. (Wisdom 7:15–21)

This Biblical framework naturally encouraged the savants of the Renaissance to look for parallels and reinforcements among their highly esteemed classical authorities. Among the Greeks we find these notions most crystallized in the works of Plato. According to his poetically expounded mythology, the charioter of the *Symposium* and of *Phaedrus*, the soul imprisoned in the body, with good fortune, may remember the world of ideas and this arouses the desire in man to elevate himself above the physical existence and to open a channel of communication with the transcendental world, the divine.

> If a man makes right use of such means of remembrance, and ever approaches to the full vision of the perfect mysteries, he and he alone becomes truly perfect. Standing aside from the busy doings of mankind, and drawing nigh to the divine, he is rebuked by the multitude as being out of his wits, for they know not that he is possessed by a deity. (*Phaedrus* 249c–d; Plato 1963, 496).

Plato distinguished between four such channels, as he called them, sacred enthusiasms, or furies. As none of these forms of communication with the transcendental is a logically concievable experience, we can call them mystical apprehensions. Among them the first two (religious enthusiasm and prophetic fury) are rather passive operations. They happen to man without the active cooperation of the medium who is suddenly enlightened through epiphanic revelation. The other two—furies of love and poetry—are more active and inspire individual acts, leading even to a creative process. Thus man becomes the imitator of divine creation and eventually a partaker of the transcendental reality. At this point Plato clearly differentiates between the uselessness of the imitative poet who creates without sacred elevation and the high quality output of the inspired bard. One should remember this distinction in adopting the commonplace about Plato's condemnatory opinion of painters and poets:

> There is a third form of possession or madness, of which the Muses are the source. This seizes a tender, virgin soul and stimulates it to rapt passionate expression, especially in lyric poetry. [. . .] But if any man come to the gates of poetry without the madness of the Muses, persuaded that skill alone will make him a good poet, then shall he and his works of sanity with him be brought to nought by the poetry of madness, and behold, their place is nowhere to be found. (*Phaedrus* 245a; Plato 1963, 492)

It is obvious that such mystical experience cannot be classified as part of the common human knowledge, which normally derives from discursive logic. Yet it is still some kind of knowledge, in my definition, occult knowledge, that is, a secret learning which is a privilege of the hypersensitive elect.

At this point it may be worth recalling Edgar Wind's distinction between the three senses of the term *mystery*. According to him it refers to rituals, figurative understanding, and magical practices (1968, 6 and the whole of chapter 1). These three phases, naturally, could never be strictly separated from each other; however their interrelatedness also comprised some sort of internal evolution. Originally 'the mysteries' meant collective ritualistic practices, such as the rites of Eleusis at which the ancient philosophers (such as Diogenes Laertius, Heraclitus, Anaxagoras, and others) looked with distrust and irreverence as befitting only the vulgar multitude. Plato's opinion, however, was more ambiguous. On the one hand he spoke with irony about the possibility of such hierophany, according to his famous maxim: "Many are the thyrsus-bearers but few are the bacchoi."[3] But on the other hand he himself emphasized that the final end of wisdom was the purgation of the soul from the follies of the body and that the true philosopher's occupation "consists precisely in the freeing and separation of soul from body" (*Phaedo* 67d; Plato 1963, 50). While this separation happens naturally in death, the wise man has to try to achieve it while still alive. For Plato a rational excercise, the art of dialectic, was a feasible alternative way to cleanse the soul and achieve communion with the Beyond (Wind's phrase). In this sense, in philosophy, 'the mystery' is to be understood figuratively.

Plato's chief follower, Plotinus, was more permissive concerning the possibility of syncretic approaches to philosophy and religion. Although he claimed that "the gods must come to me, not I to them,"[4] he also approved the significance of manifest symbols for those who are still on the outside but aspire to enter.

Although Plato himself did not care much for magic, its hellenistic revival resulted from the inner logic of his theory of enthusiasms. In addition to the four sacred madnesses, inevitably was added a fifth channel through which one could contact the transcendental. If poetic inspiration could be defined as a *mystère littéraire* (Festugière 1932, 116ff.), the mystical exaltation ought to have been achieved also by means of incantations, application of sacred names and numbers, or other magical-ritualistic procedures. Plotinus, and especially his disciples, the hellenistic "Platonici" (Porphyry, Iamblichus, Proclus, and Synesius) accomplished a complex program of syncretism that resulted in the fact that magic became gradually readmitted as a handmaid of philosophy and, as Wind wryly remarked, "soon rose to become her mistress" (6). In this context magic may be defined as that type of human action that, exploiting occult knowledge, connects man's intellect with the supernatural and through this connection man tries to exercise his will in the spirit world.

It is well known to what extent the neopletonist philosophers of the Renaissance came under the spell of this syncretic, theological understanding of magic, especially since they did not see an unbridgeable divide between this hellenistic inheritance and the Christian doctrines. The final goal remained the same: the deification of man, a program which was corroborated by the biblical doctrine according to which man was created after the image of God and shared all God's characteristics. The most important among those characteristics were omniscience and omnipotence, which all magi craved. Christian magic seems to have followed Plato's logic in the *Phaedo*, namely that while man normally could expect the union with the divine only after death, magic tried to overcome the existential limits of the human species and elevate the individual soul to the world of ideas during earthly life. Nothing expressed this objective better than Pico della Mirandola's passionate words in *De hominis dignitate*:

> Who would not long to be initiated into such sacred rites? Who would not desire, by neglecting all human concerns, by despising the goods of fortune, and by disregarding those of the body, to become the guest of the gods while yet living on earth, and, made drunk by the nectar of eternity, to be endowed with the gifts of immortality though still a mortal being? (section 16, Pico 1948, 233)

This was the program that the Renaissance magi became obsessed with and this became the lifelong aspiration of the English mathematician John Dee, too.

To sum up the set of definitions established so far: first of all, mystical experiences constitute the widest category within which one finds occult knowledge, a somewhat more systematic body of doctrines developed on the basis of mystical experiences. Occult knowledge is thus a synthetic amalgam of traditionally transmitted lore and its philosophically organized explanation. And, as we can safely claim that only a smaller circle of the recipients of mystical experiences became conscious of occult wisdom, an even smaller circle among those would attempt to express active, magical will. Depending on the magical program and the evoked agents of the magus, one can thus distinguish between white and black magic.

THE ORGANIC WORLD MODEL

After the preliminary definitions we need to identify the intellectual framework that provides the theoretical basis for a magically oriented natural philosophy. First and foremost it is a hierarchical world picture, since in a uniform cosmos there is no transcendental sphere. A further prerequisite is the belief in the organic, or even occult, mystical correspondences between the elements of this hierarchical universe. Typical systems of such occult correspondences are astrology and alchemy. The latter has an important offspring, spiritual alchemy, which interprets the transmutation of metals on an allegorical-emblematic level and aims at the purification of the human soul.

We may also add that without the speculative Greco-Hellenistic philosophy no such complexity of European magical lore could have developed. All Christianized magical thinking can be traced back to the derivations of Platonism or Plotinus' doctrine of emanations. I do not want to describe in detail the organic world picture; it is enough to refer to classical works that contributed to our understanding of that world model, so different from our own based on the Cartesian cosmos and the achievments of the Scientific Revolution. It was Arthur O. Lovejoy who in 1936 first employed the concept of "the Great Chain of Being" in cultural history (cf. Lovejoy 1960), which later became popularized in E. M. W. Tillyard's controversial *The Elizabethan World Picture* (1946) and further explained in a great number of scholarly monographs, including S. K. Heninger's important books (1974 and 1977). Although the concept of the Great Chain of Being—since it suggested a grand narrative or a universal formula in which scholars hoped to distill the essence of the premodern world picture—has been recently challenged, in my opinion, with ample fine tuning, it is still tenable, as is shown by the contemporary influential theory of Jurii Lotman who derived his cultural semiotics from a typology of world models, contrasting the medieval vertical with the modern horizontal ones.[5] Instead of repeating the already known features of this premodern world model, here I would rather like to recall the evolution of the ways it was imagined and visualized throughout the centuries up to the great paradigm shift of the seventeenth century.

The central idea and metaphor was summarized by Cicero in his commentary to the dream of Scipio as follows:

> Since from the Supreme God Mind arises, and from Mind, Soul, and since this in turn creates all subsequent things and fills them all with life, and since this single radiance illuminates all and is reflected in each, as a single face might be reflected in many mirrors placed in a series; and since all things follow in continuous succession, degenerating in sequence to the very bottom of the series, the attentive observer will discover a connection of parts, from the Supreme God down to the last dregs of things, mutually linked together and without a break. And this is Homer's golden chain, which God, he says, bade hang down from heaven to earth.[6]

The chain metaphor obviously recapitulated Plotinus' concept of emanations; however, it also relied on Aristotle's natural philosophy since it was the latter who produced a graphically conceivable picture concerning the structure of the universe by dividing it into the sublunary and translunary spheres.[7]

Cicero's visual metaphor was further developed and Christianized by Pseudo-Dionysius, the Areopagite who inserted the orders of angels into the Chain. His popularity was unshaken during the Middle Ages and his system gained a most sophisticated form in Aquinas' scholastic theology. From the time of scholasticism more and more specialized works tried to explain and further develop the design of the Great Chain of Being and this culminated in the natural philosophy of the Renaissance, including thinkers such as Agrippa, Paracelsus, Fludd—and John Dee. These "scientific" descriptions are not easy to follow for the modern reader, but fortunately we also have literary-artistic visions as well as graphic illustrations showing how the fundamentally unchanged world model gained more and more refined explanations and representations up to the seventeenth century.

Hartmann Schedel's late medieval world chronicle offered a naively "realistic" scheme of the hierarchies of the world, and this approach was preserved until the early decades of printing, as can be seen from the illustration in the 1493 edition (Figure 2.1).[8] The spheres of the created world are surrounded by the hierarchies of spirits and angels and the whole structure of the cosmos is kept in place by the four principal winds.

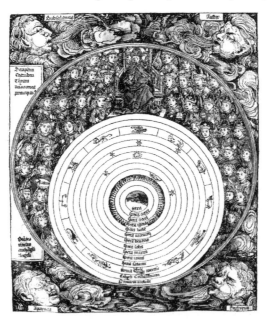

Figure 2.1   A late medieval representation of the seventh day of the Creation, resulting in the Great Chain of Being. Hartmann Schedel, *Weltchronik* (Nürnberg, 1493), fol. 5ᵛ. Somogyi Library, Szeged [Inc 10].

In Charles de Bouelles' *Liber de intellecu* (1510) we find a more exact table: a chain-like structure registers the hierarchies, avoiding the representation of realistic objects. The diagram actually offers two parallel columns, one representing the Great Chain of Being—that is, the macrocosm—while the other chain shows the corresponding levels of cognition and sensation—that is, the functions of the microcosm (Figure 2.2). Bouelles, a well-known occult philosopher of the early sixteenth century and one of the chief authorities on number symbolism, corresponded with Jacques Lefèvre d'Étaples, Germain Ganay, Trithemius, and others. It is worth noting that his books on secret numbers, mystical geometry, and the seven ages of the world—including the one this illustration is taken from—were featured in Dee's library in seven editions, both in Latin and in French.[9]

Renaissance magic naturally issued from the idea of the Great Chain of Being and its correspondences. It is not by chance that the Renaissance magi so often referred to the system, such as Agrippa in his introduction to *De occulta philosophia*:

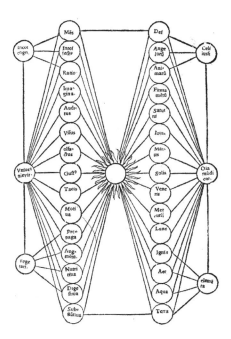

FIGURE 2.2   Representation of the "Grait Chain of Being" from Charles de Bouelles, *Liber de intellectu* (Paris, 1510), 42ᵛ. Herzog August Bibliothek, Wolfenbüttel [E 391 Helmst 2o].

Seeing there is a threefold world, elementary, celestial and intellectual, and every inferior is governed by its superior, and receiveth the influence of the virtues thereof, so that the very original, and chief Worker of all doth by angels, the heavens, stars, elements, animals, plants, metals, and stones convey from himself the virtues of his omnipotency upon us, for whose service he made, and created all these things. (1.1; Agrippa 1997, 3)

Needless to say, Agrippa was one of Dee's main inspirations in turning to the occult philosophy. What the English Doctor could not know was, that after his death there was to come yet another exalted, last soar of the magical philosophy which was to produce the most fascinating and beautiful illustrations that kept alive the splendor of this intellectual endeavor long after it became invalidated by the great paradigm shift effected by the Scientific Revolution. Dee's compatriot Robert Fludd was one of the last great occult philosophers of the Renaissance, and in the early decades of the seventeenth century he further refined the organic world model and created the following captivating diagram (Figure 2.3). At the foot of the scheme one finds the earth as the base of material existence, at the top the Holy Trinity represents pure intelligence. God and the earth are connected by a reversed, "formal pyramid," which indicates the diminishing amount of intelligence alongside the downreaching chain. While "formality" (standing

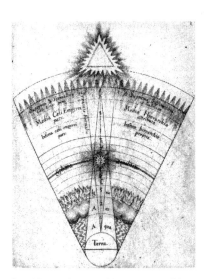

Figure 2.3   The "formal" and "material" pyramidal components of the universe. Robert Fludd, *Utriusque cosmi . . . historia* (Oppenheim, 1617–1619), 1:89. Somogyi Library, Szeged [E.d. 1949].

for the purely conceptual, Platonic ideal) decreases, materiality is represented by another pyramid that is largest on the earth and narrows to zero in the sphere of pure spirituality. As Heninger notes, materiality and formality are two basic paradigms of existence and they structure the cosmos in a symmetrical frame (1977, 28).

These notions were so strong that they survived the Middle Ages and continued to dominate the scientific concepts of the Renaissance. Philosophers such as Ficino devoted long passages to describe the angelic hierarchies and their relation with the material world:

> Seraphim speculate on the order and providence of God.
> Cherubim speculate on the essence and form of God.
> Thrones also speculate, though some descend to works.
> Dominions, like architects, design what the rest execute.
> Virtues execute, and move the heavens, and concur for the working
> of miracles as God's instruments.
> Powers watch that the order of divine governance is not interrupted
> and some of them descend to human things.
> Principalities care for public affairs, nations, princes, magistrates.
> Archangels direct the divine cult and look after sacred things.
> Angels look after smaller affairs, and take charge of individuals as
> their guardian angels.[10]

What is more, as we know from Lovejoy, the metaphor of the Chain of Being did not immediately disappear after its scientific foundations had been discredited. The aesthetic beauty of symmetry and divine order captured the imagination of poets from Dante until the Enlightenment. In the Age of Reason, Alexander Pope celebrated the hierarchy of beings as follows:

> Vast Chain of Being! Which from God began,
> Natures ethereal, human, angel, man,
> Beast, bird, fish, insect, what no eye can see,
> No glass can reach! from Infinite to thee,
> From thee to nothing . . .
> *Essay on Man* (1733), quoted from Abrams et al. 1986, 1:2269.

From the concept of the chain of being followed another important characteristics of the premodern world model, that is, its supposed organic character. As opposed to the seventeenth-century paradigm in which the world was compared to a machine or a clock, wound up and allowed to run by God, in the late Renaissance the cosmos had been likened to a living organism governed and moved by sympathies, drawn by likeness and analogies.[11] The *spiritus mundi* entirely filled the universe within which each layer of the hierarchy was mirrored in the other, analogously functioning tiers. The orders of angels were duplicated in the celestial and planetary hierarchies, which in turn governed the elemental spheres of the material world. This intricate system of correspondences was extremely old. It had been present long before Aristotle, preceding even the Platonic and Pythagorean mathematical theology. Its roots had reached as far as the Egyptian and other Eastern philosophies. Correspondences characterized magical and astrological speculations from the beginnings, as can be seen in the ancient text of the *Smaragdine Table*:

> That which is beneath is like that which is above: and that which is above, is like that which is beneath to worke the miracles of one thing. And as all things have proceeded from one, by the meditation of one, so all things have sprung from this one thing by adaptation.[12]

This concise maxim named the spheres above and beneath but also referred to the correspondences between the two worlds, the large and the small, that is, the macro and microcosms, the latter being man who was seen as a miniature model of the universe. The most important elements of this concept can best be viewed in contemporary diagrams and illustrations.

Both classical and biblical sources spoke of the double nature of man, namely that he was composed of the material and of the intellectual worlds. His microcosm was connected with the macrocosm through the four elements as well as through the intelligences. The occult side of these correspondences was manifest in the notions of astrological determinism, which presupposed the unity and organic nature of the world.

One of the most compact representations of these correspondences is found in a 1472 publication of Isidore of Seville. The key words placed in the circular diagram—Mundus–Annus–Homo—underline the unity of cosmos and man existing in time. The combination of the elements and qualities with the cycle of time, the yearly seasons within a geometrical compound, is so perfect that the famous Warburg Institute has selected this emblem as its own device. Since this diagram is so well known, I have chosen another, impressively elaborate version from 1555, from one of the books John Dee also possessed. His personal acquaintance Oronce Finé, the French mathematician, devised it for his *De mundi sphaera, sive Cosmographia* (Figure 2.4). Like on Isidor's diagram, Finé also sets up the four elements and the four qualities, but connects them

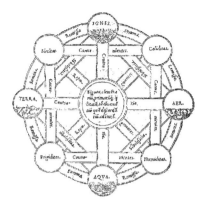

FIGURE 2.4   The expanded tetrad of the elements and qualities. Oronce Finé, *De mundi sphaera, sive cosmographia* (Paris: Vascosanus, 1555), 2ᵛ. Herzog August Bibliothek, Wolfenbüttel [13.8 Astron /2/].

according to a complicated system of correspondences showing "convenientes," "contraria," and "repugnantes," summarizing the whole as follows: "Figura elementarium, primarumquae qualitatum, tam convenientium quam discordantium ad invicem."[13]

    While the diagram of Isidore and Finé provides the theoretical framework for expanding on the occult correspondences, another medieval illustration leads us to one of their concrete applications: the astrological effects on man's body (Figure 2.5: Gregor Reisch, *Margarita philosophica*

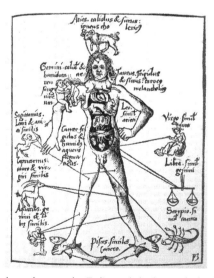

FIGURE 2.5   Correspondences between the Zodiac and the human body. Gregor Reisch, *Margarita philosophica nova* (Strassbourg, 1504), 165ᵛ. Herzog August Bibliothek, Wolfenbüttel [Li 5881].

nova, Strassbourg, 1504). It is important to note that John Dee's imagination was no doubt fertilized by the above illustrations, since he not only possessed Finé's treatise, but also the exquisitely beautiful Reisch edition (R&W 1385); as for the works of Isidore, he had three valuable manuscripts (R&W M94a, M114k, M119).

Woodcuts like the above, deriving from medieval manuals, became extremely common in Renaissance almanacs and emblem books, continuing their career well into the early modern era. An emblematic treatment of the microcosm is attractively visualised in Henry Peachem's *Minerva Brittana* (1610, cf. Figure 2.6) and many more complex diagrams can be

FIGURE 2.6   Homo microcosmus. Henry Peachem, *Minerva Britanna* (London, 1612), 190. Reproduced from Heninger 1977, 153.

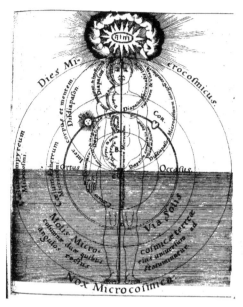

FIGURE 2.7   Man—Cosmos—Day—Night. Robert Fludd, *Utriusque cosmi . . . historia* (Oppenheim, 1617–9), 3:275. Somogyi Library, Szeged [E.d. 1049].

found in the large, seventeenth-century encyclopaedic works, such as the publications of Robert Fludd or Athanasius Kircher (Figures 2.7 and 2.8).

The microcosmic man Fludd's diagram evokes was yet another important ingredient of the organic world model: the cosmic harmonies of mathematics and music. The octave or diapason sounding on the monochord refers to the harmony that had been subject to philosophic

FIGURE 2.8   Zodiacal-man. Athanasius Kircher, *Ars magna, lucis & umbrae* (Roma, 1646), 396. Somogyi Library, Szeged [E.b. 1].

speculations since Pythagoras. On this particular illustration the two parts of the body, belonging to the day and to the night, are kept together by the *spiritus mundi*, represented by the monochord. On it, following the proportions of the golden mean, one can see the stages of the descension and ascension of the soul. The macrocosm and the microcosm are alike divided into three empires: the elemental, the ethereal, and the empyrean. The parts of the body correspond to these orders.[14] Kircher's zodiacal man is important because, according to scholarly literature, this author was the last to offer such speculative diagrams in a strictly scientifically orientated monograph (Godwin 1979b, 92).

From the above simplified presentation, I believe that we can draw the conclusion that the theoretical framework of occult and magical natural philosophy was provided by the principles of the Great Chain of Being, the notion of correspondences, and the analogical interpretations of the macro- and microcosms. It is true that not all theorists of the organic world picture proceeded to deal with magic, but the reverse can be safely claimed: no magic could be imagined without the organic world model.

THE DOCTRINE OF EXALTATION

Finally, before moving on from the area of definitions and demarcations, a brief elaboration is needed concerning the term and concept of *exaltatio*, the doctrine according to which man—with the help of certain techniques, including magic—could bring himself into such a state that enables him to leave the body and seek the company of the Deity.

I have decided to employ the term *exaltatio* to describe this program of deification, according to which a mystically elevating state can be achieved through the grace of God, by the efforts of the individual, or by accidental fortunate circumstances. In the latter two cases the exaltation needs catalyzers or supernatural help.

For Ficino the experiencing of beauty could launch the soul upward into the world of ideas, but he himself was most intrigued by the possibility that, in constructing talismans, the magus himself could mobilize demonic or angelic agencies. This option was even more emphasized by Pico della Mirandola and Cornelius Agrippa. As Pico wrote in the *Oration*, "Thou, constrained by no limits, *in accordance with thine own free will,* in whose hand We have placed thee, shalt ordain for thyself the limits of thy nature" (section 3, Pico 1948, 225, emphasis mine). And in order to corroborate this view, he cited biblical loci, classical authorities (referring to the Greek mysteries, Plato, Pythagoras, Chaldean oracles), as well as Christian scholars (Pseudo-Dionysius, Duns Scotus, Aquinas, Albertus Magnus). As he observed, the result was invariably the same, a miraculous exaltation:

> We shall measure therefrom all things that are and shall be and have been in indivisible eternity; and, admiring their original beauty, like the seers of Phoebus, we shall become her own winged lovers. And at last, roused by ineffable love as by a sting, like burning Seraphim rapt from ourselves, full of divine power we shall no longer be ourselves but shall become He Himself Who made us. (section 16, Pico 1948, 234)

Paracelsus went even further in expanding his vision about the infinite possibilities of the magus:

> Thoughts create a new heaven, a new firmament, a new source of energy, from which new arts flow. [. . .] When a man undertakes to create something, he establishes a new heaven, as it were, and from it the work that he desires to create flows into him. [. . .] For such is the immensity of man that he is greater than heaven and earth. (*Astronomia magna;* Paracelsus 1928–1933, 12:183 [1951, 45])

The above quotations do not involve the expression *exaltation,* which in fact was rather exceptional in classical and humanist Latin. The sense in which I use it, however, can be extracted from dictionaries of the Latin language. The great Teubner, for example, gives the following division for the connotations of *exaltatio*:

> ☞I. 'actio sursum levandi, extollendi, elevatio' (A/ a proprie [hic afferuntur etiam ei loci, quibus sensus quidam myst. vel transl. per planam alleg. accedit]: 1/ in universum [variarum rerum allevatio]: a/ corporaliter: astrorum; b/ incorporaliter: vocis *"tuba vocis exaltatio in prædicatione divina"* [Is. 58, 1]; 2/ peculiariter: de crucis sive Christi in cruce elevatione; B/ translate de conditione [syn. ascensio; opp. humilitas]: 1/ bono sensu: *"ædificavit Moyses altare et vocavit nomen eius 'dominus exaltatio mea'"* [Exod. 17, 15]. Ascensio super templum moraliter exaltatio cordis sanctorum ad sanctitatem [Matth. 5]; 2/ in malam partem: superbia, elatio. *"Exaltatio oculorum est dilatatio cordis"* [Prov. 21, 4].—☞II. de statu eius, qui exaltatus est, i.q. altitudo, sublimitas (A/ dei, Christi; B/ de eximietate facundiæ: *viro laudabilis*

prudentiæ et clementiæ singularis, eloquentiæque exal tationis eximiæ).—
☞III. de actione profundius reddendi: *"exaltetur manus tua"* (Cassiodorus, Psalm 9, 33).[15]

Among these explanations for our purpose the two most important ones will be I/A, which includes the mystical, figurative meaning of elevation, and I/B, which denotes a change of status or condition the opposite of which is humility. This elevation can happen through the grace of God (see the quotation from Exodus) or as a reward of human excellence (as in Matthew 5:11–12: "Blessed are ye, when [men] shall revile you, and persecute [you], and shall say all manner of evil against you falsely, for my sake. / Rejoice, and be exceeding glad: for great [is] your reward in heaven: for so persecuted they the prophets which were before you" [*gaudete et exultate quoniam merces vestra copiosa est in cælis*][16]).

The expression—as most signs that have symbolic connotations—envelops negative meanings, too (*in malam partem*). It may stand for *superbia* or *elatio,* that is, pride and conceit. As we shall see in the forthcoming analyses, all of these meanings will play an important role in the concept of magical *exaltatio.* Passive as opposed to active elevation on the one hand, assertive enthusiasm as opposed to conceitful delusion on the other, all contribute to the complicated cultural history of occult aspirations.

There are a great number of phrases in the texts dealing with the deification of man that characterize the magical exaltation: *elatus, elevatio, exultatio, furor, illuminatio, inspiratio.* I have chosen *exaltatio* as a collective term for all these primarily because of its connotations in modern European languages—think of the French term *l'exaltation* [praise, elevation, admiration], or the German *exaltiert,* or the English *exalted.* Beyond the everyday meanings one should remember that the term *exaltatio* in astrology refers to the position of a planet in the zodiac where its power is the greatest. Alchemy also uses this term. For example, Edward Kelly in his *Theatro astronomiae terrestri* (Hamburg, 1676) speaks about the "exaltation of Mercurial water" (1999, chapter 7); and according to the conclusion of the *Practise of Mary Prophetess in the Alchemicall Art* the sister of Moses "Joyned with three seeds she does aspire To be exalted in the Fire."[17]

In an alchemical treatise published in 1680 and attributed to George Ripley, one can also read about the "First Matter" that contains the four elements "pure in their Exaltation."[18] Furthermore, according to the 1612 lexicon of Martin Ruland, exaltation is an operation by which a substance is raised into a purer and more perfect nature (Ruland 1984, 138). The same dictionary points out the relationship between *exaltatio* and *sublimatio*, which is not only a chemical process but also a key term in spiritual alchemy that indicates the purification process of the soul, sometimes compared to the resurrection of Christ.

Relying on the rich net of connotation, I consciously use *exaltatio* somewhat ambiguously in the sense that a person can reach the state of exaltation either by accidental circumstances or by his/her own will. And this initiative can spring from deep faith as well as from self-conceit. In my opinion the vague borderline between mysticism and magic can be found in the transitory area leading from passive happening to conscious action.

The last remark of my introduction should be devoted to a very important caveat. No one should think that the significance of *exaltatio* is restricted to being an abstract term of philosophy, thus constituting a trend of speculative thinking. The program of deification combined with magic had far-reaching consequences for those who adhered to it. The occult outlook not only determined their thinking, the metaphysical goal also customized their behavior, social interaction, strategies of self-fashioning, the iconography of their gestures, as well as their poetic imagination. In the ensuing chapters I hope to demonstrate this complexity with the example of John Dee.

Part 2

Input

"In many bokes and sundry languages . . ."

3

The Sources of Renaissance Magic

The library of John Dee has fascinated researchers of his life and work. Since the bookstock has been dispersed, the main sources by which to assess it have been the handwritten catalogues that remained unpublished until recently.[1] Frances Yates referred to this fabulous collection many times and advocated that its catalogue be published.[2] Peter French analyzed its contents and tried to measure the scope of the subcollection dealing with magic (1972, 40–61). Nicholas Clulee did the same, only with greater accuracy, helped by the proofs of Roberts and Watson's magisterial edition of the catalogues that, with important studies and indices, finally appeared in 1990. This book has proved to be such an indispensable source that hardly a decade after its printing it has become a rarity in secondhand bookshops and among antiquarians.

Roberts and Watson accomplished an important work not only in reconstructing Dee's library but in showing the way of interpreting the various impacts of such a storehouse and representative selection of sixteenth-century knowledge. They collected as many extant copies as it was possible from the scattered collection, and by examining the inscriptions of possessors as well as the marginalia, they offered insights into the books and the thoughts of their owner. William Sherman continued their work and from the outset looked at the books not as treasured items on shelves in the study of their possessor, but rather as social agents that played an important mediatory role in the politics of reading and writing.

Thanks to research in the past fifteen years, it has become possible to assess with unprecedented accuracy the traditions Dee set out to follow, subvert, or rewrite, casting a fresh eye upon often conflicting historio-graphical interpretations.

As I have indicated in the preface, in the present part of my book I will look at the various available sources at the disposal of Renaissance magi by way of rereading a few eminent texts that were also in the possession of the English Doctor.

Nicholas Clulee has called our attention to the fact that Dee's thinking changed radically throughout his career, and he also repeatedly warned that the contents of Dee's library should not be uncritically hypothesized as immediate sources for his works. In fact, the acquisition of a book would not mean that its owner immediately incorporated it into his own thought. This is all true. However, in the following section, I am not going to take into consideration the chronology of Dee's own intellectual evolution; rather I shall turn to this in the third part. In the present section I shall trace magical ideas relating to the doctrine of *exaltatio* according to that sup-posed genealogy of wisdom as believed by Dee and his contemporaries. As is well known, in spite of its late Hellenistic origin, in the sixteenth century the *Corpus hermeticum* was considered to be the most ancient non-Judeo-Christian source that could authenticate those biblical loci about the dig-nity of man. Due to this firm Renaissance conviction, I find it appropriate to start our review with the writings of Hermes Trismegistus.

Traditions of Classical Magic

Frances Yates and the Rediscovery of Renaissance Magic

Since cultural history, like epic narratives, consists of intricate, intertwin-ing plot elements, it seems advisable to begin the tale in medias res. To start to map John Dee's intellectual horizon, the second half of the fif-teenth century will be an appropriate point. By this time Renaissance humanism had consolidated itself, which meant the recovering of the cultural and philosophical heritage of Antiquity. Parallel with that, a new infrastructure of intellectuals was developed by the formation of *academias* as an alternative network to the medieval universities.[3] Perhaps the most important among these private academies was the Florentine neoplatonist circle presided over by Marsilio Ficino and sponsored by the Medici princes. The importance of the Florentine Academy, naturally, has been known since the emergence of Renaissance studies.[4] Frances Yates, how-ever, in her book *Giordano Bruno and the Hermetic Tradition* (1964) contributed observations about the interests of the Florentine philosophers that resulted in a thorough reconsideration of Renaissance magic; something that had been seen as a highly suspect and superstitious occupation turned out to seem a respected and ambitious program, fully in harmony with the man-centered world picture of the Renaissance.

Not that Yates was the first to notice the gravity of magic in early modern thought. Since the time of Burckhardt it had been noticed by others, and the meticulous works of Thorndike, Kristeller, Walker, and several others grounded the reassessment of magic. It was nevertheless Yates who, with great erudition, pointed out that the Florentine neoplatonists, and notably Ficino, not only concentrated on Plato and the Platonici in trying to create a syncretic classical-Christian philosophy, but that an important group of their sources consisted of the obscure and irrational texts of the so-called hermetic tradition.

This textual lore came to the attention of the neoplatonists first of all by chance, then due to a colossal philological error. Ficino himself told the story in the preface of his Plotinus commentary addressed to Lorenzo il Magnifico: in 1560 a monk from Macedonia had brought the manuscripts of the *Corpus hermeticum* to Prince Cosimo. The chance element in this story relates to the fall of Byzantium in 1453, which started a landslide effect: monks, humanists, scholars were fleeing from the Turks and taking refuge in Italy, often carrying with them important manuscripts and other cultural treasures. The political changes gave a thrust to Greek studies in Italy (note, for example, the activities of Cardinal Bessarion who gave his valuable collection of Greek manuscripts to the library of the San Marco in Venice and who himself greatly contributed to the spreading of Greek studies as well as to reconciling classical philosophy and Christian theology in Western Europe).

Related to this historical accident was the ensuing philological gaffe, namely that old Cosimo became so excited about the hermetic texts that he ordered Ficino to interrupt the Plato translations and to undertake the Latin rendering of Hermes' writings: "mihi Mercurium primo Termaximum, mox Platonem mandavit interpretandum."[5] This extraordinary situation inspired Dame Frances to the following exclamation: "There are the complete works of Plato, waiting, and they must wait whilst Ficino quickly translates Hermes, probably because Cosimo wants to read him before he dies. What a testimony this is to the mysterious reputation of the Thrice Great!" (Yates 1964, 13).

While Ficino worked on the translation, he also cross-referenced what classical and Christian authorities had to say on the hermetic writings.

It seems that he had weighty enough sources to conclude that the writings of Hermes Trismegistus belonged to the most ancient divine revelations in the possession of mankind. In fact, he became convinced that they were of the same age if not older than God's teachings communicated to and through the biblical Moses.

Before turning to the hermetic treatises, it might be useful to recall in a few words the modern textual history of the *Corpus hermeticum*. Reitzenstein's pioneering edition of one text, the *Poimandres* (1904), was followed by Walter Scott's four-volume complete publication (1924–1936), which, although today no longer considered to be textually reliable, still contains numerous interesting observations and comparisons. The mid-twentieth-century large-scale edition of A. D. Nock and A.-J. Festugière (Nock 1945–1954) is still considered definitive, and Festugière's complementary studies also belong to the most important interpretations of these texts (1950–1954). Parallel to these editions, Kristeller discovered the relationship between the hermetic texts and the Italian humanists of the Cinquecento (1937–1945; 1943). His research was rounded out by the studies fostered by the Warburg Institute (by then in London): after Raymond Klibansky's *The Continuity of the Platonic Tradition during the Middle Ages* (1939), it was D. P. Walker who first associated directly neoplatonist philosophy, hermetic lore, and Renaissance magical interests in his *Spiritual and Demonic Magic from Ficino to Campanella* (1958). Frances Yates also worked within this intellectual milieu but her Bruno book of 1964 demonstrated the individualistic features of her approach to hermeticism and magic.

Another publication of the *Hermetica* should still be mentioned: Brian Copenhaver's English translation (1992), which not only offers a highly accurate text but also broad contextual—philological, social, and cultural—interpretations for the understanding of Hermes' writings. It should be mentioned that Copenhaver contributed important articles to the assessment of the debates concerning the Yates thesis (1978; 1988; 1990), and in the dedication of his *Hermetica* edition he paid tribute to the achievement of Yates and two other great Renaissance scholars: "Many bear the wand, but few become bacchoi: Frances Amelia Yates, Daniel Pickering Walker, Charles Bernard Schmitt."

While the studies of Scott and Festugière had no direct relation to Renaissance research, and Kristeller touched upon the questions of Renaissance magic only peripherally, Yates broadened Walker's rather narrowly defined scope of interest and placed magic in the wider contexts of early modern cultural history. She also intended to give a general explanation for this rather surprising phenomenon and, while doing so, came to far-reaching conclusions that called for a radical reinter pretation of the history of Renaissance science and intellectual development. Her significance in the reintegration of the *Hermetica* into early modern intellectual history was correctly summarized by Brian Copenhaver as follows:

> accepting Festugière's analysis and calling 'the critical and historical problem of the Hermetic literature [. . .] irrelevant [because . . .] they would have been entirely unknown to Ficino and his readers,' Yates made 'the great Egyptian illusion' and the chronological misconceptions eventually resolved by Casaubon [the] major themes of her study, which focuses on figures of the late fifteenth and sixteenth centuries, from Ficino through Bruno and somewhat beyond. [. . .] Needless to say, the *Hermetica* soon became required reading for many students of early modern thought and letters whose interests were otherwise quite far from the fascinating puzzles of Hellenistic, Roman, and Egyptian religion and philosophy. (1992, lviii–lix)

Yates' understanding of hermeticism was closely related to Walker's thesis, according to which the philosophy of Ficino encouraged a new interpretation of magic, drawing inspiration, as in contrast to medieval magic, from Hellenistic occultism. Apart from Plato, Ficino's readings consisted of Plotinus, Porphyry, Iamblichus, Proclus, and the later neoplatonist Psellus—and also the hermetic treatises, Pythagorean number mysticism, Chaldean and Sybilline oracles, and Orphic hymns, all of which together constituted an ancient *prisca theologia* that was considered to be as authentic and valuable as the biblical revelation. This was the philological error of Ficino and his contemporaries: namely that they turned with the greatest reverence to textual materials that, by and large, were not older than the Hellenistic culture of the second and third centuries.

This is why Ficino tired in his attempt to reconcile Christianity and the neoplatonic-hermetic tradition. Thus his neoplatonism was more theology (as shown by the title of his *Theologia Platonica*) than natural philosophy, and consequently his demonology, astrology and magic must also be interpreted from a religious perspective.

According to Walker, as a result of Ficino's theological outlook, Renaissance magic developed in two directions: partly into an entirely "white," in Walker's terminology, spiritual magic, and partly into a more complex demonic magic, which, from the viewpoint of Christian dogmas, was of more heterodox nature. In this second tradition—which included authors such as Trithemius and Agrippa—the use of Hellenistic-neoplatonic sources was complemented by other, more medieval, elements of magic.

Continuing Walker's investigations, Frances Yates found the impact of the hermetic texts prevailing in Ficino's works, to which the Florentine philosopher's younger colleague, Pico della Mirandola, added elements of Jewish cabala. From this dual heritage issued the special ideology that Yates called the "hermetic tradition" (see also Copenhaver's summary, 1988, 79–83; and 1990). According to Yates, this hermeticism not only contributed to the formation of the Renaissance image of man, but also to the evolution of the Scientific Revolution. Needless to say, this claim presented a great challenge to those science historians who, brought up in schools based on the Cartesian cogito, were eagerly looking in each and every epoch only for signs of progress towards the final victory of rationalism.

As well as the challenge to the history of science challenge, another aspect of the Yates thesis concerned the importance of the hermetic tradition to the development of Renaissance philosophy. Yates asserted that among the followers of Ficino, hermeticism became a coherent hermetic-cabalistic system that evolved into a religious trend offering an alternative way to individual purification and self-redemption. This reformed occult philosophy provided a higher prestige to that kind of magic which, in the fifteenth century, emerged from a suspect, semi-legal status to a discipline that could give important impetus to the examination of nature and to the conducting of daring experiments.[6]

Due to the so-called hermeticism debate inspired by the Yates-thesis, our understanding of Renaissance magic is now much more refined than the propositions of Dame Frances themselves were thirty-five years ago. We must not forget, however, that this improvement has in no small part resulted from her often contradictory stimulation. All of those scholars who have been working on the correction of Yates's sometimes exaggerated and simplified ideas were, after all, inspired by her to accomplish a complex and interdisciplinary task, which has been furnishing new results ever since.

It was also Frances Yates who located Dee in the context of Renaissance hermeticism and, in fact, pinpointed him as being the prototype of the Rosicrucian magus. This rather schematic Dee image has been radically augmented during the past fifteen years; however Yates's insistence that the natural philosophy of Renaissance magic cannot be fully appreciated without a careful assessment of neoplatonic and hermetic occultism is still a pertinent admonition to Dee scholars.

In the following subchapters I shall revisit those source materials of Renaissance magic that—according to our present knowledge—led the

Florentine neoplatonists to include magic as an important ingredient of their Christian-humanist ideology.

Hermetic Magic

The manuscript (now known as the Florence MS Laurentianus 71, 33) given by the Macedonian monk to Ficino was a fourteenth-century copy of fourteen short treatises that the Florentine philosopher translated and in 1471 published under the title *Mercurii Trismegisti Liber de Potestate et Sapientia Dei, e Græco in Latinum traductus à Marsilio Ficino . . . Tarvisii.* As the first discourse was called *Poimandres*, Ficino titled the whole collection of the *Corpus hermeticum* "Pimander" (Ficino 1576, 1836; Garin 1988, 15–20; Yates 1964, 14 ff.).

Following his usual habit, the translator prefixed an *Argumentum* to the texts in which he displayed the genealogy of Hermes Trismegistus and asserted his date to be identical with that of Moses. He concluded from this "fact" that the wisdom of Hermes was part of the same divine revelation as the canonized texts of the Old Testament. He justified his view by citing the affirmative opinion of the early Christian writer Lactantius, whose approval, in his view, well balanced Augustinus' condemnation of another hermetic text, that of the *Asclepius*.[7]

The first treatise of Ficino's translation introduces the divine Poimandres (spirit of the unlimited power, that is Nous) who appears to Hermes Trismegistus in his dream. The Thrice Great Prophet requests him as follows:

> "I wish to learn about the things that are, to understand their nature and to know god." I said. Then he [Poimandres] said to me: "Keep in mind all that you wish to learn, and I will teach you." Saying this, he changed his appearence, and in an instant everything was immediately opened to me. I saw an endless vision in which everything became light—clear and joyful—and in seeing the vision I came to love it. (CH 1.3–4; quoted in Copenhaver 1992, 1).

This situation is well known in the literature of mysticism: the narrator receives inspiration in a trance-like state and communicates with the transcendental world through intuitive revelation. In the vocabulary of *Poimandres,* the expressions of light and shadow, enlightenment and radiation, dominate:

> After a little while darknesse arose separately and descended—fearful
> and gloomy—coiling sinuously so that it looked to me like a snake.
> Then the darkness changed into something of a watery nature, inde-
> scribably agitated and smoking like a fire. [. . .] But from the light [. . .]
> a holy word mounted upon the watery nature, and untempered fire
> leapt up from the watery nature to the height above. (ibid.)

Apart from the conflicting interpretations of textual scholarship (Copenhaver
1992, 97–102), in more general terms the orchestration of this treatise
recalls Plato's world of ideas, the neoplatonic doctrine of emanation, and
also Genesis in the Bible. Could this syncretic approach have inspired John
Dee in his craving for omniscience through divine revelation? He certainly
had several versions of the *Corpus hermeticum* in his library (see note 15
below) and the mystical-epistemological tour of the soul was not alien to
his own program. In connection with a desire for knowledge, Dee was also
interested in the primordial beginnings: the mythology of creation, the
Golden Age, and the question of Fall and rebirth prominently feature in
his angelic conversations (Dee 1659, 92 ff.).

According to Poimandres, the elements of nature have arisen "from
the counsel of god, which, having taken in the word and having seen the
beautiful cosmos, imitated it" (I.8). The actual creator thus was not the
Mind [*nous*], but rather by his spoken word [*logos*] he gave birth to a
Second Mind [*demiourgos*]. This craftsman-like creator in turn created
seven governors who "encompass the sensible world in circles" (I.9).

As the Hungarian classical philologist Tamás Adamik notes, the
genre of *Poimandres* is a vision with an unmistakably characteristic
structure (Adamik 1997, 177). It is introduced by the appearance of
Poimandres and Hermes' address to him; then follows a three-part revelation. After the story of the creation of the cosmos (4–11), man's
creation is recounted (12–23). In spite of similarities with Genesis, in
Poimandres man is endowed with much greater power than Adam. It
seems as if this man could receive even the fruit of the Tree of Knowledge—and without any punishment!

> Mind, the Father of all, who is life and light, gave birth to a man like
> himself whom he loved as his own child. The man was most fair: he
> had the father's image; and god, who was really in love with his own
> form, bestowed on him all his craftworks. And after the man had
> observed what the craftsman had created with the father's help, he also
> wished to make some craftwork, and the father agreed to this. Entering
> the craftsman's sphere, where he was to have all authority, the man

observed his brother's craftworks; the governors loved the man, and each gave a share of his own order. (1.12–3)

After this, man "broke through" into the vault of the created world and, when he looked at his own image in the earthly waters, came to like it and wished to stay there. Nature thus "took hold of her beloved, hugged him all about and embraced him, for they were lovers" (1.14). Man thus remained on the earth as part of nature, but he also preserved in himself the original, divine constitution. Because of this, his character is uniquely dual, different from all other creatures:

> Because of this, unlike any other living thing on earth, mankind is twofold—in the body mortal but immortal in the essential man. Even though he is immortal and has authority over all things, mankind is affected by mortality because he is subject to fate. (1.15)

Anthropology then is followed by eschatology (24–26): Poimandres advises Hermes about how he can perfect himself in striving to ascend to higher and higher spheres. The first recommendation is to adhere to asceticism. As a result, the human being rises up through the cosmic framework, through seven zones, surrendering the psychological muzzles of material existence, from evil machinations and arrogance to recklessness and deceit. Due to the teachings of Poimandres, Hermes also perceives that the fate of man is not death, since he might have power to gain immortality. He also recognizes that humanity is sleeping in ignorance and that it may be his mission to wake them up and spread the new wisdom:

> Then he [Poimandres] sent me forth, empowered and instructed on the nature of the universe and on the supreme vision, after I had given thanks to the father of all and praised him. And I began proclaiming to mankind the beauty of reverence and knowledge. (1.27)

Here there is apparent a compelling genealogy in the hermetic writings, transmitted through Ficino to John Dee. In the *Hermetica* man appears to be a close relative, a brother of the craftsman-demiurge, and his wisdom combines reverence and knowledge that could be paraphrased as theology and science. Although the theoretical *Hermetica* does not feature overt magical elements (cf. Copenhaver 1992, xxxiii; Festugière 1967, 59–60; Fowden 1986, 57–75), I believe that Yates was right in presuming that the Renaissance philosophers—and Dee certainly among them—were attracted by the potential combination of miraculous deeds and spiritual exaltation. An illuminating proof of this expectation might be a hitherto unnoticed remark in Ficino's argumentum to the *Pimander*:

> Among philosophers he [Trismegistus] first turned from physical and mathematical topics to contemplation of things divine, and he was the first to discuss with great wisdom the majesty of God, the order of demons, and the transformation of souls. Thus he was called the first author of theology. . . . (Ficino 1576, 1836; translated in Copenhaver 1992, xiviii)

Here Ficino sets up a taxonomy of wisdom that displays a dualism of science and theology but at the same time acknowledges a dynamism, an evolution from the first to the second. No doubt, Ficino envisioned himself moving along this line (cf. Allen 1994, 97–100), and as we shall see, Dee's intellectual history can be described in the same paradigm: "from science to magic," the highest form of which was no longer a set of active operations [*magia naturalis*], but rather a conscious and open reception of the divine revelation—"conversations with the angels" about the majesty of God and the transformation of the soul.

The thirteen tracts following *Poimandres* constitute a heterogeneous mix of tone, language, and philosophy. They are, however, connected by recurring characters (Nous, Hermes, Agathodaimon, Asclepius, Ammon, Tat, and Isis), a loose Egyptian framework (for some scholars a mere decoration, for others part of the synthetised traditions), and a loosely defined hermeticism that, according to Festugière, was no more than "a certain turn of mind that lies in bending every philosophical inquiry in the direction of piety and knowledge of God" (1967, 39).

The study of the original hermetic lore has developed during the past two decades as much as (if not more than) Dee studies. Copenhaver gives an admirably concise and clear account of the divers conflicting concepts and traditions amalgamated here: theoretical and technical, contemplative and pragmatic, religious and magical, literary and cultic, gnostic, Greek, and Egyptian (Copenhaver 1992, lviii). In spite of this critical variety, except for Reitzenstein who voted for a definite Egyptian origin, the first modern textual editors and interpreters such as Scott, Nock, and Festugière all thought that the hermetic literature by and large consisted of eclectic, late Hellenistic Greek philosophy with traces of Judaism and even less Zoroastrianism. Festugière sharply differentiated between optimist and pessimist gnosis on the one hand, and between theoretical and popular hermetica on the other. His views remained so dominating after the publication of his "monumental deposit of hermetic studies" (Copenhaver's expression, cf. Festugière 1950–1954; 1954; 1967; 1972) that an occasion to improve them could arise only with the discovery of new source materials, especially the Coptic Nag Hammadi texts and the Armenian *Definitions*.[8] This was largely done by Jean-Pierre Mahé, who reestablished the Egyptian ancestry of the *Hermetica* seventy-five years after "Reitzenstein's Egyptomania" (Copenhaver's expression). The last weighty word in the debate was that of Garth Fowden, who—although he spoke of "the Egyptian Hermes"—managed to establish a golden mean between the extreme positions of Festugière and Mahé. The strength of his case lies in his caveat concerning the characteristics of a syncretic culture in which the individual elements are not easy to separate.

Since I am interested in the possible impact of hermetic thought on Renaissance occultism and particularly on John Dee's philosophy, this later development of hermetic studies is of less importance. From a methodological aspect, however, the strong commitment of Fowden and Copenhaver to syncretism will be very important.

Although Copenhaver emphasized that the magical aspects of the theoretical *Hermetica* are insignificant compared to the astrological-alchemical magic of the practical or technical tracts that were never considered integral parts of the *Corpus hermeticum* (1992, xxxii), he himself recalled that the lack of magic in the *Corpus* may reflect more the biases of later editors than those of the authors. William Grese pointed out the same: "It is not known when the collection was made, why it was made, or what was excluded. The lack of more references to magical practices may reflect more the selection of texts that have survived than the actual situation in antiquity" (Grese 1988, 49). At this point, it may be useful to recall some further notices of Copenhaver. In harmony with Frances Yates (1964, 40 ff.), Copenhaver also acknowledged the magical importance of the "god-making" passages of the *Asclepius* (23–24, 37–38), furthermore he emphasized that "instead of a theory of magic, the theoretical *Hermetica* present a theory of salvation through knowledge or *gnosis*, yet this theory was the product of a culture that made no clear, rigid distinction between religion and magic" (1992, xxxvii). Finally, we should also bear in mind that neither the age of Hellenism nor the Renaissance made such a distinction between philosophical and technical treatises as did Festugière in calling the latter "popular," which meant inferior, in fact obscure, gibberish.

Ficino and his contemporaries did not know about many of the hermetic texts now considered to be component parts of the *Corpus hermeticum.* On the other hand, they had access to a great amount of magical literature deriving from the original technical hermetica, including Arabic sources, such as Al-Kindi, Abu Ma'shar, Jabir (Latinized as Geber, the alchemist), and others who spoke much about Hermes and whose writings were accessible throughout the Middle Ages. The *Tabula smaragdina*, the *Picatrix,* and various treatises bearing the name of Hermes (*The Book of Hermes on the Six Principles of Nature, Book of Propositions . . . said to be by the Philosopher Termegistus,* etc.) also circulated from the eleventh century[9] and there is no reason to think that the learned neoplatonists would not have associated the two groups of sources that all claimed to be revealed writings of Hermes Trismegistus.

Let us now return to that text that was known to Ficino, and although it survived in Latin, it was not disassociated from the Greek corpus of hermetic writings. It was the *Asclepius,* which had been spoken of by many classical and medieval Christian authorities and was also mentioned by a number of medieval philosophers, such as Albertus Magnus, Bernardus Silvestris, John of Salisbury, Alain de Lille, Vincent of Beauvais, Guillaume d'Auvergne, and others.[10] This tract was often considered to be a synopsis of Egyptian religion and contained important magical ideas as well. It received bad and good critiques during its career until Ficino and his readers—according to Frances Yates—considered it "to be the Mosaic piety of the Egyptian Genesis, and the Christian piety of Egyptian regeneration would have rehabilitated in their eyes the Egyptian religion of the *Asclepius*" (1964, 41). She also added: "The rehabilitation of the *Asclepius,* through the rediscovery of the *Corpus hermeticum,* is, I believe, one of the chief factors in the Renaissance revival of magic" (ibid.). It is time to look then at the magical contents of the *Asclepius.*

The introduction of the text describes a situation when Hermes Trismegistus, Asclepius, Tat, and Ammon meet in an Egyptian temple where the four men receive exaltation and revelatory teachings through the mouth of Hermes on the nature of the cosmos and that of man.

Scott thought the text falls into three, almost independent parts. The first being a coherent, well-structured treatise on the trinity of God, the world, and man (*De tota summitate: Deus, Mundus, Homo*); in this the stress falls on the role of man. The second part represents dualist gnosis and deals with the origin of evil (*De origine mali*). The third one is a highly corrupted text, the leitmotif of which is the relationship between the gods and man, which is why it is usually referred to as *De cultu deorum.*[11]

Ficino's attention was caught primarily by two motives in the *Asclepius.* The first was its anthropocentric approach, which described man's importance and potential power almost with the erudition of the humanists. The following sentences became a quasi-bible of Renaissance moral philosophers and provided important ideological support for magical theories, too:

> *Propter haec, o Asclepi, magnum miraculum est homo . . .* —Because of this, Asclepius, a human being is a great wonder, a living thing to be worshipped and honored: for he changes his nature into god's, as if he were a god; he knows the demonic kind inasmuch as he recognizes that he originated among them; he despises the part of him that is human nature, having put his trust in the divinity of his other part. [. . .] Everything is permitted him: heaven itself seems not too high, for he measures it in his clever thinking as if it were nearby. [. . .] He is everything, and he is everywhere.—*Omnia idem est, et ubique idem est.* (*Ascl.* 6; quoted from Copenhaver 1992, 70)

One of the most intriguing sections of *Asclepius* claims that the omnipotence of man, the possibility of his *exaltatio*, is proved by the fact that he himself is capable of creating living gods. As Trismegistus explains:

> And since this discourse proclaims to us the kinship and association between humans and gods, Asclepius, you must recognize mankind's power and strength. Just as the master and father [. . .] is maker of the heavenly gods, so is mankind who fashions the temple gods who are content to be near to humans. (*Ascl.* 23)

Then we learn that

> The figures of gods that humans form have been formed of both natures—from the divine, which is purer and more divine by far, and from the material of which they are built, whose nature falls short of the human. [. . .] Always mindful of its nature and origin, humanity persists in imitating divinity, representing its gods in semblence of its own features, just as the father and master made his gods eternal to resemble him. (ibid.)

As it turns out, the sage here refers to statues, not simple representations, but rather "statues ensouled and conscious, filled with spirit and doing great deeds, [. . .] statues that make people ill and cure them, bringing them pain and pleasure as each deserves" (*Ascl.* 24). This notion recurs once again towards the end of the treatise:

Let us turn again to mankind and reason, that divine gift whereby a human is called a rational animal. What we have said of mankind is wondrous, but less wondrous than this: it exceeds the wonderment of all wonders that humans have been able to discover the divine nature and how to make it. Our ancestors [. . .] discovered the art of making gods. To their discovery they added a conformable power arising from the nature of matter. Because they could not make souls, they mixed this power in and called up the souls of demons or angels and implanted them in likeness through holy and divine mysteries, whence the idols could have the power to do good and evil. (*Ascl.* 37)[12]

Let us imagine what John Dee would feel if he happened to read or remembered his reading of the above passage on the holy mysteries of calling up the souls of demons or angels, while preparing himself for a session to meet Madimi or Nalvage. The quoted paragraphs of the *Asclepius* can be considered a very powerful statement about the *exaltation* of man and they indeed captured the imagination of the Renaissance philosophers and magi.

To understand their enthusiasm, we must remember that the Renaissance of the humanists was a retrospective epoch. As Frances Yates suggested, "the great forward movements of the Renaissance all derive their vigour, their emotional impulse, from looking backwards" (1964, 1). The revived classical view of a cyclical history—even if counterbalanced by the eschatological linearity of Christianity—made the humanists constantly aware of the lost Golden Age and the need for researching and studying the past as far back as one could reach in time.

By the fifteenth and sixteenth centuries more and more thinkers and scholars entertained the idea that the Golden Age could be restored on earth in the material life of humans, provided one could restore the pristine wisdom, the ancient theology. The Florentine neoplatonists were greatly concerned with this, and one can say that no matter how advanced was their new, man-centered ideology, it gained its energy through a determined search of the past, highly appreciative of everything that was ancient and antiquated.[13]

Most of the humanists were engaged with a well-defined classical heritage—that of Greco-Roman philosophy and literature. Some of them, on the other hand, tried to reach back to an antedeluvian, pristine wisdom which they sought in Pythagorean number mysticism, the Chaldean oracles, Jewish speculations, and Egyptian magic. One of the most esteemed sources in this respect was the *Corpus hermeticum*, although much was to be learned from the *Sybilline Oracles*, the *Orphic Hymns*, and from those later commentators who in the Hellenistic era were preoccupied with the *prisca theologia*.

I have already recalled the impetus that led to the hermetic interest of Ficino's Florentine Academy, as well as the ideological background of the philological misrepresentation by means of which they examined these writings as testimonies from the times of Moses. This firm belief was not shaken until 1614 when the Protestant Isaac Casaubon—interestingly, the father of Meric, who published the documents of Dee's spiritual magic, a system partly derived from the *Hermetica*—philologically proved that the hermetic texts included biblical and Greek diction and etymologies that disproved their supposed ancient age.[14] Preceding this denominational as well as textual polemic, however, the sixteenth century saw the triumphant process of the hermetic texts: prior to 1614 Ficino's 1471 edition was republished on twenty-two occasions by various European presses, and, parallel with this, other humanist editors produced further publications. To select just a few representative works from Copenhaver's list (1992, lxix), in the first half of the sixteenth century Italian, French, Dutch, and Spanish versions were published; the first Greek critical edition was prepared by Turnebus in 1554 (*Mercurii Trismegisti Poemander, seu de potestate et sapientia divina. Aesculapii definitiones ad Ammonem regem . . .* , Paris); important commentaries were offered by Lefèvre d'Étaples (1494, 1505), Lodovico Lazzarelli (*Crater hermetis*, 1494, published in d'Étaples 1505), Francesco Giorgi (in his *De harmonia mundi totius*, 1525), then by Hannibal Rosselli (4 volumes, Cracow, 1585–1590), and Francesco Patrizi, who embedded his new translation into a large and complicated work of neoplatonist philosophy (Ferrara, 1591, Venice 1593) under the title: *Nova de universis philosophia, libris quinquaginta comprehensa: in qua Aristotelico methodo non per notum, sed per lucem et lumina ad primam causam ascenditur. [. . .] Postremo methodo Platonico rerum universitas a conditore Deo deducitur. [. . .] Quibus postremo sunt adiecta Zoroastris oracula ex Platonicis collecta: Hermetis Trismegisti libelli, et fragmenta: Asclepi discipuli tres libelli: Mystica Aegyptiorum . . .* etc.

Even well after 1614 one could see enthusiastic testimonies for Hermes Trismegistus, such as in the writings of the "last polymath," Athanasius Kircher, or in Newton's secret alchemical notebooks.

Needless to say, John Dee had an impressive collection of various editions and commentaries on the *Hermetica*.[15] At least in this respect he certainly was well equipped to connect himself with that peculiar trend of Renaissance humanism that avowed the dignity of man and worked on a mystical-theological program to realize the magical *exaltatio*.

Neoplatonism and Classical Theurgy

One aspect of the hermeticism debate reacted against the thesis posited by Frances Yates that the hermetic tradition played an almost exclusive role in fostering the new magical ideas of the Florentine neoplatonists. More recent studies have pointed out the importance of other intellectual trends; for example, Michael Allen has been systematically concentrating on the influence of Plato himself and that of the neoplatonists (Plotinus, Porphyry, Iamblichus), while Brian Copenhaver—in harmony with Allen—called attention also to the medieval magical heritage (Proclus, Psellus, as well as Patristic and scholastic Christian writers)—which by no means should be understood as being homogeneous.[16]

The anti-Yatesian criticism in the hermeticism debate does not mean that Yates would have entirely neglected questions related to Hellenistic or medieval magic. She devoted long passages and chapters to topics such as the infamous medieval magical primer, the *Picatrix*, and its possible influence on Ficino. But she interpreted Ficino's magic as something that turned away from this "rude and primitive" medieval inheritance and elevated magic onto a prestigeous level, justified by the scholarly and philosophical apparatus of neoplatonist humanism (1964, 80, 108).

It must be recognized that Yates was simplifying when she postulated a sharp dichotomy between medieval and Renaissance magic, since the medieval lore, at least a large portion of it, was nothing but a derivation of the classical heritage incubated by Arabic schools. She was also reluctant to see that Ficino, when he had interpreted magic enveloped into the humanist ideology, had also relied on the praxis of medieval magic, and his operations with talismans, for example, were not necessarily less primitive or naive than that of his medieval predecessors.

Let us now have a quick look at the magical ideas of the so-called Platonici, a textual heritage that also featured abundantly in John Dee's library[17] but received comparably the smallest attention from Yates and the Yatesian interpretation of Renaissance magic. Since my main concern here is the theme of *exaltatio* in relation to magical practice, I shall concentrate on those passages that presupposed, described, and eventually approved magical practices in order to come—as Proclus put it—"to directly experience the Primordial and Divine Powers" (*De sacrificio et magia*, quoted in Iamblichus 1989, 149).

Those who considered themselves true philosophers have always spoken with contempt of magic as something that is contrary to reasonable thinking and suits only the ignorant mob. Plato and his followers, such as Plotinus, were no exceptions to this attitude. It is easy to find passages in their works that condemn or ridicule magic and mystical rituals.[18] Still, as Brian Copenhaver claimed, "if one wishes to find the philosophical and scientific roots of Renaissance magical theory—as distinguished from the genealogy of the magus—one looks not to the eclectic pieties of Hermes Trismegistus but to the neoplatonists" (1988, 84).

As we have already seen with the help of Edgar Wind's explanations (see pg. 23), some elements in Plato's mysticism led to a development in philosophy inclining towards the reintegration of dialectics and religion and turned the philosopher into a hierophant. Although Iamblichus is credited as having fathered the first comprehensive scheme of occult philosophy (see Ronan's introduction in Iamblichus 1989, 4), most of the Hellenistic philosophers, beginning with Plotinus, became sensitive to issues of the reversed emanation, that is, the ascension of man and the catalyzing of this ascension by magical means. The latter intention was of course connected with their concepts of demons and demonology, which is by no means an easy subject in relation to the philosophical schools of the Hellenistic period.

There is no place here to give a comprehensive survey of classical demonology or the scholarly literature written on the subject; let it be enough to mention that the whole history of neoplatonism was ambiguous in this respect, and Plato was no exception. He often spoke of the gods, but the nature of his gods can be understood in several ways. P. Merlan (in Armstrong 1995, 32 ff.) distinguishes among three possible interpretations: that the gods are used as myths or literary devices, or that they are derivations of the first principles, or that they are theologized, personified versions of the principles. In Plotinus, the second hypostasis (i.e., the transcendent source of reality) contains ideas, intellects, and gods. The question of demons arose in connection with the problem of evil; according to Plato and Plotinus, the One could not contain anything corrupt, so evil came to being through the imperfections of the emanations.

The demon world, however, soon became heterogeneous, accommodating various sorts of spirits. Plato spoke of demons in connection with the *daimón* of Socrates, and in the *Symposium* attributed a whole system of demonology to Socrates' teacher, Diotima (202e–203a). It is worth quoting from these passages because the wise woman gave quite an extended classification of spirits with functions that have important resonances in the history of magic:

[Diotima] . . . spirits, you know, are half-way between god and man. [. . .] They are the envoys and interpreters that ply between heaven and earth, flying upward with our worship and our prayers, and descending with the heavenly answers and commandments, and since they are between the two estates they weld both sides together and merge them into one great whole. They form the medium of the prophetic arts, of the priestly rites of sacrifice, initiation, and incantation, of divination and of sorcery, for the divine will not mingle directly with the human, and it is only through the mediation of the spirit world that man can have any intercourse, whether waking or sleeping, with the gods. And the man who is versed in such matters is said to have spiritual powers, as opposed to the mechanical powers of the man who is expert in the more mundane arts. There are many spirits and many kinds of spirits, too. . . . (203a, Plato 1963, 555)

Preceding the above explanation, Diotima is said to have accomplished a magical act that would later accord with Agrippa's description of the mighty magus, commanding the governing powers of nature: "a woman who was deeply versed in many [. . .] fields of knowledge. It was she who brought about a ten years' postponement of the great plague of Athens on the occasion of certain sacrifice . . ." (201d).

It was Xenocrates, who, expanding Plato's notions on demons, established a dichotomy between good and evil spirits. He also set up a tripartite hierarchy of these beings: some had simply always existed as demons; a second class consisted of souls of men that, after death, had separated from their bodies, becoming demons; the third category consisted of souls, still remaining in the body (Armstrong 1995, 35).

Plotinus followed Xenocrates' typology (*Enneads* III.4–5) and at one point, in spite of his general scepticism concerning interaction with spirits, even asserted that demons can be invoked:

Even the Celestials, the Daimones, are not on their unreasoning side immune: there is nothing against ascribing acts of memory and experiences of sense to them, in supposing them to accept the traction of methods laid up in the natural order, and to give hearing to petitioners . . . (IV.4.43, Plotinus 1991, 330)

The *Enneads*, of course, have many intriguing passages concerning the state of *exaltatio* and man's intercourse wih the Deity as well as with demons. The most cited passages can be found in IV.4, which is titled by

Porphyry as "Questions Concerning the Soul, II." Here Plotinus examines the upward journey of the soul in relation to the nature of the universe, which he describes as a homogeneous and organic unity filled with and ruled by correspondences. In sections 30–31 he raises the problem of astrology of which he had a generally derogatory opinion. He certainly denied that the stars, as higher intelligences, would have memory or sensation; on the other hand, he did not exclude the possibility that the stars could have an influence on human destiny. This would result from the organic nature of the cosmos being filled with occult correspondences. "Our problem embraces all act and all experience throughout the entire Cosmos— whether due to nature, or effected by art," says Plotinus (IV.4.31) and in the following sections he describes the World Soul (One-All) that is

> a sympathetic total and stands as one living being; the far is near; it happens as in one animal with its separate parts: talon, horn, finger, and any other member are not continuous and yet are effectively near; intermediate parts feel nothing, but at a distant point the local experience is known. (4.32, Plotinus 1991, 319)

Since this united cosmos is ruled by order and harmony (following the ordinance of numbers), "The Universe is immensely varied, [. . .] it must contain an untellably wonderful variety of powers, with which, of course, the bodies moving through the heavens will be most richly endowed" (4.36). True magic follows from this order, it is "the primal mage and sourcerer—discovered by men who thenceforth turn those same ensorcellations and magic arts upon one another" (4.40).

Plotinus was definitely cautious in his assessment of magic. The only notion he accepted without reservation was the universal correspondences, which, at least indirectly, admitted the concept of sympathetic magic. Speaking about these sympathies, he stated that "the prayer is answered by the mere fact that part and other part are wrought to one tone like a musical string which, plucked at one end, vibrates at the other also" (4.41), and that

> the art of doctor or magic healer will compel some one contre to purvey something of its own power to another centre. Just so the All: it purveys spontaneously, but it purveys also under spell; a petition brings to some one part the power laid up for each: the All gives to its members by a natural act, and the petitioner is no alien. (IV.4.42, Plotinus 1991, 329)

Ficino later made use of his ideas to develop the method of talismanic magic in *De vita coelitus comparanda*.[19]

In *Enneads* IV.3 there is a much discussed paragraph that seems to connect Plotinus to the magic described in the hermetic *Asclepius*, namely his interpretation of supposed human potential to create living gods:

> Those ancient sages, who sought to secure the presence of divine beings by the erection of shrines and statues, showed insight into the nature of the All; they perceived that , though this Soul is everywhere tractable, its presence will be secured all the more readily when an appropriate receptacle is elaborated, a place especially capable of receiving some portion or phase of it, something reproducing it, or representing it and serving like a mirror to catch an image of it. (IV.3.11, Plotinus 1991, 264)

Although most historians of philosophy deny Plotinus' involvement in magical practices and few ascribe any great importance to the Egyptian-Persian influence in his philosophy, the above passages could easily catch the attentive but philologically less sharpened eyes of Renaissance thinkers, such as Ficino or even John Dee. One should add, that in Porphyry's famous *Life of Plotinus* which was known and used throughout the early modern period, some of the biographical data could support the conjectures concerning a syncretic Plotinian-hermetic-oriental derivation of the *prisca theologia*, comparable to the methods of the pious magi of the Renaissance.

To begin with, Porphyry argues that the first teacher of whom Plotinus really approved was the Alexandrian sage Ammonius. Although next to nothing is known about his philosophy (Armstrong 1995, 196 ff.), he, as a teacher, had also been associated with the philosophical sect of hermeticists. As Garth Fowden recently suggested, in the second and third centuries of the Roman Empire, a characteristic intellectual elite crystallized that was educated in Greek philosophy but had become dissatisfied with pure philosophizing. They formed small sects that transmitted oral teachings and Ammonius Saccas might have been the leader of such a group (Fowden 1986, 112–29). According to Fowden, Ammonius represented that common denomintor from which Plotinus developed a systematic philosophical doctrine while the supposed hermetic groups produced only fragments, accidentally surviving products of mystical contemplation bordering on theosophy and religion. The figure of Ammonius may be a symbolic embodiment of the overlap between hermeticism and neoplatonism as well as within hermeticism between philosophical and technical writings as has been pointed out in recent scholarly literature (see Grese 1988).

One should also note another similarity between Hellenistic neo-platonism and hermeticism: Scott and Festugière both pointed out what should *not* be looked for in the *Hermetica*. There is neither a canonized body of texts preserving the revelation of God, nor any traces of theurgic practice, that is, a set of rites and sacramentalism (cf. Scott 1924–1936, 1:7). These shortages interestingly coincide with what Armstrong characterised as Plotinus' mystical "religion": "There is no place in it for rites or sacraments, nor are there any methods of prayer or meditation or devices for concentrating and liberating the mind such as are used by both theistic and non-theistic mystics" (Armstrong 1995, 260).

Let us return to Porphyry's *Life*. He furthermore informs the reader that Plotinus became so interested in Eastern, Persian, and Indian philosophy that he undertook to participate in Emperor Gordian III's campaign against the Persians (ch. 3). Although this episode is dismissed by Armstrong with claims that "his thought is entirely explainable as a personal development of Greek philosophy, without any need to postulate Oriental influences" (1995, 200), two other incidents shed light on a more syncretic nature and eventual magical practices in the master's life. In chapter 10 of Porphyry's *Life* we learn that Plotinus' only enemy, Olympius of Alexandria, had tried to practice star magic against the master but Plotinus had such a strong soul power that the harmful magic rebounded on Olympius, who then stopped his machinations. According to the other episode (related in the same chapter) once an Egyptian priest came to Rome and offered to invoke Plotinus' personal *daimón*. When Plotinus agreed, they went to the Iseum and the Egyptian conjured up the spirit, who, to the amazement of the participants, turned out to be a real god. The priest told Plotinus, "You are singularly graced; the guiding-spirit within you is not of the lower degree but a God" (ch. 10, Porphyry 1991, cx). The séance was unfortunately interrupted because a jealous helper strangled the apotropaic fowls used in the divination, so no conversation could ensue with the protecting god. Still, Plotinus himself remained so impressed, that he wrote a treatise "On Our Allotted Guardian Spirit" (*Enneads*, III.4). Although these episodes do not undeniably prove that Plotinus himself ever performed magical ceremonies, they certainly may have kindled the fantasy of the Renaissance readers of Porphyry's *Life* and could have contributed to the concepts of early modern demonology.[20]

Among the followers of Plotinus, it was Iamblichus of Chalcis (242/ 3–325 A.D.) who developed a systematic occult philosophy. His philo-

sophical thought was characterized by a new approach to religion, as
A. C. Lloyd formulated it: "to describe the change in anthropological
terms—it was no longer merely the myth which was regarded as philosophically relevant but the ritual" (1995, 277). Copenhaver referred to
him and the tendency he represented noting that "a Syrian writing in
Greek could embrace with the word philosophy a body of practical,
religious literature that bore little trace of the rational analysis still implied by φιλοσοφια" (1988, 83). However this can hardly belittle his
striving to grasp the essence of *exaltatio* in terms that would suit both
intellectual thinking and intuitive enlightenment. This theurgy was not
only to unite philosophy and religion, but also receptive contemplation
and active magic. As Lloyd recalled Bidez's classic observation, "the ap-
pellation was intended 'to go one better than the theologian and remind
people that the theurgist does not limit himself to talking about the gods
but knows how to act.' "[21]

To Plotinus' neoplatonism Iamblichus added elements of Egyptian
mysticism, or at least what was thought to be Egyptian mysticism, and
he also became interested in the Chaldean tradition. As a consequence,
he adopted the view that the religious activities of the initiates were more
effective than those of philosophers. This was quite a sharp turn from the
standpoint of his predecessors in neoplatonist philosophy who ranked
intellectual inquiry and the enlightenment resulting from it either as the
goal of life or at least the best means to it (cf. Lloyd 1995, 295 ff.). This
debate can best be seen in the controversy between Iamblichus and
his immediate predecessor, Porphyry: Iamblichus' main theological-
philosophical work *De mysteriis* was in fact an answer to Porphyry's *Letter
to Anebo*, a rather sceptical work, denying that the practice of theurgic
rites could lead to salvation. Iamblichus' views expressed in *De mysteriis*
corroborate the common perception that he was not only a deeply religious philosopher but also a clairvoyant, who claimed to have raised
phantoms by the intervention of the gods. His consideration about the
mutually interrelated nature of knowledge and intuitive revelation (a
union with the deity, i.e. *exaltatio*) runs as follows, undoubtedly suggesting the superiority of intuition over reason:

> You may not think all the authority of the energy in theurgic operations
> is in our power, and that you may not suppose the true work of them
> consists in our conceptions. [. . .] Nevertheless, efficacious union [with
> divine natures] is not effected without knowledge; yet knowledge does
> not possess a sameness with this union. (II.11, Iamblichus 1989, 62)[22]

He treated daemons and spirits quite extensively throughout his work and saw them as important engines of revelation and catalyzers of the union:

> may it not be natural to divinity to extend a phantasm from itself? But how can that which is firmly established in itself, and which is the cause of essence and truth, produce in a foreign seat a certain deceitful imitation of itself? By no means, therefore, does divinity either transform himself into phantasms, nor extend these from himself to other things, but emits, by illumination, true representations of himself, in the true manners of the souls. (II.10, 61)

One can easily imagine Dee's thrill when he encountered the following passage in *De mysteriis*:

> A god, an angel, and a good daemon instruct man in what their proper essence consists. [. . .] Angels and daemons always receive truth from the Gods, so that they never assert any thing contrary to this. . . . (II.10, 59)

The functioning of a spirit contact is explained in one of the next chapters. This is again something John Dee could adopt as important guidelines for his own "angelic conversations":

> He who [appears to] draw down a certain divinity, sees a spirit descending and entering into some one, recognizes its magnitude and quality, and is also mystically persuaded and governed by it. (III.6, 69)

In the rest of the work Iamblichus surveys various modes of divination, such as incantations, specific inspirations, and touching dead bodies, and devotes lengthy chapters to weighing the possibilities of astrology, that is, the influence of the stars on individual lives and the ways of getting to know this influence. A part of his work corresponding to the typology of divination is the typology of sacrifices. These sacrifices are the true catalyzers of *exaltatio* that help to attain a state in which divination can be successful. His definition of true enthusiasm is the following: "There is a time when we become wholly soul, are out of the body, and sublimely revolve on high, in conjunction with all the immaterial Gods" (V.15, 114). As we shall see, this definition not only corresponds with the aspirations of Plato, Plotinus, and the unknown author(s) of the *Corpus hermeticum*, but also with that of the Renaissance magi, most eloquently expressed in Pico's *encomium*, but also echoed in Dee's various writings, including his *Mathematicall Praeface*.

Before concluding this subchapter on the classical traditions of magic, one more name must be mentioned, that of Proclus, who in recent research increasingly features as a possible major source for Renaissance magic.

Proclus (410/12–485 A.D.) is perhaps the best known among the fourth- and fifth-century neoplatonists of Athens. He came from Constantinople via Alexandria to the seat of Plato and studied under Plutarch of Athens and Syrianus, becoming acquainted with Orphic and Chaldean theology, too. In spite of the expansion of the, by now, official and enforced Christianity, he remained a defender of pagan worship, even followed the Chaldean rituals and observed the Egyptian holy days (Lloyd 1995, 304 ff.). It is no surprise that he was also believed to have been able to conjure up luminous phantoms and spirits, just as his predecessors Plotinus and Iamblichus did. Although he left behind a voluminous corpus of philosophical writings (including the *Elements of Theology* and a series of commentaries on various books of Plato), for the moment, however, only two small fragments are of interest, those directly dealing with divination and magic.

The first had been known only in Ficino's Latin translation (which the Italian called "Proculi opusculum de sacrificio interprete Marsilio Ficino Florentino") until Joseph Bidez unearthed the Greek original and published it in the sixth volume of his *Catalogue des manuscrits alchimiques Grecs*.[23] Recently two English translations of the Greek original were produced by Brian Copenhaver (1988) and Stephen Ronan (1989). Copenhaver also prepared a superb edition of Ficino's Latin[24] and included Bidez's Greek text making a complex comparison possible. The other fragment has been preserved in Michael Psellus' *Accusation against Michael Cerularius before the Synod* and has recently been translated by Stephen Ronan under the title "On the Signs of Divine Possession."[25]

Although two very short fragments, they offer a condensed syncretic essence of classical (that is, Hellenistic-neoplatonic) magical concepts without excluding the occult notions of the *Hermetica*. One of the main themes of the first fragment is the notion of sympathy, likeness, and analogy, which provides the framework for the workings of occult correspondences as well as for the practice of magic:

> So by observing such things and connecting them to the appropriate heavenly beings, the ancient wise men brought divine powers into the region of mortals, attracting them through likeness. For likeness is sufficient to join beings to one another. (lines 17–20, Proclus 1988, 103)

The organic system of the universe is asserted by the statement of line 46: "Thus all things are full of gods. . . ." The theoretical framework is connected with the occult practices invented by mankind: "The authorities on the priestly art have thus discovered how to gain the favor of powers above, mixing some things together and setting others apart in due order" (lines 70–73, Proclus 1988, 105). This process was the case in alchemy, as is well known, but Proclus also employed it to account for the creation of living statues of gods, as we have already learnt from the *Asclepius*.[26] Proclus also touches upon ritual or ceremonial magic. He mentions that through consecrations and other divine services people "achieved association with the [daemons], from whom they returned forthwith to actual works of the gods" (lines 92–93, 105).

Copenhaver's impressive philological inquiry (1988) has proved that the examples of natural and ceremonial magic mentioned in Proclus' fragment can be encountered in most authorities of Renaissance magic, especially in the works of Ficino and Agrippa. Thus he has convincingly established Proclus' magical treatises among the sourceworks of Renaissance occultism.

The other fragment in Psellus' paraphrase (as published in É. des Places' *Oracles Chaldaiques*) touches upon the "physiology" of *exaltatio*, that is, the sacred enragement, and connects it with the evocation of spirits. As Psellus sums up, Proclus claims that

> there are men who are possessed and who receive a divine spirit. Some receive it spontaneously, like those who are said to be 'seized by God' either at certain periods or intermittently and on occasion. There are others who work themselves up into a state of inspiration by deliberate action. In order for a Theagogy and an inspiration to take effect, they must be accompanied by a change of consciousness. (Proclus 1989, 150)

When divine inspiration comes, there are cases where the possessed become completely beside themselves and unconscious; others, conversely, show remarkable strength. His last advice suggests that it is "necessary to begin by removing all the obstacles blocking the arrival of the Gods and to impose an absolute calm around ourselves in order that the manifestation of the spirits we invoke takes place without tumult and in peace" (ibid.).

—∞—

Although the neoplatonist philosophers hardly ever mentioned the hermetic texts and vice versa, and, consequently, most students of the

Hermetica have been reluctant to see a direct neoplatonic influence in the texts, one must admit that the two traditions were not so separate and irreconcilable as first appears. I would like to refer to two textual instances that corroborate this view, one from Iamblichus' *De mysteriis*, the other from the practice of the late enthusiastic follower, the Renaissance neoplatonist Marsilio Ficino.

As for Iamblichus, he reflected on Porphyry's wry remark that Egyptian wisdom is basically Hellenistic philosophy (see the *Letter to Anebo*, VIII.35–38 in Porphyry 1989, 19) by drawing a detailed parallel between the two:

> For the books which are circulated under the name of Hermes contain Hermaic opinions, though they frequently employ the language of the philosophers: for they were translated from the Egyptian tongue by men who were not unskilled in philosophy. [. . .] The Egyptians do not say that all things are physical. For they separate the life of the soul and the intellectual life from nature, not only in the universe but also in us. [. . .] They likewise arrange the Demiurgus as the primary father of things in generation; and they acknowledge the existence of a vital power, prior to the heavens, and subsisting in the heavens. (Ibid. VIII.4, 132–33)[27]

A particularly interesting aspect of the above section is that Iamblichus refers not only to the theoretical hermetica here, but also mentions the technical aspects, including astrology, the interpretation of the zodiac, the decans, and naming the leading planets.

Iamblichus' approach suggests that later neoplatonists in fact did not see the Hermetica and their own philosophy as isolated from each other, as many modern intellectual historians have suggested. In the fifteenth century, in setting himself to revive the pagan achievements of neoplatonism, Ficino certainly thought likewise. He, for example, found it very appropriate to unite the two traditions, namely the philosophy of emanations and the spirit-lore of the Platonici on the one hand and the mythology of *exaltatio* drawn from the *Corpus hermeticum* on the other. It was not coincidental that he decided to expand his *Hermetica* translation into an anthology of neoplatonic mysticism, the contents of which were preserved in Ficino's *Opera* as follows: "Dionysii Areopagitae translatio cum suis argumentis" (Ficino 1576, 2:1–1128); "In divinum Platonem epitomae" (1129–1533); "In Plotinum Philosophum ex Platonici familia nati" (1534–1800); "Expositio Prisciavi & Marsilii Theophrastum defenso, ac phantasia, & intellectu" (1801–1835); "Mercurii Trismegisti Pymander, de potestate ac sapientia Dei item Asclepius de voluntate dei" (1836–1870); "Iamblichus de mysteriis Aegyptiorum, Chaldeorum, atque Assiriorum" (1873–1907); "Proclus de anima & daemonum [commentariis in Alcibiadem Platonis primum]" (1908–1928); "Proclus de sacrificio & magia" (1928–1929); "Porphyrius de occasionibus sive causis ad intelligibilia nos ducensibus" (1929–1932); "Porphyrius de abstinentia animalium [de animi ascenta & descenta]" (1932–1938); "Psellus de daemonibus" (1939–1944); "Pithagore aurea verba & symbola" (1978–1979).

Here one finds those late neoplatonists (Iamblichus, Proclus, Porphyrius, Psellus) whom Brian Copenhaver identified as being Ficino's main inspirations, together with the tracts of the *Corpus hermeticum*, or, as Ficino translated it, "Mercurii Trismegisti Pymander, de potestate ac sapientia Dei item Asclepius de voluntate dei."[28] And if we decide to look for John Dee's possible sources of hermeticism, we find that he had the entirety of this literature at his disposal, not only a copy of Ficino's *Opera* (R&W 204), but also a beautiful 1516 Aldus edition of Ficino's "anthologia esoterica" (R&W 256)[29] that is now kept in the Folger Library and preserves Dee's marginalia on Iamblichus and the other Platonici as well as on the hermetic treatises (cf. Clulee 1988, 277n. 75; Håkansson 2001, 213; Harkness 1999, 228).

MEDIEVAL MAGIC

Medieval magic has not been excluded from the recent radical reinterpretation and revaluation of magical and occult lore. As with intriguing questions related to the *Hermetica* or Renaissance magic, the research of the Middle Ages has also led to the discovery of new texts as well as to the development of new theories on the meaning and the use of those texts. If we want to classify the medieval traditions of magic as possible input for Dee, again we shall have to look into his library catalogues because this is where we have a good chance of encountering missing links between his collection and the presumable sources of his magic.

One category is well represented and clearly visible in his collection: medieval texts that engaged in the definition and classification of magic, often either condemning it entirely or refuting just some of its branches.[30]

The second category would be those scholarly works oriented towards scientific questions whose authors restricted themselves to *magia naturalis,* optics, and alchemy. The best example in this category would be Roger Bacon, who, as Nicholas Clulee has shown (1971, 1973, 1988), was one of Dee's favorite authors, especially in his early career. Bacon's works were widely represented in Dee's library,[31] but belonging to this category one could also mention Al-Kindi's *De radiis* (R&W M149b, DM 42); Arnaldo de Villa Nova (*Opera*, R&W 299); Ramon Lull (*Opera*, R&W 1421; *Arbor scientiae*, R&W 1415; *Ars magna*, R&W 1418); and Johannes de Rupescissa's *De quintae essentiae* (R&W 1436).

A third group of sources would be medieval mystics, reflecting on the hierarchical world model, angelology, spiritual illumination, and related subjects. The following great authorities should be mentioned here: first and foremost Pseudo-Dionysius, whose complete works Dee possessed in an 1556 edition that survives with his heavy annotations (R&W 975, cf. Harkness 1999, 113 ff.). A work of similar scope was *De omnibus rebus naturalibus* by Pompilius Azalus, a 1544 Venice edition of which belonged to Dee (R&W 134) and also survives with his emphases and annotations. These notes indicate that the Doctor purchased this copy as early as 1550, probably during his visit to Paris and—then, or later on— he heavily glossed the chapters on angels (Roberts & Watson) 1990, 83; and Harkness 1999). Among medieval mystics a writer of great importance for Reformation millenarism and chiliasm was Joachim of Fiore. His apocalyptic visions can be compared in many ways with that of Dee's angelic conversations and in fact Dee had a considerable collection of Joachim's works, including his *Opera* (R&W 436, 706, 2028).[32]

Finally, the most obscure and problematic group of possible source texts are those proliferated from the thirteenth century and dealt with divination and various forms of ceremonial magic. In this category we face a strictly unpublishable manuscript lore that until recently has been neglected as trash and bogus literature. However, lately, largely inspired by the pioneering studies of Richard Kieckhefer, it has increasingly come to the forefront of attention.[33] And there are good reasons to believe that John Dee's angelic magic had much to do with this murky and mysterious tradition. It was Stephen Clucas (1998, 200?) who recently has most emphatically pointed out this possibility, analyzing carefully a great number of medieval manuscripts of ritual magic and comparing them with Dee's own ritual magic as developed in his *Spiritual Diaries*. It was also Clucas who has noticed in Dee's library catalogue that the Doctor in fact possessed such manuals of medieval ceremonial magic.[34]

Having set up a general typology of medieval magic, I would like to state that in *magia naturalis* there was little or no trace of the mysticism and theological orientation of magical *exaltatio* that characterized the Hellenistic neoplatonic philosophers or the hermetic writings. All this does not mean that the hermetic tradition was totally absent in the Middle Ages. Although we find few hints concerning it in the official discourse of theological schools and universities, ancient magical lore did find shelters in which to survive. To discover those we have to look at the evidence concerning medieval ceremonial magic.

Medieval Ceremonial Magic

If the concepts of this magic were mainly platonic, the actual practices had a much more dubious origin. We gather more and more evidence about the existence of a complex magical lore during the Middle Ages which in certain respects reached back to the Hellenistic period or even earlier, without having much in common—admittedly—with the conceptual ideas of Hermes Trismegistus or the Platonici. Arthur Waite called this lore "ceremonial magic" (1961 [1911]) and recently it has been Richard Kieckhefer who has done the most to examine this textual heritage (1989).

As in my earlier discussion of the relationship between the philosophical and the technical *hermetica*, I have to restate my suspicion concerning the possibility of maintaining a clearly visible borderline between the high (the more or less accepted *magia naturalis*) and "underground" (perhaps a better expression than the rather problematically used adjective "popular") magic of the Middle Ages.[35]

An interesting feature of this corpus is that among the medieval documents of ceremonial magic a great many treatises survived under the name of Hermes—some of them are alchemical, while others deal directly with conjurations and divination by means of manipulations using angelic names. It seems reasonable to associate at least some of these texts with the technical hermetica recently studied by Fowden (1986) and Grese (1988). The technical hermetica certainly offered a great deal of practical information from alchemical operations to various ritualistic spells, conjurations, enumerations of demons, and the like. Although most of them (such as the Egyptian-Greek papyri and the Coptic library) were unknown to the Renaissance magi, it is also true that—as I have just mentioned—many similar texts did circulate in the Middle Ages as a rather secret and illegal body of literature associated with the name of Hermes.

Already Waite has noticed that these two groups of texts could have had some connection with each other: "Between the most ancient processes, such as those of Chaldean Magic, and the rites of the Middle Ages, there are marked correspondences and there is something of common doctrine. The doctrine of compulsion, or the power upon superior spirits by the use of certain words, is a case in point" (Waite 1961, 9). Then he adds: "The Ceremonial Magic of certain Graeco-Egyptian papyri offers the closest analogies with the processes of the Kabalistic school" (ibid.).

Lynn Thorndike, in his *History of Magic*, described the scope of the popularity of this literature and summarized their main contents. He identified a large number of thirteenth- to seventeenth-century manuscripts that contained alchemical and magical treatises associated with Hermes (among them, *The Book of Hermes on the Six Principles of Nature, and Book of Propositions . . . said to be by the Philosopher Termegistus*; cf. Thorndike 1923–1958, 2:214–29). It is interesting to notice that these writings enjoyed a partly positive reception. For example, Robert of Chester's Latin translation (from the year 1144) of an Arabic alchemical treatise under the name of Hermes described the supposed author as one of the three "Hermeses," namely Enoch, Noah, and himself, the Triplex, who was at once king, philosopher, and prophet (Thorndike, 215). Another fifteenth-century manuscript, containing a treatise on the fifth essence ascribed again to Hermes, characterized the author as "the prophet and king of Egypt, [who] after the flood of Noah, father of philosophers, had [the text] by revelation of an angel of God to him sent" (219). This is reminiscent of the Enochian legends, suggesting that some privileged men after the Fall or the Flood were entrusted by God to possess divine wisdom and teach mankind the skills and technologies of survival. As we shall see later, this motive constituted a central theme in John Dee's angel magic.

Thorndike also mentions specific treatises of theurgy and necromancy under the name of Hermes, which treated magic images, incantations, and spells using the names of God. These were strictly condemned by the scholastic philosophers and scientists: Albertus Magnus included them in his list of evil books on necromantic images often of which Christians were to beware, and Guillaume d'Auvergne, bishop of Paris, although he mentioned Hermes and Asclepius approvingly, generally considered this necromantic-hermetic literature to be dangerous.[36]

The above scholastic authors condemned even more strongly another group of similar literature that survived under the name of Solomon, legendary king and savant of the Jews. Treatises with such titles as *De figura Almandel, Clavicula Solomonis,* and *Ars Notoria Solomonis* circulated in great numbers from the thirteenth century until the seventeenth century and contained invocations of angels for the purpose of seeking communion with God, as well as mystic figures and magical prayers

(Thorndike 1923–1958, 2:279–90; Clucas 200?; Fanger 1998). They often stated that the Creator revealed this art through an angel to Solomon, and it was useful for acquiring all the liberal and mechanical arts in a short time. In fact, the Solomonic art is more than that. In the *Liber sacer*, or *Liber juratus of Honorius*, which consists of ninety-three chapters and is supposed to be derived from a conference of magicians who decided to condense all their knowledge into one single volume, one learns about a variety of topics, among others how to compose of the great name of God of in seventy-two letters, how to redeem the soul from purgatory, how to get your wish from any angel, how to learn the hour of one's death, how to control spirits by words or seals, and many more mundane goals, such as how to open closed doors, catch thieves, and find lost treasure. Interestingly, two chapters, 91 on the apparition of dead bodies and 92 on the creation of animals from earth, were omitted, as contrary to the will of God.

In spite of this tactful caution of its authors, Albertus Magnus automatically included them in the list of evil books, and Guillaume d'Auvergne called them "cursed and execrable" books (cf. his *De legibus*, quoted by Thorndike, 1923–1958, 2:281). Roger Bacon classified the Solomonic literature as something that "ought to be prohibited by law" (Thorndike, 279), and in his famous epistle "concerning the marvelous power of art and of nature" wrote as follows:

> It ought to be denied, which is claimed by some, that Solomon and other wise men composed these books—for books of this sort are not received by the authority of the Church but only by seducers who accept the naked letter and themselves compose new books and multiply inventions and inscribe renowned titles on their works. . . . (Bacon 1923, 19)

One cannot fail to notice that this illicit literature in many respects points back to the technical hermetica (Fanger 1998a); however, they also reveal a more immediate source, namely the early cabalistic literature with its concentration on characters and magic names (Kieckhefer 1998). Gerschom Scholem provided us with a full account of the development of this early medieval Jewish mystical literature (Scholem 1974 [1946]) and he also gave illuminating hints concerning the continuous popularity of this kind of magic, in spite of and against the development of rationalistic philosophy. Mystics and philosophers, as he suggested, were "both aristocrats of thought; yet Kabbalism succeeded in establishing a connection between its own world and certain elemental impulses operative in every human mind. It did not turn its back upon the primitive side of life, that all-important region where mortals are afraid of life and in fear of death, and derive scant wisdom from rational philosophy. Philosophy ignored these fears, out of whose substance man wove myths, and in turning its back upon the primitive side of man's existence, it paid a high price in losing touch with him altogether" (Scholem 1974, 35). One could add to this concept two points: to begin with, Scholem's dichotomy between rational philosophy and the cabala could be applied to other forms of mystical wisdom, such as Pythagoreanism, gnosticism, and hermeticism. Second, beside the fears and anxieties of "the primitive side of life," which were better answered by mysticism than philosophy, one should also take into account the desire for deification, the drive for *exaltatio* that has never ceased to be a major ambition of humankind. And this ambition characterized certainly not only the popular register of culture but caught the highest minds, too.

Returning now to the mixed textual lore of medieval ceremonial magic, by observing that these works were in constant use in the form of manuscript literature as late as the sixteenth and seventeenth centuries, one can see a continuity between the medieval and the Renaissance traditions of divinatory magic. One can also easily accept the possibility that the great Renaissance magi, a Trithemius, an Agrippa, or a John Dee, did not model their magical practices only on the venerable philosophical sources of the neoplatonists, or that of the "real" Hermes Trismegistus; they also must have tried out the illicit methods at their disposal, extracting them either from medieval or from contemporary underground sources.

As opposed to the medieval teachers, what encouraged them to do so? On the one hand, undoubtedly their increased self-confidence, catalyzed by the rediscovered hermetic tradition. On the other, the complexity of the traditions. In spite of the condemnations of the medieval authorities, tracts of ceremonial magic all claimed to be pious and to aspire to magical exaltation. The Solomonic *Liber juratus*, for example, described itself as follows:

> This is the book by which one can see God in this life. This is the book, by which anyone can be saved and led beyond a doubt to life eternal. [. . .] This is the book which no religion possesses except the Christian, or if it does, with no advantage.[37]

With their enlarged self-confidence, the Renaissance magi could see and acknowledge Christian piety in places where their medieval predecessors expressed abhorrence and disgust. In this attitude the Renaissance magi were, of course, also encouraged by their extensive classical learning, whether Christian or pagan. They could take courage from the Christian concept of the angelic hierarchies elaborated by the Pseudo-Dionysius, who also spoke much about the possibility of religious *exaltatio* and a union with God during earthly existence. He wrote about the souls that

> by means of angels as good leaders, they can be uplifted to the generous Source of all good things and, each according to his measure, they are able to have a share in the illuminations streaming out from that Source. (*The Divine Names* 696c, in Pseudo-Dionysius 1987, 73).

The Renaissance magi could easily find similar passages in the works of the neoplatonists, in the hermetic treatises, or, even, in such murky medieval tracts as the infamous *Picatrix*. If we take a look at that text, we shall have made an almost full circle, to arrive at the connecting link between Hellenistic and Arabic hermeticism and medieval ceremonial magic, which all seem to have inspired Renaissance neoplatonic magic.[38] This text is the only one, however, among my examples in this book that does not feature in Dee's library catalogue nor does he mention the title of the *Picatrix* in any of his writings. Nevertheless, I find it useful and necessary to include it among the input sources of Dee for the following reasons: as I shall show in the next chapter, the *Picatrix* definitely influenced many of the great Renaissance magi who were Dee's most important sources: Ficino, Trithemius, and Agrippa. Dee himself was interested in Arabic magical literature, as many of his references show (see, for example, his treatment of *alnirangiat* in the *Mathematical Preface*; cf. Clulee 1988, 167), not to mention his highly treasured *Book of Soyga*, the "Arabik Book" that Harkness recently identified as an English-Latin compendium of astrology and ceremonial magic (1999, 44–45). Even if Dee did not read the *Picatrix* itself, he must have been familiar with it through his other readings and its concept of exaltation may have been amalgamated with his own ideology of deification by means of magical science.

Magical Exaltatio in the Picatrix

I would like to call attention to the fact that the earliest surviving copies of the *Hermetica* are medieval codices, which indicate the uninterrupted interest in hermeticism even during the Middle Ages.[39] There is another medieval textual lore, however, that not only testifies to the survival of hermetism but also demonstrates the active use of this tradition, a kind of medieval rewriting or recycling of the *Hermetica*. This is the fascinating *Picatrix*, which may, or may not have been known to John Dee.

The Hungarian scholar Miklós Maróth noted concerning the *Picatrix* as follows: "[it shows] that the neoplatonic interpretation of the world was still feasible for certain groups, outside the circles of scholastic philosophers. Those who today could be called 'the practicioners of the occult' " (Maróth 1995, 24). In the Middle Ages this magical treatise was attributed to an Arabic scholar, Maslama al-Magriti; today it is rather seen as a compilation, *summa*, that documents the interest of Arabic science in hermeticism. Alphons, King of Castile, had it translated into Spanish in 1256 and this later became the basis of a Latin translation. Until the twentieth century no printed edition was known, the surviving manuscripts deriving from the later Middle Ages.[40] According to the Latin text, Picatrix (Buqratis, Picatris) is none other than the author of the book: *liber, quem sapientissimus philosophus Picatris in nigromanticis artibus ex quampluribus libris composuit* (a book on magical arts compiled from several others by the wisest philosopher, Picatris).

The *Picatrix* is good evidence that Hellenistic neoplatonism—like other elements of the Greek philosophy—returned to Europe via Arabic mediation. This text is similar to previously mentioned medieval magical sources in that it discusses at length the ways of sympathetic magic, among them astrology. It suggests that a constant energy radiates from the stars to the Earth and influences the happenings here. In the *Picatrix* magical-astrological observations are mixed with philosophical considerations:

> These two sciences [i.e., magic and alchemy] aim at boosting a desire to study. But this goal can be reached only by the philosophers, those men who are familiar with all the fields, branches and steps of wisdom. These two sciences are at the end of philosophy like a conclusion drawn from premises in a syllogism. Mark this well, because I have just revealed to you a marvellous secret. (*Picatrix* 1.1)[47]

The material world is full of occult sympathies drawn from the corresponding stars and planets. With appropriate knowledge and skills the researcher can discover and use these energies, says the *Picatrix*. It is most important to know the hidden correspondences. If, for example, someone wants to exploit the energy of Venus, he has to know what animals, plants, metals, and stones belong to her, and he must use those when trying to contact the demon of that planet.

So far this is not radically different from the sympathetic magic of the *Liber secretorum Alberti Magni* and other similar treatises capitalizing on the concept of the organic world model. The peculiar feature of the *Picatrix* is that, reaching back to the hermetic tradition, it pays great attention to the spirits and demons of the universe. What is more, the explanation of the spiritual hierarchies is done in an elaborate symbolic-mythological framework that also derives from the Hellenistic ideology. The cornerstone of magic in the *Picatrix* is the assumption that man can contact the decans and the demons of the planets by using magic talismans as mediators. Talismans—by the power of images and inscriptions—capture the virtue of the planetary demon even to the point of conjuring it up. To illustrate this with the example of Venus, the researcher needs to know the symbolic attributes of Venus and these will be used to form the image on the talisman, which has to be made of the appropriate metal, and will have to be used only in the astrologically appropriate moment.

The *Picatrix* also discusses a great number of correspondences, related to the various talismans described in the first part of the treatise. Here follow description of the images of a few planets:

> Two images of Saturn:
> "The form of a man with a crow's face and foot, sitting on a throne, having in his right hand a spear and in his left a lance or an arrow."
> "The form of a man standing on a dragon, clothed in black and holding in his right hand a sickle and in his left a spear."
> Two images of Jupiter:
> "The form of a man, sitting on an eagle, clothed in garment, with eagles beneath his feet. . . ."
> "The form of a man with a lion's face and bird's feet, below them a dragon with seven heads, holding an arrow in his right hand. . . ."
> An image of Mars:
> "The form of a man, crowned, holding a raised sword in his right hand."
> An image of Sol:
> "The form of a king sitting on a throne, with a crown on his head and beneath his feet the figure (magic character) of the Sun."
> An image of Venus:
> "The form of a woman with her hair unbound riding on a stag, having in her right hand an apple, and in her left, flowers, and dressed in white garment." (Picatrix, 2.10).[42]

While the first part of the treatise provides the necessary information on talismans and the way they should be made, the second part deals with the correspondences of the macrocosm and the microcosm and this is where we find passages relating to the role of man as a potential magus. These suggest that astrological determinism can be suspended if man (by means of magic) learns how to master nature:

> Man is a small world, similar to the great cosmos, consisting of a complete, living and sensible body and a sensible soul. [. . .] He possesses divine power [. . .] can make miracles and can manufacture miraculous images. [. . .] God ordained him to become the inventor of all sciences, with a prophetic faculty to understand everything and to recognize the valuable in everything. . . . (1.6; Ritter and Plessner 1962, 35–38).

Eugenio Garin compared this image of the human being to the hermetic magus, even to Pico's oration on the dignity of man (1983, 50).

The fourth book of the *Picatrix* contains an interesting mythological fable that is a direct reference to the magical deeds of Hermes Trismegistus. According to the text he was not only the first to create magic talismans, but through his magic power founded a wondrous city in Egypt:

> There are many among the Chaldeans who can create magic images, and they claim that Hermes was the first to make such [talismans] and by their help he regulated the Nile. [. . .] It was also who founded a city in Eastern Egypt which was 12 miles long, with a palace in the middle and with a gate on each of the four sides. He attached the image of an eagle to the eastern gate, a bull to the western, a lion to the southern, and a dog to the northern. Then he infused a living spirit into the images which then could speak with voice and none could enter without their consent. [. . .] In the middle of the palace he built a tower and in it he placed a shining body which produced every day light of different color while on the seventh day returned to the first one. [. . .] Around the city he placed statues. By the power of these the inhabitants remained virtuous, free from vickedness and vices. The name of the city was Adocentyn. (4. 3)[43]

In the description of this marvellous city Garin finds a predecessor of sixteenth- and seventeenth-century utopias, such as those of Filarete and Campanella. Frances Yates furthermore emphasized the relationship of this text to the motif of the magical, man-made statues in the *Asclepius*. I could add that the ambition to reveal the great secrets of Nature could also be compared to the vision of Hermes Trismegistus before Poimandres, described in *Corpus hermeticum* 1:

> When I wanted to reveal the secret working of the world and the process of creation, I found a dark cave, full of shadows and winds. I could see nothing and I was unable to light my torch. Then I saw a beautiful creature in my dream who said: "Put your torch under a glass jar in order to protect it against the winds and then it will shine in spite of the storm. Thus you will be able to penetrate even into the underworld region." (3.6; Ritter and Plessner 1962, 198)

Yates and Garin highlighted two different, although complementary, aspects of the *Picatrix*. For Yates its importance lay in the links with the hermetic literature and ideology. She emphasized how the medieval text had moved forward from a philosophical vision towards practical magic, the construction of talismans in order to exalt their users. As she wrote, "The work is thus a most complete text-book for the magician, giving the philosophy of nature on which talismanic and sympathetic magic is based together with full instructions for its practice. Its objects are strictly practical; the various talismans and procedures are used to gain specific ends, for the cure of various diseases, for long life, for success in various enterprises, and so on" (Yates 1964, 54). Garin appreciated the theoretical depth, the attachment to the speculative neoplatonic philosophy: "[I]t puts all the vast inheritance of ancient and medieval magic and astrology into, on the one hand, the theoretical neoplatonic picture, and on the other the hermeticist one" (Garin 1983, 48). Both emphasized, however, that the motive of bold human inquiry and the ambition to research nature had been crucially important in the grounding the notion of the dignity of man by the time of the Renaissance. The secret magical lore preserved by the Arabs provides a connecting link with both the magical theology of the Florentine neoplatonists and the experimental natural-ceremonial magic of the sixteenth century.

John Dee, as a truly versatile Renaissance man, was equally interested in science, technology, and inquiry into the occult. He could thus take inspiration from all the intellectual trends summarized in this chapter of medieval magic. Indeed, he seems to have researched the path of *magia naturalis* advertised by Roger Bacon and Albertus Magnus as well as the techniques of talismanic magic originally worked out in the *Picatrix*, until he came to crave a direct communication with God and the spirit world, somewhat along the lines of *Clavicula Solomonis* and its type of literature.

Keeping a chronological track of possible sources, in the following chapter I shall examine the elements of Florentine neoplatonism that undoubtedly contributed to the formation of Dee's program of *exaltatio*.

4

Florentine Neoplatonism
and Christian Magic

John Dee's library catalogues as well as his marginalia and scholarly references show that in his syncretic magical system one of the main inspirations undoubtedly came from the neoplatonist magi, especially Ficino and Pico. In the part of my book entitled "OUTPUT" I shall discuss textual parallels and influences. Here I intend only to summarize briefly the ideas and iconography of magical *exaltatio* as seen in some works of Ficino and Pico.

FICINO'S TALISMANIC MAGIC

Ficino's translations of Plato were published in Florence between 1462 and 1468, sponsored by the Neoplatonic Academy of Lorenzo de' Medici, il Magnifico. These publications exercised a major influence on the subsequent development of Renaissance philosophy as well as on the early modern history of magic. Ficino's scholarly output was complex and versatile, far exceeding the present sketch of pre- and early modern Western magical traditions. From the angle of this narrower scope, his ideas on beauty, love, and celestial correspondences are of particular interest.

The philosophical discussions of beauty and love go back as far as Plato himself and his mentor, Socrates. The former treated these questions in his dialogues *Symposium* and *Phaedrus*, and came to the conclusion that the catalyzer of love was beauty, which appeared in the physical as well as in the metaphysical spheres of existence. Thus religious desire

79

could also be explained as the analogy of the soul's craving for perfect beauty. This explanation proved to be congenial for many Renaissance theologians, too, such as Cardinal Bembo, one of Castiglione's protagonists in his *The Courtier*. Ficino himself remained evasive in defining the borderline between theology, philosophy, and even pious, white magic. The common ground among the three areas seemed to be a curious blend of a philosophy of beauty and love, a poetical theology, and a theory of magic based on the sympathetic love among the elements of the universe.[1]

The Florentine philosopher wrote extensive commentaries on Plato's works that he later collected under the title *Theologia platonica* (1482). In this work Ficino expanded his philosophy of beauty. As Tibor Klaniczay summed up: "beauty is nothing else but the symbol of divine perfectness, that is the reflection of God in the sensible world, a visible aspect of Truth. Beauty derives from a creative act of the divine, consequently Man, who can also create beautiful things, becomes partaker of the divine attributes" (1975, 14). And this is precisely the point of the amalgamation of philosophy and magic in Florentine neoplatonism. And also at this point we can detect Ficino's great synthetizing ambition, how he enriched Plato's philosophy with that of the other neoplatonists as well as with his admired hermetic lore. To begin with, let us remember the command of the creative Mind, *Nous* from the eleventh tract of the *Corpus hermeticum*:

> Thus, unless you make yourself equal to god, you cannot understand god; like is understood by like. Make yourself grow to immeasurable immensity, outleap all body, outstrip all time, become eternity and you will understand god. Having conceived that nothing is impossible to you, consider yourself immortal and able to understand everything, all art, all learning, the temper of every living thing. Go higher than every height and lower than every depth. (1.20, in Copenhaver 1992, 41)

As we shall see, this concept of hermetic deification will not only echo in Ficino's philosophy, but also become one of the most important commonplaces of Renaissance magic, expounded in innumerable fifteenth- and sixteenth-century works, from Pico through Reuchlin, Agrippa, Giorgi, Lazzarelli, Gohory, Paracelsus, Postel—whose works were important readings of John Dee.

In his commentary on the *Symposium*, Ficino identified magic with love. In fact he called love "a magus":

> Why do we think love is a sorcerer? Because in love there is all the
> power of enchantment. The work of enchantment is the attraction of
> one thing by another because of a certain similarity of their nature. The
> parts of this world, like the parts of a single animal, all hanging from
> one author, are joined to each other by the mutuality of one nature.
> [...] From their common relation a common love is born, and from
> that love a common attraction, and this is true enchantment. (*In
> convivium Platonis de amore*, 6.10; Ficino 1944, 91/199)

Using this general framework, Ficino relied on a wide range of
sources—from the Neoplatonici through the *Asclepius*, even the Latin
Picatrix—in order to integrate and elevate magic onto the rank of venerable science. He not only translated and propagated the magical views
of the Platonici and the *Corpus hermeticum* in his already mentioned
Anthologia esoterica (Ficino 1497, 1516), but he also developed one of the
most ambitious theories of astral magic in his late work, the *Three Books
on Life (De vita triplici...,* 1489*)*. Brian Copenhaver characterized this
book as follows: "Ficino took natural magic to be as much the province
of the natural philosopher as cosmology, astronomy, matter-theory. The
wisdom of the *magus* and the learning of the *philosophus* were distinguishable but interdependent parts of the same enterprise..." (Copenhaver
1988a, 274).

In the remaining part of this subchapter I shall concentrate on this
work of Ficino, which, according to Copenhaver, was "the fullest Renaissance exposition of a theory of magic and the most influential such
statement written in post-classical times" (ibid.).[2]

De vita... consists of three books. Its first part, *De studiosorum sani-
tate tuenda*, was written in 1480 and deals with the ways of preserving
the good health of scholars. The second book, *De vita procurenda*, treats
the possibility of prolonging human life. This was written last among the
three books, completed just before publication in 1489. From the viewpoint of magic, the third part is the most important and most discussed:
De vita coelitus comparanda, which is about the capturing of the celestial
povers.

Ficino dedicated the whole work to Lorenzo de' Medici and in
this dedication mentioned important facts pertaining to his whole scholarly career:

> I had two fathers—Ficino the doctor and Cosimo de' Medici. From the
> former I was born, from the latter reborn. The former commended me

to Galen as both a doctor and a Platonist; the latter consecrated me to the divine Plato. And both the one and the other alike dedicated Marsilio to a doctor—Galen, doctor of the body, Plato, doctor of the soul. Therefore, for a long time now I have practiced the medicine salutary to souls under Plato: after translating all his books, I straightaway composed eighteen books concerning the immortality of souls and eternal happiness, so to the best of my ability repaying my Medici father. Thinking I ought next to repay my medical father, I have composed a book *On Caring for the Health of Learned People.* In addition, after this, learned people desired not only to be healthy for a while, but also, being in good health, to live a long time. And so I then gave them a book *On a Long Life.* But they distrusted terrestrial medicine and remedies in a matter of such importance; and so I added a book *On Obtaining a Life Both Healthy and Long from Heaven,* so that from the very living body of the world, a more vigorous life might be propagated as if from a vine into our own body, which is in a way a part of the world's body. (Gen. Proem., Ficino 1989, 103–105)

The program is clear: based on the doctrine of correspondences, Ficino offers medical methods that utilize cosmic forces for maintaining the human body and prolonging human life. The first book contains relatively little magical material; it concentrates instead on the correspondences of the macro- and microcosms. Complying with the concept of the four elements and the four humors, Ficino tries to define the nature of scholars and outline the dangers following from their way of life. Separate chapters are devoted to the threats of coitus, overeating, and getting up late. Next to the body, Ficino pays attention to psychology as well: he enlists cosmic rules that should be observed by the melancholic learned persons.

The second book was dedicated to Filippo Valori, a Florentine nobleman in the service of the Medicis who sponsored the publication of this book as well as the Plato translation. This treatise also starts with medical advice derived from the doctrine of correspondences and discusses how to regulate the bodily fluids and the body's temperature, what diet is good for the elderly, and what the advantages of ascetic life are. The book already introduces various magical concepts, offering recipes that follow the popular medieval concepts of sympathetic magic, including chapters 10 ("On Gold, Foods Made of Gold, and the Revitalization of Old Man") and 19 ("The Medicine of the Magi for Old People"). Also in this book we come across the leitmotif of Book Three, which led Ficino to the ground of Christian neoplatonic magic. This is nothing other than the notion that astrological influences have medicinal effects, as is explained by mythological characters in chapter 13 ("What means of fomenting all the parts of the body the elderly may receive from the planets") and 15 ("Mercury addresses the elderly and counsels them about pleasure, odors, song, and medicines"). One should note that old people are counseled to converse while traversing the green fields under the leadership of Venus (chapter 14) and, if their body dries out, to "choose a young girl who is healthy, beautiful, cheerful, and temperate, and when you are hungry and the Moon is waxing, suck her milk" (ch. 11, Ficino 1989, 197). As Frances Yates ironically remarked: "We might be in the consulting room of a rather expensive psychiatrist who knows that his patients can afford plenty of gold and holidays in the country, and flowers out of season" (1964, 63).

Book Three is dedicated to Matthias Corvinus, the Hungarian Renaissance ruler, who on several occasions unsuccessfully invited Ficino to his court. According to Ficino's dedication,

> The ancient philosophers [. . .] judged, as I suppose, that the elements and all that is composed therefrom would be known by them in vain, and that the motions and influences of the heavens would be too aimlessly observed, if the knowledge of both, taken jointly together, did not eventually lead to life and happiness for themselves. Thoughts of this kind profited them, as it seems, first of all in the present life; for Pythagoras and Democritus and Apollonius of Tyana and all who have made this their special study have by using the things they knew attained good health and long life. (Proem 3, Ficino 1989, 237)

These introductory words indicate that the following treatise belongs to the territory of astrological medicine, and one should also note that Ficino emphasizes the importance of utilizing celestial forces for maintaining the body in this earthly life—a typical Renaissance concern!

The next passage of the dedication also reveals Ficino's source and inspiration in writing this book:

> Now among the books of Plotinus destined for the great Lorenzo de' Medici I had recently composed a commentary on the book of Plotinus which discusses drawing favor from the heavens. With all this in mind, I have just decided to extract that one (with the approval of Lorenzo himself) and dedicate it especially to your Majesty. (Ficino 1989, 239)

The first chapter of this famous book again recapitulates some basics of the organic world picture and the correspondences: the celestial powers, the World Soul, the planets, and the demons. Ficino, following Plotinus and the hermetic tradition, asserts that each planet and the houses of the zodiac have their demons and governing angels, which translate the will of the World Soul (*Anima mundi*) toward the inferior spheres.

The system of will transfer (in Plotinus, "emanation") sustains the harmony of the world (chapter 2), a notion which became a central component of the Renaissance world model, primarily due to Ficino and the other neoplatonist philosophers. As the miniature model of the cosmos, the human soul is capable of absorbing the strength of the World Soul through the rays of Sol or Jupiter. This is how one becomes of solar or jovial temperament (chapter 4). The point is that all these astral forces can be used for medical purposes in order to improve man's physical and mental functioning (chapter 10).

In chapter 13 Ficino introduces the concept of talismanic magic, probably borrowed from the *Picatrix*: "On the power acquired from the heavens both in images, according to the Ancients, and in medicines." The following chapters enlist the various planetary and stellar forces and the talismanic images corresponding to them. Chapter 16 treats the question of the rays from which images are thought to obtain their force. After the "flames without light" (Ficino 1989, 321) penetrate the metals and gems embellished with the magic images, they "imprint in them wonderful gifts, since indeed they generate supremely precious things in the womb of the earth" (323). This is as when the rays of a beautiful eye generate great love in one who beholds that eye (as Ficino already had explained in his *Symposium* commentary).[3] Chapter 18 describes talismans already known since Antiquity and in some of them elements of Dee's hieroglyophic monad can be recognized. It is even more so in chapter 19, which advises on the construction of a general image, representing the whole cosmos. As we shall see, again, in this respect Dee's *Monas* was the ultimate achievment (see chapter 6 below, p. 161 ff).

Beginning with chapter 21, Ficino adds to the treatment of powerful images a description of powerful words, incantations, magical prayers and he offers a seven-grade typology of celestial influences according to the seven planets. The theoretical introduction is followed by practical advice: how to find our place in the web of astral influences, how to defend against the harmful domination of Saturn, how to capitalize on Jupiter's benevolent strength (chapter 22). The next chapter gives the following counsel: "To live well and prosper, first know your natural bent, your star, your Genius, and the place suitable to these; here live. Follow your natural profession" (Ficino 1989, 371). The influence of the talismanic magic of *Picatrix* is quite obvious here: the complex of prerequisites—place, astrological and physical correspondences (zodiac, planetary position, materials, colors, and odors) and the magical images on the talismans and the accompanying incantations—all follow the traditions of hermetic and Arabic authors.

Beginning with chapter 24 further pieces of advice are gathered and directed to scholars specifically: "By what system people dedicated to learning may recognize their natural bent and follow a manner of life suitable to their guardian spirit."

The closing, twenty-sixth chapter summarizes astrological magic returning to the theoretical plane again: "How by exposing lower things to higher things, you can bring down the higher, and cosmic gifts especially through cosmic materials." Ficino's wording is a clear product of Renaissance neoplatonism inspired also by hermetic magic:

> As Plato teaches, echoing Timaeus the Pythagorean, the world has been produced by the Good itself the best it could possibly have been. It is therefore not only corporeal but participating in life and intelligence as well. (3.26, Ficino 1989, 385)

The definition of the magus and the encomium of magical practices follow this tone, concluding again with an equation between magic and love:

> Agriculture prepares the field and the seed for celestial gifts and by grafting prolongs the life of the shoot and refashions it into another and better species. The doctor, the natural philosopher, and the surgeon achieve similar effects in our bodies in order to both strengthen our own nature and to obtain more productively the nature of the universe. The philosopher who knows about natural objects and stars, whom we rightly are accustomed to call a Magus, does the very same things: he seasonally introduces the celestial into the earthly by particular lures just as the farmer interested in grafting brings the fresh graft into the old stock. [. . .] The Magus subjects earthly things to celestial, lower things everywhere to higher, just as particular females everywhere are subjected to males appropriate to them for impregnation, as iron to a magnet to get magnetized, as camphor to hot air for absorption, as crystal to the Sun for illumination, as sulphur and sublimed liquor to a flame for kindling, as an egg-shell, empty and full of dew, to the Sun for elevation, or rather the egg itself to the hen for hatching. (3.26, 387)

His own definition Ficino strengthens by the authority of Plotinus and Hermes Trismegistus:

> Plotinus uses almost the same examples in that place where, paraphrasing Hermes Trismegistus, he says that the ancient priests or Magi used to capture in statues and material sacrifices something divine and wonderful. (3.26, 389)[4]

This locus is a good example to show with what determination Ficino tried to amalgamate his different sources: Plato, the Platonici, and the hermetic tradition. While moderns scholars are usually sceptical about Plotinus' approval or even knowledge of the *Corpus hermeticum*, Ficino thinks him to have paraphrased Hermes. This claim is not void of cultural politics, though: Plotinus' opinion was more acceptable for Christian authorities than that of Hermes Trismegistus, so it could serve as a mediator for the Christianization of the *Hermetica*.

> But now let us get back to Hermes, or rather to Plotinus. Hermes says that the priests received an appropriate power from the nature of the cosmos and mixed it. Plotinus follows him and thinks that everything can be easily accomplished by the intermediation of the Anima Mundi, since the Anima Mundi generates and moves the forms of natural things through certain seminal reasons implanted in her from the divine. [. . .] The Anima Mundi can easily apply herself to materials since she has formed them to begin with through these seminal reasons, when the Magus or a priest brings to bear at the right time rightly grouped forms of things. [. . .] Sometimes it can happen that when you bring seminal reasons to bear on forms, higher gifts too may descend, since reason in the Anima Mundi are conjoined to the intellectual forms in her and through these to the Ideas of the Divine Mind. (3.26, 391)

In Ficino's interpretation, then, magic is nothing else but the capturing and manipulation of supernatural forces in order to free man's soul and intellect from the burden of the material world. The goal is to unite the human spirit with the divine not only after death but during earthly life, in the form of *exaltatio*. The roots of this concept originated in neoplatonic hermeticism but for the Renaissance philosopher the platonic concepts of Supreme Good, creative Nous, and the transmitting demons could be easily associated with Christian doctrines: God, angels, and the human soul. Ficino's purpose was precisely this association: the Christianization of neoplatonism and hermetic magic. A good example of this process can be seen in his commentary on Plato's *Symposium*, when his discussion of demons involves the Pseudo-Dionysian discourse on angels:

> The good daemons, our protectors, Dionysius the Areopagite is accustomed to call by the proper names, Angels, the governors of the lower world, and this differs very little from the interpretation of Plato. [. . .] Plato does not in the least bind spirits of this kind within the narrow limits of the spheres, as he does the souls of earthly creatures in bodies, but asserts that they are endowed with such great virtue by the supreme God that they are able to enjoy the vision of God at once, and they are able without any labor or care to rule and move the globes of the world according to the will of their father, and by moving them, easily govern lower creatures. Therefore it is rather a difference in words between Plato and Dionysius than a difference in meaning. (*In convivium Platonis . . .*, 6.3; Ficino 1944, 79/186)

Florentine neoplatonism was not the only trend in Christian philosophy to assimilate the teachings of Plato. Its intellectual novelty was nevertheless the emphasis on magical possibilities (through the synthesis of the Platonici and hermeticism) that was to enable humankind to assume a more central and important role than previously had been permitted in the framework of medieval Christian philosophy.

A look at the critical history of *De vita . . .* can refine the character of Ficino's magic so far outlined. The first extensive analysis was done by D. P. Walker (1958) whose views were further developed by Frances Yates in her book on Bruno under the heading "Ficino as Christian-Renaissance magus" (1964, 62–84). Her thesis was grounded on a reading of *De vita . . .*, and this well fitted the concept of the dignity of Renaissance man as established by Cassirer.[5] As Cassirer suggested, the Renaissance preserved the idea of the Great Chain of Being, but the great innovation was that man's place changed—from fixed to movable. As a result the neoplatonists thought man could climb up the Chain, even up to God. This possibility intensely occupied Renaissance philosophers who tried to validate the idea from the works of Plato and other pagan sources, mixing them with the ideas of Christian mystics, such as the works of Pseudo-Dionysius.

This philosophical *exaltatio* was supposed to be comparable to a reverse emanation in Plotinus' system, first described by Plato in his *Symposium* and the *Phaedrus*. The human soul encaged in the material body does not entirely forget about its supernatural origin and keeps longing for it.[6] And when the human perception encounters something beautiful, this earthly beauty reminds the soul of its divine heritage, and the soul then longs even more strongly for the heavenly perfection. And if the soul is strong and disciplined enough, it can break out of the prison of matter and can dine with the divinity: the *exaltatio* happens.

One of Ficino's important theoretical works was his commentary on Plato's *Symposium*,[7] where he Christianized Plato's theory of love and also articulated the doctrine of the deification of man. In this process the catalyzing agents are Plato's four furors or "sacred madnesses"—prophetic, religious-mystical, poetical, and love (cf. *Phaedrus* 244a–249c), which are able to lift the soul from—in Ficino's wording (7.13–14)—dissonance to harmony and from variety to unity. The first step is done by poetic madness:

> The Soul cannot return to the One unless it itself becomes one. The whole soul is filled with discord and dissonance; therefore the first need is for the poetic madness, which through musical tones arouses what is sleeping, through harmonic sweetness calms what is in turmoil, and finally, through the blending of different things, quells discord and tempers the various parts of the soul. (7.14; Ficino 1944, 231)

The other madnesses follow and complete the elevation of the soul, climaxing in Christian, holy love:

> Finally, when the soul has been made one, it recovers itself into the One which is above essence, that is God. This the heavenly Venus completes through Love, that is through the desire for the divine beauty, and the passion for Good. So the first kind of madness tempers dissonant and unharmonious parts. The second makes the tempered parts one out of many. The third makes it one above all parts; and the fourth into One which is above essence and above the whole. (7.14, 232)

To sum up: Ficino laid down the theoretical framework of his magic in his commentaries on Plato and Plotinus by means of "re-platonizing" Pseudo-Dionysius and amalgamating it with a syncretic mix of classical traditions. The magical praxis of *exaltatio* using astrological talismans was, on the other hand, grounded in his *De vita coelitus comparanda* and again can be considered to be the result of the fusion of various earlier practices.

According to Frances Yates the most dominating intellectual force on Ficino's development of neoplatonic magic was Egyptian-Hellenic hermeticism. Based on this assumption she coined the historical category "Renaissance hermeticism," which she considered to be the most important intellectual achievement of the fifteenth and sixteenth centuries. Research over the past few decades in many ways has broken with Dame Frances' thesis, philologists above all demonstrating that the magic of Ficino was more complex, relying on sources outside hermeticism, such as the Platonici, Arabic and Jewish sources of the Middle Ages, and medieval sympathetic magic.[8]

Taking all this into consideration, one has to conclude that the category of hermeticism must either be enlarged ad infinitum to accommodate all the signficant phenomena Frances Yates tried to bring under this label; or it has to be understood as a well-defined but by no means generally influential intellectual trend. However, I would still like to emphasize with Yates what an important inspiration the doctrine of ascension/*exaltatio* meant for the forging of the man-centered world picture of the Renaissance.

If the Yates thesis, including her model of the "Rosicrucian Enlightenment," has become outdated in current historical research, even today's historians have to face the facts according to which occult philosophies produced an amazing amount of written, printed, and illustrated material during the sixteenth and seventeenth centuries in genres ranging from philosophical tracts to spiritual diaries, from poetry to learned theology, not to mention the popular imagination of the age as manifested in anecdotes, broad sheets, *volksbuchs,* and intriguing plays on the stages of Europe. And also there remains the surprising fact that neither the occult philosophies nor their complex iconography disappeared after the scientific recolution.

Compared with this variety of the Western esoteric tradition, Yates was also right to point out that Ficino's magic was largely restricted to a pious and limited version of talismanic lore. The purpose of the next subchapter is to show what giant steps were taken in Renaissance magic after Ficino's initial experiments, resulting in the fact that in the second half of the sixteenth century John Dee could encounter a more enlarged and complicated magical world picture than Ficino had dreamt of seventy-eighty years earlier.

The first step in this development was undertaken by Pico della Mirandola who integrated Jewish cabala into neoplatonic-hermetic magic, as manifested in his *De hominis dignitate.*

PICO'S ENCOMIUM OF *EXALTATIO*

Ficino always made a point of detaching himself from dark or evil magic, calling his own system theology. This division of magic into white and black had been in use since Antiquity. The word *magia* originally referred to the practices of Persian priests, and the abused version of this practice was identified as "black magic."[9]

Greek philosophers, such as Plotinus, differentiated between *theurgy* and *goétia* (Dodds 1951), while Christian theologists talked about *mira* and *miracula* as opposed to wicked *maleficia* and *veneficia* (Flint 1991, 33). The Catholic Church, in spite of the the careful distinguishing of many theologians, did not like theurgy either. It is almost surprising that Ficino never encountered a conflict with the church because of his experiments with magic; his disciple, Pico, on the other hand, had to face serious charges of heresy several times during his short life (1463–1494).

As I shall show later, the typologizing of magic always depended on subjective motivations, and the labelling of esoterically oriented minds either as venerable magician or wicked witch and conjuror always belonged to the repertoire of power politics.

No doubt, with his bold ideas and gestures Pico provoked the suspicion of church authorities. The dangerous elements of his philosophy were as follows: he articulated the doctrine of the dignity of man in a more inflammatory way than his master, Ficino; he openly advocated magic as being a suitable means for the elevation (*exaltatio*) of man to the level of God; and, last but not least, in professing magic he introduced a new methodology taken from the Jewish cabala. In this section I briefly outline the system of cabala and its connecting points to Christian mysticism, then examine Pico's cabalistical magic as a life program given to the people of the Renaissance.

Cabala and 'exaltatio'

Cabala is the theosophy of the Jewish religion, that is, a mystical-philosophical system. The word itself means "received doctrine" or "tradition." Opinions differ about the origins of this tradition. Believers speak about a time even before the revelation given to Moses; historians connect it to Merkabah mysticism beginning in the first few centuries B.C., then flourishing in the Hellenistic period. The historically distinct cradle of the cabala is the early Middle Ages (eighth and nineth centuries), and its real flourishing starts from the twelfth century.[10]

The two fundamentally important texts of the cabala are the *Sefer Yetsirah* or the "Book of Formation," and the *Zohar* or the "Book of Splendor." Neither of them is possible to date precisely. The *Sefer Yetsirah* is supposed to have been written between the second and the sixth centuries A.D. The Zohar is a much later development; it must have been compiled toward the end of the thirteenth century, in spite of its claiming the authorship of Simeon ben Yohai, a scholar of the first century A.D.

No matter the exact dates of composition, these books obviously relied on earlier oral or textual traditions, and what seems to be rather certain is that the roots of cabala reach back to the period more or less coinciding with the creation of the other great corpuses of mystical literature: the *Corpus hermeticum* and the early Christian gnostic literature. Thus the Jewish cabala also sprung from that cosmopolitan and decadent atmosphere of the decaying Roman Empire where religious systems almost freely mixed, became open to mysticism, and sought individual revelation. Most of these experimental trends were influenced to some extent by Hellenistic neoplatonism as well as the Eastern mystical lore, from Egyptian magic through Persian Zoroastrianism to the early Christian gnosticism. All of these tried to explain the creation of the material world from the divine Mind (variations on the emanation theme) and they also tried to provide man with a key to be able to transfer himself between these two worlds, the material and the supernatural.

Among all these religious and theosophical efforts, Jewish cabala stands out because of its coherent system. Although there was a great variety even within Jewish mysticism, after the synthetizing schools of Samuel Abulafia (1240–1292) and Abraham Gikatilia (1247–1305), the system attracted Christian thinkers, too.[11] As has been recently demonstrated, this medieval Jewish mysticism excercised a great influence on medieval ceremonial magic, especially on its "underground" angelology. But it was some of the great Renaissance humanists—especially Pico and Reuchlin—who rediscovered this lore for themselves and established the Christian cabala as an important trend in Renaissance cultural history.

The most important key to the ideas of the cabala is the *Sefirot*, or the system of divine emanations. According to the doctrine that was grounded in the *Sefer Yetsirah*, God—that is, *En-Sof* the infinite—fills and contains the universe at the same time. Since God is infinite, it cannot be comprehended. In order to demonstrate its existence, God then became active and creative, emanated from itself. This process is described by the sefirotic tree, which consists of ten sefira, usually arranged in a special order:[12]

Kether (the Supreme Crown of God)
Binah (Intelligence)————————*Hokhman* (Wisdom)
Gevurah or *Din* (Power)————————*Hesed* (Love or Mercy)
Rahamin or *Tifereth* (Compassion or Beauty)
Hod (Majesty)————————*Netsah* (Endurance)
Yesod (Foundation)
Malkhuth (Kingdom)

With the appearance of Kingdom the emanation is completed, the Spirit becomes manifested in the material world. The characteristic arrangement of the sefirot is often called the Tree of Life, where the stages of emanation are grouped in triads, forming three columns and three tiers. The right side is the "Black Column," standing for mercy, which is positive, active, and male. The left side is the "Silver Column," standing for severity and is negative, passive, and female. In the middle one finds the column of equilibrium, standing for grace and divine will. The three tiers represent the three aspects of the divine nature: the upper three sefirot constitute the Divine Spirit, the next three the Divine Soul, while the lower three the Divine Will (Halevi 1979, 6 ff.).

Graphic representations of the sefirot became common by the time of the Renaissance. One of the much reproduced early prints is from Paulus Ricius' *Portae lucis* (Augsburg 1516), which shows a Jewish cabalist, deep in meditation, holding the sefirotic tree in his hand.[13] To illustrate the structure of the sefirotic tree, I am referring here to Cesare di' Evoli's diagram, which was printed in his *De divinis attributis* in 1573. The woodcut clearly represents the triads composed of the elements of the sefira (Figure 4.1), and, needless to say, John Dee had this volume in his library.[14]

During the emanation this threefold nature manifests itself in four phases, which is why the cabala is said to consist of four worlds. This has to be understood in such a way that the ten sefirot are repeated four times, or that the emanation repeats itself on four occasions. The first ten sefirot constitute the world of Manifestation, or *Atsilut*, that is, the primal emanation of the divinity. The next emanation is Creation, or *Beriah*, the Throne, or *Merkabah* with the highest angels. This is followed by the world of Formation, or *Yetsirah*, the domain of the angels and the world of Making, or *Asiyah*, the spiritual archetype of the material sphere,

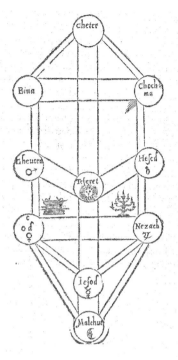

FIGURE 4.1   The Sephirotic Tree. Cesare d' Evoli, *De divinis attributis, quae sephirot ab hebraeis nuncupata* (Venice, 1573), 8ᵛ. Herzog August Bibliothek, Wolfenbüttel [98.9 Theol /2/].

something like Plotinus' hypostasis of Nature (Scholem 1974, 272). The threefold and fourfold connections of the sefirot are repeated in each subsequent world until the Spirit unites with Matter. Aspect four is as important as the aspect three, since—as we learn from the Zohar—the tree has four parts (root, trunk, branch, and fruit), there are four elements, and the most special name of God (the Tetragrammaton) also consists of four letters: JHVH (Halevi 1979, 8–9).

The theory of the four worlds has roots in the Book of Isaiah: "Even every one that is called by My Name [*Atsilut*]: for I have created [*Beriah*] him for My Glory, I have formed [*Yetsirah*] him; yea, I have made [*Asiyah*] him" (43:7). The teachings of the sefirot thus are not only a cosmogony but also a means for biblical exegesis that was used for the interpretation of the *Pentateuch*, the Books of Moses. One of the most important episodes in these books was, of course, the appearance of humankind, the mission of Adam on earth. The same threefold and fourfold logic was then applied to the explanation of man, too. According to the four worlds, the microcosm of man also has a fourfold structure. As the cabalists explained, there were four Adams: most superior was Adam Kadmon, the Divine Man who is mentioned in the vision of Ezekiel:

> And above the firmament that was over their heads was the likeness of a throne, as the appearance of a sapphire stone: and upon the likeness of the throne was the likeness as the appearance of a man above upon it.
> And I saw as the color of amber, as the appearance of fire round about him. . . . (Ezek. 1:26–27)

This man of *Atsilut* is the first reflection of God who has all the potential for will, intellect, compassion, and action. According to the cabala, all creatures derive from this Adam Kadmon, including the angels and archangels. No wonder such notions also gave rise to ambitions of *exaltatio* and catalyzed efforts to contact the world of angels.

The next Adam is of *Beriah*, who was created on the sixth day. He still possessed fully the emanation of God and the angels became jealous of him. This Adam existed already as an independent intellect; however, he had not yet been tested. The examination took place in Eden, the World of Formation where the male and female principles were separated. After the Fall, the fourth Adam came to life, the mortal, who had to interact with the sphere of Matter and had to justify himself in the World of Making.

As Scholem explains, the sefirotic tree is anthropomorphic and the simile of man is often used to describe the sefirot.

> "The Biblical word that man was created in the image of God means two things for the Kabbalist: first, that the power of the Sefiroth, the paradigm of divine life, exists and is active also in man. Secondly, that the world of the Sefiroth is capable of being visualized under the image of man the created. From this it follows that the limbs of the human body are nothing but images of a certain spiritual mode of existence which manifests itself in the symbolic figure of Adam Kadmon, the primordial man." (1974, 215)

As I have mentioned, the cabala is not only cosmology and anthropology; primarily it is teaching, a key to understanding and illumination. As opposed to the interpretation of the Torah, the recorded and public teaching, the cabala was an esoteric knowledge, reserved only for a select few.[15] By the Middle Ages we see the development of patterns of ecstatic-prophetic and meditative illumination that became highly individual techniques, sometimes involving only the mystical relationship of a master and a disciple.

Another, very important feature of the cabala was, however, that it more strictly attached itself to the codified text than any other form of mysticism. In the Bible creation happens through words and the truthful testimony of God is also handed down in writing. Thus the cabala has closer ties with the structures of verbal expression than to mystical or symbolic imagery, and its system in a way becomes a whole philosophy of language.[16] The three most important manipulative techniques of the cabala—in fact, adapted from earlier procedures of Hasidism—were *gematria, notarikon,* and *temurah*, all of which combined theology, language philosophy, and number symbolism. The first associated numerical values with the letters of the Hebrew alphabet, thus allowing certain associations on the basis of equal numerical meanings. Therefore the name of Adam could be equated with that of the Tetragrammaton. *Notarikon* was the interpretation of the letters of a word as abbreviations of whole sentences, while *temurah* meant the interchanging of letters according to certain systematic rules.

The ultimate goal of all these practices was to reach illumination, or *exaltatio*. The cabalist—through various exercises and meditation—prepared for an inner journey by the end of which he was supposed to reach the unification of the split, dualist universe. The earthly man, the *tahutonim*, that is, one of those "who live below," was to have a glimpse of the *elionim*, the world of those "who live above." Alongside other, platonically oriented philosophies, the cabala also professed the dignity of man, capable of encompassing both lower and upper worlds. The cabalistic techniques promised the acquisition of external and internal sensation, reaching downward and upward alike, even bridging different worlds, if necessary. This faculty is especially useful when divine emanation has to be steered to areas where further development is needed or chaos rules and where, due to this, the community lacks a mystical encouragement.

I hope, even this sketchy outline of the cabala shows those areas where Christian humanists, already engaged in Platonic and hermetic mysticism, could take interest. Those were the concepts of emanation and ascension, the man-centered creation myth, the interpretation of Adam as a demigod or demiurge, and, above all, the efforts to unite man with his creator.

Because of the above parallels, it is not surprising that from time to time syncretizing efforts took place between the Jewish, the Christian, and the Arabic-Muslim philosophies. Philo of Alexandria, the scholar who developed the Jewish religion into a highly conceptual philosophy in the first century A.D. applied neoplatonism to systematize the description of the religious experience. Philo used Greek philosophy to corroborate monotheism, for himself a sacred doctrine. By bringing together the Law of Jahve and the Law of the *Logos,* he tried to modernize the Rabbinic tradition. His notions of emanation and divine radiation later became incorporated in the works of the medieval Jewish philosophers, with the modification that the work of creation and government was not the work of God directly, but rather required the help of mediators, such as angels. As the Platonic ideas became angels in Christianity, a similar development took place in Jewish theology, too. This is why the *Zohar* speaks of "mediators" and the ten ranks of angels (as opposed to the nine angelic hierarchies in Pseudo-Dionysius).

Pico's "Oration," Cabalistic Magic, and Exaltatio

Considering the historical circumstances, Pico almost seems predestined to discover Jewish cabala for the purposes of Christian neoplatonism and to try to integrate its magic into the expanding system of Renaissance occultism. During the Middle Ages not only was the cabala basically hidden from gentile scholars, but so were traditional rabbinic teaching, and even, by and large, the Hebrew language. This happened partly because Christians did not trust the Jews, even suspecting that they consciously forged those passages of the Old Testament that were suitable for Christological explanations and Christian typological symbolism. Because of this atmosphere, those who became interested in the Hebrew language could not expect much support from Church institutions or the universities. Although in 1311 Pope Clement V encouraged the study of Hebrew, Arabic, and Sirian languages, even at the time of the Synod of Basel in 1432, Hebrew departments were not present within strongholds of Christian learning such as the universities of Paris, Oxford, Bologna, and Salamanca (Lloyd Jones 1983, iv ff.). Another cause hindering the development of Hebrew studies in Europe was the attitude of the Jews themselves who considered it to be sacrilegious to share sacred knowledge with gentiles.

The spread of humanism and the new ideas of the Renaissance finally changed this situation. The humanist slogan "Back to the Sources" generated efforts to research Hebrew and all the available texts surviving in this language. The study of the Bible was continued on the basis of new, philological methods with the aim of cleaning the Holy Writ of the distortions of the previous centuries. From this time on the "three sacred tongues" (Latin, Greek and Hebrew) were of equal importance.

Two Renaissance popes, Nicholas V and Sixtus IV, accumulated significant collections of Hebrew manuscripts and encouraged translations from Hebrew to Latin. The Florentine neoplatonists rejoiced concerning this incentive since it fully coincided with their efforts to widen syncretically the theological and philosophical background of Christianity.[17]

In summing up the motivations behind the heightened interest in Hebrew studies, the following reasons ought to be taken into consideration: primarily there was a Christian-humanist motivation to incorporate the third sacred language in the humanistically enlarged Christian tradition. Another important aspect was that until the Reformation froze the boundaries of religious thinking, many humanists had hopes about a new universal religion in which Christianity, Islam, and Judaism could be merged. I shall soon discuss the questions of these heterodox ideas, which strongly characterized the works of Christian cabalists from Pico through Reuchlin to Postel, since traces of them can be found among Dee's angelic prophecies, too. Last but not least, the attention of the Florentine neoplatonists and their followers were turned toward Jewish culture because of certain similarities between the cabala and the hermetic doctrines of *exaltatio*.[18]

We should remember that Renaissance humanists thought the hermetic writings were as old as the books of Moses. While calling the *Corpus hermeticum* "a book about the power and wisdom of God," Ficino became interested in certain rabbinical texts for the sake of comparison. But he did not know Hebrew and was unaware of the full system of the cabala. Pico, on the other hand, took the decisive step of bridging the separate traditions. In 1485, during a journey in Germany, Rudolf Agricola praised him as a "man who is well versed in all languages, in Latin, Greek, Hebrew, Chaldean, Arabic, and furthermore he is a theologian, a philosopher, a poet and in all excellent" (quoted by Secret 1985, 25). Although modern scholarship has doubts about the perfection of Pico's knowledge of Hebrew (for example, Lloyd-Jones 1983), his familiarity with the cabala enabled him to develop hermetic-neoplatonic magic by infusing a cabalistic cosmogony into the hermetic mythology. From a parallel analysis of the two, he concluded that according to Trismegistus as well as the cabala God created the world by means of words.

In 1486 Pico went to Rome and advertized his nine hundred theses, in which he called for a public scholarly discussion of the possibility of

creating a syncretic theory that could accommodate all religions and philosophical schools in order to make the Christian doctrines even more perfect. The theses were not unanimously approved, and a year later Pico had
to defend himself from charges of dangerous heterodoxy. This polemical
material nevertheless shows the twenty-three-year-old philosopher to have
been a broad-minded humanist, interested in a wide range of topics, including mathematics, geography, medicine, and other sciences.[19]

The theses, or theorems, were divided into larger sections, the first few
of which dealt with Christian, Arabic, Aristotelian, and Platonic philosophers: "Conclusiones secundum doctrines latinorum philosophorum et
theologorum," "Conclusiones secundum doctrinam Arabum," "Conclusiones
secundum grecos, qui peripateticam sectam profitentur," "Conclusiones
secundum doctrinam philosophorum, qui Platonici dicuntur." In the next
section Pico offered his own arguments for the reconcilability of Aristotelism
and Platonism ("Conclusiones numero quingentae secundum opinionem
propriam"). Most startling was the last section—"Questiones ad quas
pollicetur se per numeros responsurum"—in which he included subsections dealing with the mysticism of Zoroaster and the Chaldeans, magic in
general, the mystical hymns of Orpheus, and, finally, seventy-one theses on
the Hebrew cabala: "Conclusiones cabalisticae numero 71, secundum
opinionem propriam, ex ipsis Hebreorum sapientium fundamentis
Christianam Religionem maxime confirmantes."

Pico advertised twenty-six theses on magic, which scholarship refers
to as the *Conclusiones magicae*. In the first thesis Pico employs the ma-
neuver of his mentor, Ficino, separating himself from the outset from
black, diabolic magic. "Magia naturalis licita est, et non prohibita . . ."
states the second thesis (Pico 1973, 78), and in the third he claims that
magic is part of science. The following theses deal with questions of
magic and the cabala, and claim that there are no more suitable means
for proving the divinity of Christ than these: "Nulla est scientia que nos
magis certificet de divinitate Christi, quam Magia et Cabala"(*Conclusiones
magicae* 9, in Pico 1973, 79).

The nine hundred theses were to be introduced by a preface, an
oration on the dignity of man. Although the theses were never published,
the *Oratio . . .* was permitted to appear in 1487. This pamphlet is the
peak of Pico's early career, perhaps his whole scholarly output. The views
expressed in it became emblematic images of Renaissance ideology.[20]

According to the *Oratio . . .* there are two kinds of magic: one is
harmful and is the work of demons, while the other is pure natural
philosophy. The latter helps man to extend and exploit his potential to

the ultimate limits. The treatise starts with the famous saying of Hermes Trismegistus, "Magnum, o Asclepi, miraculum est homo," and this is the maxim that urged Pico to venture into his philosophical investigation concerning the divine nature of man:

> When I weighed the reason for these maxims, the many grounds for the excellence of human nature reported by many men failed to satisfy me—that man is the intermediary between creatures, the intimate of the gods, the king of the lower beings, the interpreter of nature, but little lower than the angels. [. . .] Admittedly great though these reasons be, they are not the principal grounds, that is, those which may rightfully claim for themselves the privilege of the highest admiration. For why should we not admire more the angels themselves and the blessed choirs of heaven? At last it seems to me I have come to understand why man is the most fortunate of creatures and consequently worthy of all admiration and what precisely is that rank which is his lot in the universal chain of Being—a rank to be envied not only by brutes but even by the stars and by minds beyond this world. (Section 1; Pico 1948, 223)

In the following sections he argues that the divine nature of man has roots in God's desire to have a creature of universal potential who can fully appreciate the work of creation:

> When the work was finished, the Craftsman kept wishing that there were someone to ponder the plan of so great a work, to love its beauty, and to wonder at its vastness. Therefore, when everything was done (as Moses and Timaeus bear witness), He finally took thought concerning the creation of man. [. . .] He therefore took man as a creature of indeterminate nature and, assigning him a place in the middle of the world, addressed him thus: "Neither a fixed abode nor a form that is thine alone nor any function peculiar to thyself have we given thee, Adam, to the end that according to thy longing and according to thy judgement thou mayest have and possess what abode, what form, and what function thou thyself shalt desire." (Sections 2–3, 224)

This special status, the concentration of potential and possibilities, then ordain man to shape his fate with full freedom and even elevate himself directly to God:

> We have made thee neither of heaven nor of earth, neither mortal nor immortal, so that with freedom of choice and with honor, as though

the maker and molder of thyself, thou mayest fashion thyself in whatever shape thou shalt prefer. Thou shalt have the power to degenerate
into the lower forms of life, which are brutish. Thou shalt have the
power, out of thy soul's judgement, to be reborn into the higher forms,
which are divine. (section 3, 225)

From this statement Cassirer postulated the novelty of the Renaissance
world picture in comparison with that of the Middle Ages: the so-called
man-centered ideology is nothing but the idea of man capable of *exaltatio*,
of moving upward along the Great Chain of Being and becoming the
partner of the Creator. Pico himself must have felt rapture from his own
thoughts because the following passages reach an exalted poetical intensity:

> O supreme generosity of god the Father, O highest and most marvelous
> felicity of man! To him it is granted to have whatever he chooses, to
> be whatever he wills. [. . .] And if, happy in the lot of no created thing,
> he withdraws into the center of his own unity, his spirit, made one with
> God, in the solitary darkness of God, who is set above all things, shall
> surpass them all. (section 4, 225)

After corroborating his thesis about the privileged place of man by
citing the Bible and classical authors, he poses the question: "what ought
we to do to achieve ascension?" Following the Apostle Paul and Dionysius
the Areopagite he suggests that the first step is purification (cf. Völker
1958, passim). This will lead to illumination and perfection. Pico's argumentation is quite eclectic: the variety of his sources indicates that the
new theology will have to be an amalgamation of the great world religions and that Christianity will have to be renewed with the help of
classical philosophy. He refers to Jacob's ladder and the example of Job
from the Old Testament, then he mentions the Egyptian mythology of
Osiris to which he adds a few thoughts from Empedocles.

Then he outlines the hierarchy of human learning, setting up the
following triad: moral philosophy—natural philosophy and dialectics—
theology. This threefold division corresponds to the neoplatonic concept
of sensual, rational, and intuitive knowledge. On the highest level one
finds the Peace that springs from the understanding of the One and
Primordial Truth, no matter whether it is the result of Christian,
Pythagorean, or cabalistical meditation:

> This is that peace which God creates in his heavens, which the angels
> descending to earth proclaimed to men of good will, that through it

men might ascend to heaven and become angels. Let us wish this peace for our friends, for our century. (section 14, 232)

Pico draws a parallel between the process of initiation in Moses and in the Greek mysteries before he comes to a conclusion by restating the program of ultimate sacred *exaltatio*:

> Who would not long to be initiated into such sacred rites? Who would not desire, by neglecting all human concerns, by despising the goods of fortune, and by disregarding those of the body, to become the guest of the gods while yet living on earth, and, made drunk by the nectar of eternity, to be endowed with the gifts of immortality though still a mortal being? (section 16, 233)

The second part of the *Oratio . . .* , after having introduced the state of rapture through sacred illumination, is devoted to a detailed methodology of achieving the desired ascension to God. Here Pico supports Apollo's precepts derived from the oracle of Delphoi ("Nothing too much," "Know thyself," "Thou art" [i.e., the theological greeting, ε_]); then he offers an imposing outline of various philosophical schools, beginning with the teachings of Pythagoras, Socrates, Chaldean magic, and Zoroaster, continuing with Christian philosophers (Augustinus, John Scotus Erigena, Thomas Aquinas, Albertus Magnus), the Arabs (Averroes, Alfarabi, Avicenna), and finishing with the Greek platonists (Theophrastus, Ammonius, Porphyry, Iamblichus, Plotinus, Proclus, and others). At this point he openly attests syncretism:

> I have so prepared myself that, pledged to the doctrines of no man, I have ranged through all the masters of philosophy, investigated all books, and come to know all schools. Therefore, I had to speak of them all. (section 26, 242)
> [. . .] This has been my reason for wishing to bring before the public the opinions not of a single school alone but rather of every school. (section 28, 244)

After this methodological introduction, Pico discusses in a detailed way his sources belonging to heterodox or apocryphal philosophical trends, such as the hermetic writings, Pythagorean mysticism, and the Jewish cabala. Finally he adds his own conclusions:

> I have not been content to add to the tenets held in common many teachings taken from the ancient theology of Hermes Trismegistus,

many from the doctrines of the Chaldeans and of Pythagoras, and many from the occult mysteries of the Hebrews. I have proposed also as subjects for discussion several theses in natural philosophy and in divinity, discovered and studied by me. (section 29, 245)

Hereafter Pico summarizes his nine hundred theses which he orders in six groups: the first group covers the correspondences between Plato and Aristotle whom Pico does not see as irreconcilable as many of his contemporaries thought (section 29). The second group offers seventy-two new propositions concerning natural philosophy and metaphysics derived from the parallel study of both Plato and Aristotle (section 30). The third great topic is Pythagorean number mysticism (section 31); the fourth is the area of magic (sections 32–33); the fifth touches upon the cabala (sections 34–37); and, finally, in the sixth group Pico explains his own ideas concerning the prophetic verses of Orpheus and Zoroaster (section 37).

For our present concern, we should concentrate on the propositions relating to magic and the cabala. He continually emphasizes the difference between white and black magic, that is *mageis* and *goétia*. Here he cites Porphyry to assert that the word *magus* in Persian means the interpreter of the gods. From the history of white magic he mentions the ancients (Zalmoxis, Zoroaster, Plato, Apollonius, Hostanes, and Dardanus), the Arab Al-Kindi, and medieval authorities (Roger Bacon and Villiam of Auvergne). All of them practiced a magic that "rouses [the magus] to the admiration of God's works which is the most certain condition of a willing faith, hope, and love" (section 33, 249). Pico uses a metaphor that reminds one of Ficino: "As the farmer weds his elms to vines, even so does *the magus* wed earth to heaven, that is, he weds lower things to the endowments and powers of higher things" (ibid.). Pico's image suggests an ambition to join the sypathetic magic of the Middle Ages with the new, hermetic theology.

But how to avoid the mixing of the two magics, white and black? How can the magus preserve his purity during the concrete operations? This is to be achieved with the help of the mystical lore of the Jews, the cabala.

> I come now to the things I have elicited from the ancient mysteries of the Hebrews and have cited for the confirmation of the inviolable Catholic faith. [. . .] Not only the famous doctors of the Hebrews, but also from among men of our opinion Esdras, Hilary, and Origen write that Moses on the mount received from God not only the Law, which he left to posterity written down in five books, but also a true and more occult explanation of the Law. (section 34, 250)
>
> [In it t]here is the mystery of the Trinity, there the Incarnation of the Word, there the divinity of the Messiah. . . . (section 36, 252)

Although the *Oratio*... does not say more about the connection of magic and the cabala, from the *Conclusiones magicae* one can see that for Pico it was the cabala that could ensure the safe handling of magic. The reason for this was that the cabala dealt only with the sacred names of God and the angels, with the sacred letters of the "holy tongue," and so because of its medium could not turn in any dangerous direction.

As we know, John Dee had an 1532 edition of Pico's nine hundred theses (R&W 974, B121). What could he have found crucial in them and in the introductory *Oratio*...? To begin with, certainly the bold and daring spirit advocating philosophical and theological syncretism and at the same time fervently rejecting the charges that his experiments could be termed as black magic. Dee also might have been attracted by the lofty, sometimes nearly poetical diction of the introduction in describing the *exaltatio*—a style toward which he himself often tended. As for the theses, they were written in Dee's favorite scientific genre, a series of theorems such as he used to express his ideas in the *Propaedeumata aphoristica* and the *Monas hieroglyphica*. Furthermore, in Pico's work he could find references to a mix of classical, Arabic, and Christian authors, and he also could gain inspiration to look into the hermetic writings as well as the cabala. Last, but not least, in the *Oratio*... one finds some of Dee's crucial iconographical-ideological motifs, like the mention of Jacob's ladder and several references to Enoch's translation from earth to the throne of God and his conversations with angels.

—◊—

To summarize, in the magical ideology of the Florentine neoplatonists, we can see that the texts I have reread as Dee's possible sources were rich in theoretical observations and programmatic recommendations, although they provided little in the way of technological advice in practical directions. This could follow because of several reasons, including the natural caution of theologians and the fact that natural science in fifteenth-century Italy was not in the forefront of investigations. Thirdly, the neoplatonist orientation, in fact, worked against the pursuit of systematic experimentation, since Platonism always favored theoretical speculations and metaphoric expression as opposed to more rationalistic Aristotelianism. In this respect even Pico, who tried to reconcile Plato and Aristotle, is more a Platonist than an Aristotelian, at least in this early period of his career. Later, when he started criticizing judicial astrology, for example, his argumentation became more critical and analytical (*Disputationes adversus astrologiam divinatricem*, 1496).[21]

The sixteenth century brought significant changes in the status as well as in the practice of Renaissance magic. For a while the Scientific Revolution found it inspiring to incorporate magical ideas: this transitional period from the organic to the new mechanical world picture can be dated from the 1510s to Newton's synthesis at the end of the seventeenth century.

Beside the Scientific Revolution, other cultural-historical factors, such as the revolution in Renaissance art and esthetics, the great religious Reformation, the period of eschatological-chiliastic prophecies, and the information explosion resulting from printing, all contributed to the spreading and changing of magical concepts. In the next chapter I shall look at the symbolical-metaphorical systems of a few sixteenth-century magical thinkers—Trithemius, Agrippa, Paracelsus, and Postel—who belonged to the generation immediately preceding Dee and whose works seem directly to have influenced the intellectual development of the English Doctor.

5

Occult Philosophy, Symbolism, and Science

During the sixteenth century the pious and speculative magic that characterized the works of the earlier Renaissance humanists, such as the Florentine philosophers, radically changed from the enthusiastic study of the ancient texts containing the *prisca theologia* to an ambition to influence and manipulate the supernatural powers.

When recognizing this, one has to be careful not to jump to early conclusions. The changes did not occur as a line or development from Florentine hermeticism to Agrippan magic, as Frances Yates tried to make us believe. While undoubtedly appreciating the neoplatonist magi, the next generation also capitalized on dark medieval practices that were quite unimaginable to their humanist mentors. Later I shall propose a hypothesis as to why these changes took place, but first let us see some of the details of this new magical pattern in early modern European thinking.

TRITHEMIUS AND ANGEL MAGIC

John Dee admittedly found Trithemius' *Steganographia* to be the greatest inspiration in his own recourse to magical philosophy and theology. In 1562 he visited Leuven, one of his favorite cities, a center of learning which he had already visited several times before. Perhaps it is here that he wrote the unpublished "Cabbalae Hebraicae compendiosa tabella" (Roberts and Watson 1990, 76), which shows his rising interest in the cabala and angel theology. At that time he purchased manuscripts of astronomical and astrological interest (R&W M119, M120), some books on Hebrew grammar (R&W 1600, 1612), and Jacques Gohory's deeply hermetical *De usu & mysteriis liber* (Paris 1550), which dealt with number symbolism and preserves Dee's annotations on the Monad. Probably this is the intellectual context from which the idea of the *Monas hieroglyphica* sprang and it must have been catalyzed by his acquaintance with the work of Trithemius, as we learn from Dee's letter written to his patron, Sir William Cecil, dated from Antwerp in February of the following year.[1]

This letter is an excellent specimen of Dee's humanist style where personal information, scholarly speculations, and passages considering the politics of patronage are melded together:

> Briefly to place before your eyes the chief of my requests, thus standeth my case. [. . .] Wherein our country hath no man hable to set furth his fote, or shew his hand: as in the science *De numeris formalibus,* the science *De ponderibus mysticis,* and the science *De mensuris divinis:* (by which three the huge frame of this world is fashioned) [. . .] after my long serche and study, great cost and travaile have fallen under my perseverance and understanding. (Dee 1854, 6–7)

The quoted passage clearly shows the directions of Dee's scholarly interest at that time: formal mathematics, occult mysticism, and the question of divine measures—all aspects that feature in the *Monas hieroglyphica*. In the following section Dee speaks about his own plans: he prepares to publish a work of his own but is still in search of a suitable printer. After politely asking for further sponsorship from Cecil, he comes to the most important piece of information:

> Already I have purchased one boke, for which a thowsand crownes have ben by others offred, and yet could not be obteyned; a boke whose use is greater than the fame thereof is spread; the name thereof to you is not unknowne. The title is on this wise, *Steganographia Trithemij.* . . . (9–10)

We learn furthermore that he employed a Hungarian nobleman to copy this book, which ultimately would become a present to his patron: "I give unto your Honor, as the most precyous juell that I have yet of other mens travailes recovered" (11).

Johannes Trithemius (1462–1516), the Abbot of Sponheim, is one of the most important Renaissance thinkers who devoted himself consciously to the study of angelology, seeking to syncretize the medieval traditions with that of the new neoplatonist philosophy.[2] At first sight his *Steganographia* (written in 1499 but published only in 1606) looks to be a work on writing systems and cyphers; in fact, is an interesting example of applied magic.[3] In Trithemius' system, alchemy, cabalistical number symbolism, and magic are united and magic is interpreted as the means of *exaltatio*, the theologically justifiable mystical elevation to God.

This clearly seems to be connected with Pico's theory of magical illumination, but Noel Brann in his new monograph on Trithemius' magic differentiates among his sources according to Patristic and medieval demonology on the one hand and medieval and early modern defenses of magic on the other (1999, 13–33). Brann discusses Trithemius' demonological vision and occult vision in separate chapters, suggesting that his angelology had stronger ties to the medieval monastic heritage, while his complex occult philosophy was more the product of the Renaissance.

In a letter addressed to his humanist friend, Arnold Bostius, Trithemius himself heralded his *Steganographia* as follows:

> [it will] teach very profound, marvelous, and incredible things to all who are ignorant of them, things which have never been heard of by this age. [. . .] If ever published, will be marveled at by the entire world. . . [4]

As he informed Bostius, the first book would deal with a hundred ways of secret writing, the second with ways of sending messages through great distances "without words, without writing, even without signs"; the third book would demonstrate a new and extremely fast way of teaching Latin; while the last book would be devoted to the transmission of thoughts from one person to another, totally secretly, even in the company of others.

The author had considerable misfortune with his letter to Bostius: because of the death of the adressee it was misdirected and became public, appalling many conservative church authorities, even humanists. A further blow was the visit of the famous French humanist and philosopher of the Great Chain of Being, Bovillus (Charles de Bouelles), to Sponheim, where Trithemius tried to convince him about his magical ideas. Bovillus, although not insensitive to the hermetic philosophy,[5] seems to have disapproved totally of what was presented by Trithemius. As he wrote to their mutual friend, Germaine de Ganay, another humanist interested in magic, the unaccustomed names of spirits and the demonological procedures described in the *Steganographia* terrified him, and his overall conclusion was that Trithemius was "a magician who is not in the least degree distinguished in philosophy."[6] In this letter he also went into details concerning the Abbot's angelic magic, which consisted of designating the names of spirits for conjurations according to various ranks (emperors, dukes, counts, and servants) and associating them with the twelve regions of the world as well as the forty winds of the universe. At this point Bouelles remarked that Trithemius seemed to him to be better representing the ancient demon-conjuring Zoroaster than the demon-shunning Christian saints.

Although Bouelles' critique was quite devastating to the reputation of Trithemius, one can imagine to what extent Dee, who possessed ten books by Bovillus including *De intellectu* in the 1510 edition (R&W 311), became interested in the author of the *Steganographia*. In fact, his hierarchies of angels in the *48 claves angelicae* (Dee 1584) and his invocations in the *Tabula bonorum angelorum; Fundamenta invocationum* (Dee 1588) had close kinship with the system of Trithemius.

Abbot Trithemius was not deterred from his devotion to angelic magic by the criticisms. Just the opposite, in his last years he went on defending, expanding, and explicating his magic in his autobiographical tract, *Nepiachus*, his appendix to his main work, *Clavis steganographiae*, and in various letters written to patrons and fellow scholars. Brann summarizes this last phase of Trithemius' career as follows: "The apologetic strategy adopted by Trithemius went beyond arguing for a mere toleration of magic by Christians, after removing magic from the exclusive domain of the demons, of putting it in the service of Christian theology. [. . .] In this more sublime sense, Trithemius determined, the essential affiliation of magic is not with the secular arts and sciences, but with the religious quest for God" (1999, 90).

In Trithemius' magical system, alchemy, magic, and cabalistical number symbolism are intermingled, and—similar to Pico's strategy—he defends magic by relegating it to the sphere of the highest intellectual activities. As he describes *exaltatio*:

> The alchemists make promises with reference to compoud bodies, but they err; they are deceived, and they deceive everyone who willingly listens to them. They want to imitate nature and to divide what is exclusively a whole, since they do not understand the basis of virtue and nature. [. . .] Our philosophy is not earthly but rather celestial so that we might perceive that highest principle, which we call God. [. . .] The mind is free; it does not follow motion, but rather a supercelestial principle by which it was created and by which it communicates so much. (*Epistolarum familiarum*, 1536, 90–93; quoted by Baron 1978, 95)

Trithemius had a discordant personality, similar to the other protagonists of my book who contributed to the development of Renaissance magic. On the one hand, he was a widely read and highly cultured humanist who also had a visionary, perhaps somewhat frantic mind, for whom the ultimate evidence could only be supernatural revelation. This dilemma could be associated with what Deborah Harkness calls the "crisis of the Book of Nature" (1999, 64–71). However, for Ficino, Pico, and also for Trithemius, this revelation did not result from sacred simplicity, but rather from the cognitive faculties of the human intellect. According to the train of logic of the following quotation, Trithemius appears as almost a forerunner of the rationalism of Hobbes and Locke, except, of course, for his clinging to the final revelation:

> Study generates knowledge; knowledge bears love; love, likeness; likeness, communion; communion, virtue; virtue, dignity; dignity, power; and power performs the miracle. This is the unique path to the goal of magic perfection, divine as well as natural. (*Epistolarum familiarum*, 92; Thorndike's translation, 1923–1958, 6:439)

The quotation embraces knowledge, *exaltatio*, and power, constituting a "holy trinity" of the magi. The scholarly way of illumination for Trithemius leads through mathematics and Pythagorean number symbolism, enriched by the numerology of the cabala. In this respect his main sources were Pico and the greatest Hebraist of the Renaissance, Reuchlin, who devoted two books to the occult mysteries of the cabala[7] and to whom Trithemius referred as his mentor.

The speculative theology of Trithemius was built on a paradigm that aimed at developing the variety embedded in the duality of the world through the trinity into a sacred unity. The soul, aspiring toward this sacred sphere, could elevate itself to the metaphysical world only by comprehending the mysteries of nature, especially of numbers. Although, according to his letter to Ganay, quoted above, Trithemius seemed not to approve of practical alchemy, he extensively referred to the *Tabula smaragdina*, which he interpreted not simply as an alchemical recipe, but as a concise mystical cosmology. In this context he repeatedly used the term *reformatio magica*, "referring to a passage of the soul, on the model of alchemy, through a series of purgative stages to a state of godlike sanctity and 'enlightenment' " (Brann 1999, 116). As we shall see, Dee, in the middle period of his career, employed similar syncretism in constructing the hieroglyphic monad, fusing mathematics and alchemy in order to achieve spiritual *exaltatio*.

One of Trithemius' last works could have influenced the later Dee in constructing his own vision of the angelic world. In 1508 the Abbot of Sponheim addressed a treatise to Emperor Maximilian of Habsburg[8] in which explained the seven secondary gods or demons moving the seven planets and also offered prophecies concerning world history up to the twentieth century.[9] Although Trithemius maintained that the human mind was free from the influence of the stars, in his scheme of planetary history (partly borrowed from the thirteenth-century Paduan alchemist Pietro d'Abano) each of the seven planetary spheres is governed by an angel who is also responsible over a historical period, lasting 354 solar years and four lunar months. The angels of the planetary spheres are as follows: Orifiel for Saturn, Anael for Venus, Zachariel for Jupiter, Raphael for Mercury, Samael for Mars, Gabriel for the Moon, and Michael for the Sun (Brann 1999, 134; Thorndike 1923–1958, 6:441). This scheme again may remind us of Dee's *De heptarchia mystica*. Although the Doctor employed different angel names, he also divided his angels into ranks of Kings, Princes, Subjects, and Servants, and one of his admitted aims was to learn about the future history of mankind.

Right after the time of writing his *De septem secundeis* in 1509, Trithemius received yet another visitor with whom he discoursed about magic and the occult sciences. The visitor was the still young German humanist Heinrich Cornelius Agrippa von Nettesheim, who a year later dedicated the first edition of his main work, *De occulta philosophia* (1510), to the aging master.[10]

AGRIPPA'S TRIPARTITE MAGIC

If Trithemius' magical experiements pointed much beyond the humble beginnings of Florentine Renaissance magic, Agrippa (1486–1535) could be termed as the Renaissance magus par excellence. He also relied in many respects on the achievments of his predecessors—ancient philosophers, medieval scholars, and contemporary humanists alike. Nevertheless he was able to create a unique system distinguishing him from everyone else dabbling in magic and cabalistical mysticism.

His main works show a curious chronological mismatch: the *De occulta philosophica* was written in 1510, but its definitive edition was published only in 1533, not much before Agrippa's death. His other major work, *De incertitudine et vanitate omnium scientiarum et artium atque excellentia verbi dei declamatio*, on the other hand, was published twice before that and the paradoxical fact is that while *De occulta philosophia* was meant to be a huge primer in magic, the much slimmer and highly ironic *De incertitudine* . . . in many respects refuted and disavowed his other work published only two years later. Since the two books are almost exact opposites of each other, cultural historians have pondered why the author allowed the publication of his enthusiastic affirmation of magic to happen after he had expressed his scepticism about the topic (Keefer 1988, 618). Before examining this question, I would like to set myself to a general survey of *De occulta philosophia*, naturally concentrating on the theme of *exaltatio*.

De occulta philosophia

Following Dionysius the Areopagite, Agrippa maintained that the universum consists of three worlds: the elemental, celestial, and spirit-worlds. Agrippa classified magical operations according to these spheres, too. His system of magic, however, as Keith Thomas emphasized, needed not only the cosmos of the medieval *magia naturalis*, but also the emphases of Renaissance neoplatonism, such as the doctrine of the dignity of man and the classical notion that the spirit world and the elemental world could melt into each other: "The potentialities open to human ingenuity were greatly enhanced by the tide of Neoplatonism which swept through Renaissance Europe" (Thomas 1971, 265).

The first book of *De occulta philosophia* dealt with elemental, or natural magic, and mostly concerned itself with the sympathies inherent in the organic world model. Next to the questions of magia naturalis, however, already on the first pages of the book are references to magical *exaltatio*. Agrippa refers explicitly to magic in a more direct way than Ficino or Pico:

> Seeing there is a threefold world, elementary, celestial, and intellectual, and every inferior is governed by its superior, and receiveth the influence of the virtues thereof, so that the very original, and chief Worker of all doth by angels, the heavens, stars, elements, animals, plants, metals, and stones convey from itself the virtues of his omnipotency upon us, for whose service he made, and created all these things: wise men [i.e. *magi*] conceive it no way irrational that it should be possible for us to ascend by the same degrees through each world, to the same very original world itself, the Maker of all things, and First Cause, from whence all things are, and proceed; and also to enjoy not only these

virtues, which are already in the more excellent kind of things, but also besides these, to draw new virtues from above. Hence it is that they seek after the virtues of the elementary world, through the help of physic, and natural philosophy in the various mixtions of natural things, then of the celestial world in the rays, and influences thereof, according to the rules of astrologers, and the doctrines of mathematicians, joining the celestial vertues to the former: moreover, they ratify and confirm all these with the powers of divers intelligencies, through the sacred ceremonies of religion. (1.1; Agrippa 1997, 3)[11]

When discussing the connections of natural sympathies and the spirit world, Agrippa arrives at the question of talismanic magic already treated by Ficino. For example, if you want to capture the power of the Sun, seek those things that are solar:

> amongs vegetables, plants, metals, stones, and animals, these things are to be used, and taken chiefly, which in a solary order are higher. So thou shalt draw a singular gift from the Sun through the beams thereof, being seasonably received together, and through the Spirit of the World. (1.34, 105)

Chapter 37 summarizes the system of the Great Chain of Being, giving at the same time an exact definition of magic. Citing the Platonists, Hermes Trismegistus, and Jarchas the Brahmin,[12] he states that everything existing in the elementary world has a counterpart in the celestial sphere, too. The middle nature, or quintessence that keeps together the Chain of Being, is generated in turn by the ultimately superior highest Archetype:

> Now the first image of God is the world; of the world, man; of man, beasts; of beasts, the zeophyton i.e. half-animal and half-plant; of plants, metals; of metals, stones. And again in things spiritual, the plant agrees with a brute in vegetation, a brute with a man in sense, man with an angel in understanding, an angel with God in immortality. Divinity is annexed to the mind, the mind to the intellect, the intellect to the intention, the intention to the imagination, the imagination to the senses, the senses at last to things. (1.37, 110)

This chapter also emphasizes the bi-directional nature of this organic communication, which suggests the understanding of the entire cosmos as a homogeneous whole. This homogeneity is exploited by magic:

Hence everything may be aptly reduced from these inferiors to the stars, from the stars to their intelligences, and from thence to the First cause itself; from the series, and order whereof whole magic, and all occult philosophy flows. (ibid.)

As we shall see, John Dee spoke about the cosmos as a well-tuned lyre on which the magus can play. His thought might go back to Agrippa, who also states in Chapter 37 that

> For so inferiors are succesively joined to their superiors, that there proceeds an influence from their head, the First Cause, as a certain string stretched out [. . .] of which string if one end be touched, the whole doth presently shake, and such a touch doth sound to the other end, and at the motion of the inferior, the superior also is moved, to which the other does answer, as strings in a lute well tuned. (1.37, 111)

Based on the doctrine of sympathies, then, natural magic can manipulate powers from this world as well as from the world of demons (1.39). Witchcraft using magical power, the wearing of magic rings and amulets, even the some practices of raising the dead are treated under this field of occultism (1.42–48).

After discussing the general features of the tiers of the cosmos, Agrippa comes to treating of the microcosm, man. Here he speaks of those human faculties that are capable of magical operations. Among others, he mentions the power of dreams that arise either from the memories of real experiences or can be sent by spiritual agencies. As a consequence, our emotions may greatly intensify even to the extent of changing our physical shape, transposing our body to faraway places or influencing magically other human beings. He underscores here the communicative power of language:

> It being showed that there is a great power in the affections of the soul, you must know moreover, that there is no less virtue in words, and in the names of things, but greatest of all in speeches. (1.69, 211)

Uttered words have magic power, especially proper names: "That proper names are very necessary in magical operations, almost all men testify" (1.70, 213). Stronger than proper names are "sentences," such as enchantments, invocations, orations, conjurations, and the like (1.71). Book One closes with a review of these, which are treated again under ceremonial magic in Book Three.

Book Two starts with a discussion of mathematical magic, and discusses the power of numbers:

> Severinus Boethius saith, that all things which were first made by the nature of things in its first age, seem to be formed by the proportion of numbers, for this was the principal pattern in the mind of the Creator. Hence is borrowed the number of the elements, hence the courses of times, hence the motion of the stars, and the revolution of the heaven, and the state of all things subsist by the uniting together of numbers. Numbers therefore are endowed with great and sublime virtues. (2.2, 237)[13]

Mechanics and optics are based on abstract mathematical science and are capable of creating wonders. Such were the automata of Dedalus, the speaking statues of Hermes Trismegistus,[14] the flying wooden dove of Arthita, and all the optical miracles reported by classical and medieval authorities (2.1). This enthusiasm for mechanics and optics would be very important in forming John Dee's *Mathematical preface*, too. Dee himself created such a "mechanical wonder," a flying scarabeus that was used at a school drama performance in Cambridge and earned for its creator the fame of "conjuror," as Dee often complained (e.g., Dee 1851, 5).

This Agrippan *magia naturalis* is the territory that links theological magic with the new, rising, natural sciences. This is the terrain in which the occult fantasies of Roger Bacon through to Leonardo da Vinci, della Porta, and Francis Bacon were almost freely mixing with surprisingly rational propositions. Take, for example, Agrippa's sober remark:

> Therefore [people] seeing any wonderful sight, do impute it to the Devil, as his work, or think it is a miracle, which indeed is a work of natural, or mathematical philosophy. [. . .] But here it is convenient that you know, that as by natural virtues we collect natural virtues, so by abstracted, mathematical, and celestial, we receive celestial virtues, as motion, life, sense, speech, soothsaying, and divination, even in matter less disposed, as that which is not made by nature, but only by art. (2.1, 234)

The second part of the quotation also shows that rationally approachable natural science only partially excites Agrippa. His main concern is the manipulation of natural and supernatural forces by magical means, which in this chapter he identifies with abstract, mathematical formulas. And since the most divine kind of numerology is the cabala, Book Two extensively deals with the possibilities of synthetizing Christian philosophy and Jewish number symbolism. Chapter 2.27 offers a memorable image of the microcosm, based on mathematical-poetical iconography:

> Seeing Man is the most beautiful and perfectest work of God, and his image, and also the lesser world; therefore he by a more perfect composition, and sweet harmony, and more sublime dignity doth contain and maintain in himself all numbers, measures, weights, motions, elements, and all other things which are of composition. [. . .] From hence all the ancients in time past did number by their fingers, and showed all numbers by them; and they seem to prove that from the very joints of man's body all numbers, measures, proportions, and harmonies were invented; hence according to this measure of the body, they framed, and contrived their temples, palaces, houses, theaters; also their ships, engines, and every kind of artifice. [. . .] Moreover God himself [. . .] made the whole fabric of the world proportionable to man's body; from hence it is called the great world, man's body the less. (2.27, 345)

Book Three of ceremonial magic begins with passages emphasizing the importance, power, and usefulness of religion. Interestingly, Agrippa does not classify magic within the larger system of religion, just the opposite: "The religious operation obtains no less efficacy which ofttimes of itself alone is sufficiently powerful for us to obtain this deifying virtue . . ." (3.3, 449). And, of course, needless to say, magic in association with religious rites has no other purpose than to achieve the *exaltatio*:

> Now we will declare a mystical and secret manner, necessary for everyone who desireth to practice this art, which is both the beginning, perfection, and key of all magical operations, and *it is the dignifying of men* to this so sublime virtue and power, for *this faculty requireth in man a wonderful dignification*. (3.3, 448; emphasis mine)

Since a true magus needs to know God as much as possible, lengthy theological discussion is inserted here on the nature of God, on his names and their power (3.12), about the heavenly spirits (3.15), then of about three types of intelligences and *daemons* (undoubtedly based on Iamblichus and Proclus, cf. 3.16) and the types of malevolent demons (3.18). In discussing Dee's angel magic, it will be useful to return to these chapters for further scrutiny. Another chapter on the language of angels also points toward Dee's occultism. This language, according to the ancients, could be nothing but Hebrew, since "that was the first of all, and came from heaven, and was before the confusion of languages in Babylon [. . .] and seeing all tongues have, and do undergo various mutations, and corruptions, this alone doth always continue inviolated" (3.23, 530). As opposed to the above view, Agrippa speaks about the angelic language without trying to tie it to any existing human idiom: "that instrument, whatsoever the virtue be, by which one spirit makes known to another spirit what things are in his mind, is called by the apostle Paul the tongue of angels" (ibid.).

As for concrete magical operations, the magus needs to be in contact mostly with inferior spiritual orders. Agrippa, just like Faustus in the legend, was most interested in the possibility of regulating natural forces by occult means:

> I have seen and known some, writing on virgin parchment the name and seal of some spirit in the hour of the Moon: which when afterward he gave to be devoured by a water frog, and had muttered over some verse, the frog being let go in the water, rains and showers presently followed. I saw also the same man[15] inscribing the name of another spirit whith the seal thereof in the hour of Mars, which was given to a crow, who being let go, after a verse muttered over, there followed horrible thunders with thick clouds. Neither were those names of spirits of an unknown tongue, neither did they signify anything else but their offices. Of this kind are the names of those angels, Raziel, Gabriel, Michael, Raphael, Haniel. . . . (3.24, 532)

Since Agrippa devoted all three of his books to the overlapping systems of the macro- and the microcosms, Book Three also has chapters relating directly to man. While Book One discussed the elemental composition of the body and Book Two pondered the mystical numerology of its proportions, Book Three concentrates on the act of creations and on the power of the human intellect. The ideology of this part follows quite closely Pico's *Oration,* adding to it the description of concrete magical procedures.

The creation of man is presented more on the basis of the *Corpus hermeticum* than on the Bible. Agrippa's man is strong and determined, before everything he needs to know himself (as if following the ancient Platonic advice: know thyself!)—but this knowledge should lead to the perfect knowledge of God, too: "Whosoever therefore shall know himself, shall know all things in himself; especially he shall know God, according to whose image he was made" (3.36, 580). The process of deification, or *exaltatio*, is compared here to spiritual alchemy, the kind of transmutation already mentioned by the Arabic philosopher, Geber:

> And Geber in his Sum of Alchemy[16] teacheth, that no man can come to the perfection of this art, who shall not know the principles of it in himself; but how much the more everyone shall know himself, by so much operateth greater and more wonderful things, and will ascend to so great a perfection, that *he is made the son of God,* and *is transformed into the image which is God, and is united with him, which is not granted to angels,* the world, or any creature, but to man only. (3.36, 580; emphasis mine)

The hermetic *exaltatio* of Ficino and Pico here is explained with the precision of a scientist:

> Man being united to God, all things which are in man, are united, especially his mind, then the spirits and animal powers, and vegetative faculty, and the elements are to the matter, drawing with itself even the body [. . .] even until it be glorified into immortality. (3.36, 580)

From this special status of man it follows that it is difficult to learn about the nature of the two components of his existence: the immortal soul and the mortal body. It is especially difficult to find out what happens to these after death. Agrippa devotes a number of chapters to the theories concerning the immortality of the soul and he touches upon those instances when dead souls cannot rest and return to this world. The magical aspect of this problem, according to Agrippa the highest degree of ceremonial magic, is the calling of these spirits by magicians for help in various worldly matters: "By what ways the magicians and necromancers do think they can call forth the souls of the dead" (3.42). It was especially because of this part of *De occulta philosophia* that Agrippa was known in the Renaissance as a sorcerer and a dangerous heretic. This must be the reason why he became Faustus' teacher in Marlowe drama and why a notorious sixteenth-century compendium of black magic was published as "The Fourth Book of Cornelius Agrippa." This book came out sometime after Agrippa's death, and scholars have ruled out that he could have written it. Johann Weyer, the "doctor of witches," also rejected this possibility. "The Fourth Book" nevertheless relies on Agrippa's genuine work and this similarity must have contributed to the bad reputation of the German humanist.[17]

John Dee's library catalogue proves that he possessed the 1550 Basel edition (R&W 742) which contained the spurious "Fourth Book" as well as other important treatises on ceremonial magic, such as Peter of Abano's *Heptameron*, "Ratio compendiaria Magiae naturalis ex Plinio," "Disputatio de Fascinationibus," "De incantatione et Adiuratione, Epistola incerti authoris," Trithemius' Apologetical Letter from the preface of his *Steganographia* as well as his *Octo questionum*, and, finally, "Diversa divinationum genera." To put it simply, quite a primer in magical and divinatory practices.[18]

According to the literature of magic, *necromantia*, or the calling of dead spirits, belongs without dispute to the terrain of black, diabolical practices. Agrippa himself wrote so in *De occulta philosophia*, yet in spite of this, he treats the subject at suspicious length. He classifies necromancy into two categories: *nekyomantia*, which raises the dead body and employs the blood of the deceased, and *skiomantia*, in which case only the shadow of the spirit is invoked.

> To conclude, it worketh all its experiements by the carcasses of the slain, and their bones and members, and what is from them, because there is in these things a spiritual power friendly to them. Therefore they easily allure the flowing down of wicked spirits, being by reason of the similitude and propriety very familiar: by whom the necromancer strengthened by their help can do very much in human and terrestrial things, and kindle unlawful lusts, cause dreams, diseases, hatred and such like passions. (3.42, 606)

Witches, says Agrippa, can easily use these unfortunate souls "for the effecting of their witchcrafts, alluring these unhappy souls by the apposition of their body or by the taking of some part thereof, and compelling them by their devilish charms" (ibid.).

After having plunged into the appalling details of black magic, Agrippa then returns to sacred theurgy and tries to include even the act of raising the dead within the highest level of white, ceremonial magic:

> He which would restore the souls truly to their bodies, must first know what is the proper nature of the soul from whence it went forth, with how many and how great degrees of perfection it is replenished. [. . .] To conclude, by what influences the body may be knit together again for the raising of the dead, requireth all these things which belong not to man but to God only, and to whom he will communicate them, as to Elishai who raised up the son of the Shunamite; so also Alcestis is reported to have been raised by Hercules; and Apollonius Tyanensis restored a dead maid to life. (3.42, 606)

The general conclusion of the monumental work restates the sacred and dignified nature of magic, which aims at using the secrets of nature for the glory of the Creator. On the one hand, Agrippa mentions magic as a kind of natural science, requiring systematic research:

> Some of these things are written in order, some without order, some things are delivered by fragments, some things are even hid, and left for the search of the intelligent, who are more acutely contemplating these things which are written, and diligently searching, may obtain the complete rudiments of the magical art. (3.65, 677)

On the other, however, he emphasizes the need for purity because the secrets of the art coded in special symbols cannot be comprehended otherwise. Those who are deserving will be rewarded with incredible gifts: "those virtues will appear to you, which in times past Hermes, Zoroaster, Apollonius, the others, who wrought miracles, obtained" (ibid.).

Although, according to some scholars, Agrippa's work lacks originality and is in many places confused and fragmentary, one can consider it the most comprehensive, encyclopedic *summa* written in the Renaissance. In it the author tried to present whatever he could gather from a great many different traditions of magic: classical sympathetic magic and demonology, late Hellenistic hermeticism, Arabic magic, medieval *magia naturalis,* and ceremonial magic framed by the ideology of Florentine Neoplatonism, especially its doctrine of *exaltatio* and the dignity of man.

Like most humanists, Agrippa included a great many examples in his work which are rather surprising for the modern reader. It seems that, like other humanists, the author had no scruples about the tales and anecdotes of the classical authorities. The stories of Pliny and other unreliable sources make a sharp contrast to Agrippa's own serenity and lofty enthusiasm.

Agrippa's magic is perhaps more a theology than natural science; nevertheless, it shows a great deal of rationality and analytical faculty in discussing many questions (see the chapters on mechanics and optics and on language and the psyche). Intellectual historians belonging to the Warburg school tried to approximate Agrippa's magic to science and discuss it as a subchapter in the history of Renaissance natural philosophy, a grounding of the Scientific Revolution (cf. Yates 1964, and 1979, 37–49; Debus 1978, 13, 19; Webster 1982, 27), but one should note that by the 1980s this opinion became greatly refined.[19] During the hermeticism debate, science historians argued that the occult philosophy played only a marginal role in the development of the Scientific Revolution. Though it may be true from a strictly scientific viewpoint, the general intellectual historian still feels bemused by Agrippa's occasional efforts to draft hypotheses in a clear and concise language. On these occasions he also shows his irony which gleams like that of the greatest humanists:

> According to the opinion of Synesius, seeing there are the same accidents to things, and like befall like; so he which hath often fallen upon the same visible thing, hath assigned to himself the same opinion, passion, fortune, action, event, and as Aristotle saith, the memory is confirmed by sense, and by keeping in memory the same thing knowledge is obtained, as also by the knowledge of many experiences, by little and little, arts and sciences are obtained. After the same account you must conceive dreams. [. . .] By this means shall a diviner be able by little, and little to interpret his dreams, if so be nothing slip out of his memory. (1.59 "Of divination by dreams," 186)

This humanist irony occasionally appears in the chapters of *De occulta philosophia*, but its real feat can be observed in his other famous work, *De incertitudine et vanitate omnium scientiarum*. Although the latter does not appear in Dee's library catalogues as a separate item, it is difficult to imagine that—with several copies of *De occulta philosophia*—he would not have known about it, especially since many chapters of *De incertitudine . . .* were attached as appendix to *De occulta . . .* (under the title: "The censure or retraction of Henry Cornelius Agrippa, concerning magic, after his declamation of the vanity of sciences, and the excellency of the word of God," Agrippa 1997, 689).[20] Since *De incertitudine . . .* also excercised great influence on the imagination of the sixteenth century, I shall discuss it, too.

De incertitudine et vanitate omnium scientiarum

Charles Nauert devoted a voluminous study to the philosophy of Agrippa and developed the following thesis as the backbone of his argument: the appearance of magical themes in Renaissance philosophy displayed the crisis of early modern thought and the very same crisis can be detected in the fact that Agrippa's two main works were so much the opposites of each other (cf. Nauert 1965). Nauert's monograph was written at the height of the so-called mannerism debate that characterized the 1960s and early 1970s.[21] At one point in this debate even the whole Reformation was interpreted as a crisis phenomenon of the Renaissance. I do not think that the entirety of Agrippa's magic could be interpreted as a product of crisis; rather, *De occulta philosophia* represents one of the peaks of the occult philosophy as developed by the sixteenth century. If we speak about crisis, I see it in one specific area, indeed. Although Agrippa and others tried to meticulously separate white from black magic, that proved to be a futile effort and subsequently led to a feeling of uncertainty and discomfort. Combined with other aspects of the growing intellectual crisis toward the end of the sixteenth century, these opinions can naturally be interpreted as characteristic features of mannerism.

In any case, when trying to find clues for the contradictions in Agrippa's work we must proceed to a more refined micro-analysis of *De incertitudine. . .* [22]

The general tone of the work, which consists of over one-hundred short chapters, is sarcastic irony, found first in the preface where the author compares himself to Hercules, brave enough to attack the sciences. And he is aware of the expected consequences:

> I well perceive what a bloody battle I have to fight with them hand to hand, and how dangerous this fight will be, seeing that I am beset on every side with an army of so mighty enemies. O with how many engines will they assail me, and with how many shames and villainies will they load me? [. . .] The obstinate Logicians will cast against me infinite darts of syllogisms; the long-tongued Sophisters, which wrest to every part their talk, with intricate snares of words, like a bridle, will stop my mouth. The Musicians with their many tunes will make me a laughing stock through the streets, and with jarring sounds and unpleasant ringing of pans, basins and dishes will trouble me more than they are wont at their weddings which be twice married [. . .]. The vain worker in the art Perspective will engrave and depaint me more brutish and deformed than an ape, or Thersites; [. . .] the monstrous Gunner will cast against me the revenging flames of Jupiter, and the fire of lightning. [. . .] The monstrous Magicians will transform me, as it were another Apuleius or Lucian, into an ass, yet not of gold, but perchance of dirt. The black Necromancer will persecute me with spirits and devils; [. . .] the circumcised Cabalists will wish me their foreskin; [. . .] the almighty Bishops will reserve my sins for everlasting fire. [. . .] The obstinate Divine Sophistical Doctors will call me heretic, or compel me to worship their idols; our grim masters will enforce me to recant. . . . (Agrippa 1575, Av–iAii^v)

In the second half of the preface Agrippa reveals his motivation in attacking all the human sciences:

> Now, Reader, thou perceivest through how many dangers I shall pass. Yet I hope easily to escape these assaults if you, supporting the truth, and setting envy apart, shalt come with a gentle mind to the reading of these things. Beside this, I have the Word of God wherewith to defend myself. [. . .] Furthermore, in many, and almost in all places of study, a perverse custom and damnable use is grown, in that they bind with an oath the scholars which they receive to teach, never to speak against Aristotle, Boethius, Thomas, Albert, or against any other of their scholars, being accounted as a god, from whom if a man differ a finger breadth in thought immediately they will call him heretic, a sinful person. [. . .] These then so unadvised giants and enemies of the holy scriptures are to be assaulted, and their fortresses and castles ransacked; and to declare how great a rashness and presumptuous arrogance it is to prefer the schools of philosophers before the Church of Christ. (Ai^v)

After this strictly orthodox introduction, he rejects scientific research in general. Referring to the doctrines of deification that several authors associate with the advancement of learning, Agrippa states that learning plays no part in salvation and in fact hinders it. He provides two arguments: since all sciences are based on certain basic principles, without those knowledge collapses, meaning that finite investigation cannot grasp the infinite truth. Furthermore, all scientists are tyrants, who enforce their opinion on men rather than offering honest and convincing reasoning.

In a similar style, the following chapters condemn logic, natural philosophy, politics, church government, medicine, law, even theology:

> Lastly it resteth to speak of divinity. [. . .] But let us speak first of scholastical divinity, which doctrine was first made by the Sorbonistes of Paris, with a certain mixture of God's worde and philosophical reasons, fashioned like two bodies, as if were of the Centaurs kind. [. . .] Hereof it is come to pass that the high science of school divinity is not free from error and naughtiness, so many sects, so many heresies have the wicked hypocrites and hair-brained sophisters brought up. (chapter 97, 168^v–171^v)

In the middle of the work several chapters are devoted to the magical arts. These (chapters 41 through 48) were also appended to the 1533 edition of *De occulta philosophia*, perhaps to camouflage the radicalism of that work. Interestingly, although he criticizes the practices dealing with magic, he finds little condemnable in the principles of the occult arts. "Of Magic in general" Agrippa says:

> Magic therefore comprehending all philosophy, natural and mathematical, joins the powers of religions to them. Hence also they contain in them goetia, and theurgia, for which cause many divide magic into two parts, viz. natural and ceremonial. (chapter 41, quoted from Agrippa 1997, 689)

The greatest danger of magic, he says furthermore, is that even if it is practiced without the intention of *goetia* or necromancy, wicked spirits may arise instead of the invoked angels. As we shall see, Casaubon argued similarily when condemning John Dee's angel magic. Although Agrippa is more permissive concerning theurgy, he finally calls it futile: "Now many think that theurgia is not unlawful, as if this be governed by good angels" (chapter 46, Agrippa 1997, 699). Interestingly, he cites Porphyry to deny the possibility of magical *exaltatio*:

> Of this theurgia, or magic of divine things, Porphyry disputing at large, at length concludes that by theurgical consecrations the soul of man may be fitted to receive spirits, and angels, and to see God: but he altogether denies that we can by this art return to God. (ibid.)

Here he mentions his own *De occulta philosophia* which he interprets in a new light: "Here is great need of caution, as we have lately discoursed at large in our books of Occult Philosophy" (ibid.). In fact, as I have quoted, in *De occulta . . .* he spoke about magical deification—and the cabala—in the loftiest tone. Here he calls it "pernicious superstition, by the which they gather at their pleasure, defaming the Scriptures, they calumniate the Law of God, and by the supputations of words, syllables, letters, numbers impudently extorted, they assay to bring violent and blasphemous proofs for their unbelief" (chapter 47, Agrippa 1997, 701–02). Let us remember that in the second book of *De occulta . . .* Agrippa did his best to fuse Christian number symbolism and the cabala, developing complicated tables of the principal sacred numbers, always giving the corresponding Hebrew letters, too ("The name of Jehovah with ten letters collected; The name of Jehovah with ten letters extended . . . " 2.12, Agrippa 1997, 288).

The title of chapter 100 in *De incertitudine . . .* is "De verbo Dei" and admits only the Scripture as the receptacle of truth. However, as

Keefer observes, Agrippa does not speak merely about the truth of the Word (that is, Christ, the *Logos*), he also introduces here the concept of a type of illumination which the occult sciences can substitute. To be precise, this illumination can fulfill what magic is incapable of:

> [This faith] truly is much higher and more stable than all the credulity of human sciences by as much as God himself is more exalted and more truthful than men. Nay rather God alone is truthful, and every man a liar. [. . .] Indeed God alone contains the fountain of truth, from which he must drink who desires true doctrines: since there is not, nor can be had, any science of the secrets of nature, of the separate substances, much less of God their author, unless it is revealed by divine inspiration. (chapter 100, Agrippa 1575, 177^v)

The quotation suggests that faith is not the ultimate goal, rather a means that opens the gates of sacred illumination and allows man to peep through this entrance into the supernatural world. A passage from chapter 98 seems to confirm this reading. Here Agrippa writes of interpretive theology, acknowledging that he himself does not belong to those elect who have this divine gift. He can only interpret the prophecies, thus trying to get nearer to God. There are, however, more ways than one to interpret prophecies. Agrippa rejects "defining, dividing, and compounding" Aristotelians because God "cannot be defined, or divided or compounded" (quoted by Keefer 1988, 634). The more acceptable way lies

> midway between this and the prophetic vision, which is the agreement of the truth with our purged intellect, like a key with a lock. As our intellect is most desirous of all truths, so it is perceptive of all intelligibles, and therefore it is termed the passive intellect [*intellectus passibilis*] by which even if we do not perceive in a full light the things which the prophets set forth, nonetheless the gate is opened to us, [. . .] and it is granted us to read and understand, not with outward eyes and ears, but to perceive with better senses, and with the veil taken away. . . . (Chapter 98, Agrippa 1575 71^v-172)[23]

The allusions to the New Testament are obvious here,[24] but the reader well versed in hermetic literature can immediately add a complementary text from chapter 13 of the *Corpus hermeticum*, the so-called hymn of light:

> Powers within me, sing a hymn to the one and the universe. Sing together, all you powers within me, for I wish it. Holy knowledge, you

enlightened me. [. . .] I thank you, god, power of my energies; through me your word hymns you; through me, O universe, accept a speech offering, by my word. (13.18; Copenhaver 1992, 53)

Chapter 102 of *De incertitudine* . . . is a perplexing digression on the praise of asses (*Ad encomium asini digressio*). Here Agrippa praises the simple ass on which Jesus rode into Jerusalem. Knowledge is the invention of the Serpent, so it is reasonable that Christ invited no rabbis and learned priests as his apostles, rather simple working men who themselves were "asses."

The conclusion of the work also refers to the asses, and Agrippa calls the pious reader thus:

Wherefore O ye asses, [. . .] be you loosed from the darkness of flesh and blood. If ye desire to attain to this divine and true wisdom, not of the tree of the knowledge of good and ill, but of the tree of life, cast aside the sciences of man. Now entering not into the schools of philosophers and sophisters, but into your own selves, ye shall know all things: for the knowledge of all things is compact in you. . . . (Peroratio, Agrippa 1575, 186)

After putting on this tone of the propagator of holy simplicity and naive illumination, in the last paragraph Agrippa takes yet another turn. By alluding to the wisdom of Solomon and the apocryphal Book of Wisdom, he echoes the hermetic teachings once more:

It is he that hath given me the true knowledge of those things which are, that I might know the disposition of the compass of the earth, the virtue of the elements, the beginning, consummation, middle, and revolutions of times, the course of the year, the disposition of the stars, the natures of living creatures, the anger of beasts, the force of the winds, the thoughts of men, the difference of plants, the virtue of roots, and finally I have learned all things which be hidden or unknown, for the Artificer of all things hath taught me wisdom. (Peroratio, Agrippa 1575, 187[v])[25]

What is this if not a reminiscence of the *exaltatio* of the magus? This biblical locus, not entirely fitting in with the general tone of *De incertitudine* . . . , makes us aware of Agrippa's possible multiple intentions, showing the work to be much more complex than it looks at first sight. This becomes even clearer if we discover with Keefer Agrippa's conscious misquoting: "In the Vulgate the last words of this passage are 'omnium enim artifex docuit me sapientia.' Agrippa, adding one letter, writes 'sapientiam'—and wisdom becomes, not his teacher, but the content of what he is taught, not an aspect of God, but an instrument of his own desire for power over nature" (Keefer 1988, 640).

After this one could ask if Agrippa really became a sceptic, or rather had he something to hide on the pages of *De incertitudine* . . . ? Pondering this question, Frances Yates noticed some interesting textual parallels (1979, 42–44). She mentioned *The Golden Ass* of Apuleius where the hero has to turn into an ass to rid himself of earthly drag before entering mystical initiation. Similarly, Agrippa leaves behind secular sciences before the sacred illumination. Yates entertained the thought that Agrippa's ambivalent attitude in *De incertitudine* . . . could be interpreted as covert subversion. There were too many attacks against him with charges of black magic, so with a witty humanist treatise he discredited the branches of scholasticism unappreciated by the new learning. With this he testified to his Christian faith and othodoxy.[26] The rejection of traditional sciences by no means guaranteed pious orthodoxy. Faustus, in Marlowe's drama, does something similar and his arguments in his first soliloquy are quite close relatives of Agrippa's sarcastic criticism. Still, out of desperation, Faustus ends up making a pact with Satan. In the light of this possible outcome of the disillusionment with the human sciences, Agrippa's subversion gains unresolved significance.[27]

Agrippa's scepticism could be rooted in, at least partly, the humanist literary traditions, too. In this respect two possible parallels can be mentioned. The first is Cusanus' *De docta ignorantia* (*Of learned ignorance*, written in 1440), which explains in a quasi-naive manner that learned ignorance "is a practice and style of mystical contemplation that depends upon a prior committment to rational knowledge and to the investigation of nature" (Koenigsberger 1979, 125). The second parallel is the *Praise of Folly* (*Encomium moriae*, 1511), written by Agrippa's contemporary and fellow-humanist, Erasmus of Rotterdam. In the *Praise of Folly* Erasmus mocked monastic life as well as scholastic sciences in a manner quite similar to *De incertitudine*. . . . The allegorical woman personifying Folly discredits not only the corruption of the church and the stupidity of the monks, but she also rejects sciences from grammar through mathematics to magic. The conclusion of the work is again similar to that of Agrippa: the only firm truth can be found in the Gospels. Erasmus also entertains thoughts on sacred illumination; here he speaks of the "madnesses" of Plato and his concept of illumination is not far from the concepts of Ficino and Pico discussed earlier.[28]

One can also see interesting biographical connections between Erasmus and Agrippa. While the former was working on the *Praise of Folly* in the house of Thomas More near London, Agrippa also traveled in England (1510). There is no evidence that the two humanists met at that time but later they corresponded on various occasions. In 1530 Erasmus recommended to Agrippa a student who wished to pursue studies in the occult philosophy. In this letter Erasmus also mentioned that he had heard of *De incertitudine . . .* as a "bold work." Agrippa quickly answered, calling himself an Erasmian and a faithful Christian, and asked for Erasmus' opinion about his work. The scholar of Rotterdam replied only three years later, already after the publication of *De occulta philosophia*. Erasmus politely praised Agrippa's scholarship, but made his intention clear that he would not be involved in the debate concerning the German's magical work.[29] In this correspondence we see an Erasmus different from that younger and more enthusiastic scholar who had passionately defended the Christian-cabalist Reuchlin a few decades ago—at about the time when he himself had alluded to neoplatonic *exaltatio* in the *Praise of Folly*. By the 1530s he had become distrustful of number symbolism and other magical and mystical practices.[30]

We have come closer to the ideological context and the literary models of *De incertitudine . . .* , but so far we have not been able to explain Agrippa's strategy in publishing his two works in the described manner. His argumentation quite certainly rules out that his purpose with *De incertitudine . . .* was merely to open an ideological safety valve, although the 1533 edition of *De occulta . . .* , especially its paratext, the various prefaces and dedications, definitely reveal some ironic and subversive gestures. In the general preface, "To the Reader," Agrippa emphasizes that *De occulta . . .* was a product of his foolish youth: "I wrote this being scarce a young man, that I may excuse myself, and say, whilst I was a child, I spake as a child, I understood as a child" (Agrippa 1997, lii). Realizing what logical question would arise from this remark, he immediately puts it up himself: "You may blame me again, saying, behold though being a youth didst write and now being old hast retracted it; what therefore hast thou set forth?" (ibid.). Then he tries to convince the reader that his only purpose with the late publication was to eliminate the danger resulting from the circulation of corrupted manuscripts and prints.

As opposed to this, in his next preface, dedicated to Prince Hermann, Archbishop of Cologne, Agrippa presents his work as a valuable gift to the patron, which has been amended: "You have therefore the work, not only of my youth, but of my present age, for I have corrected many errata, I have inserted many things in many places, and have added many things to many chapters" (Agrippa 1997, lx).

Swinging in the opposite direction, in the first chapter, Agrippa humbly says, again:

> I know not whether it be an unpardonable presumption in me, that I, a man of so little judgement and learning should in my very youth so confidently set upon a business so difficult, so hard, and intricate as this is. (1.1; Agrippa 1997, 3)

And, as we already know, in the ensuing several hundred pages of the book the author provides an elaborate and lofty encomium of the magical arts concluding with the appendix, which is his retraction of magic, using the chapters from *De incertitudine*. . . .

I think that among scholars dealing with this problem Michael Keefer has come nearest to a solution. He has introduced an ingredient in the examination of intellectual magic that has not been much discussed previously, but which I myself find central for the understanding of the occult philosophy, including John Dee's seemingly paradoxical thoughts.

The first element in Keefer's argument is that both of Agrippa's works concentrate on the same notion: the mystical rebirth and the revelatory, illuminative understanding that leads man in his earthly life to comprehend God. To put it simply, the question of *exaltatio*. In this respect Agrippa found a corresponding harmony between the Gospels and the hermetic treatises: for him Matthew, Saint Paul, the fourth and thirteenth tracts of the *Corpus hermeticum*, Plato and Plotinus, and also some medieval mystics spoke of the same thing. As Keefer propounds, in respect to the *exaltatio*, the two works of Agrippa show only a seeming contradiction. The real dilemma for Agrippa must have come, Keefer continues, when he discovered yet another source aspiring for revelatory rebirth, but this source was terrifying and detestable for the devout philosopher. This line of magic pointed toward the Faust legend and its archetype, the story of Simon Magus.

Simon is mentioned in the Acts of the Apostles as somebody who tries to purchase for money the knowledge bestowed by Jesus upon the Apostles. Peter, however, calls him a charlatan and chases him away (Acts 8:9–25). Here we also learn that Simon "used sorcery, and bewitched the people of Samaria, giving out that himself was some great man" (Acts 8:10). The people, entirely taken with him, believed that "this man is the great power of God."

In early gnostic literature the character of Simon became inflated, and the tradition of the early church considered him to be the first gnostic.[31] According to the legend he was touring Palestine with thirty disciples and a woman called Helena. Finally he turned up in Rome and contested Saint Peter in magical power. First he was defeated in raising the dead, then he tried to fly over the city, but after Peter's fervent prayers he fell. Simon also called his lover, Helena, an incarnation of the Divine Wisdom (Ennoia) who had been captured by her creatures and imprisoned in matter. She had various reincarnations, including Helen of Troy, and, finally, Simon freed her from the body of a harlot of Tyrus. László Kákosy, the Hungarian Egyptologist, points out that this bizarre creation myth interestingly echoes the mystical program of gnosticism, that is, the liberation of the spirit from crude matter (1984, 21).

Patristic sources unanimously stated that Simon's power derived from Satan. All this would not deter the notorious sixteenth-century rebel, Doctor Faustus from expressing his committment to magic in a terminology deriving from Simon.[32] As Keefer has noticed, Agrippa also used Simon's terminology, although not on purpose, and perhaps this was the reason why he became so horrified when recognizing Simon's teachings in his own argumentation, which he intended to follow the *Corpus hermeticum*. As we read in chapter 44 of his book on ceremonial magic,

> There is no work in this whole world so admirable, so excellent, so wonderful, which the soul of man, being associated to his image of divinity, which the magicians call a soul standing and not falling, cannot accomplish by its own power without any external help. Therefore the form of all magical power is from the soul of man standing and not falling. (3.44; Agrippa 1997, 614; also quoted by Keefer 1988, 648)

The whole of this chapter is close to tracts 4 and 13 of the *Corpus hermeticum*, but the expression "soul standing and not falling" can only be found in relation to Simon Magus. As Pseudo-Clementine wrote,

> By nation [Simon] is a Samaritan; by profession a magician, yet exceedingly well trained in Greek literature; desirous of glory, and boasting above all the human race, so that he wishes himself to be believed to be an exalted power, which is above God the Creator, and to be thought to be Christ, and to be called the *Standing One*. (Recognitiones II.7; quoted by Keefer 1988, 646)

At some point Agrippa had to realize that his work inescapably implied an affiliation between the sacred and the demonic quite contrary to his lengthy effort to clearly separate the two. He was looking for the divine and in successive stages he created a syncretic vision of magical hermeticism and the Holy Writ, scientific investigation and faith, pagan rituals and Christianity, finally to end up with the conceited demonology of Simon. As Keefer concludes: "If Hermetic rebirth and the ideas of Simon Magus are indistinguishable, then the whole effort is compromised: the breaking down of oppositions has been allowed to go too far" (Keefer 1988, 650). Recognizing this, Agrippa may have written the following sentences on jugglers in chapter 48 of *De incertitudine*. . . . These words, significantly, constitute the last sentences of the 1533 edition of *De occulta philosophia*, too:

> But let us return to that magic, part of which is an art of juggling, i.e. delusions, which are made according to appearance only, by which magicians show phantasms, and play many miracles by circulatory frauds. [. . .] And now there is by magicians raised a great company of heretics in the Church, who as Jannes and Jambres resisted Moses, do in the like manner resist the apostolical truth. The chief of these was Simon the Samaritan . . . [. . .] But of magic I wrote whilst I was very young three large books, which I called Of Occult Philosophy, in which what was then through the curiosity of my youth erroneous, I now being more advised, am willing to have retracted, by this recantation. [. . .] For whosoever do not in the truth, nor in the power of God, but in the deceits of devils, according to the operation of wicked spirits persume to divine and prophesy, and practising through magical vanities, exorcisms, incantations and other demoniacal works, brag that they can do miracles, I say all these shall with Jannes and Jambres, and Simon Magus, be destinated to the torments of eternal fire. (Agrippa 1997, 706)

The abominations of Simon Magus were, of course, well known and publicized also in contemporary popular, moralizing literature. George Whetstone in his *The English Myrror* summarized Simon's overweening pride as follows:

> Simon, enuying the miracles the Apostle did by grace, he continually studied to doe the like by magicke, and in the ende he grew so famous, as in the time of the Emperour Nero, he was so reuerenced in Rome, as between the two bridges over Tiber, his Images were set up with this superscription, *To Simon the holy God:* Simon being drunken with this admiration of the people, arrogantly offred to contend with S. Peter in doing of myracles. . . . (Whetstone 1586, 60–61)

From a pure moralistic viewpoint Simon's machinations were heresy and damnable pride, but seen with the ambitions of a Renaissance magus, this archetypal narrative embraced the dangerous borderline between holy *exaltatio* and arrogant conceit.

Agrippa's work, then, subverted itself, and in this respect we may accept Nauert's proposition to see in it a product of crisis. This was not, however, the crisis of Renaissance thought, rather, an inherent, built-in contradiction of the doctrine of magical *exaltatio* that Agrippa finally recognized. Although he naturally could not resolve the contraditction, the very fact that he was able to articulate it clearly marked an important step in the history of Western magic. The intellectual dynamism of many of his followers—such as Paracelsus and John Dee—can be seen to have derived from the ambivalence between the sacred and the demonic. And this incertitude catalyzed the birth of such great literary characters as Doctor Faustus and Prospero.

In the title of this chapter I proposed the investigation of magic in relation to the natural sciences. As may be seen, my concern was not that of the traditional historian of science, but I hope to have shown that neither were Agrippa's concerns for traditional scientific experiments or theories. For him magic meant a sacred science of the supernatural in which the highest form of knowledge was revelatory illumination. This science was not the analytical approach of the scholastic natural philosophers; however it did not entirely exclude certain scientific approaches, such as the inclusion of mathematics and astronomy. But even these subjects were filled with symbolic imagery which substituted for induction and deduction.[33]

John Dee's natural philosophy was of a similar approach to the physical world. Before I examine it in detail, we shall have to become acquainted with two more topics crucial to the formation of his occult worldview: on the one hand the philosophy and ideology of Paracelsus and on the other the ideas of apocalyptic prophesying that made Enoch a central character in sixteenth-century intellectual discourse.

PARACELSUS, ALCHEMY, THEOSOPHY

In the previous chapter I tried to show how Agrippa's synthetic magic combined the comprehension of the world with a theological approach, uniting *magia naturalis* and ceremonial magic. In the fifteenth century—under the influence of neoplatonism with its theological concerns for the supreme beauty and the supreme good—the figure of the magus was often associated with artistic creation. "Divine" painters or sculptors, even poets, were thought to be able to create something out of nothing just like a god. By the sixteenth century the image of the creative man was extended to natural scientists, too, and the word *magus* became at least partly synonymous with the word *scientist*. As Paracelsus wrote, "as God created the heaven and the earth, so also the physician must form, separate, and prepare a medicinal world" (*Archidoxa* 10.8; quoted from Paracelsus 1894, 90).

This new type of magus emerged with Trithemius, in whose thought mystical operations such as the conjuration of angels mixed with very practical technical purposes, like telecommunication and distance learning, which also needed the consideration of contemporary scientific ideas. Agrippa in his tripartite magic designated a branch of science for the investigation of each world. The lowest, physical world was to be researched by physics and medicine. Mechanics, for example, had always been intriguing for those who dabbled in magic since man-made machines reminded one of the act of divine creation and coincided with the superhuman ambitions of Renaissance man. I have already mentioned the living statues of Hermes Trismegistus and the *automata* of Heron (page 53 ff), which were seen as magical wonders just as much as the production of gold in alchemy. There were especially three branches of science that became tinted with occult ideas—astrology, alchemy, and *magia naturalis*—and it seems that all important scientific fields had their mystical extension. Applied astronomy could be either navigation or occult astrology; applied chemistry could be metallurgy or occult alchemy; applied mathematics could be algebra or occult numerology. In the background of great scientific discoveries, such as Copernicus' heliocentric world model or Miguel Servet's theory of the circulation of the blood, we find inspiration from magical and hermetic theories.[34]

The most spectacular intertwining of hermeticism, magic, and science can be seen in the natural philosophy of Philippus Aureolus Theophrastus Bombastus von Hohenheim, commonly known as Paracelsus (1493–1541), whose works constituted one of the most important sections in John Dee's magical library.

Since Paracelsus primarily practiced medicine, it is quite understandable that his magic was nearest to natural science; however, one should also note that his works abound with theological and speculative arguments. He exercised strong and manifold influence on the intellectual discourse of the sixteenth and seventeenth centuries, in spite of the fact that his violent temper and arrogant style made him largely unacceptable to his contemporaries. The following generations, however, discovered in him a prophetic master, and "Paracelsianism" became one of the catchwords during the time of the Scientific Revolution.[35]

It has been a relatively recent finding of Dee scholarship to discover the great impression that Paracelsus exercised on the English Doctor. Frances Yates almost entirely neglected this aspect; Peter French briefly mentioned it but did not go into details (1972, 60–61, 76–78, 127–28); and, most amazingly, Nicholas Clulee had only one mention of the German mystic (1988, 141). Dee's interest in Paracelsus has been brought to light only by the publication of his library catalogues and the editors, Roberts and Watson, devoted considerable attention to this (1990, 11, 36). From the inspection of the catalogues it has turned out that between 1562 and 1582 Dee purchased 92 editions of Paracelsus in 157 copies, in both Latin and German. The only dated survivor among these is a German edition (R&W 1476) that is heavily annotated by Dee. He, in fact, set up separate subsections for his Paracelsica in the library catalogues, such as "Paracelsici libri compacti" (R&W 1461 ff.) and "Paracelsici libri latinè compacti" (R&W 1502 ff.). As a result of this discovery, Deborah Harkness makes more mention of Paracelsus in her new study on Dee's cabala and alchemy (1999, 63, 147, 199–203, 217–25) but even her review is far from being complete. A full comparison of Paracelsus and Dee would also exceed my present study, so in the followings I shall concentrate on Paracelsus' occult natural philosophy and his views on *exaltatio*.[36]

Although I have not intended to elaborate on Paracelsus' complicated and legend-ridden biography, it may be instructive to note that his career seems to have emblematized his disparate and contradictory thoughts. Academia and exile, professorial chair and homelessness, appreciation and poverty in his life; philosophical depth and cheap vulgarity, intellectual subtlety and arrogant mocking, religious enthusiasm and blasphemy in his works. He reached the zenith of his professional career in the mid-1520s when he became a professor as well as a town physician in Basel and for a while could enjoy the peaceful company of fellow scholars and disciples, such as Johannes Oporinus, his assistant in the Basel years and the later editor of Vesalius' anatomy (1543). This was when he wrote his most important medical works. After he had publically burned the books of Avicenna in Basel, he again had to set out on the road, and changes in his fortune steered his interest from medicine toward hermetic philosophy and esoteric theology. In the last years of his life, he returned to practical medicine (the *Grossen Wundarznei*, his monumental work on surgery was published in 1536) while he was also working on his mystical synthesis, represented by *Astronomia magna* and *Philosophia magna*, two treatises exceeding 700 pages (1536/1537). He died in 1541, his last three years remaining very obscure. He must have possessed titanic energies: the Sudhoff and Matthiessen critical edition amounts to over eight-thousand pages and his theological writings are still partly unpublished.

Let us examine several of Paracelsus' works, beginning with the nine books of *Archidoxa*, which date from his early creative years (about 1526) and present his medical philosophy without some later characteristic developments. For example, the mention of the three primary substances, salt, mercury and sulphur, is entirely lacking from it. It nevertheless contains the germs of Paracelsus' basic ideology and since Dee had seven editions of this work, it is worth examining.[37] Another work under a similar title is the *Archidoxis magica*. Although Sudhoff treats it as of spurious origin, in the sixteenth and seventeenth centuries this work was one of the most popular among those attributed to Paracelsus. Huser also accepted it as authentic and included it in his edition of 1589–1591. The work is a compendium of alchemy, talismanic magic, and ceremonial magic in popular Paracelsian rhetoric. In 1656 it was translated into English by Robert Turner, who a year earlier had also translated and published Agrippa's *Fourth Book of Occult Philosophy*. Turner, in his preface, advertised the work to the English reader as follows: "This little Treatise presents you with the rare secrets of Alchymy, and the miraculous cures of diseases by Sigils and Lamens, made in their proper seasons, and attributed to the nature of Celestial Bodies" (A3[r]).[38] He also noted:

> [A]s this author will tell you, and woful experience daily shews: how frequently, and familiarly did those blessed Angels visibly communicate with the holy men and Magicians of Old! though now such is the wickedness of our age, that they have almost quite forsaken us. (Paracelsus 1975, A5[v])

No doubt, Dee would have appreciated this remark since he must have read the treatise with great interest specifically for its concern with the occult philosophy. And indeed, he had several copies of this text.[39] The third book to be looked at is Paracelsus' monumental philosophical-magical-theosophical synthesis, the *Astronomia magna*, or "Die gantze

Philosophia Sagax der Grossen und Kleinen Welt" (the whole philosophy of the macro- and microcosms).[40] Dee had a copy of this work, too (Frankfurt 1571; R&W 289), which interestingly appears at an earlier section in the catalogue instead of together with the other "Paracelsica." If we single out just the aforementioned three books, it already indicates that Dee was in possession of a substantial package of works containing Paracelsus' mystical natural philosophy and system of magic.

As I have mentioned, the *Archidoxa* is an early work, but it already contains those leitmotifs that explain Paracelsus' expectations about the ideal doctor, as advertised in his later great works, the *Opus Paramirum* and the *Paragranum*. To begin with, for him the true physician must nest his practical knowledge in a higher, theosophical theory, and needs to know not only about man's body but about the whole created universe of which the microcosm is only a miniature model:

> It is to learn the mysteries of Nature, by which we can discover what God is and what man is, and what avails a knowledge of heavenly eternity and earthly weakness. [. . .] For although many things are gained in medicine, and many more in the mysteries of Nature, nevertheless after this life the Eternal Mystery remains, and what it is we have no foundation for asserting, save that which has been revealed to us by Christ. (Paracelsus 1894, 4)

Along with contextualizing medicine in theology and theosophy, Paracelsus also emphasized from the outset the importance of experience, which is to be gained from the study of nature rather than from the study of ancient authorities. He never tired of mocking and scolding Galen and Avicenna; however, we must be aware that his concept of experience—just as in the case of Dee—was nearer to Roger Bacon's *experientia* than to Francis Bacon's deductive reasoning: "We have drawn our medicine by experiment, wherein it is made clear to the eye that things are so" (5); "and let no one wonder at the school of our learning. Though it be contrary to the courses and methods of the ancients, still it is firmly based on experience, which is mistress to all things, and by which all arts should be proved" (9).

These quotations warn us that the two traditional standpoints of science historians will not work in the case of Paracelsus: those who called him a confused charlatan were certainly wrong, but those who tried to purge him of his magical concepts and mystical philosophy and, thus, include him in the pantheon of science history as a venerable pharmacist were equally mistaken. Marie Boas noticed this problem in the 1960s, describing Paracelsus' thought as "combined iconoclasm with appeal to 'experience,' primarily mystic experience. He attacked reason because it was opposed to magic, and magic was to him the best key to experience" (1962, 177). For these reasons he despised the ancient authorities but found a perfect synthesis between science and mystical illumination among biblical characters: Adam, the forefather, and his descendant, Enoch. As we shall see, these two became extremely important for Dee, too. And among Paracelsus' works it is the *Archidoxa* which for the first time raises the questions of primordial knowledge:

> As long as we have the power and knowledge, we possess the capacity of sustaining our life. For Adam attained to such an advanced period of life not from the nature or condition of his own properties, but simply from this reason, that he was so learned and wise a physician, who knew all things in Nature herself. . . . (Paracelsus 1894, 70)

Adam's knowledge was emblematized by his mystical language, which provided him with a direct means of communication with God and with the angels. And it was Enoch who was the last man privileged to be able to learn the *lingua adamica*, the key to perfect knowledge so much sought by Renaissance philosophers who all aspired to be among the new elect of the *pansophia*. Many of them, with Paracelsus in the forefront, indeed became convinced that they had come into the possession of universal wisdom:

> The celestial treasure, in these last days of grace, has been freely revealed to me from on high, which, indeed, make a true Adam and paradoxic physician, according to the days of Enoch, in the intellects of a new generation. [. . .] There is no doubt, that in that very great multitude of men, mentioned in the fourth book of Esdras, the Lord God will reserve for Himself a small number of certain elect persons, who will desire faithfully to pursue my Theophrastic doctrine, to love the truth, and help their neighbours in their destitution and diseases, for pure love of God. . . . (83)

Antirationalism, magic, and experience are also mixed together in the *Archidoxis magica*. Paracelsus advises even theologians to study magic instead of stupid reasoning, but not to practice it, however just "to know the virtues and effects thereof":

Those things which are impossible to be searched out by humane reasons, by this Art, to wit, Magick, it may be found out and known: wherefore it is the most occult and secret wisdom; and reasoning against it is nothing else but extreme folly. It were therefore very necessary that the Divines would learn to know something of this Art, and be experienced in Magick what it is. (Paracelsus 1975, 81)

The *Archidoxis* divides into three main parts. The first is a study in applied alchemy, explaining how to use it for medical purposes such as producing the perfect healing tincture. It deals with the variety of metals, their astrological spirits, and also with the circumstances of the transmutation, the fire, the furnace, and the glass. The third part is applied talismanic magic: Paracelsus gives detailed illustrations regarding how to construct magical images that would cure specific illnesses, such as leprosy, gout, contractures, or discomforts like menstruation. These magic seals recall Ficino's talismanic magic, or even more that of the *Picatrix*, in which the underlying theory presupposes a sympathetic correspondence between earthly living organisms and the macrocosm, governed by the houses of the zodiac. The middle section addresses topics of ceremonial magic, conjurations, enchanting, enthusiastic imagination, spirits and devils, possessions, and also such practical questions as how to find hidden treasures.

The work is not without contradictions. While in the third part he approves the use of magic seals and characters, in a chapter of the middle section called "Of occult philosophy," Paracelsus speaks against all the great Renaissance magi: "we will write therefore in most briefe and plain words, the most occult and secret things, which neither Cornelius Agrippa, nor Peter de Abano, much less Tritemius, never understood or wrote of" (Paracelsus 1975, 31). Here he seems to follow Agrippa's strategy in *De incertitudine* . . . : he does not deny mystical *exaltation* but tries to separate it from all earthly imperfections. As he states, the only source of true magic is the Scriptures:

We do intend to treat of the greatest and most occult secrets of Philosophy, and of all those things which do appertain to Magicke. Clearly and fully demonstrating and setting forth every thing that may be investigated, effected and brought to pass thereby: this Philosophy in the practice thereof is much abused, by Ceremonies and other abuses, and hitherto the foundation thereof hath been built falsely upon the sand. [. . .] It is therefore necessary that the foundation of these and of

all other Arts be laid in the holy Scriptures, upon the doctrine and faith
of Christ; which is the most firme and sure foundation. (29–30)

Reading all this, one can agree with Andrew Weeks' repeatedly stressed
argument: "Most of the medical-theoretical work is as much religious as
scientific" (1997, 41). Although a deep religiousness definitely distinguishes the natural philosophy of Paracelsus, his theology was by no
means orthodox; rather it was as iconoclastic, noncomformist, and heterodox as any of the great occult thinkers. He approximated the Reformation in his antipathy to ceremonies and rituals, but his thinking was
too idiosyncratic to shift from Catholic orthodoxy to Lutheran dogmatics. His religious individualism can be compared to that of Miguel Servet,
Giordano Bruno, Guillaume Postel, or John Dee.[41] His *Astronomia magna* is the clearest manifesto of his esoteric philosophy.

Like Agrippa, Paracelsus approached and explained the dignity of
man from two directions: the viewpoint of the Scriptures and the viewpoint of hermetic rebirth. As for the biblical message,

> From Holy Scripture comes the beginning and guidance of all philoso-
> phy and natural science, and it must be taken into account before
> anything else; without this fundament all philosophy would be ex-
> pounded and applied in vain. Consequently, if a philosopher is not
> born out of theology, he has no cornerstone upon which to build his
> philosophy. For truth springs from religion, and cannot be discovered
> without its help. (*Astronomia magna,* I,12:32;[42] Paracelsus 1951, 196)

And similarly, later on:

> Let man not be surprised that God is with him, and that he can
> perform miracles on earth by virtue of His power, for man is of divine
> nature. "All of you are gods and sons of the Most High," says Holy
> Writ. (I, 12:328; Paracelsus 1951, 195)

For to become "gods," man also needs hermetic knowledge, which gives
the key to the secrets of the universe by the help of personalized Wisdom.
Man, just like in Hermes Trismegistus or in Pico's *Oratio . . .* appears as
the greatest miracle, the book of all mysteries: "Man is the book in which
all the mysteries are recorded; but this book is interpreted by God" (*Liber
Azoth*[43] *sive de ligno et linea vitae,* I,14:547–48; Paracelsus 1951, 44).
"How marvellously man is made and formed if one penetrates into his
true nature. [. . .] Where else can Heaven be rediscovered if not in man?

[. . .] God made His Heaven in man beautiful and great, noble and good; for God is in His Heaven, i.e., in man" (*Opus Paramirum*, I,9:219–20; Paracelsus 1951, 44–45). And, indeed, it is the presence of God in the microcosm that permits man to become himself a creator of miracles:

> Thoughts create a new heaven, a new firmament, a new source of energy, from which new arts flow. [. . .] When a man undertakes to create something, he establishes a new heaven, as it were, and from it the work that he desires to create flows into him. [. . .] For such is the immensity of man that he is greater than heaven and earth. (*Astronomia magna*, I,12:183; Paracelsus 1951, 45)

When man undertakes to create something miraculous, it happens by the help of magic: "After all, God has permitted magic, and this is a sign that we may use it; it is also a sign of what we are" (*Die Bücher von den unsichtbaren Krankheiten*, I,9:271; Paracelsus 1951, 138), and in Paracelsus' works we also come across with magic, corresponding to all three worlds of Agrippa, from *magia naturalis* up to gnostic spiritual rebirth. In the *Archidoxis magica* he states that the physician needs to know the original cause of all diseases, which may result from three areas: material things ("evil meat or drink"), celestial or heavenly influences, and supernatural causes ("inchantment or some Magical Sorceries").[44] These three areas demand corresponding medical practices: material magic needs "to know the secrets of Herbs and Roots, etc.," celestial influences are treated with medical astrology, and sorcery can be fought only by magical remedies (ibid.).

Physicians with magical power are comparable to the Saints of God who also worked miracles:

> As God awakens the dead to new life, so the 'natural saints' who are called magi, are given power over the energies and faculties of nature. For there are holy men in God who serve the beatific life; they are called saints. But there are also holy men in God who serve the forces of nature, and they are called magi. God shows his miracles through His holy men, both through those of beatific life and through those of nature. . . . (*Astronomia magna*, I,12:130; Paracelsus 1951, 139)

A characteristic of celestial magic is that it makes man a ruler over the stars. It is all the more important because in Paracelsus' medicine astrological influences and corresponding cures are of central importance. At this point astrological power, Wisdom, and the deification of man are intertwined: "The wise man is the man who live by divine wisdom and is an image of Him in whose likeness he was created. [. . .] He who imitates the image of God will conquer the stars" (*Astronomia magna* I,12: 41–42; Paracelsus 1951, 155–56).

Celestial magic is crowned by angelic magic. Paracelsus here is more cautious than Agrippa was; nevertheless he clearly professed the magical potential of man:

> He who inherits God's wisdom walks on water without wetting his feet; for in the true art inherited from God, man is like an angel. But what will wet an angel? Nothing. Similarly, nothing will wet the wise man. God is powerful and He wills it that His power be revealed to men and to angels in the wisdoms of the arts. He wills it that the world and the earth be like Heaven: (*De fundamento scientiarum sapientiaeque*, I,13:306; Paracelsus 1951, 163)

One notices another parallel with Agrippa here: the ultimate end of true magic is Christian exaltation, which is also signified by the steps of spiritual alchemy. Paracelsus uses the term *rebirth* just like his colleague from Nettesheim. Paracelsus' most elevated thoughts on *exaltatio* can be found again in the *Astronomia magna*:

> But if the whole heart is to be filled with love of God, all opposition to God must withdraw from the soul, and that which is not divine must go, to the end that it may be all pure, untainted by any other thing, separated from all the rest, perfectly clean and pure itself. (I, 12:299; Paracelsus 1951, 199)
>
> Our Father in Heaven teaches us in the reborn body, and not in the old body, and in this reborn man he teaches us heavenly wisdom . . . (316–17)
>
> Man is born of the earth, therefore he also has in him the nature of the earth. But later, in his new birth, he is of God and in this form receives divine nature. Just as man in nature is illuminated by the sidereal light[45] that he may know nature, so he is illuminated by the Holy Ghost that he may know God in his essence. For no one can know God unless he is of divine nature. (326)

As I have pointed out, in Agrippa's work the phenomenon of *exaltatio* received an almost scien tifically precise analysis. Paracelsus did likewise, and this is the subject-area where anthropocentric, Christian-esoteric natural philosophy can be best understood. The reborn man of Paracelsus is called in the alchemical treatises *corpus glorificationis*, and this is nothing else but the primordial man of *prisca theologia*, and the Adam Kadmon of the cabala.[46] Paracelsus' views on spirits and the soul also point back to the *prisca theologia*. According to him, "as man is built, so is built God after whose image he was created."[47]

For Paracelsus *astronomia* means not only cosmology, but primarily the description of man who is built in harmony with the macrocosm. Consequently, he presupposes close connections between the spirits populating the outer skies and the ones living in man's inner heaven.[48] And as man has two bodies (the elemental and the sidereal), so has he also two spirits in which rebirth takes place. These souls are bathed in the mystical Light of Nature (*lumen naturae*), which is identified with the Wisdom of Nature, corresponding loosely to Ficino's *anima mundi* (see Kämmerer 1971, 29; Müller-Jahncke 1985, 72). The seat of spirits in the body is the soul, thus Paracelsus does not divert from the traditional Platonic triad: body—soul—spirit, but he completes it with the elements of the "alchemical trinity," *sal, mercurius, sulphur.*

Using this triad, Elizabeth Ann Ambrose (1992) describes Paracelsian ontology and gnoseology with the terms *Cosmos—Anthropos—Theos*. These three stages mean not only the three paradigms of existence (world—man—God) but also include the steps man uses to know the world and God. The process starts with a phase of submerging in the material, then concludes with a spiritual ascension. Man is born in a structured *cosmos* and has to suffer separation (the alchemical *separatio* is one of Paracelsus' favorite terms), then, due to *Theos*, he can again build up his primordial homogeneity.[49]

Cosmos is the incarnation of the divine, the *corpus* of God which is the self-expression of the Supreme Being (Paracelsus calls it *Yliaster*) through the *Logos*, by the help of thought and will. Such a complicated process involving enormous creative energy is not without dangers and the possibilities of flaws, the German Doctor realized. He mentioned that the *mysterium magnum* might result in deformed incarnations. A good example for that is man, and especially, woman.[50] The dualism of spiritual and physical existence can best be seen in the context of *Anthropos*: this is a necessary but hazardous separation from which reintegration by the help of *lumen naturae* is chancy, not guaranteed. This reintegration is of course nothing else but the mystical rebirth, the *exaltatio*, provided the self is able to achieve it.

At this point it is instructive to look at Paracelsus' concept of evil. He suggests that without the stage of the purely material, and the experience of godlessness, one cannot recognize the Creator, the Supreme Being.[51]

Among scholars it has become a commonplace to speak about the interconnectedness of Reformation theology, gnosticism, the *prisca theologia,* and the cabala. According to Jung, all these whirl around the idea of the primordial man, whose once existing perfectness and power should be reestablished by the reborn mystic ([1942] 1983, 129–32). For Paracelsus the road to this idea led through mystical medicine and alchemy, which was framed by a theological synthesis, and influenced by Ficino, Pico, Reuchlin, and Agrippa. In his theological works one finds ample evidence for this:

> [R]emember that you must take unto yourselves the teachings of the cabala. For the cabala builds on a true foundation. Pray and it will be given you, knock and you will be heard, the gate will be opened to you. [. . .] Everything you desire will flow and be granted to you. You will see into the lowest depths of the earth, into the depths of hell, into the third heaven. You will gain more wisdom than Solomon, you will have greater communion with God than Moses and Aaron.[52]

This quotation indicates Paracelsus' indebtedness to the hermetic magicians and Christian cabalists of the Renaissance, but also points toward various schools rising up from his legacy, ranging from John Dee's scientific application in his hieroglyphic monad to a purely spiritual alchemical theosophy in Jakob Boehme.

Paracelsus not only synthetized Renaissance occultism, but he also suffered from the inherent contradiction of the magical worldview, just as we have seen in the case of Agrippa. It was again Jung who first noticed this: "Paracelsus was, perhaps most deeply of all, an 'alchemical philosopher' whose religious views involved him in an unconscious conflict with the Christian beliefs of his age in a way that seems inextricably confused. Nevertheless, in this confusion are to be found the beginnings of philosophical, psychological, and religious problems which are taking clearer shape in our own epoch" (1983, 110). As Keefer (1988) discovered the contradictions in Agrippa's ideology of rebirth, Jung in 1941 pinpointed the contradictions of *exaltatio* as the main problem of the hermetic magus. And as Keefer associated the dark side of *exaltatio* with the heresy of Simon Magus, Jung compared Paracelsus' arrogance with that of an other archetypal heretic, Doctor Faustus.

Paracelsus never questioned the power of magic and alchemy because according to him these were agents of the *lumen naturae,* which in turn was nothing but revelative illumination about God's rationally incomprehensible truths. Achieving this revelation meant the deification of man: "God has given us the eternal body to the end that we mortal men on earth may become immortal" (*De honestis utriusque divitiis*, II,1:249; Paracelsus 1951, 203). The true physician should become such an immortal man. Speaking of the office of such divine practicioners, Paracelsus cried out: "I under the Lord, the Lord under me, I under him outside my office, and he under me outside his office" (*De caducis*, I,8: 267; Jung 1983, 117).

The outspokenness of this statement is breathtaking and reminds Jung of the later Angelus Silesius:

> I am as great as God,
> And he is small like me;
> He cannot be above,
> Nor I below him be.
> (Jung 1983, 117)

This is the kind of attitude that many scholars identified with the man-centered spirit of the Renaissance, which endowed humankind with divine dignity. And this spirit manifested itself most dramatically in magic and alchemy. "*Deus et Homo* in a new and unprecedented sense!" concluded Jung in rapture. But he also saw the traps on the road of the magus who had said "I under the Lord," but really thought "the Lord under me": "Man takes the place of the Creator. Medieval alchemy prepared the way for the greatest intervention in the divine world order that man has ever attempted: alchemy was the dawn of the scientific age, when the daemon of the scientific spirit compelled the forces of nature to serve man to an extent that had never been known before. It was from the spirit of alchemy that Goethe created the figure of the 'superman' Faust, and this superman led Nietzsche's Zarathustra to declare that God was dead" (Jung 1983, 128).

Jung also speaks of Agrippa's crisis, manifesting itself in *De incertitudine.* . . . In its preface, the magus of Nettesheim wrote with greatest outburst of intensity:

> This Agrippa spareth none, he condemneth, knows, is ignorant, weeps, laughs, is angry, pursueth, carps at all things being himself a philosopher, demon, a hero, a god,—and all things.[53]

According to Jung, Paracelsus was not a split character to such an extent, but his arrogance and extremist diction derived from the unresolved tension between his Christian piety and his Agrippan attitude of "philosopher, demon, hero, and god." According to Jung "the Christian and

the primitive pagan lived together in [Paracelsus] in a strange and marvellous way to form a conflicting whole. [. . .] His spirit was heroic,
because creative, and as such was doomed to Promethean guilt" (1983,
189). This guilt resulted from Paracelsus' conceited hubris which generated discomfort: although subjectively he thought of himself as a faithful
Christian, even a good man since his whole life was spent helping the
physically wretched, he could never overcome his bad consciousness and
an inferiority complex.

To what extent can we find Jung's insights helpful today, when trying
to comprehend Paracelsus' concept of *exaltatio* and enter into a dialogue
with the work of this enigmatic philosopher? Jung's opinion of course
reveals his own preoccupations and his own personal characteristics. That
he started dealing with alchemy after a serious private crisis and that he
wrote his Paracelsus essay in 1941, at the height of the great demonic
war, should throw a special light on his cultural historical paradigm
embracing Paracelsus, Faust, Goethe, and Nietzsche.

In our analysis today we can hardly appreciate Jung's opinion that
the history of alchemy is more or less identical with an age-old case study
in psychiatry. Consequently, we do not need to look for signs of mental
distractions in the works of the Renaissance magi. On the other hand,
Jung also juxtaposed the outlook of Christianity and rational scientific
investigation and interpreted alchemy as something that first tried to
bridge the two, yet later indeed contributed to their separation.

Furthermore, Jung's reading of Paracelsus offers one more lesson to be
observed in our postmodern age. Namely, he highlighted the unnerving
ambiguity that not only characterized Paracelsus himself, but can also be
seen in the whole history of Western magic and occult philsophy. How can
we account for the fact that an ancient and venerable, basically stable and
conservative tradition could produce such representatives whose synthetizing
works prove to be trampled by contradictions, paradoxes, and discrepan-
cies? The Platonist philosopher would say only that this is the consequence
of the Fall. The human spirit besieges infinity, but it is unattainable. Now
and again it approaches only to fall back again, ad infinitum.

The modern cultural historian must be more cautious in drawing
conclusions but may venture to suggest that this striving, this self-
destroying subversion, has been responsible over centuries for the dynamism of European culture. Paracelsus' endeavors for synthesis clearly
show that traditions are never homogeneous or clear-cut or isolated.
Subversion, antagonisms, and variety on the one hand and lasting tradition on the other are equally important segments of culture.

ENOCH, SCIENCE, APOCALYPTIC PROPHECY

We have come to the last theme among the intellectual impacts that contributed to the formation of John Dee's doctrine of *exaltatio*. This was an idiosyncratic attitude of certain sixteenth-century intellectuals who gained inspiration from the hermetic Renaissance of the Florentine neoplatonists and who themselves contributed to various chiliastic and apocalyptic tendencies of the Reformation and to the general religious climate of early modern Europe.

As attitudes are often shaped by role models embedded in mythologies or ancient wisdom, in this case we also find such elements, including fables, images, and characteristic iconography. Let us start from Paracelsus' already quoted remarks concerning the wisdom and magic power of Adam and his descendant Enoch (see above, p. 136). The latter was relatvely little discussed until the Renaissance, however in the sixteenth century he was made into a sensational biblical figure, and Dee himself felt much obsessed with his character.

In the Old and New Testaments Enoch is rather briefly mentioned. We learn that there were two Enochs, the first was Cain's son (Gen. 4:17) who thus belonged to the third generation of humankind. The second, "real" Enoch derived from Adam's son Seth; his father was Jared who beget Enoch in the year 622 after the Creation (Gen. 5:18–19). Enoch lived 365 years; at the age of 65 he beget Methuselah, then he "walked with God: and he was not; for God took him" (Gen. 5:24). Saint Paul in his epistle to the Hebrews remembered that "by faith [Enoch] was translated that he should not see death" (Heb. 11:5). Finally the epistle of Jude briefly mentions that "Enoch, the seventh from Adam, prophesied of these, saying, Behold, the Lord cometh with ten thousands of his saints" (Jude 14).

There is much more apocryphal and pseudepigraphical[54] material on Enoch in the Judeo- and the Christian traditions alike. The historiography of this literature is interesting and complicated. Though the text of the so-called Book of Enoch was in fact not known to Europeans until the eighteenth century, there was a great interest in Enoch from the sixteenth century on, as we can see in various mystical trends of humanist literature. It is important then to examine Dee's sources for the Enochian legends.

At present there are three known collections associated with the name of Enoch. *1Enoch* is the so-called Ethiopic Apocalypse of Enoch, the full text of which survived only in the Ethiopic language and was brought to Europe in 1773 by the Scottish Africa traveler J. Bruce. The original book might have been written either in Hebrew or in Aramaic. Some fragments have survived in Aramaic (among the Qumran scrolls), in Greek (an eighth-century manuscript found in a Christian grave in Egypt, plus some quotations in the *Chronographia* of Georgius Syncellus), and in Latin, found also in an eighth-century manuscript.[55]

1Enoch consists of the following themes: after the introduction, Chapters 6–36 relate the story of the fallen angels, how they intercoursed with women and corrupted all men, and how Enoch tried to intervene on the angels' behalf before God. The second part contains apocalyptic visions concerning the final judgement of the righteous and the wicked, while the third part (Chapters 72–82) is an astrological treatise that undoubtedly inspired the medieval astrological tracts to be discussed below. The fourth part contains dream visions about the future of Israel and tells the history of mankind from Adam to the Flood. The fifth part is Enoch's testament. From the viewpoint of Dee's mystical writings, the first part of the work, also known as the Book of the Watchers, is particularly interesting, because it is a kind of angelology (Charlesworth 1983, 5).

2Enoch is the so-called Slavonic Enoch. It survived in old church Slavonic manuscripts, but the origin and history of those even nowadays is totally obscure (cf. F. I. Andersen's summary in Charlesworth 1983, 91–100).

3Enoch is a fascinating Hebrew text, belonging to the body of Merkabah mystical literature (fifth through tenth centuries, A.D.) that survived in various fourteenth- to sixteenth-century manuscripts, and one of its chapters (48BCD) was also printed in Cracow, in a Hebrew publication of 1579 (information on *3Enoch* by P. Alexander in Charlesworth 1983, 223–53).

Since Dee had no interest in orthodox Christian texts and the Slavonic book of Enoch was not known to Western Europe in the time of the Renaissance, this text can be neglected in our investigation. More interesting is the case with the other two versions. Although we have no evidence of Dee's relationship with Jewish scholars or rabbis, one should not forget that a few years after some parts of *3Enoch* had been printed in Cracow, Dee spent several months there and might have had access to this publication, in which he could read in Chapter 48A about the right hand of God that rewards the rightous; in 48B about the seventy names of God (the list wrapped in a literary imagery not dissimilar from Dee's own visionary writings); and, finally in 48C about a short account of the elevation of Enoch, the story arranged cabalistically along the Hebrew alphabet:

Lamed: "I took him"—Enoch the son of Jared, from their midst, and brought him up with the sound of the trumpet and with shouting to the height, to be my witness. . . . (48C:2)

Peh: "I appointed him"—over all the storehouses and treasuries which I have in every heaven, and I entrusted to him the keys of each of them. I set him as a prince over all the princes, and made him a minister of the throne of glory, to deck and arrange it. . . . (48C:3–4; in Charlesworth 1983, 311)

The above passage, as well as *1Enoch*, contains all those motifs— Enoch being chosen to see God face to face; being entrusted with the knowledge of all sciences and a *clavis universalis*; and, finally, being elected to be the minister of "the throne of Glory to deck and arrange it"— which truly corresponded to Dee's burning desires to obtain universal knowledge and attain *exaltatio*, that is, to converse with angels and perhaps see the Creator face-to-face. Although it is most unlikely that he would have had access to the full text of the Book of Enoch, he certainly must have been aware of the long medieval tradition as well as the new Renaissance attraction to Enoch, who became one of the emblematic figures of the omniscient magi.

References to Enoch's exaltation abounded in Christian literature throughout the centuries. He featured in the writings of the Church fathers and the early theologians and then in some medieval treatises, although his fame was eclipsed during the Middle Ages. According to Thorndike (1923–1958, 1:342–45), Alexander Neckam in the twelfth century spoke as if Christendom had some acquaintance with the Enoch literature. He also pointed out that Hildegard of Bingen's visions had interesting parallels with that of Enoch. In his *Speculum naturale*, Vincent of Beauvais (thirteenth century) also referred to the Book of Enoch with reverence, but perhaps even more important is that corpus of pseudo-Enochian literature that in the Middle Ages attributed to him the privilege of being the inventor of astrology and alchemy. In these treatises Enoch was also identified with Hermes Trismegistus, or called "one of the three holy Hermeses." This is the claim in the "Treatise on fifteen stars," which survives in many medieval manuscripts (Thorndike, 1:340), and it is repeated by Robert of Chester's *Liber de compositione alchemiae* (published in Dee's lifetime in Paris, 1564); and by the thirteenth-century manuscript "Hermes Mercurius Triplex on the six principles of things." Enoch's lore on angels was echoed in the whole of spurious medieval manuscript literature of ceremonial magic, including the "Book of Venus,"

the *Liber Juratus*, the *Liber lunae,* and the various versions of the "Book
of Toz" (Thorndike, 2:220–27). It also appears, that Roger Bacon (whom
Dee unconditionally admired for his engagement in the magical-
mechanical arts), highly regarded Enoch and mentioned him in his *Secre-
tum secretorum* as equal being to Hermes (Clulee 1989, 209).

These occasional and more or less illicit mentions gained a new
dimension during the late fifteenth century—undoubtedly due to the
Florentine neoplatonists' enthusiasm for hermeticism. Enoch and Hermes
Trismegistus became role models for magically oriented humanists who
were obsessed with the practical methods for achieving *exaltatio*, even to
the extent that they claimed themselves to be the reincarnation of those
ancient sages.[56] A notable example was Giovanni Mercurio, the wandering hermetic magus who around 1501 visited France and had his sensational appearance recorded by Trithemius. Mercurio left no writings of
his own, but accounts of his activities reported that he had declared
himself to be the heir of Apollonius of Tyana, the ancient magician. After
Mercurius Trismegistus he also called himself Mercurius Secundus and,
according to Trithemius, promised "great, strange, and exceedingly marvelous things."[57] Although Trithemius claimed similar magical power for
himself, he was ready to see in Mercurio a charlatan, a fraud, at best a
convenor of evil spirits. He exploited the example of the Italian in order
to show how narrow and uncertain was the dividing line between real,
pious magic and necromancy (Brann 1999, 66). Not everybody, however,
was so critical of Mercurio. In 1505 Jacques Lefèvre d'Étaples, the her-
metically oriented humanist, published a work in Paris by the Italian
mystic, Lodovico Lazzarelli titled *Crater hermetis*, together with the
Pimander and the *Asclepius*, that is, the basic texts of hermetism.[58] Lazzarelli
(1450–1500) belonged to the humanist circle of Ficino and Pontano and
later turned into an apostle of the hermetic tradition. This conversion
was greatly influenced by Giovanni Mercurio, who in 1484 appeared in
Rome and roamed the streets with a crown of thorns and preached a
mystical renovation of Christianity. Lazzarelli remembered this encounter
in a work assuming the form of a letter by Enoch, in which he called
himself "Lodovicus Enoch Lazarellus Septempedanus, once a poet but
now by new rebirth the son of true wisdom" (Thorndike 1923–1958,
5:438). Thus, it seems, Lazzarelli considered himself to be a reincarnation
of Enoch and his ideas of hermetic rebirth can be compared to those of
Agrippa and Paracelsus, as mentioned above.[59]

Another sixteenth-century humanist who became involved with the
questions of Enoch and hermetic rebirth was Guillaume Postel, one of

John Dee's personal acquaintances. They met in early 1551 in Paris, where Dee had been staying since July 1550 and where in September he had lectured on Euclid. The title of his talk was "Prolegomena et didacta Parisiensa in Euclidis Elementorum Geometricorum librum primum et secundum" (Dee 1851, 25). According to his recollections from 1592,

> I did undertake to read freely and publiquely Euclide's Elements Geometricall, Mathematicè, Physicè, et Pythagoricè; a thing never done publiquely in any University of Christendome. . . . (Dee 1851, 7)

Here Dee also gives a long list of eminent scholars whom he met during his stay in Paris. Among the names of Pierre Mondoré (the king's librarian), Oronce Finé (a famous mathematician), and Pierre de la Ramée (the reformer of logic), one also finds Guillaume Postel, who in many ways can be considered as one of the closest intellectual relatives of the English Doctor.[60]

Postel (1510–1581) had a career similar to that of Dee.[61] Coming from a poor family, on attending school he was characterized by an extreme thirst for knowledge, often even forgetting to stop reading for the sake of eating.[62] As we also know from about Dee, "I was so vehemently bent to studie, that for those yeares I did inviolably keepe this order; only to sleepe four houres every night; to allow to meate and drink two houres every day; and of the other eighteen houres all was spent in my studies and learning" (Dee 1851, 5). Postel quickly learned Greek and Hebrew and later, during a trip to Constantinople, Siriac and Arabic. Like Dee, he also became a devoted collector of books although his even less stable life did not allow him to gather such a large collection as Dee's. The first sentences of William Bouwsma's monograph on Postel give a good introduction to his significance in the history of Renaissance humanism: "Postel is at once one of the most interesting and one of the most puzzling figures of the sixteenth century. His spectacular career and the wide range of his interests and activities have frequently attracted the attention of historians, and his name appears in the most various connections. He was the most learned Christian cabalist of his day, one of the earliest systematic Arabists in western Europe, a pioneer in the comparative study of language, and a humanist of distinction" (1957, v).

These thoughts have been repeated almost verbatim about John Dee, too. The two men had not only their humanist and scholarly interests in common. Both were deeply interested in the occult and the cabala, and both of them had a particular mystical conversion or illumination that concluded in a radical turn in their careers.

Parallel with his humanistic and philological interests, Postel's chief concern was the religious reformation of the world. He hoped that through rational reasoning non-Christians could be convinced of the superior truths of Christ. He was also looking for a human instrument to be the missionary of his project and he thought of the Jesuits. In 1544 he went to Rome, met Ignatius Loyola, and asked for admittance. Although Postel had only a brief encounter with the Society of Jesus (a year later Ignatius felt compelled to set up a committee to examine the religious heterodoxy of the Frenchman), Rome proved to be of crucial importance. In 1546 he met an Ethiopian priest who described for him the Book of Enoch, which existed only in that language. Postel became quite enthusiastic about apocryphal literature in general—he translated James' *Protoevangelium* and proposed that the Pope adopt the *Zohar* and the Book of Enoch as the keys to the Scriptures—and also often cited Enoch, since "its esoteric character and messianic emphasis were exactly the sort of thing to appeal to Postel" (Bouwsma 1957, 36).

His interest in Enoch may have led him to a preoccupation with reincarnation (cf. Secret 1990), which manifested itself in 1547 in Venice. There he met an almost illiterate elderly lady serving in the Hospital of Saints John and Paul, in whom Postel recognized the incarnation of the *anima mundi* or the divine radiation, the Shekhinah of the cabala. He called her "mater mundi" and the "New Eve" (Bouwsma 1957, 15 ff., 155–60; Kuntz 1981, 73 ff.) and he was fixated on her until his death in 1581. Mother Joana (or Zuana) died in 1549, and two years later an even more dramatic event occurred in Postel's life. He was celebrating Christmas, when he suddenly fell ill, suffered terrible awe and tremor until Mother Joana appeared to him, announcing that she would occupy his body as she had promised at their last meeting:

> I shall send you two beautiful gifts in our garments, and you shall be our first born son, who shall cause to be understood by Intellect and Reason the truth of our mysteries. (*Le prime novo del altro mondo,* Venice, 1555; quoted by Bouwsma 1957, 157)

Postel recorded the incarnation of the "Venetian Vergin" in his body as follows:

> Two years after her ascension into heaven, her spiritual body and substance sensibly descended into me and sensibly extended throughout my body, so that it is she and not I who live in me. (*Les très merveilleuses victories des femmes,* Paris, 1553, 20; Bouwsma 1957, 158)

Although Postel felt heavenly peace and bliss after the initial shock, one cannot be surprised at the wry observation of the modern historian: "The leap from simple desire to full belief in the actuality of an incarnate feminine principle and her first born son, not to mention the identification of himself with the latter, is considerable; and it is hardly surprising that his strange convictions bewildered his contemporaries [. . .] and these beliefs raised doubts about his sanity" (Bouwsma 1957, 165). As Bouwsma explains, Postel in fact saw himself as the incarnation of a "lower Messiah," a new Elias, the governor of the feminine sphere. As he himself wrote, "It is entirely necessary that there should be a lower Messiah, the image of the Wife, subordinate to her husband, and of the body subordinate to its soul . . ." (*Restitutio rerum omnium*, Paris, 1552; Bouwsma 1957, 163). Postel in fact called himself a reborn, or restituted, man, a herald of the last epoch when all things would be renewed to their primal perfection and Satan would be defeated for all before the final apocalypse.

Giovanni Mercurio, Lodovico Lazzarelli, and Guillaume Postel seem to have accomplished—at least in their subjective reality—all that to which Agrippa and Paracelsus were only aspiring, and which John Dee stubbornly tried to achieve during his decades-long "angelic conferences." The latter will be the subject of the next part of this book.

Part 3

Output

"Glyms or Beame of Radicall Truthes"

6

The Ideology and Occult Symbolism of
Dee's Natural Philosophy

I have devoted the previous part of this book to the examination of
magical *exaltatio* as it appeared and reappeared in Western thought from
classical Antiquity through the Middle Ages up to the sixteenth century—undertaking this by looking at books that were in the personal
library of John Dee. To a certain extent I have revisited the Yates thesis
and thus laid a special emphasis on the great magi of the fifteenth and
early sixteenth centuries, whose activity strongly contributed to the rise
of the much-discussed "man-centered" world picture of the Renaissance.
Their texts demonstrate that *that* "man-centeredness" by no means meant
religious scepticism, let alone atheism.[1] Instead, we could rather speak of
a new type of religiosity, some individual and idiosyncratic versions of
which are clearly distinguishable from the official branches of the Reformation. Historians often call these religious attitudes heterodoxy, or
interconfessionalism.

As I have shown, the idea that man had a special role in creation and
had been endowed with godlike faculties directly relating him to the
Supreme Being had been emphasized since earliest times. And as is also
clear, these thoughts have always been associated with mysticism, gnosticism, and symbolic magic. I am aware that it is impossible to explain
a very complex cultural phenomenon, such as the Renaissance, by reduc-
ing it to a product of a single intellectual impulse (that was the special
weakness of Frances Yates and her uncritical followers); still, I am nevertheless quite convinced that the magical vogue started and made acceptable by the Florentine neoplatonists became a particularly important

catalyzer in helping Western humankind break out of its medieval intellectual framework. Later, in the early modern period, this interest in magical *exaltatio* spread widely, became differentiated and popularized, influencing the Scientific Revolution on the one hand while on the other incorporating itself into the discourse of various religious denominations. Thus it became the property of much larger communities than it had been in the time of humanism and its patronage system. Another important contribution to this popularization was the expansion of book publishing. This meant not only more and cheaper books, but the technical development fostered a fascinating trend in magical illustrations that filled the works of Heinrich Khunrath, Michael Maier, Robert Fludd, Athanasius Kircher, and the later editions of Jakob Boehme.

With my references to Simon Magus and the appearance of the Faustian archetype, I argued that the doctrine of *exaltatio* had inherent subversive contradictions that may have led to total or partial self-destruction, too. I am convinced that the dynamism of the reborn European culture followed from these contradictions: from the tension between affirmation and negation, construction and demolition, tradition and subversion. Renaissance magic clearly shows this dichotomy. Because of this I can hardly believe early modern magicians who confidently asserted the possibility of separating white from black magic. It was only self-defense and propaganda in claiming that they were entirely free from all dark temptations. But why should we want to expel the examination of those murky experiments from the study of our cultural heritage? Cultural history is not to be purged; rather it should be interpreted and comprehended. As I suggested in connection with Paracelsus, Christian magic—and the doctrine of *exaltatio*—is more like a heroic torso, a gallery of broken dreams; still, it exercised an admirable influence on modern Western mentality.

I want to argue that John Dee fully integrated with this tradition, in fact that he was a prominent representative of it from the later sixteenth century. So much has been written about his career and works that I can do without the obligatory sketch of his biography and a general review of his writings. Let us plunge into the texts, a selection of his "output" that has pertinence for the notion of *exaltatio*. I am going to look at his *Propaedeumata aphoristica*, the *Monas hieroglyphica*, *The Mathematicall Praeface*, and the spiritual diaries as representing repeated efforts, successive stages, and sometimes different underlying theories in order to attain that pristine knowledge which leads man during his earthly life to the full comprehension of the universe, the manifestation of God's infinite intellect.

ASTROLOGY: *PROPAEDEUMATA APHORISTICA*

According to recent analyses, especially Nicholas Clulee's definitive interpretation, Dee's early career was dominated by his fascination with mathematics and medieval *magia naturalis* (Clulee 1988, 19–75; Heilbronn 1978, 50–105). As for geometry, his continental trip to the Low Countries and to Paris in 1550 and 1551 was spent under the sign of Euclid, though his account of the successful Paris lecture betrays an interest in mystical occult lore, too. He described Euclid as "Mathematicè, Physicè, et Pythagoricè," and even if at this point he was not yet aware of neoplatonic hermetism, he could refer to Proclus and the contemporary Jacques Lefèvre d'Étaples as representatives of a Pythagorean frame of thought. The evidence we have indicates that Dee from the earliest years of his scholarly career was occupied by an ambition to seek and acquire perfect knowledge, which necessarily made him aware of esoteric concerns.

Given his early interests, it should not be surprising that his first major work, the *Propaedeumata aphoristica* ("An aphoristic introduction [. . .] concerning certain virtues of nature, dedicated to Gerard Mercator, distinguished mathematician," London, 1558, 1568; modern edition: Dee 1978), dealt with the connections of geometry and astrology. It is not clear from where Dee acquired his expertise in traditional astrology, but as we know, in the same year of the publication of the *Propaedeumata,* he was invited to determine the astrologically most suitable day for the coronation of Elizabeth I. His interest in astrology may have been rooted in the studies he had pursued in Louvain during the years 1547 and 1548. He met there scholars—Gemma Frisius, Gerard Mercator, Caspar à Mirica, and Antonio Gogava—who were eminent representatives of a syncretic Renaissance science tinted with occultism and alchemical-astrological studies. He came home with valuable astronomical instruments, made by Mercator. Still earlier, however, "First, from Lovayne did the favourable fame of my skill in good literature spread, that thereupon divers noblemen came from the Emperour Charles the Vth, his court at Bruxelles to visit me at Lovayne . . ." (Dee 1851, 6).

The *Propaedeumata* shows that Dee tried to approach prognostication on a strictly scientific ground, astrology being treated here as applied mathematics. While the neoplatonist magi of the early Renaissance tried to control the influence of the stars through talismanic magic and ritual incantations, Dee thought to accomplish this task by the help of mathematically constructed optical mirrors. In this scientific program his predecessors were Ptolemy himself and the medieval authorities on optics:

the Arab al-Kindi (*De radiis stellarum*), Urso Salernitanus, Robert Grosseteste, and Roger Bacon (cf. Clulee 1988, 52–69; Harkness 1999, 71–77; Szulakowska 2000, 37–43).

The nature of my present investigation does not require a digression into Dee's mathematical reasoning. The point is that for the improvement of astrology he needed the exact number of stellar constellations. While traditional astrologers usually differentiated between 120 constellations, Dee in his book consisting of 120 aphorisms, determined a number of 25,341. Dee tried to derive astrology from nature alone, avoiding demonic intelligences that haunted even his learned contemporary Giordano Bruno. According to Clulee, the early natural philosophy of Dee was built on a naturalistic concept of the world and man, in which the dualism of natural and supernatural was not particularly emphasized. The *Propaedeumata* represents an eclectic synthesis, argues Clulee, that cannot be directly linked with neoplatonic hermetism as the representatives of the Warburg school and Yates saw it. He is undoubtedly right that Renaissance occultism was not a homogeneous and monolithic subject and that it was rooted in many medieval sources, too. But as Harkness recently noticed, by 1550, "during his visit to Paris [Dee] became more acutely aware of the enormous potential, and the enormous difficulties, associated with the study of the natural world" (1999, 82). And in my opinion, from the time of his earliest writings this awareness pushed him in a more and more mystical direction as the only means of promising true *exaltatio*. I can see this attitude among the aphorisms of the *Propaedeutama*, as well.

The title page itself is characterized by iconographical elements of esoteric symbolism summarizing the occult correspondences of the universe. The frontispiece shows an architectural construct with the four elements at its four corners; at the centre of the columns the two main characters of the alchemical process can be seen (Sol and Luna); the central icon is a modified astrological-alchemical sign of Mercury that can represent all the planetary metals. This is stated by the motto written in the ribbon: "*STILBON, acumine praeditus est instar omnium planetarum*" (MERCURY, endowed with a sting, is like all the planets). This combination of Mercury seems to be Dee's invention; it appears here for the first time and later becomes the central motif of his major work, the hieroglyphic monad. The lower motto refers to connections between Christianity and occult philosophy: "And there shall be signs in the sun, and in the moon, and in the stars" (Luke 21:25). The upper motto offers one of Dee's favorite maxims: "Let him who does not understand either be silent or learn" (cf. Figure 6.1).

FIGURE 6.1   Frontispiece of Dee's *Propaedeumata aphoristica* (London, 1558). Reproduced from Dee 1978 [facsimile].

The book is dedicated to Mercator and mentions that the catalyzer of the work was his friend's recent letter in which he asked about his projects. Remembering their philosophical studies ten years earlier in Louvain, he decided to comment on the problems they were discussing at that time. Admittedly, thus, the *Propaedeumata* is the synthesis of the studies of the past ten years, including his intellectual encounters in Louvain and Paris. The treatise clearly demonstrates Dee's working methods and the characteristic structure of his works (at least before the spiritual diaries). All of his surviving scholarly works were written in haste and in a short time, usually after a long period of gestation. He liked the concise, aphoristical expression; thus, his writings look like drafts or outlines for larger—but never written—works.[4]

The first aphorism is a general thesis of ontology, asserting Dee's monistic, nature-oriented interest:

> As God created all things from nothing against the laws of reason and nature, so anything created can never be reduced to nothing unless this is done through the supernatural power of God and against the laws of reason and nature. (I, Dee 1978, 123)

Aphorism II introduces the principle of *magia naturalis* and in Aphorism X we are assured about the realistic and legal possibility of magical transformation of the world. Although Dee avoids speaking about Man the Magus, his program implicitly involves the prospect of *exaltatio*:

> The entire universe is like a lyre tuned by some excellent artificer, whose strings are separate species of the universal whole. Anyone who knew how to touch these and make them vibrate would draw forth marvellous harmonies. In himself, man is wholly analogous to the universal lyre. (XI, 126–27)

This thesis refers to the analogy between the macro and microcosms, and although one cannot say that the correspondences of the Great Chain of Being were the intellectual property of neoplatonism and hermetism, Dee's words evoke their atmosphere. Clulee is right to emphasize that Dee's scientific reasoning shows no relationship to the Florentine synthesis; however, in my opinion, his contextual aphorisms nevertheless point in that direction. He mentions, for example, the cabala (XVIII). Like Ficino, he praises the healing power of music (XXIII), and even speaks about talismans (XXVI). He also treats alchemy as *astrologia inferior* (LII), not unlike Paracelsus, and praises the mystic monad, constructed by himself.

Furthermore, in Aphorism LXXIII he speaks about "the assidious mage" who can discover the great harmony of the world. He illustrates the correspondences by the paradigm of Sun—gold—and human heart and here he speaks of anatomical magic. In LXXVII he again uses parallels from alchemy and the cabala: "What is seven times properly separated is prepared also to be seven times joined for the making of that most famous philosopher's stone."[5]

The concluding aphorisms again show openness toward hermetic neoplatonism. Although according to Clulee the reference to Hermes Trismegistus in CXIX comes not from Ficino but from the late Hellenistic *Iatromathematica*, which was used throughout the Middle Ages (1988, 45), he also accepts that by the time of writing the *Propaedeumata* Dee already had the basic primers of hermeticism: Ficino's edition of the *Corpus hermeticum*, Giorgi's *De harmonia mundi totius*, Reuchlin's *De verbo mirifico*, and Agrippa's *De occulta philosophia*. One should take Clylee's caveat seriously, namely that the acquisition of a book does not immediately mean its appropriation; still, while re-reading the aphorisms, I am inclined to find in them the natural philosopher who is just about ready to abandon scientific humanism for the sake of hermetic mysticism.

During the six years between writing the *Propaedeumata* and the *Monas*, Dee's intellectual arsenal became enriched with important elements. This is the time when he started establishing his collection of Paracelsica and his occult studies were also boosted by his long travel on the continent in 1563 and 1564.[6] The next subchapter will look at the *Monas hieroglyphica*, considering its sources and its importance as Dee's full-fledged manifesto for the study of magic *exaltatio*.

ALCHEMY: *MONAS HIEROGLYPHICA*

On September 8, 1563, one of the many bemused observers of the coronation of Maximilian II as King of Hungary was Doctor John Dee, the English mathematician, promotor of ascending British imperialism, and later notorious visitor of East-Central European courts with a strange, mystical-chiliastic message based on his conversations with angels. The Hungarian coronation city, Pozsony or Pressburg, present-day Bratislava in Slovakia, was just one stop on Dee's long European journey, which included visits to Zurich, Padova, Venice, and Urbino. The English humanist's main purpose was to meet leading intellectuals on the continent, such as Conrad Gessner and Frederico Commandino; he consulted with the former and with the latter he prepared a joint publication.[7] From Pozsony, through Germany, he moved back to Antwerp where he spent the whole of January 1564 finishing his major work, the *Monas hieroglyphica,* which was published in March by the well-known printer Willem Silvius. The spectacular pageant of the Hungarian coronation so much impressed the Doctor that he decided to dedicate the whole work to "Maximilian, by the grace of God the most wise King of the Romans, of Bohemia and of Hungary" (title page, Dee 1964, 113). A passing reference in Dee's memoirs, almost thirty years later, from 1592, suggests that after the publication he returned to Vienna with the intention of personally presenting his work to the Emperor:

> [15]64. Junij 14, after my return from the emperors court, her Maiestie very gratiously vouchsafed to account her self my scholar, in my boke written to the Emperor Maximilian, entitled *Monas Hieroglyphica*. . . . [8]

As Robert Evans (1973, 52–3) has noted, Maximilian seems to have been interested in esoteric subjects while his religious views were ambiguous.

Dee's work itself is a slim volume, introducing and explaining a magic diagram, which is supposed to demonstrate all visible and metaphysical aspects of the universe in the form of a geometrical-alchemical-philosophical image. We have good reason to say that it was to function as a revelatory mandala in order to propel the soul's flight, that is, to bring the viewer into the state of *exaltatio*, an intuitive understanding of the cosmos and a unification with the wisdom of God.

Dee himself explained the layers of his mystical meaning in the lengthy introduction addressed to Maximilian. As he wrote, his monad is explained "mathematically, magically, cabalistically, and anagogically" (Dee 1964, 155), but these four layers of meaning ought to be completed with two more: the alchemical and the linguistic aspects that seem to link intricately with the others.

The text of the *Monas hieroglyphica* is nothing else than twenty-four theorems explaining the diagram. This explanation constitutes two planes of argumentation: the first acquaints the reader with the geometrical elements and the mystical-mathematical-cabalistic meanings of the diagram; the second outlines the potential capabilities of Man the Magus, in relation to his privilege to recreate the lost unity in the split, dualist existence.

The title page in a comely manner incorporates the full diagram, surrounded by an architectural composition and several emblematic and philosophical phrases. As I have shown, Dee had already used the monad on the frontispiece of his previous work, the *Propaedeumata aphoristica*, and there are similarities between the two title pages. However, it should be noted that while in the *Propaedeumata* the hieroglyphic monad served only as emblematic decoration and the text did not provide its interpretation, this new book was entirely devoted to the explication of this mystical device. There is also a great difference between the two versions of the diagram, the later being much more refined and placed in an egg-shaped oval—this is what Dee used for the second edition of the *Propaedeumata*, too (cf. Figure 6.2). Although Dee retained one of the mottos—"Qui non intelligit, aut taceat, aut discat" (He who does not understand should either be silent or learn)—he replaced the key biblical quotation from Luke 21-25, which referred to astrology, with Genesis 27: "May God give thee of the dew of heaven and of the fat of the earth." This promise may have seemed to prefigure the kind of mystical synthesis of heavenly, occult knowledge, and earthly well-being the hermetic magus so much craved (see Figure 6.3).

FIGURE 6.2   Frontispiece of the 2nd edition of Dee's *Propaedeumata . . .* (London, 1568). Reproduced from Dee 1978 [facsimile].

FIGURE 6.3   Frontispiece of Dee's *Monas hieroglyphica* (Antwerp, 1564). Herzog August Bibliothek, Wolfenbüttel [223.3 Quod /1/].

It is notable that no apparent model has been identified so far for Dee's cosmogram, which, as I have said, seems to be his own invention. We can hardly trace graphic or diagrammatic sources because the time of composition fell so much before the great vogue of symbolic and emblematic illustrations, the kind that fill occult and scientific books from the early seventeenth century on. Khunrath, Fludd, Maier, Kircher, and others, in fact, often used and further elaborated Dee's monad.[9]

The first serious scholarly commentator of the hieroglyphic monad (after Tymme's pioneering interpretation of the 1610s), C. H. Josten, admitted his uncertainty about the sources:

> It has not been possible to identify any ancient author as the principal source of Dee's ideas on the monas and on numbers. [. . .] Trying to determine why Dee chose to name the universal principle of transmutation, and his symbol thereof, *monas*, i.e. essential oneness, one recalls the *una res* of the *Smaragdine Table*; but a more immediate source is perhaps to be found in chapter iii of book II, of Henry Cornelius Agrippa's work *De occulta philosophia*, which chapter is titled "De unitate, & eius scala." (Josten 1964, 106)

Next to these, Josten mentions Ioannes Pierius Valerianus' *Hieroglyphica* (Basel, 1556), in which there is a woodcut of Mercury carrying a ram while the accompanying text interprets this as the astrological symbol of restored health.[10] Although Dee possessed an 1567 edition of this work (R&W 114, published three years after Dee's *Monas*), he does not seem to have had either Horapollo or Francesco Colonna's *Hypnerotomachia Poliphili*, or any other books directly touching upon Egypt or hieroglyphics.

On the other hand, he did have several other works in which interesting passing remarks discussed the Egyptian writing system. One such volume was his copy of Alberti's *De architectura libri decem* (1523 edition, R&W 607) in which he could have read:

> [The Egyptians'] reason for expressing their sense by these symbols was, that words were understood only by the respective nations that talked that language, and, therefore, inscriptions in common characters must in short time be lost. [. . .] The manner of expressing their sense by symbols, they thought must always be understood by learned men of all nations, whom alone they were of the opinion that things of moment were fit to be communicated." (quoted in Daly 1998, 22)

In his article on the *monas* Michael T. Walton cited Meric Casaubon's opinion that Dee was "a Cabalistical man, up to the ears[11] and applied cabalist writers—Pico, Agrippa, and Postel—to extract the precise meaning of the cosmogram. His view—"Dee's treatment of the Monad's interpretation as an art of writing which revealed all astronomical knowledge, both the greater astronomy of the heavens and the lesser astronomy or alchemy"—is corroborated by Dee's text in the preface addressed to Maximilian, according to which

> [T]his our holy language, which I have called the real cabbala, [. . .] which was born to us by the law of the creation, is also a more divine [gift], since it invents new arts and explains the most abstruse arts very faithfully. [. . .] I know well (O King) that you will not shrink away in horror if I dare proffer this magic parable in your royal presence. (Dee 1964, 135)

One cannot help noticing, though, that neither Dee nor his interpreter, Walton gave any indication of the exact origin of the monad's graphic design.

Nicholas Clulee has analyzed the *Monas hieroglyphica* at perhaps the greatest length, but even he has not been able to identify sources or really close parallel texts among Dee's readings. He noticed the concept of the metamorphosis from the "horizon temporis" to the "horizon aeternitatis" in Dee's thought, which is nothing but the *exaltatio*, although he did not call it so. He cited Pliny, Trithemius, and Pico among those who voiced similar notions and finally concluded: "I believe that it is from Roger Bacon that Dee derived the basic inspiration to seek an integral knowledge of nature" (Clulee 1988, 121). To strengthen his argument, he recalled Dee's lost treatise from 1557 titled *Speculum unitatis*, written in defense of Roger Bacon. Relying on Bacon's *Tractatus brevis et utilis*, Clulee argued that Dee had been able to receive information about ancient theology and hermeticism through purely medieval sources. But then he also added that Dee himself had interpreted his cosmogram in evolving turns from a diagram of natural magic in the 1550s to a summary of a universal grammar by the 1560s. In this context the monad should be seen as a pythagorean or cabalistical formula generating the spiritual transformation of the soul and its mystical ascent from the material to the supercelestial realm.[12] At this point Clulee turns to Renaissance sources that could reveal concepts of magic for Dee, "far less natural than that he encountered in Roger Bacon" Clulee 1988, 128). These sources primarily meant the neoplatonic philosophers—Ficino, Pico, and Agrippa—whom Frances Yates called "the hermetic magi."

Here I would like to argue that Dee, possessing and heavily annotating Ficino's *Index eorum* . . . (R&W 256), had a compact primer in neoplatonic hermetism at hand that could provide him with a wide spectrum of that philosophy in a single textbook. As I have stated above, merely by looking at the contents of this compendium (reprinted and expanded in his *Opera* of 1576 which Dee also possessed), one can conclude that Ficino's ideal of magic must have been a synthesis between the hermetic lore and the so-called Platonici.[13] The collection unites the two kinds of corpus in the following order: "Dionysii Areopagitae translatio cum suis argumentis" (Ficino 1576, 2:1–1128); "In divinum Platonem epitomae" (1129–1533); "In Plotinum Philosophum ex Platonici familia nati" (1534–1800); "Expositio Prisciavi & Marsilii Theophrastum defenso, ac phantasia, & intellectu" (1801–1835); "Mercurii Trismegisti Pymander, de potestate ac sapientia Dei item Asclepius de voluntate dei" (1836–1870); "Iamblichus de mysteriis Aegyptiorum, Caldeorum, atque Assiriorum" (1873–1907); "Proclus de anima & daemonum [commentariis in Alcibiadem Platonis primum]" (1908–28); "Proclus de sacrificio & magia" (1928–29); "Porphyrius de occasionibus sive causis ad intelligibilia nos ducensibus" (1929–32); "Porphyrius de abstinentia animalium [de animi ascenta & descenta]" (1932–38); "Psellus de daemonibus" (1939–44); "Pythagore aurea verba & symbola" (1978–79).

Here one finds those late neoplatonists (Iamblichus, Proclus, Porphyry, Psellus) whom Brian Copenhaver (1988 and 1990) identified as Ficino's main inspirations—together with the tracts of the *Corpus hermeticum*, or, as Ficino translated, "Mercurii Trismegisti Pymander, de potestate ac sapientia Dei item Asclepius de voluntate dei." And if we are looking for John Dee's possible sources of hermetism, it is enough to look at this collection, in which Chapter 4 of the *Corpus hermeticum* in its title mentioned a monad: "Mercurii ad Tatium Crater, sive Monas." The very first sentence of the text refers to *that* magical language/grammar that Walton, Clulee, myself, and now Harkness have considered as the main idea behind Dee's *monas*:[14]

> Since the craftsman made the whole cosmos by reasoned speech, not by hand, you should conceive of him as present, as always existing, as having made all things as the one and only and as having crafted by his own will the things that are. (4.1; quoted from Copenhaver 1992, 15)

The passage then speaks about man's exaltation: "The man became a spectator of god's work. He looked at it in astonishement and recognized its maker" (4.2). And "God shared reason among all people" (4.3). In the conclusion of the chapter, Hermes explains the mystery of the unit of oneness, the monad:

> The monad, because it is the beginning and root of all things, is in them all as root and beginning. Because it is a beginning, then, the monad contains every number, is contained by none, and generates every number without being generated by any other number. (4.10; Copenhaver 1992, 17)

This is exactly how Dee's monad works: it represents oneness but one can derive from it all numbers, all letters, in fact all (alphanumeric) systems of information. Ficino's commentary to this locus emphasizes the *exaltatio* of man catalyzed by numbers: "Mox unitatis, & numerorum analogia, ad veram monadem cogitandam, verosque naturæ numeros nos elevat. Haec Crater" (Ficino 1576, 2:1842–43).

Recently Håkan Håkansson has studied Dee's annotations in the Greek *Corpus hermeticum* and emphasized that it was the gnostic themes of these texts towards which Dee directed his attention in his marginal notes. Håkansson corroborates my view that in Chapter 4 the "Crater sive Monas" image could represent for Dee that kind of divine illumination he associated with the magus-adept in the *Monas hieroglyphica*.[15]

Ficino's compendium included the editor's most radical esoteric work: *De vita triplici*. Although Dee did not annotate this part of the book, this may result from the fact that he possessed *De vita* in two other editions (R&W 779, 896) which have not survived.[16] If we compare John Dee's speculations and the third part of the work, that is, *De vita coelitus comparanda*, which contains the author's boldest occult deliberations, we notice first of all a great deal of similarity between them concerning the general aims of magical operations. A program drawn up in one of Ficino's chapters strikingly resembles the English Doctor's ultimate goal with his monad:

> But why, then, should we neglect a universal image, an image of the very universe itself? Through it, they seem to hope for a benefit from the universe. The adherent of these things, if he can do it, should sculpt an archetypal form of the whole world. (3.19; Ficino 1989, 343–45)

Although mostly concerned with talismanic images representing the classical deities of the planets, Ficino also thought highly of mathematical and geometric entities that could serve as a sign repertoire for the construction of the universal image:

> To keep you from distrusting figures too much, astrologers will order
> you to remember that [. . .] numbers and figures, to obtain celestial
> gifts, they are very powerful. For in the heavens, lights, numbers, and
> figures are practically the most powerful of all. [. . .] For thus figures,
> numbers, and rays, since they are sustained by no other material, then
> deservedly they claim the most dignity in the primary—that is the
> celestial—levels of the cosmos. (3.17; Ficino 1989, 329)

Then he arrived at concrete geometrical elements, praising their power to
express universal harmony: "Proportions constituted out of numbers are
almost figures of a sort, made, as it were, out of points and lines" (3.17,
331). And finally, he offered geometrical shapes for his talismans in a way
that might have inspired Dee to construct his monad out of circle and
straight lines forming a cross:

> The recent authorities on images have accepted as the general form for
> these a round shape in imitation of the heavens. The more ancient
> authorities, however, as we have read in a certain Arabic miscellany,
> used to prefer above all other figures that of a cross for the following
> reason. [. . .] Above all a cross, like a plane, possesses length and breadth.
> This figure of the cross is primary; also, of all the figures, it is rectilinear
> in the highest degree, and it has four right angles. (3.18, 335)

As we know, Dee also added a geometric form (two semicircles) to the
diagram, which was to represent the element of fire, corresponding to
the fiery zodiacal sign of Aries. Referring to the appropriate time of the
operation, Ficino also pointed out the importance of Aries:

> But when exactly should he imprint it? When the Sun has reached the
> first minute of Aries [. . .] because a particular Lot of the world being
> reborn, so to speak, is revolved through the same position in every year.
> At this time, therefore, he should construct the figure of the world.
> (3.19, 343–45)

These textual parallels not only include the very geometrical base, but
also Dee's intention to offer the monad as a mystical object for revelative
contemplation. A similar goal is designated by Ficino for his talismanic
images: "Nor should one simply look at it but reflect upon it in the mind"
(3.19, 347). And since he renders "reflection" into seven steps—in harmony with the number of the planets—it is interesting to see that after
four elementary stages or functions, the three higher ones relate to different

human intellectual activities. The fifth is the sphere of imagination ("Fifth are the strong concepts of the imagination—forms, motions, passions"—Mars), the sixth is discursive logic ("the sequential arguments and deliberations of the human reason"—Jupiter), while the seventh could be called intuition ("the more remote and simple operations of the *understanding*, almost now disjoined from motion and conjoined to the divine"—Saturn).[17] This is the concept that Thomas Hoby in his translation of Castiglione's *The Courtier* also named "understanding":

> In our soul there be three manner ways to know, namely, by sense, reason, and understanding: of sense ariseth appetite or longing, which is common to us with brute beasts; of reason ariseth election or choice, which is proper to man; of understanding, by the which man may be partner with angels, ariseth will.[18]

The idea of the reborn world comes up often in Dee's later mystical writings, the private diaries. The importance of this idea for Ficino has recently been demonstrated by Michael Allen. In *Nuptial Arithmetic* he examined Ficino's commentary on the famous "Fatal Number" section in Plato's *Republic* (Book VIII). In the complex analysis of Ficino's number symbolism, Allen points out that "Ficino was in no position to follow his brother Platonist Pico della Mirandola into the arcana of cabalistic gematria with its substitutions, [. . .] still such intellectual consequences were the next logical steps" (Allen 1994, 144).

Drawing a conclusion from the above remark, I am suggesting that Ficino's cited passages of *De vita coelitus comparanda* can be treated as Dee's main and immediate textual source for constructing the monad, and if Pico's cabala was the next logical step deriving from Ficino's magic, then Dee took the following two logical steps: first, constructing a geometrical-cabalistical-magical cosmogram, then abandoning the whole enterprise and turning directly to angel magic.

—m—

The theorems of the *Monas hieroglyphica* explain the cosmic image on two planes: the geometrical, cabalistical, and anagogical interpretations—including astrological, alchemical and linguistic insights—highlight how the elements and proportions can give a mystical but strictly scientific expression of the ultimate cause of the World, the Oneness. The second plane refers to Man, the Magus who goes through a mystical transmutation of "understanding," the *exaltatio.*

As for the elements and mystical proportions of the monad, interpreters have pointed out the mathematical (cabalistic as well as geometrical), astrological, alchemical, and linguistic components. In the theorems,
Dee mostly concentrates on the mathematical aspects and adds explanatory charts to show how the combination of simple forms (straight line,
circle, point, crossing lines at right angles) can symbolize the general
principles of the natural cosmos. As he explains in Theorem VI,

> We see Sun and Moon here resting upon a rectilinear cross which, by
> way of hieroglyphic interpretation, may rather fittingly signify the ter-
> nary as well as the quaternary: the ternary [in so far as it consists] of
> two straight lines and one point which they have in common and
> which, as it were, connects them; the quaternary of four straight lines
> including four right angles [. . .]. And so here the octonary offers itself
> in a most secret manner, of which I doubt whether our predecessors
> among the magi ever beheld it, and which you will especially note. The
> magical ternary of the first [of our] forefathers and wise men consisted
> of body, spirit, and soul. Thence we see here manifested a remarkable
> septenary, to be sure of two straight lines and a point which they have
> in common, and of four straight lines separating themselves from one
> point. (Dee 1964, 157; cf. Figure 6.4)

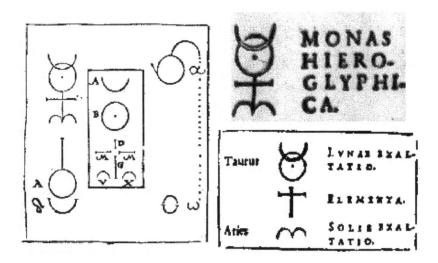

FIGURE 6.4 Compositional schemes of the Monad. Compiled by Gy. E. Szőnyi from the illustrations of the *Monas hieroglyphica*, copy of Wolfenbüttel [223.3 Quod /1/].

A near-contemporary interpreter Thomas Tymme (who planned an English translation of the *Monas* although we have only his preface to the projected edition) included the alchemical aspects in his explanation of the work's number symbolism:

> By the word TERNARIE is meant the first matter of the Philosophers stone, which are there in.
> By the QUATERNARIE is meant the 4 Elements: Water, Earth, Fire & Air.
> By the QUINARIE is understoode Quintessence.
> By the SEPTINARIE is understoode the 7 heavenly Planets [. . .] by whiche are meant Gold, Silver, Lead, Tynn, Iron, Copper & ☿ or Quick Silver.
> By the BINARIE is understoode common quick Silver, which is not the Mercury of the Philosophers, and therefore being without that Mercury it is rejected as a false Medicine. . . .
> By the OCTONARIE is understoode the 8 parts of Alchimy: Calcination, Dissolucion, Coniunccion, Putrifaccion, Separacion, Coagulacion, Sublimacion, & Fixacion.
> By the DENARIE is meant the Multiplicacion of Gold & Silver, by the perfection of the Medicine, from 1 to 10, from 10 to 100, & so by the Number to a Number Infinite by Arithmeticall proporcion. (Tymme 1963, 27–28)

Dee himself refers to the alchemical importance of the monad when he identifies the double semicircles at the bottom of the diagram with the astrological sign of Aries: this is nothing other than the sign of fire providing heat for the transmutation (X–XI; Dee 1964, 161). The egg-shaped frame of the diagram furthermore refers to alchemy, as it may stand for the alembic of the adept, also called the egg of the philosophers. Here Dee again calls attention to the interrelatedness of astrology and alchemy (*astronomia inferior*, XVIII).

In Charles Nicholl's interpretation, mystical geometry, number symbolism, and alchemy make the monad "a cosmogram of astrological import, [and on the other hand it] works as a talismanic synopsis of the alchemical process" (1980, 45). The alchemical plane of reference incorporates the doctrine of *exaltatio* or deification of man in Dee's natural philosophy. As Nicholl suggests, the creation of the alchemists' Mercury—that is, the quintessential, perfect Mercury in the final phase of the Work—leads to the liberation of the spirit, too, because the process of (spiritual) alchemy entails two transformations: while it captures the celestial energies and channels them into the material, it also elevates the soul and leads it back to the supernatural spheres from the prison of the material substance. Elaborating on this process, in the preface written to Maximilian, Dee interprets his "magic parable" as follows:

> This, our hieroglyphic monad possesses, hidden away in its innermost centre, a terrestrial body. [The monad] teaches without words, by what divine force that [terrestrial body] should be actuated. When it has been actuated it is to be united (in a perpetual marriage) to a generative influence which is lunar and solar. [. . .] When this Gamaaea has (by God's will) been concluded, the monad can no longer be fed or watered on its native soil, until the fourth, great, and truly metaphysical revolution be completed. When that advance has been made, he who fed [the monad] will first himself go away into a metamorphosis and will afterwards very rarely be held by mortal eye. This, O very good King, is the true invisibility of the *magi*, which has so often been spoken of. . . . (Dee 1964, 135–37).

In developing a philosophy of the alchemical *exaltatio* of man, Dee's masters were undoubtedly the hermetist magi Ficino, Agrippa, and Paracelsus. Agrippa in *De occulta philosophia* (1533) claimed that

> magicians affirm, that not only by the mixture and application of natural things, but also of images, seals, rings, glasses, and some other instruments, being opportunely framed under a certain constellation, some celestiall illustration may be taken, and some wonderful thing may be received; for the beams of the celestiall bodies being animated, living, sensuall, and bringing along with them admirable gifts and a most violent power, do, even in a moment, and at the first touch, imprint wonderful powers in the images, though their matter be less capable. (2.35; Agrippa 1997, 373)

Similarly, Paracelsus in his Astronomia magna wrote,

> The Magus can transport many meadows of heaven into a small pebble, which we call 'Gemaheu,' or 'Imago,' or 'Character.' For these are containers in which the magus keeps sidereal forces and virtues as in a box. (Paracelsus 1589–1591, 10:376)[19]

All the Renaissance magi tried to clarify through natural-philosophical speculations the nature of that transcendental material, or radiation, or agent that transferred the energy of the *anima mundi* to the talismans. These philosophers also strongly asserted the bidirectional nature of this process: if the magus can draw the power of the World Soul to base matter, so can he elevate himself above the material world.

In the alchemical process the catalyzer is the pure mercury, "the celestial messenger" (Dee 1964, 177). The transmutation means the meeting of two worlds, represented as a marriage, where the "terrestrial body" is the material of the *Gamaaea* or talisman by the help of which the magus can boost its elevation. The talisman—because of its inscription—is also a character or sign of the heavenly language, the exploration of which is the ultimate goal of the magus. This aspect of metaphysical linguistics has only recently been explored: following Clulee's train of thought, Umberto Eco in his book on *The Search for the Perfect Language* connected Dee's interest in the reconstruction of a mystical and universal language to Postel's similar objectives (1995, 185–90). As he pointed out, the view that the three sacred languages (Hebrew, Greek, Latin) developed from a common geometrical-numerological base was put forward by Postel in his *De originibus* (1553). The Frenchman there claimed that "every demonstration of the world" came from point, line, and triangle, and that sounds themselves—following the principles of Pythagoras—could be reduced to geometry.[20]

In the theorems Dee, who of course had *De originibus* in his library,[21] exercised various manipulations on the monad (rotation, dismantling, combination and permutation of its elements), not unlike cabalistic, numerology works on and with the Hebrew characters. The preface to Emperor Maximilian clearly refers to this "science":

> The science of the alphabet contains great mysteries, since He, who is the only Author of all mysteries, has compared Himself to the first and last letter (which is to be understood not only for the Greek language, but also for the Hebrew and Latin ones). How great, then, must be the mysteries of the intermediate letters? [. . .] We have demonstrated that the shape of all letters are derived from points, straight lines and the circumferences of circles. [. . .] By the same process we discover clearly enough that the first humans could not have established out of such mystical principles that very stupendous fabric of the Hebrew letter and the Nekudoth had not the afflation of the divine power been most [effectively] present. (Dee 1964, 125–27)

From this it would follow that his intention in the construction of the Monad was not only the creation of a mystical emblem for contemplation, *compare w/ Ficino (242/43)*

a mandala, but also a "geometrical automaton" that could generate the alphabet of all languages and thus would represent the universal principle of language.

Theorem XXII of the *Monas hieroglyphica* wonderfully unites in a concise maxim the interconnectedness of metaphysical semiotics and *exaltatio*:

> The Logos of the creative universe works by rules so that man, godly-minded and born of God, may learn straightforward work and by theological and mystical language. (Dee 1964, 201)

This mystical language, then, like the inscription on a talisman, can transmit the energy of the World Soul and, conversely, can illuminate the magus with intuitive understanding. Does not this, again, remind us of Ficino's aphorism from *De vita*: "Nor should one simply look at it but reflect upon it in the mind?"[22] And if one moves from "looking" to "reflecting," the meditation over the revelatory cosmogram-mandala can accomplish the magical *exaltatio* spoken of in the *Tabula smaragdina*: "It ascendeth from the Earth into Heaven, and againe it descendeth into the Earth, and receiveth the power of the superiours and inferiours. So shalt thou have the glorie of the whole world."[23]

By no means exhausting all the possible magical connotations of the *Monas hieroglyphica*, I would conclude by comparing the first two great works of John Dee. One can clearly see the continuity between them as well as the innovation Dee added to the *Monas*. When writing the *Propaedeumata*, Dee was primarily still a scholar only superficially interested in the occult philosophy. By the time of the *Monas* Dee had turned into a hermetic magus, albeit one who had not entirely abandoned his earlier scholarly objectives and who still had the ambition of uniting the "old science" (Roger Bacon) with the "new philosophy" (Ficino, Agrippa, and Paracelsus) and "linguistics" (Postel). The connecting link between the two works was his ever present desire to acquire a superior knowledge that could lead him to the comprehension of the nature and intentions of the Logos. In this sense the *Monas* represents the ultimate step toward pure theology, the term meaning, of course, not orthodox dogma but a highly intriguing and idiosyncratic interconfessionalist vision.

MAGIC: *THE MATHEMATICALL PRAEFACE*

As I have already emphasized, Dee's career was characterized throughout by the pursuit of perfect knowledge and this crystallized in the search for the *lingua adamica* from the time of his constructing the hieroglyphic monad.

From this point on, Dee became more and more imbued with a spiritual-cosmic vision and this concern can clearly be felt even in his most practical work, the lengthy *Preface* to the English translation of Euclid's *Elements* (1570).[24] This introduction was to serve the popularization of mathematics in the vernacular and show how it could support the arts and crafts. Dee in fact created a whole new scientific terminology, at the same time giving a retrospective summary of his previous scientific studies. To a superficial reading, it seems that the *Preface* is nearer to the old, scholarly Dee of the *Propaedeumata* than to the magus of the *Monas*. Evidence of this is that while he mentions his work of 1558, he neglects to refer to his "hieroglyphics" (Clulee 1988, 146–48). Because of this, Roberts and Watson call this work a "retrospective" endeavor (1990, 9–10), also noticing that while the *Monas* was secretive, speaking to a small number of elect, the *Preface* is much more open, ecumenical, programmatic, and didactic. Interestingly, the literature Dee cites is relatively outdated, mentioning from among his books only those he had bought before 1560.

In this respect, the beautifully executed emblematic frontispiece can also be considered conservative; it has no esoteric motives, only scientific elements and figures. The ten-fold division contains six portraits of classical philosophers and scientists, and four emblematic pictures representing the subjects of the quadrivium (cf. Figure 6.5).

FIGURE 6.5   Frontispiece of Euclid's *Elements* with Dee's *Mathematicall Praeface* (London, 1570). University of Chicago, Department of Special Collections, reproduced from Dee 1975, 35.

It should also be noticed, however, that by that time his mind was already fixed on the "Otherworld," and Clulee suggests that the Doctor's new preoccupation can definitely be felt as a subtext of his main discourse. On the frontispiece, this subtext is indicated by the emblems of the Sun and the Moon, while at the bottom of the page one sees Mercurius carrying his winged staff with two serpents twined around it.

In the text itself, according to his new orientation, Dee develops a diction occasionally using phrases recalling the neoplatonists. He praises harmony, mathematics, and proportions in passages that at times soar up like prayer, like in the chapter explaining the laws of Archimedes:

> Thou onely, knowest all things precisely (O God) who hast made weight and Balance, thy Judgement: who hast created all things in Number, Waight, and Measure. [. . .] And for as much as, of Number and Measure, the two Artes (auncient, famous, and to humaine uses most necessary) are, all ready, sufficiently knowen and extant: this third key [the weight], we beseech thee that it may come to the nedefull and sufficient knowledge, of such thy Servantes, as in thy workmanship, would gladly finde, thy true occasions whereby we should glorify thy name, and shew forth thy wondrous wisdom and Goodness. Amen. (Dee 1975, b.iiij^v)

Such passages indicate that Dee by no means wanted to write a simple engineers' handbook; rather, he considered the mathematician a magus, capable of *exaltatio*. According to Knoespel (1987), this highly rhetorical diction identifies Dee's writing as premodern scientific discourse, since— as opposed to the language of the Scientific Revolution—it still heavily relied on images, allegories, and analogy, and the mixing of mathematical formulas with biblical quotations and religious eulogies.[25] In this vision the applied mathematician was not yet liberated from logocentrism and he appeared as the priest of science, even of culture:

> All thinges (which from the very first originall being of thinges, have bene framed and made) do appeare to be formed by the reason of Numbers. For this was the principall example or patterne in the minde of the Creator. O comfortable allurement, O ravishing perswasion, to deale with a Science, whose subject is so auncient, so pure, so excellent, so surmounting all creatures, so used of the Almighty and incomprehensible wisdome of the Creator, in the distinct creation of all creatures [. . .] by order, and most absolute number, brought, from Nothing to the Formalitie of their being and State. (Dee 1975, *j)

From such an ideological platform Dee wanted not only to educate his readers but to offer a kind of mystical initiation into science. His deep veneration of the mathematical arts resulted from his conviction that the proportions and balances as well as the cabalistical numerological correspondences taught the secrets of God's creative mind. Because of this logic, he emphasized the importance of the vernacular translation in a peculiar way. Although he never spoke against the official seats of learning, the universities, he also suggested that initiation into mystical knowledge was not a sole privilege of the higher schools of education. The adept must learn, but university position could not guarantee the proper intuition also needed by the scientist.

In the *Mathematicall Praeface . . .* Dee created a hierarchy of sciences that culminated in *Archemastrie*, a discipline he characterized as follows:

> This Arte, teacheth to bryng to actuall experience sensible, all worthy conclusions by all the Artes Mathematicall purposed, & by true Naturall Philosophie concluded. [. . .] And bycause it procedeth by *Experiences,* and searcheth forth the causes of Conclusions, by *Experiences:* and also putteth the Conclusions them selves, in *Experiences,* it is named of some, *Scientia Experimentalis.* [. . .] But wordes, and Argumentes, are no sensible certifying: nor the full and finall frute of Sciences practisable. (Dee 1975, A.iij^v)

Historians of science have often interpreted the above passage as evidence that Dee professed the experimental and practical disciplines and, what is more, advocated science in the vernacular, so in this respect he could be regarded as an important forerunner of the Scientific Revolution. But at this point one should remember Allen Debus' caveat from the 1970s: "In reality sixteenth-century natural magic was a new attempt to unify nature and religion" (1978, 13). And, indeed, by putting Dee's "Scientia Experimentalis" in the wider context of the work, we must be cautious about this carefree deduction. Immediately after the above passage Dee introduces the chief auxiliary sciences of *Archemastrie*, which according to him are

> the *Science Alnirangiat,* great Service. Under this, commeth *Ars Sintrillia,* by Artephius, briefly written. But the chief Science, of the Archemaster, as yet known, is an other OPTICAL Science: whereof, the name shall be told when I shall have some (more just) occasion, thereof, to Discourse. (Dee 1975, A.iij^v)

Although Dee apparently had no more occasion to expand on these sciences and never gave a clear definition of optics as he understood it, in the next chapter—following Clulee's investigations—I shall suggest that these sciences were more magical activities than experimental natural sciences. Under optics, in fact, we can find *scrying*, crystal gazing, which by 1570 was definitely on the horizon of his interest (see Harkness 1999, 63–78). And Dee's purpose with this kind of optical magic, no doubt, was to attain to great, superhuman knowledge. Clulee tried to derive Dee's interest in mystical intuition from Roger Bacon's works and his frequent use of the words *experience* and *experiment*. By the time he was writing the *Preface*, Dee had accumulated so much literature of modern Renaissance magic that we ought to look for the genesis of such ideas in the works of, say, Paracelsus, too. In his treatise on syphilis, the German Doctor wrote,

> The right path does not consist in speculation, but leads deep into experience. From experience the physician receives help, and upon it rests all his skill. He must have rich knowledge based on experience, for he is born blind, and book knowledge has never made a single physician. For this purpose he needs not human, but divine things, and therefore he should not treat truth light-headedly. He does not act for himself, but for God, and God bestows His grace upon him so that he may come to the assistance of his fellow men in their needs.[26]

Dee's definition of *archemastrie* is in harmony with Paracelsus' views: "There, then the Archemaster steppeth in, and leadeth forth on, the Experiences, by order of his doctrine Experimentall, to the chief and finall power of Naturall and Mathematical Artes" (Dee 1975, Aiiijᵛ).

External evidence of Dee's admiration for Paracelsus can be found in the *album amicorum* of the famous Swiss natural scientist Conrad Gesner, whom Dee visited in Zurich in April 1563. In the album, next to Dee's signature, Gesner commemorated his English guest's great knowledge of and interest in Paracelsus (cf. Durling 1965, 134 ff).

 But what was behind his burning desire to have a glimpse of the mysteries of Creation? His motivation was the same as that of the Florentine neoplatonists, and later on of Trithemius, Agrippa, and Paracelsus, that is, the new self-consciousness of Renaissance man who considered himself God's almost equal partner and asked for his share from the secrets of nature. Its logic was driven by a confidence that God could not be pleased with the praises of the simply humble, will-less, and boring creatures; rather, he would require the adoration of ennobled and all-powerful humans, suited to the label "the image of God."

With this in mind it is difficult to enroll Dee among the forerunners of the seventeenth century epistemological reform; rather, he seems to represent a return to occult universalism, which was one of the products of the ideological crisis on the eve of the Renaissance. An examination of his last intellectual period, that is, the full bloom of his angel magic, shows that he finally arrived at a conviction according to which—because of internal contradictions—rational scientific progress was not feasible for the purposes of humankind. From this dilemma he managed to create an almost perfectly consistent theory of meta-science or anti-science, whichever term one wishes to use.

7

Illuminaton and Angel Magic

Earlier Dee studies tended to separate the Doctor's "scholarly phase" from the twenty-five-year long period of "angel conferences." In fact, traditional science historians were not able to handle this phenomenon within the sphere of their subject field. Apart from two exceptional accounts of professional historians (Evans 1973; Firpo 1952), it was only in the 1980s that new efforts were made to look at the entirety of Dee's output from a unified perspective. The first decisive steps in this direction were taken by Christopher Whitby (1981/1988, 1985)[1] and Wayne Shumaker (1982, 15–53). Following these pioneers, Clulee's analysis "from science to religion" produced the first extensive and widely contextualized study, embracing Dee "the scholar" as well as "the mystical and supermetaphysical philosopher" (1988, 203–31). Clulee's example was emulated by Harkness to that extreme that she speaks about Dee's earlier scientific works as "the genesis of the angel conversations," (1999, 60–98). I would be cautious to follow her to that point, since such an approach might repeat the earlier blunder of the Yates school by explaining all and everything from one single vantage point. In this respect I would rather side with Clulee, who was careful enough to show the variety and the inconsistencies in Dee's intellectual development. As I see now, Dee must have been haunted by the same *idée fixé* during his long life, which pushed him through schools and books and acquaintances pursuing knowledge, power, and prestige. But at various stages of his career this single drive manifested itself in various forms, leading him to various subject fields and various ideological positions. Looking backward, one can say that his recourse to angel magic was a logical conclusion of his earlier efforts, but at the time of his other attempts that outcome was not at all inevitable. While pursuing results by means of the natural sciences, the Doctor's final goals were nevertheless very similar to what we identify as being supernatural and magical today. On the other hand, while becoming engaged entirely in angel magic, Dee still considered himself a scientist looking for the ultimate truths of nature.

Dee's angel—or Enochian—magic can be examined from several aspects. In the following subchapters I shall look at some of these, trying to answer the questions:

—what was the scholar's motivation in turning away from science and pursuing angel magic?

—what was the philosophy behind angel magic and the connected idea of the *lingua adamica*?

—what was the nature of Dee's practical methodology, that is, scrying, and how was it related to the program of conversing with angels?

—what were the contents of the angelic conferences, and how may a typology be established concerning these?

—what can we say about Dee's theology and religion in view of his angel magic?

Finally, in the next chapter I am going to touch upon one more, equally important aspect—the historical anthropology and sociology of Dee's occultism, which includes his relation to his scryers as well as Meric Casaubon's early explanation of Dee's spiritual magic.

Angel Magic and the Search for the Perfect Language

From the perspective of a positivistic model of science history, Dee's turning from humanism to magic was described by John E. Bailey, editor of his diary, as follows: "[Dee had] long forsaken the exact sciences, having exhausted their study; and had devoted himself to the blighting influence of occult investigations, intermingling with them in credulous simplicity what remained in him of the Christian faith" (Dee 1880, 2).

One of Dee's remarks of a confessional quality helps to explain this change. When he was finally given an audience by Rudolf II in Prague, he explained his life-long ambition in and his disillusionment with science as follows:

Hereupon I began to declare that All my life time I had spent in learning: but for this forty years continually, in sundry manners, and in divers Countries, with great pain, care, and cost, I had from degree to degree sought to come by the best knowledge that man might attain unto in the world: and I found (at length) that neither any man living, nor any Book I could yet meet withal, was able to teach me those truths I desired and longed for: And therefore I concluded with my self, to make intercession and prayer to the giver of wisdom and all good things, to send me such wisdom, as I might know the natures of his creatures; and also enjoy means to use them to his honour and glory. (Dee 1659, 231)

The quotation certainly displays scepticism and disappointment with science but also, in fact, that his transition from science to magic was not as abrupt as it seemed until recently. Based on analysis of the unpublished spiritual diaries, Yewbrey (1981) and Whitby (1981/1988, 1985) called attention to the fact that Dee started his angel magic before 1581, the usual date accepted by scholars. According to his first, previously unstudied angelic diary, he had already employed a scryer in 1579 and, commenting on this, he even added: "Ab anno 1579. hoc ferè modo: Latinè vel Anglicè (ast circa annum 1569 alio et peculiari . . . , "[12] that is:

From the year 1579 usually in this manner: in Latin, or English; (but around the year 1569 in another and special way: sometimes on behalf of Raphael, sometimes of behalf of Michael it has been most pleasing to me to pour out prayers to God: God works his wonderful mercy in me. (Yewbrey 1981, 167)

The reference to 1569 is very important because just at that time, during 1569 and 1570, Dee was also working on one of his most ambitious scientific works, the *Mathematicall Praeface*, in which he attempted a synthetical survey of all the mathematical sciences. The question thus becomes even more relevant: what was the relationship, if any, between Dee's scholarly thinking and the angelic conversations? I have already emphasized to what extent the ambition to gain omniscience motivated Dee's investigations in natural philosophy. His radical turn from science to magic, in my view, must have been in close connection with this ambition. Dee's preface to the above quoted spiritual diary started with a confession similar to the one he delivered before Rudolf:

I have from my youth up, desyred & prayed unto thee [i.e. God] for pure & sound wisdome, and understanding of some of thy truthes naturall and artificiall, such as by which, thy goodnes & powre bestowed in the frame of the word might be brought, in some bountiful measure under the talent of my capacitie, to thy honor & glory, & the benefit of thy Servants, my brethren & sistern. (MS Sloane 3188; Dee 1996, 1.4)

This burning desire for inspired knowledge led him to various fields of the natural sciences, including mathematics, geometry, astronomy, and philosophy, but we would not miss the fact that a strong theological framework was present in his thought from the very beginning of his career. His admiration for the work of creation led him to a hymnic eulogy in the *Propaedeumata*:

> The revolution of the stars has been established for the sake of that total and unceasing celestial harmony—which is a kind of first form of everything. [. . .] The most beneficient and wise Maker of the whole having ordained things in this way. (LXXV; Dee 1978, 163)

No wonder that he concluded his work with these words: *SOLI DEO HONOR ET GLORIA* (198). The same deep religious enthusiasm can be found in his later works, too. He offered the *Monas hieroglyphica* to Emperor Maximilian with the following advice:

> For all things, visible and invisible, manifest and most occult things, emanating (through nature or art) from God Himself, are to be most diligently explored in our wanderings, so that thereby we may proclaim and celebrate HIS GOODNESS, HIS WISDOM, & HIS POWER. (Dee 1964, 125)

The *Mathematicall Praeface*, too, abounds in such passages:

> The Heavens declare the Glorie of God: who made the Heavens in his wisedome: who made the Sonne, for to have dominion of the day: the Mone and Sterres to have dominion of the nyght: whereby, day to day uttereth talke: to night declareth knowledge. Prayse him, all ye Sterres and Light. Amen. (Dee 1975, biiij)

Although the theological texture of the above three quotations is homogeneous, the three works from which they were cited represent Dee's stations along his journey from science to magic. At the beginning of his career he strongly believed in the potential of the natural sciences and perhaps it was his "discovery," explained in the *Propaedeumata*, that an astrologer should calculate using over twenty-five thousand constellations for a single nativity chart, that disturbed his trust in quantitative science.

The disappointment led Dee to another trend of natural philosophy, Renaissance hermeticism, which combined neoplatonism, Ficino's talismanic magic, and Paracelsus' spiritual alchemy. This train of thought was stretched to its ultimate limits in the *Mathematicall Praeface*, where Dee laid the theoretical foundations of *archemastrie*, a universal science (Dee 1975, Aiii).

By the early 1580s he must have become disillusioned with this universal science, too, as we may see in the confession written in his spiritual diary in 1581 and later reconfirmed before Emperor Rudolf in 1584. He must have come to the conclusion that no human discipline could lead to the desired omniscience. His situation thus became quite similar to that of Doctor Faustus—we remember how Marlowe's hero cried out with great dismay about the uselessness of human sciences:

> Settle thy studies, Faustus, and begin
> To sound the depth of that thou wilt;
> Having commenced, be a divine in show,
> Yet level at the end of every art. . . .
>
> (A text 1.1.1–3)
>
> Philosophy is odious and obscure,
> Both law and physic are for petty wits;
> Divinity is basest of the three.
> Unpleasant, harsh, contemptible and vile. . . .
>
> (A text 1.1.138–41; quoted from Marlowe 1991)

Although the English Doctor did not make a covenant with the Devil, he arrived at a method of trying to gain superhuman knowledge that he himself had abhorred earlier. In general, he rejected the use of demonic magic and always passionately complained of being called a sorcerer or conjuror.[3] On the other hand, he always believed in a strong symbiosis of science and deep religious faith, which necessarily affected his scholarly work, too. In 1592, in an apology, Dee summed up his program of a combined scientific and spiritual *exaltatio* as follows:

> By the true philosophical method and harmony proceeding and ascending, (as it were) *gradatim,* from things visible, to consider of things invisible from things bodily, to conceive of things spirituall: by things mortall to have some perseverance of immortality. And to conclude: by the most mervailous frame of the *whole World,* philosophically viewed, and circumspectly weighed, numbered, and measured, most faithfully to love, honor, and glorifie alwais the *Framer* and *Creator* thereof. (published in Dee 1659, 57; also 1851, 72)

It seems, however, that at some point a disconcerting discrepancy emerged between Dee's religious convictions and his scientific program, which led him to abandon the scientific investigations entirely and turn to angel magic. In fact, this solution is remarkably logical from the Doctor's subjective vantage point. He came to the conclusion that if the human endeavor is insufficient to reveal the secrets of nature, man should turn directly to supernatural beings and gain information from them. This is how angel magic evolved as the ultimate solution to help Dee out of the failure of his scientific projects, and this is how the ex-humanist became more and more absorbed in the questions of the *lingua adamica*.

—m—

As I have pointed out in the introductory chapters, Dee, as an attentive reader of the Bible, was, naturally, well aware of those pieces of information in the sacred book that asserted the dignity of Adam in Paradise and dealt with the omniscient intellectual capacity given to Man prior to his fall.[4] A beautiful visualization of the glory of our forefather can be found in Schedel's *Weltchronik*, depicting the creation of Adam on the sixth day. While being moulded from clay, Adam is holding the hand of God, surrounded by animals as if waiting for him to give names to all the beings of the world (Figure 7.1).

FIGURE 7.1   The sixth day of Creation: Adam names the beings of the world. From Schedel, *Das Buch der Chroniken* (Nürnberg, 1493), fol. 5ʳ. Somogyi Library, Szeged [Inc 10].

If ever John Dee had the chance to see this page, four lines above the illustration he could read the well-known hermetic maxim on the dignity of man in German: "O Asclepi, wie ein gross wunderwerck ist der Mensch."

This happy state and high status was ended by the disobedience of primordial humankind, but Renaissance philosophers never stopped searching the Holy Script (including the apocrypha and the pseudepigraphica) for signs of promise and hope that Man could regain the lost dignity. Next to Psalm 8:4–6 and Wisdom 7:15–21, a section from the Book of Jesus, Son of Sirach sounded especially promising:

> The Lord endued them with strength by themselves, and made them according to his image. . . . They received the use of the five operations of the Lord, and in the sixth place he imparted them understanding, and in the seventh speech, an interpreter of the cogitations thereof. Counsel, and a tongue, and eyes, and a heart, gave he them to understand. Withal he filled them with the knowledge of understanding. . . . (Sirach 17:3–7)

The above passage suggests that one of the most important gifts of God to Man was the sacred language, through which communication with the godhead as well as understanding of the work of creation was possible. From this passage alone, the early modern thinker could infer that by recovering this lost sacred language all his ambitions and desires concerning *exaltatio* could be fulfilled. This train of thought is the key to John Dee's later scientific and philosophical investigations.

I have already shown how he suggested a way of recovering the perfect language in the *Monas hieroglyphica*. As it seems today, the monad was equally meant to serve as a mystical emblem for contemplation and also as a "geometrical automaton," which could generate the alphabet of all languages, thus contribute to the restoration of the lost universal language.

Realizing the failure of this project, Dee finally must have come to the obvious conclusion, namely, that he could not find any other way but turning to God directly:

> I have sought [. . .] to fynde or get some ynckling, glyms, or beame of such the foresaid radicall truthes: But after all my foresaid endevor I could fynde no other way, to such true wisdom atteyning, but by thy Extraordinary Gift. . . . (MS Sloane 3188, 6ᵛ; Dee 1988, 2:8; Dee 1996, 1.4)

I understand the phrase "extraordinary gift" as referring to Dee's being permitted to contact the angels and learn the divine language from them.

He saw an encouraging example of such a gift in the Old Testament. The gift he craved was similar to Enoch's privilege of learning the angelic language and being "translated" by God. According to Old Testament pseudepigraphica, it was Enoch who invented the human crafts and created writing for his descendants. Dee, on the basis of his readings on Enoch,[5] associated the learning of Jared's son with the use of a "shew-stone," a crystal ball that could be used as the connecting device in communication with angels:

> I have read in thy bokes & records, how Enoch enjoyed thy favour and conversation, with Moyses thou wast familier: and also that to Abraham, Isaac, and Jacob, Josua, Gedeon, Esdras, Daniel, Tobias, and sundry other, thy good Angels were sent, by thy disposition to instruct them, informe them, help them, yea in wordly and domesticall affaires, yea, and sometimes to satisfy theyr desyres, doutes & questions of thy Secrets. And furdermore considering the Shew stone which the high preists did use, by thy owne ordering. (ibid.)

Dee thus finally arrived at a radical method in order to gain supernatural knowledge: he employed a kind of magical divination to contact angels in order to learn directly from them the primordial perfect language, which had once been summarized for mankind by Enoch but was ultimately lost with the destruction of humankind at the time of the Flood. As Dee claimed, since Enoch he was the first human being who—by the help of angels—could have some insight into this language.

The fact is that Enoch caused quite a lot of excitement among early modern humanists and chiliasts. His portrait could be found even in such general encyclopedias, as Schedel's *Weltchronik* (Figure 7.2). Dee's direct source must have been Guillaume Postel's *De originibus* (Basel, 1553) in which the French enthusiast related his meeting with an Ethiopian priest in Rome in 1547 who described for him the Book of Enoch in detail (cf. Bouwsma 1957, 13–14). As I have mentioned in another context, Dee possessed this book, and his surviving copy in the Royal College of Physicians testifies to his fascination with it: all the passages referring to Enoch are marked and underlined (R&W 868; cf. Clulee 1988, 297n. 25).

We cannot know if Postel and Dee discussed the question of Enoch at their meeting in France in 1551 but obviously Postel's mystical and apocalyptic writings with their speculations on the origin of languages

FIGURE 7.2   The portrait of Enoch from Schedel's *Das Buch der Chroniken* (Nürnberg, 1493), fol. 10ᵛ. Somogyi Library, Szeged [Inc 10].

attracted the English Doctor into a similar circle of thought. Postel might have also drawn Dee's attention to the Hebrew *3Enoch*. He was deeply interested in Jewish scholarship, including the cabala, and translated several important works of the Judaic tradition. Already before their meeting he had published *Candelabri typici in Mosis tabernaculo jussu divino* (Venice, 1548) in which he—following Johannes Reuchlin—advertised the *Zohar*, the *Bahir*, and the cabala as Jewish treasures leading to the final verification of the evangelical truths. He also translated and edited the *Sefer Yetsirah*. Its title page claimed that it was Postel who had recovered the text from Babylon and now decided to restitute it for the edification of mankind (*Abrahami patriarchae liber Jezirah sive formationis mundi* . . . Paris, 1552). In the same year he published one more exciting text, *Restitutio rerum omnium conditarum, per manum Eliae profetae terribilis*, which suggested that the horrifying prophecies of Elijah, deriving from the language of "Saint Adam," would contribute to "the restitution" of the whole world the first example of which was his own "translation" by the Venetian Virgin (Bouwsma 1957, 276 ff.; Secret 1985, 178–86). There is no proof that Dee was aware of Postel's personal "restitution" as the first-born of the new epoch, but his rhetoric in the spiritual diaries sometimes suggests something of a similar conviction about himself.

Although Dee could not have read the Book of Enoch, he and many other enthusiasts were eagerly awaiting the return of its manuscript. Even in the seventeenth century, several codices brought from Ethiopia stirred excitement in regard to the long awaited discovery. For example, a learned Capuchin monk retrieved a manuscript that he brought to Europe and believed to be the hunted text, but in 1683 Ludolfus Hiob clarified that it was an unknown Ethiopian work called "The Book of the Mysteries of Heaven and Earth"—nevertheless a close relative of the Book of Enoch. In this atmosphere, especially considering the passages in Postel's works of which Dee must have been well aware, one cannot be surprised that even without being directly familiar with the core of Enochian literature, the English Doctor chose this biblical-apocryphal character as his role model. And it was indeed logical that Dee, who could not have had access to the sacred text of the Book of Enoch, finally turned to the angels for information. And they seem to have been good informants because Enoch's appearance in Dee's private mythology embedded in his angelic conversations shows interesting convergence with the since-discovered original Enochian literature.

For example, the first part of *1Enoch* relates the story of the fallen angels, how they intercoursed with women and corrupted all men, and how Enoch tried to intervene on their behalf before God. This book is usually referred to as the "Book of the Watchers" (Charlesworth 1983, 5). As we shall see, Dee in one of his visions called a mighty angel "the chief Watchman" and his dwelling place a "Watch-Tower"[6]—all this may have been accidental but nevertheless suggests that the Doctor's train of thought ran parallel with that of the imagery of the Book of Enoch.

Let us now examine how the Enochian mythology unfolded in his spiritual diaries through the communication of Archangel Gabriel. On Saturday, April 21, 1584, at a scrying session, Gabriel himself revealed the mythical story of the *lingua adamica* to the bemused Doctor:

> GABRIEL: Man in his Creation, being made an Innocent, was also authorised and made partaker of the Power and Spirit of God: whereby he not onely did know all things under his Creation and spoke of them properly, naming them as they were: but also was partaker of our [i.e. the angels'] presence and society, yea a speaker of the mysteries of God; yea, with God himself: so that in innocency the power of his partakers with God, and us his good Angels, was exalted and so became holy in the sight of God until that Coronzon (for so is the true name of that

mighty Devil) envying his felicity, began to assail him. [. . .] And [Man] was driven forth (as your Scriptures record) unto the Earth: where being dumb and not able to speak, he began to learn of necessity the Language in the which he uttered and delivered to his posterity, the nearest knowledge he had of God his Creatures. (Dee 1659, 92)

According to this piece of information, the prelapsarian Adam was partaker of the perfect divine knowledge and he could be set as the model and measure the magus wanted to achieve. The key to this knowledge seemed to be the reconstruction of the lost angelic language that would provide the way of return to the world of transcendental superexistence. Dee's solution was remarkably simple: according to his finally crystallized opinion, neither mathematics nor poetry could teach the language of angels. One should rather contact them and learn it from themselves.

The Archangel indeed assured the pious magus of the goodwill of the spirit world in sharing their knowledge with him:

With this that we deliver, which Adam verily spake in innocency, and never uttered nor disclosed to man since till now, wherein the power of God must work, and wisdom in her true kind be delivered: which are not to be spoken of in any other thing, neither to be talked of with mans imaginations; for as this Work and Gift is of God, which is all power, so doth he open it in a toungue of power. (ibid.)

So Doctor Dee devoted the last twenty some years of his life to this goal and, surprisingly, the scholar who was perfectly intimate with the most subtle intellectual procedures of his time chose the crudest way of contacting angels: scrying.

THE THEORY AND TECHNOLOGY OF ANGEL MAGIC

Theory and Sources

When we discuss the nature and procedures of scrying, we also cannot help noticing the connecting links between medieval science, natural magic, and this kind of uncultivated divination. So far these links have been largely neglected by science historians, but I hope to demonstrate that although Dee's recourse to the practice of crystal gazing may seem at first sight quite surprising, his decision was not at all a sudden and whimsical resolution, but just the opposite; it followed from his previous ambitions and investigations.

Although there seems to be an enormous difference between optics and scrying, I agree with Clulee and Harkness that the roots of Dee's crystal magic should be looked for in his early interest in medieval optics. In connection with optics, one should remember that this term refers to at least two strands of exploration: first, the practical study of light rays in their effect on the human eye and in their reflective and refractive behavior in relation to objects, such as glass, crystal prisms, and water; and, second, mystical concepts concerning the occult operations of light, a potent force in activating inert matter.[7] This double nature of optics can be compared to the Janus face of alchemy, which included practical procedures with chemical matter on the one hand and on the other spiritual transformation, that is, soaring up from base existence to supernatural understanding.[8]

Again similar to alchemy in which the two orientations did not separate, but rather overlapped, medieval optics was also a mixture of mystical concepts and practical observations. Thus in one of the most famous medieval Arabic treatises on optics, al-Kindi's *De radiis stellarum*, we find a concoction of theorizing from light rays to astrology (Clulee 1988, 52–69; Garin 1983). Even late medieval experimental optics— as in the works of Robert Grosseteste and Roger Bacon—was heavily influenced by neoplatonic mysticism, ideas related to the Plotinian emanations, and light imagery often borrowed from Jewish mysticism, primarily the *Zohar*. Dee was deeply influenced by these medieval opticians and his library catalogues testify what an amount of manuscripts and printed materials he collected in this field. In the following paragraphs I am going to demonstrate that each of Dee's major scientific works had some themes related to optics and that all these led toward a theory of magic.

Let us begin with the *Mathematicall Praeface* because this elaboration contained an interesting hierarchy of scientific disciplines. Dee made it clear that the ultimate end of any science should be the understanding of God's creative genius. In relation to this, Dee emphasized the cosmic significance of mathematics and suggested that the mathematical practitioner had the power to become a magus, capable of *exaltatio*, the emulation of God:

> By Numbers [. . .] we may both winde and draw our selves into the inward and deepe search of all creatures distinct vertues, natures, properties, and Formes: And also, farder, arise, clime, ascend, and mount up

(with Speculative winges) in spirit, to behold in the Glas of Creation, the Forme of Formes, the Exemplar Number of all thinges Numerable: both visible and invisible, mortall and immortall, Corporall and Spirituall. . . . (Dee 1975, *j-*jᵛ)

When mapping the hierarchy of sciences, Dee put on top a discipline called *archemastrie*. "So that, this Art, is no fantasticall Imagination: as some Sophister might [. . .] dash your honest desire and Courage, from beleving these thinges, so unheard of, so mervaylous, & of such Importance" (1975 A.iiiᵛ). As I have quoted earlier, here Dee also listed the auxiliary sciences helping the work of the Archemaster: *alnirangiat, ars sintrillia,* and *optical science* (see above, p. 177).

Nicholas Clulee has identified all three above mentioned sciences as magical practices. The expression *alnirangiat* derives from Arabic sources: the term *nīrangïyāt* meant a certain magical procedure; in the Arabic version of the *Picatrix* the term *nīrang* referred to magical incantations that were used to invoke heavenly powers. It was also used in such contexts when pictures or talismans were involved. As Clulee explains, Dee's source for this term was Avicenna's *De divisionibus scientiarum,* in which "scientia *alnirangiat*" is listed among the subordinate branches of natural science. Here it is a form of natural magic, for the manipulation of the hidden virtues of things (1988, 167). Dee possessed this work in his library and from the surviving copy we know that he underlined the word *alnirangiat* and glossed on the margin: "magicae" (R&W 395).

The next science mentioned by Dee is *ars sintrillia,* which has been connected with the name of a medieval author, Artephius, who is often referred to in a great many treatises though his identity is unclear. According to Dee's catalogue, in 1556 he possessed a manuscript that contained Artephius' *Ars sintrillia* but this treatise is no longer extant. The only clue scholars have been able to track down is a remark of Guillaume d'Auvergne who mentions a certain Artesius known for his ability to conjure up visions by placing a glossy sword over a water basin so that the glittering of the two caused the viewer to see strange sights (Clulee 1988, 168). The context of Dee's note makes this conjecture plausible since he subsequently lists "opticall science," which—also according to Clulee—is not only physics but rather crystallomancy, or as commonly known, scrying. As we have seen, Dee started his scrying experiments around the writing of the *Mathematicall Praeface* and his scientific treatise suggests that, at least at that point, he saw no fundamental contradiction between natural science and occult spirit lore.

Although Artephius' *ars sintrillia* has not been recovered, it should be remembered that Artephius, the legendary twelfth-century alchemist, was said to have lived over a thousand years due to the magic elixir he managed to distill. His story became a paradigmatic point of reference in sixteenth-century humanist mythologies and his name was occasionally associated with Enoch as well. François Secret in his studies (1979, 1990) brought together these motifs and many of our main heroes in an intriguing combination set in mid-century Paris. There is Postel, who in the 1540s worked in the Collège Royal founded by Francis I. His colleague there, Oronce Finé, the famous mathematician, extensively dealt with alchemical experiments, too, and introduced Postel to the art of "inferior astronomy." There are many references concerning alchemy in his early masterpiece *De orbis terrae concordia* (Basel, 1544), where, among others, he mentioned Arthepius, who, thanks to his alchemical studies, succeeded in living 1020 years.[9] According to the *Secret Book of Artephius*:

> I, Artephius, after I became an adept, and had attained to the true and complete wisdom, by studying the books of the most faithful Hermes, the speaker of truth, [...] when I had the space of a thousand years, or thereabouts, which has now passed over my head [...] by the use of this wonderful quintessence. (Artephius 1999, paragraph 30)

Postel's source for this legend was Roger Bacon, of whom he could have learned from Finé's recent edition of Bacon's *De mirabili potestate artis et naturae*. A few years later Dee visited Paris and met Finé, with whom he could discuss not only Euclid but also his own beloved author, Roger Bacon, while he also met Postel, who was interested in Enoch and Artephius like himself. Soon after, Postel had his "restitution" by the reincarnation of his "Venetian Virgin," and from this time on he claimed that he was reborn and endowed with the gift of extremely long life. The legend, according to which he lived over 120 years, was still remembered in the seventeenth century. It was repeated by many distinguished scholars, such as the philosopher Francis Bacon (1560–1626) and Gabriel Naudé (1600–1653), Mazarin's librarian and the historiographer of the Rosicrucians (Secret 1979, 85).

Perhaps it was his conversations in Paris that set Dee to studying the critical edition of Roger Bacon's *Epistolae de secretis operibus et naturae*. To propel his enthusiasm, he could also consult Finé's earlier publication (Paris, 1542). Dee's text appeared only posthumously in Germany,[10] but its English translation published half a century later still recalled the Doctor's editorial efforts: *Discovery of the Miracles of Art, Nature, and*

Magick. Faithfully translated out of Dr. Dees own copy, by T. M. and never before in English.[11] Here one could read about Artephius in the passage referring to the prolongation of life: "Artephius, who wisely studied the forces of animals, stones, etc., for the purpose of learning the secrets of Nature, especially the secret of the length of life, gloried in living for one thousand and twenty-five years" (Bacon 1923, 34–35).

The fame of Artephius continued also in France. His story was convoluted with that of Nicholas Flamel (1330–1418), the legendary French adept who was said to have discovered the elixir of long life himself and his followers believed that he was still alive though retired from the world, and would live for six centuries (Seligmann 1971, 123–24; Spence 1960, 162). A publication of 1624 finally introduced both Flamel and Artephius to the English readers: *Nicolas Flamel, His exposition of the hieroglyphicall figures which he caused to bee painted upon an Arch in St. Innocent's Church-yard in Paris [. . .] Together with the secret booke of Artephius [. . .] concerning both the theoricke and the practicke of the Philosophers Stone. Faithfully done into English out of the french and latine copies by Eirenaeus Orandus.*[12]

Before returning to the career of crystallomancy in the Renaissance, I would like to mention one more aspect of "opticall science" that is also pertinent to Dee's works. Already in 1558, in his first synthetizing work (*Propaedeumata aphoristica*), he mentioned "catoptrics" of which he wrote:

> If you were skilled in "catoptrics," you would be able, by art, to imprint the rays of any star much more strongly upon any matter subjected to it than nature itself does. [. . .] And this secret is not of much less dignity than the very August astronomy of the philosophers, called inferior [i.e. alchemy], whose symbols, enclosed in a certain Monad and taken from my theories, I send to you along with this treatise. (Dee 1978, 149)

Catoptrics in classical natural science meant the study of the radiation and reflection of light, and Roger Bacon in the Middle Ages devoted much work to this field. Not only in his great scholarly works did he discuss "burning mirrors" and the like, optical devices were also mentioned in his programmatic Epistle (Bacon 1923, 28–29). As we know, Dee was most interested in Bacon's work, and it was partly this influence that encouraged him to try to catch the power of the stars by the help of mirrors, which activity he interpreted as the scientific version of ancient talismanic magic.

Talismans, which had been much discussed in medieval Arabic and Latin sources, were reinvented by the Florentine neoplatonists, and their scientific application was proposed by Heinrich Cornelius Agrippa and Paracelsus.[13] Of these magical images, or "sigils" Agrippa noted:

> So great is the extent, power and efficacy of the celestial bodies, that not only natural things, but also artificial when they are rightly exposed to those above, do presently suffer by that most potent agent, and obtain a wonderful life which oftentimes gives them an admirable celestial virtue. [. . .] Such an image, best prepared to receive the operations and powers of the celestial bodies and figures, and instantly receiveth the heavenly gift into itself; then it constantly worketh on another thing, and other things do yield obedience to it. (2.35; in Agrippa 1997, 373)

Agrippa developed an intricate typology of these magical symbols ranging from direct emblematic representations of celestial demons, through traditional signs of planets, metals, and zodiacal signs, to the numerologically symbolic cabalistical characters or sigils (Figure 7.3). One of his notable examples describes the power of planetary amulets:

FIGURE 7.3   Magical sigils from Agrippa's *De occulta philosophia* (Basel, 1550), 286, 394. Herzog August Bibliothek, Wolfenbüttel [Na 146].

This fortunate Moon being engraven on Silver, renders the bearer thereof grateful, aimiable, pleasant, cheerfull, honored, removing all malice, and ill will. It causeth security in a journey, increase of riches, and health of body, drives away enemies and other evil things from what place thou pleasest; and if it be an unfortunate Moon engraven in a plate of Lead, where ever it shall be buried, it makes that place unfortunate, and the inhabitants thereabouts, as also Ships, Rivers, Fountains, Mills, and it makes every man unfortunate. (2.22, 319)

Dee could also read much about amulets and catoptrics in Pracelsus. From a 1562 Paracelsus edition, annotated by Dee in 1594, we learn that he was preoccupied with the German sage even in his later career and discussed it with his disciples, Mr. Barker and Mr. Alped. The names of his good angels, Anchorus, Anachor, and Anilos, inscribed in the same book, indicate the interrelatedness of Paracelsus and angel magic in old Dee's interests (Roberts and Watson 1990, 101; note to item 1476). Paracelsus wrote about images and defined *Gamaaea* as follows:

OF IMAGES [IMAGINUM]. This science represents the properties of heaven and impresses them on images, so that an image of great efficacy is compounded, moving itself and significant. Images of this kind cure exceptional diseases, and avert many remarkable accidents, such as wounds caused by cutting or puncturing. A like virtue is not found in any herbs.

OF GAMAHEI [GEMAHEORUM]. These are stones graven according to the face of heaven. Thus prepared they are useful against wounds, poisons, and incantations. They render persons invisible, and display other qualities which, without this science, Nature of herself cannot exhibit. (*Erklärung der Gantzen Astronomey;* Paracelsus 1894, 2:295)

Let us compare this to Dee's thesis in the *Propaedeumata*:

The stars and celestial powers are like seals whose characters are imprinted differently by reason of differences in the elemental matter. [. . .] You will therefore consider talismans rather attentively, and other still greater things. (Dee 1978, 135)

And to the already quoted passage of the *Monas*, written in 1564:

This our hieroglyphic monad possesses, hidden away in its innermost centre, a terrestrial body. It [the monad] teaches without words, by what divine force that [terrestrial body] should be actuated. [. . .] When this Gamaaea has (by God's will) been concluded, [. . .] he who fed [the monad] will first himself go away into a metamorphosis and will afterwards very rarely be held by mortal eye. (Dee 1964, 135)

As I have pointed out, in the *Propaedeumata* he only passingly mentioned talismans and instead concentrated on a scientific method that was to substitute the use of magical images. As opposed to this, the *Monas* is nothing but a magical image, a talisman that here has a double function: as earthly material it participates in the process of transmutation, and as a heavenly esoteric sign it helps the magus to soar up to the higher spheres of reality.

The above quotations from Dee redirect us to Paracelsian contexts, since in his synthetizing *Astronomia magna* the German Doctor made it clear that

Man is born of the earth, therefore he also has in him the nature of the earth. But later, in his new birth, he is of God and in this form receives divine nature. Just as man in nature is illuminated by the sidereal light that he may know nature, so he is illuminated by the Holy Ghost that he may know God in his essence. For no one can know God unless he is of divine nature. (I, 12: 326; Paracelsus 1951, 44)

And indeed, it is this similarity to God that enables man to become a creator of things, even more powerful than the upper and lower firmaments:

Now, it is no matter for astonishment that man accomplishes such things, for if it be true, as the scripture says, that ye are gods, we shall certainly be superior to the stars. [. . .] The wise man rules Nature, not Nature the wise man. For the same reason we can accomplish more than the stars. [. . .] The will of man extends over the depth of the sea and the height of the firmament. (*Erklärung der Gantzen Astronomey;* Paracelsus 1894, 2:300)

Creation, the establishment of wondrous things, happens through magic and Paracelsus in his writings introduced magic according to the three tiers of the Agrippian model, from *magia naturalis* through planetary, astrological magic up to mystical rebirth: "He who imitates the image of God will conquer the stars" (*Astronomia magna*, I,12:41–42; Paracelsus 1951, 155–56). This is simply the doctrine of Man's deification through white magic, as proposed by Agrippa in his most beautiful passage on *exaltatio*:

Therefore our mind being pure and divine, inflamed with a religious love, adorned with hope, directly by faith, placed in the height and top of the human soul, doth attract the truth and suddenly comprehend it, and beholdeth all the stations, grounds, causes and sciences of things [. . .] as it were in a certain glass of eternity. (3.6; Agrippa 1997, 455)

Previously, I have pointed out that for Agrippa the idea of deification was connected with alchemy in the form of spiritual transmutation (cf. *De occulta* 3.36). In the above passage, the phrase "glass of eternity" seems to refer to other magical arts: if it meant a mirror, then one can associate it with "catoptrics," Artephius' *ars sintrillia*; if it meant a crystal, one can think of Paracelsus' "beryl," or Dee's "shew-stone."

The main significance of the use of beryls or crystals was, of course, that by their help one could contact the spirit world, could practice angel magic, which for both Agrippa and Paracelsus was the highest kind of occult art. The former wrote of divine angelic names:

Therefore sacred words [i.e. names] have not their power in magical operations, from themselves, but from the occult divine powers working in them in the minds of those who by faith adhere to them; [. . .] who have ears purged by faith, and by most pure conversation and invocation of the divine names are made the habitation of God, and capable of the divine influences. Whosoever therefore useth rightly these words or names of God with that purity of mind, shall both obtain and do many wonderful things. (3.11; Agrippa 1997, 476)

To which Paracelsus added with his usual lofty imagery:

He who inherits God's wisdom walks on water without wetting his feet; for in the true art inherited from God, man is like an angel. But what will wet an angel? Nothing. Similarly, nothing will wet the wise man. God is powerful and He wills it that His power be revealed to men and to angels in the wisdom of the arts. He wills it that the world and the earth be like Heaven. (*De fundamento scientiarum sapientiaeque,* I,13:306; Paracelsus 1951, 163)

Once again we have arrived at Dee's most ambitious magical program: he aspired for this state of *exaltatio* in order to understand fully the work of creation and become God's partner. His whole scientific program was subordinated to this goal, and this is why he was experimenting with astrological catoptrics as well as with the monad, extracted and transmuted from talismanic magic into sacred geometry and alchemy.

It would be a mistake, however, to limit Dee's magic to sources of hermetic neoplatonism such as Ficino, Agrippa, or Paracelsus. What makes his esoteric experiments fascinating is the ease of syncretism with which he freely exploited quite distinct traditions from medieval Baconian magic through Old Testament traditions to some semi-scientific, semi-popular practices of dubious origin.

A good point of departure is the technique of Artephius (*ars sintrillia*), which operated with glittering mirrors in order to bring the viewer into a trance where logic became suspended. The ancient and venerable nature of this practice was proved in the Bible, where we read about Joseph hiding a silver chalice in Benjamin's pouch saying, "Is not this it in which my lord drinketh, and whereby indeed he divineth?" (Genesis 44:5). It should be noted, however, that such divination in the Bible is usually both condemnable and condemned: "And he made his son pass through the fire, and observed times, and used enchantments, and dealt with familiar spirits and wizards: he wrought much wickedness in the sight of the Lord . . ." (2 Kings 20:21).

Dee seems to have tendentiously overlooked such warnings, both in the Bible and in his much admired Paracelsus, where he could read in the *Astronomia magna*: "Spirits often teach those persons who deal with them to perform certain ceremonies, to speak certain words and names in which there is no meaning. [. . .] On the whole, all these spirits surpass each other in deception and lies" (quoted by Hartman 1891, 149).

In the second book of Moses we learn that the priestly garment made for Aaron contained a golden breastplate with twelve shining jewels, symbolizing the twelve tribes of Israel. This shining breastplate could also be used for purposes of divination (helping the gazing prophet to fall into a trance) and it is in this sense that medieval lapidaries refer to this locus.[14] Paracelsus also spoke about a particular way of divination by using shining surfaces. He calls it *ars beryllistica*, which aims at gaining visions from diamonds, mirrors and other glossy materials, such as black coal:

> VISIONS. This species sees in crystals, mirrors, polished surfaces, and the like, things that are hidden, secret, present or future, which are present just as though they appeared in bodily presence. (Paracelsus 1894, 2:296; also 1:171)

The most important difference between *catoptromantia* and *crystallomantia* was that in the former the operator—after proper preparations and sufficient fasting—did not want to conjure spirits in the mirror;

rather he expected visions relating to the future. In scrying, the magus definitely aimed at calling spiritual beings (angels or the spirits of already dead persons), hoping to gain information, not necessarily about the future. In both cases the use of mediums was common.[15]

It seems that Dee possessed instruments for both kinds of magic: a shining black obsidian mirror may have been used to practice *ars sintrillia* or *catoptromantia*, that is, divination from mirrors (this mirror presently is in the British Museum, donated by the eighteenth-century eccentric aristocrat Horace Walpole), while his much exploited crystal ball served the purposes of scrying.[16] What becomes perplexing for the cultural historian is that Dee, acquainted with the most complex magical theories and techniques, finally ended up practicing this crudest form of divination and, having pursued it till the last days of his life, lost no faith in it at all.

Crystallomantia, or scrying, was relatively neglected in the works of Renaissance humanists, although some mentions can be found in the works of Trithemius and others, usually in contexts reciting the anti-magical condemnations of medieval authorities and encyclopedias, as in John of Salisbury's *Policraticus* or Gregorius Reisch's *Margarita philosophica nova*.[17] It seems that by the sixteenth century, crystallomantia became most widespread in popular culture as a common form of magic. We have two groups of sources to document such practices. Humanist literature, on the one hand, relates us anecdotes of such magical habits. Nearest to Dee's scrying practice is, for example, Cardano's story about the conjuration of a scryer boy who saw angels in the crystal by the help of Saint Helena.[18] Another type of source material for the popular usage of the crystal ball (or *beryl*, or *sphera*) is the protocols of witchcraft trials and ecclesiastical visitations. In such processes a routine question of the interrogation was "Have you told anything from crystal, glass, or mirror to people?"[19]

Needless to say, scrying was strictly damned by both secular and ecclesiastical law. In England law court processes took place in 1467, 1534, and 1549, and the 1541 statute against conjuration and witchcraft definitely prohibited it (Whitby 1985, 29–30). Since scrying was mostly used for finding lost or stolen property, the temptation to overlook the law was considerate. Although such practices were strictly private, almost all astrologers and alchemists can be suspected of having exercised it. Another Elizabethan astrologer and magus, Simon Forman, kept a journal not unlike Dee's, and he noted about the year 1584: "a reasonable, good, and quiet yere; but I had certain braulles and sclaunders fell out against me aboute detecting of one that had stollen certain thinges, whereby I was like to have bin spoiled." Although it appears he was dissociating himself from scrying at this point, by 1588 he openly admitted that he "began to practise necromancy and to call angells and spirits" (Forman 1849, 17).

It is worth noting that sixteenth- and seventeenth-century manuscript literature abounds in secret diaries, notes, and copies of "grimoires" revealing the widespread magical practices of the day—most of which were rooted in the medieval Solomonic art. Journals of actual divination are nevertheless more of a rarity: interested amateurs seemingly did not get much beyond collecting and copying magical materials, prayers, incantations, and books of rituals that, at least theoretically, provided equipment to lead the readers to success in contacting the spirit world.[20] This body of literature has recently been much discussed among historians,[21] and it was Stephen Clucas who has undertaken most work in recovering possible source materials of this kind for Dee's angel magic. In his (unfortunately still forthcoming) essay on "John Dee's angelic conversations and the *ars notoria*," he examines the relationship of Renaissance magic and medieval theurgy and comes to the conclusion that medieval ceremonial magic influenced more strongly the actual practices of Renaissance divination than hitherto imagined. Concentrating on Dee's spiritual diaries, he has convincingly shown that the rituals described in the various books of *ars notoria*, *ars Solomonis*, and *liber juratus* closely correspond to Dee's actual practices as described below. What is decisive in his proposition is that although this medieval literature was strictly illicit and those who had such books would not have spoken about them publicly, one of these collections crops up in Dee's library catalogue. Dee possessed a fourteenth-century copy of the *Liber Juratus*, and the surviving copy has preserved his handwriting (R&W DM70).[22]

Although Clucas has meticulously verified the influence of medieval theurgy on Dee, he has somewhat tendentiously neglected the impact of Renaissance publications of "high magic" that Dee also carefully studied. He himself cites Dee's glosses from the spiritual diaries among which there are fewer references to spurious, medieval theurgic works than citations of distinguished humanists such as Ficino, Reuchlin, and Agrippa.[23] One should note that in one of his copies of Agrippa's *De occulta philosophia* Dee could read Pietro d'Abano's treatise on the elements of magic in which the picture of a magic seal (see Figure 7.4) has striking visual similarity to Dee's Golden Talisman.[24]

This fact should be a reminder to us not to try to explain Dee's magic, yet again, from one single type of source material. It is obvious that his, too, was a syncretic mind and had enough venerable examples

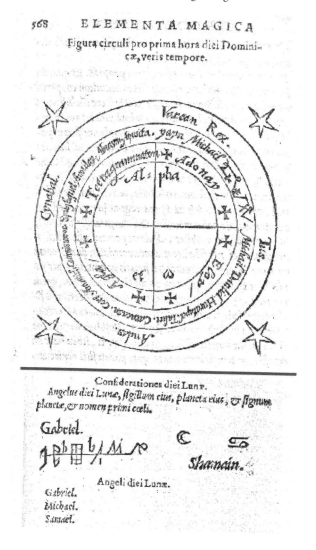

FIGURE 7.4 Pietro d' Abano's magic seal from Agrippa's 1550 edition of *De occulta philosophia* (Basel, 1550), 568. Herzog August Bibliothek, Wolfenbüttel [Na 146].

before him not to be afraid of amalgamating various traditions. No doubt, by the time of the angelic conversations he had become disappointed with most of the sciences for which he had had such an enthusiasm earlier. His former studies of the hermetic magi, however, clearly manifest themselves in his late writings, too.

This will become even more plausible if we consider the long overlap during which Dee was equally occupied with scholarly pursuits (producing the *Mathematicall Praeface* and the *General and Rare Memorials*) and mystical revelations (he started praying to God for illumination in 1569). He definitely undertook extensive and practical use of the crystal, making it a habitual action, from 1579. Already before that, on March 10, 1575, he had a chance to demonstrate "his glass" to the Queen's Majesty (Dee 1851, 17).

The first well-documented scrying session with the help of a medium, Barnabas Saul, took place on December 22, 1581 (MS Sloane 3188, fol. 8; Dee 1996, 1.6). Prior to this, Dee may have increased his interest in this area of magic during his continental journey in 1578, when he visited some German courts with the purpose of consulting medical doctors about the queen's condition. During this journey he met Leonhard Thurneysser, the famous physician, alchemist, and interpreter of Paracelsus, in Frankfurt on the Oder (Dee 1998, 4). He might have taken the meeting as an omen, since in exactly those years the learned doctor came under attack of accusations of conjuration and crystal-magic. A year later Franz Joel, a doctor from Greifswald, published a book about witches and black magic in which he openly attacked Thurneysser as a stubborn sorcerer whose source of knowledge—especially foreign languages, including Chaldeus, Hebrew, and Sanskrit—was his daemon, appearing in his "shewstone" (Kopp 1886, 1:117). Thurneysser had to write a passionate apology, very much in the manner of Dee's own "Digression Apologeticall" of the *Mathematicall Praeface* in which Dee compared the accusations against him to the attacks against his predecessors in the occult and mechanical sciences from Socrates and Apuleius, to Pico della Mirandola and Trithemius (Dee 1975, Aij^v).

As previously mentioned, Dee pursued angel magic until his death. During these years he had three steady scryers. He worked longest with Edward Kelly, whom he took on his journey to the East-Central European courts. Over the long years of common magical practice they developed a rather elaborate ritual with special circumstances and requisites that is now called Enochian magic. In the following subchapter I shall briefly summarize the practice of the "Enochian evocations."

The Choreography of the Scrying Sessions

Although there are no coherent descriptions of the scrying rituals in Dee's diaries, it is nevertheless possible to reconstruct the choreography they used. First, Christopher Whitby devoted the larger part of his Ph.D.

dissertation to the reconstruction and analysis of the "actions" (Whitby 1988/1981, 1:116–57). Later on, Geoffrey James published a selection of Dee's magical diaries in which he thematically rearranged the entries (cf. Dee 1994, 1–13, 179–91), then recently Stephen Clucas compared Dee's practices to the rituals of medieval theurgy (200?), while Deborah Harkness has also reconstructed the sessions, referring to the setting, the requisites, the angels, and Dee's audience (1999, 9–60). On the basis of the above studies one can summarize the rituals of Dee's ceremonial magic as follows.

The sessions needed two basic actors: the magus and the scryer. The magus performed the conjurations, chants and prayers which prepared the evocation of angels and spirits from the shew-stone. It was the scryer who gazed at the ball, and the apparitions spoke via his tongue. The most important requisite, thus, was the crystal ball. There are various accounts about the Doctor's different scrying instruments, and some of them have even been preserved in distinguished collections. Nicholas Clulee reproduces two items preserved in the British Museum, Dee's crystal ball and his obsidian speculum (1988, illustrations 8.1 and 8.2). The story of the descent of these magical instruments is complicated and their provenance in fact is dubious. Theodore Besterman summed up their origin in his book on crystal gazing as follows: on November 21, 1582, in his diary Dee himself refers to his great crystal ball as something that had been brought to him by his angels and looked "as big as an egg: most bryght, clere, and glorious" (cf. Dee 1581–1583, f59ᵛ). Throughout his writings, the Doctor referred to this crystal as "the shew-stone," or simply "the stone," but he also called it the "diaphanous globe" (58ʳ), the "first sanctified stone" and the "holy stone" (see Casaubon's summary in Dee 1659, #47). From his writings it is difficult to decide how many stones Dee had. The two items now in the British Museum certainly passed from hand to hand as belonging to the Doctor. The crystal ball had been included in the Cottonian Collection and was acquired by the Museum in 1700. It was described as a globe "of solid pink tinted glass, size and form of a full-grown orange" or as "a polished crystal" or as "a smoky ball" and has generally been considered as Dee's principal crystal ball.[25]

The obsidian mirror turned up in the collection of the writer, aristocrat, and father of the Gothic horror novel Horace Walpole. At his neogothic castle, Strawberry Hill, he collected all kinds of paraphernalia from the Middle Ages that belonged to mysterious magical practices. Thus, with delight he acquired a black obsidian mirror, probably of Mexican origin, which again was believed to have belonged to Doctor

Dee. Walpole described the item as follows: "Among other odd things he [the Lord Frederick Campbell] produced a round piece of shining black marble in leathern case, as big as the crown of a hat, and asked me what that could possibly be; I screamed out, 'Oh, Lord, I am the only man in England that can tell you! it is Dr. Dee's black stone.'" Later on, in 1842, the item was put up at the Strawberry Hill sale with the following description: "A singularly interesting and curious relic of the superstitions of our ancestors—the celebrated speculum of kennel coal, highly polished, in a leathern case. It is remarkable for having been used to deceive the mob, by the celebrated Dr. Dee, the conjuror, in the reign of Queen Elizabeth" (Walpole's letter and the auction catalogue quoted by Besterman 1965, 21). Although Dee in his own writings never specifies the obsidian mirror, he indeed may have had such a piece, since his most appreciated Paracelsus spoke at length about visions that could be gained by methods of "beryllistica" from shining black pieces of coal or other similar materials.[26]

In case of the tandem of Doctor Dee and Edward Kelly, the magus acted also as a scribe, meticulously recording the actions. Here follows the description of preparations preceding their very first common session:

> He [Kelly] then settled him self to the Action: and on his knees at my desk (setting the Stone before him) fell to prayer and entreaty, &c. In the mean space, I in my Oratory did pray, and make motion to god and his good Creatures for the furthering of this Action. And within one quarter of an hour (or less) he had sight of one in the stone. (Mortlake, March 10, 1582—Dee 1996, 1.8; 1998, 28)

And here is an example of the preliminary prayers:

> PRAYER. O beginning and fountain of all wisdom, gird up thy loines in mercy, and shadow our weaknesse; be merciful unto us, and forgive us our trespasses: for those that rise up saying there is no God, have risen up against us, saying, Let us confound them: Our strength is not, neither are our bones full of marrow. Help therefore O eternal God of mercy. . . . (Cracow, April 14, 1584; Dee 1659, 82)

Another very important prayer is included in the collection titled *Fundamenta invocationum* (Dee 1588), called "The Fundamental Obesance." Its tone and vocabulary are characteristic for Dee's magical diction:

> O, IEHOVAH ZEBAOTH, I John Dee (your unworthy servant) most earnestly invoke and call upon your divine power, wisdom and goodness. I humbly and faithfully seek your favour and assistance to me in all my

deeds, words, and thoughts, and in the promoting, procuring, and min-gling of your praise, honour, and glory. Through these, your twelve mys-tical Names: ORO, IBAH, AOZPI, MOR, DIAL, HCTGA, OIP, TEAA, PDOCE, MPH, ARSI, GAIOL, I conjure and pray most zealously to your divine and omnipotent majesty, that all your angelic spirits (whose mystical names are contained in this book, and whose offices are herein briefly noted) might be called from any and all parts of the universe, or at any time in my life, through the special domination and controlling power of your holy names (which are also in this book). Let them come most quickly to me. Let them appear visibly, friendly, and peacefully to me. Let them remain visible according to my will. Let them vanish from me and from my sight when I so request. Let them give reverence and obedience before you and your 12 mystical Names. I command that they happily satisfy me in all things and at all times in my life, by accomplishing each and every one of my petitions. [. . .] According to your united ministry and office O God. AMEN. Through You, Jesu Christe, AMEN. (Dee 1994, 120)

Not only the prayers, but the chaste life of the magicians, fasting, and concentrated piety were to ensure the success of the magical operations. As Uriel warned them, "There must be Conjunction of myndes in prayer, betwyxt you two, to God contynually" (March 10, 1582; Dee 1996, 1.9; 1998, 29).

Although magical primers often suggest special requisites, such as the Magus wearing a crown and a sword or a wand, there is no trace of such tools in Dee's records. On the other hand, they needed other instru-ments, the exact form and nature of which were dictated by the angels. The primary tool, naturally, was the crystal ball, but already during the early sessions Dee and his scryer received instructions to create a tablet as well as the special sigil of God, called Æmeth (Whitby 1988, 1: 118–24; cf. Figure 7.5).

FIGURE 7.5 Dee's *Sigillum dei*, or AEMETH. Based on Dee 1581–1583 [Sloane 3188], f. 30ʳ; recreated by Clay Holden, see <www.dnai.com/~cholden>.

> You must use a foure-square Table, two cubits square: Where uppon
> must be set Sigillum Dei, which is allready perfected in a boke of
> thyne. (March 10, 1582; Dee 1996, 1.19; 1998, 30)

From the context it becomes clear, that the phrase "a book of thine" meant
a certain book, called Soyga, probably a manuscript of such theurgic divination that has been identified as one of Dee's sources in developing his
Enochian magic. Uriel claimed that the book of Soyga "was revealed to
Adam in Paradise by the good angels of God" (Dee 1998, 28) and obviously Dee's ambition was to receive the same privilege through his actions.
    Uriel's further directions included conditions, such as that

> The seal is to be made of perfect wax. We have no respect of cullours.
> This seal must be nine ynches in diameter: the roundness must be 27
> ynches, and somewhat more. The Thicknes of it must be of an ynch and
> half a quarter, and a figure of a crosse must be on the back side of it. [. . .]
> The Table is to be made of sweet wood: and to be of two cubits high
> with 4 feete: with four feet of the former seals under the four feet. [. . .]
> Under the Table did seme likewise red sylk to lye foursquare: somewhat
> broader than the Table, hanging down. [. . .] Uppon this uppermost silk,
> did seme to be set the stone with the frame: right over and uppon the
> principal seal. (Dee 1996, 1.10; 1998, 30)

Not only were the instructions very detailed, but Dee also commemorated the exact circumstances of the actions:

> Note, all the tables before were by E.T. [Edward Talbot, alias E. Kelly]
> letter for letter noted out of the stone standing before him all the while:
> and the 7 Tables following wer[e] written by me as he repeated them
> orderly out of the stone. (April 28, 1582; Dee 1996, 3.10; 1998, 40)

We furthermore learn that twelve banners or flags were also needed, each
embroidered with a name of God, and, then, all this furniture was arranged in the form of "a temple" where Enochian evocation could be
practiced. Geoffrey James suggests that the sessions may have been out-
doors (Dee 1994, 181) but from the spiritual diaries one can identify in
fact a variety of locations, most of them in the studies of their various
dwelling places. The temple was constructed in the following manner:
the place of working was enclosed by a magical circle, which was called
"Terra"; the banners were propped at the circle's edge; a red silk rug was
placed in the centre of the circle; four small waxen tablets were arranged

in a square pattern in the centre of the silk rug; the table was balanced upon the wax tablets; the large wax tablet was placed on the center of the table. Then a silk tablecloth was draped over the table, covering the large wax tablet; the crystal was laid on the top of the tablecloth, balanced on the wax tablet (cf. Figure 7.6).

An extremely important part of the actions was the magus' obligation to record all the happenings, including the prayers, the conjurations, and a detailed description of the apparitions as well as the conversations with the spirits.

Performed upon the prayers, the conjurations were of several types, such as the "heptarchic conjurations," which consisted of the attributes of Kings and Princes; in fact, Dee devoted a whole book to describing and identifying the names of these angelic hierarchies (*De heptarchia mystica*, cf. Dee 1588). Another type of conjuration was the "Angelic Keys," which were dictated in the Enochian language and were later translated by Dee into English. His book *48 claves angelicae* (cf. Dee 1584) contained these sacred and powerful texts.

At this point it is necessary to examine the nature of the angelic language. In the 1970s an Australian linguist, Donald Laycock subjected it to the most thorough examination and distinguished two layers in it. The specimen of the *lingua adamica* that was communicated through

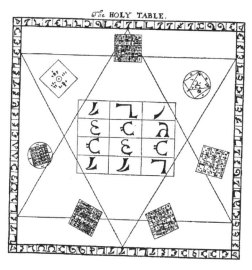

FIGURE 7.6 The "Holy Table" and its arrangement. Based on Casaubon's edition of Dee 1659, *77 and Dee 1581–1583 [Sloane 3188]; see <www.dnai.com/~cholden>.

Kelly during the first scrying sessions (known as the *Liber Logaeth*) is rich in repetition, rhyme, alliteration and other patterns characteristic of poetry and magical charms. From this Laycock has concluded that Kelly must have been in trance, "speaking in tongues," when receiving these messages. As opposed to this, the Enochian language received later (*48 claves angelicae*) appears more like a real language, generated from set elements. In Dee's diaries there is a translation provided for these texts, which would allow speculation about its grammar. We also know that these texts were dictated to Kelly letter by letter, as opposed to the earlier trance-like flow of speech. As Laycock suggests, 'this is exactly the type of text produced if one generates a string of letters on some random pattern' (op. cit., 40). Although the Enochian language appears to be very strange, it is not entirely impossible to reconstruct its morphology and syntax. Interestingly, according to Laycock, there is nothing strikingly un-English about the grammar, and he was able to compile an extensive dictionary of more than 2400 words, together with phonology and alphabet.

As for the latter, Laycock has noted that the script may have had a common origin with Pantheus' Enochian alphabet published in his alchemical handbook, *Voarchadumia* (1530, 14–15). As is well known, the British Library copy of this book belonged to Dee and preserves his extensive marginal notes. In spite of this, Laycock has reasoned that Dee's Enochian alphabet bears no relation to that in Pantheus' book although the latter may have provided the idea.[27] About the transcendental validity of the angelic language, he sceptically suggested that the angels' 'limitations are those of Kelly; their occasional sublimities, those of Dee. If the true voice of God comes through the shewstone at all, it is certainly as through a glass darkly' (Laycock 1994, 64).

The highest type of conjurations consisted of the "Invitations to the Angels of the Four Quarters" (cf. the *Tabula bonorum angelorum* and the *Fundamenta invocationum* in Dee 1588). These rituals were given by the spirit world during the sessions in Prague and Trebona, and these books contain detailed invocations to all classes of angels. The book starts with "the Great Table" from which the angels of this book have been derived—this is a table of alphabetical characters from which the names could be generated through various cabalistical permutations (cf. Figure 7.7). This table was reformed by the Archangel Raphael on April 20, 1587. The book also contains "the great circle of the quarters," the circle consisting of four triads with the twelve names of God. These names were extracted "from the four lines of the holy spirit, which govern all

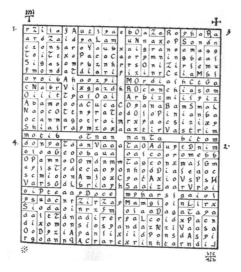

FIGURE 7.7   The "Great Table" from *Tabula bonorum angelorum*. Based on Dee 1588 [Sloane 3191]; see <www.dnai.com/~cholden>.

creatures on the earth (both visible and invisible). They are carried upon twelve banners" (Dee 1994, 119). The following chapters contain invocations to the twenty-four seniors—one call to the six seniors of each hemisphere—then come the angels of medicine (again according to quarters), then the angels of precious stones, the angels of transformation, the angels of the four elements, of natural substances, of transportation, of the mechanical arts, and, finally, of secret discovery. The collection of conjurations is preceded by a special prayer, "The Fundamental Obesance," as quoted above.

I think that nothing shows more emblematically the dramatic changes in Dee's intellectual career than his attitude toward the mechanical arts. He had always been deeply preoccupied with *magia naturalis*, that is, the creating of machines and instruments. As we remember, in his youth he himself constructed a movable toy, a "scarab," which was used in a school drama performance in Cambridge (Dee 1851, 6). Later, he became a passionate collector of mechanical, astronomical, and maritime instruments. He devoted almost poetically elevated passages to this art in his *Mathematicall Praeface*, including an eager rejection of those who called these mechanical experiments sorcery:

And for these, and such like marveilous Actes and Feates, Naturally, Mathematically, and Mechanically, wrought and contriued: ought any

honest Student, and modest Christian Philosopher, be counted, & called
a Coniurer? (Dee 1975, Ai^v)

It is ironic to see that at the age of sixty-five he was still craving for
accomplishments in mechanics, but he hoped for success only from the
angels of the mechanical arts by means of conjuration. He invoked the
angels as follows:

> This is the invitation to the four good angels of the East,
>   who are skilled and powerful in the Mechanical Arts:
> O YOU FOUR HOLY & TRUTHFUL MINISTERS of omnipotent God, our
> Creator, CNBR, NBRC, BRCN, and RCNB, who are in the Eastern part of the
> world, and who hast by our God been charged and committed with
> His ministry to practice, impart, teach, and communicate perfect skill
> in all arts mechanical, to the praise, honour, and glory of our God. I,
> John Dee, the baptized and maked slave of our Creator, faithfully,
> prudently, and powerfully desiring to be devout, do humbly require
> and vehemently petition from all of you, named above, through the
> omnipotent wisdom of the same, our God and Creator, and through
> this holy and mystical Name, HCNBR, that at whatever time in the
> future of my entire life, that I would call you by name or invoke any,
> each, or all of you through this name of God, HCNBR, that you imme-
> diately come to me and appear to me, benignly, peacefully, personally,
> and visibly, and that you be friendly and favourable to me, and that
> you discharge, implement, and make perfect immediately, truly, plen-
> tifully, manifestly, and perfectly any and all of my petitions concerning
> the Arts Mechanical as well as other mechanical conclusions and ex-
> periments. Through this mystical name of God, HCNBR, AMEN. (Dee
> 1994, 168)

From the above prayer it can also be clearly seen that the angelic names
were generated through simple permutations of groups of letters.

In order to proceed with the account of Dee's ritual magic, mention
needs to be made of the orders of angels, who were the most important
agencies of this type of theurgy. The question of angelology, as it developed from the speculations of Pseudo-Dionysius through the scholastic
philosophers to the Renaissance theologians and white or black magicians, is an extremely difficult subject.[28] Apart from the writings of medieval
theologians on angelology—with which he was also familiar[29]—Dee could
rely on a number of Renaissance authors whose works he kept in his
library. Agrippa's *De occulta philosophia* was a primary source, where in
chapter 3.24 he would find the names of spirits and that how they related

to the planets and the zodiac, and the ranks of good and evil spirits. Similarly, in Trithemius' treatise *De septem secundeis* he found information about the planetary angels governing history. The Doctor had no fewer than three copies of this work and there is no doubt that he consulted it thoroughly.[30] Paracelsus, then, provided another tradition of interpreting angels, associating them with elemental spirits. All these could support the ambitions of the scholar concerning the feasibility and safe Christian framework of contacting the spirit world. And, beyond these learned sources, there was also the secret medieval lore, the Solomonic *ars notoria*, which heavily relied on angel magic composed of rituals and cabalistic manipulations with the Hebrew angelic names.[31]

It is also true that innumerable sources warned against the dangers of angel magic, especially that evil spirits could take the form of benevolent daemons and thus deceive even the pious practitioner. It is also true, that such passages could be found even in the writings of Agrippa and Paracelsus, but, as I have already mentioned, Dee seems to have not been bothered by these caveats. His confidence and trust in his angels could never be shaken.[32]

James set up the following typology of the angelic hierarchies (Dee 1994, 183–87). The evocations were used to summon three interrelated hierarchies of angels. First was "the Heptarchical Royalty" which were believed to govern "all earthly actions, & disperse of the will of the Creator." These angels were related to the seven planets and the seven days of the week. In second rank there were "the Angels of the Aires" which ruled the various countries of the world. One conjured them "to subvert whole countries without armies, to get the favour of all the human princes, & to know the secret treasure of the waters, and the unknown caves of the earth." These angels were primarily related to the twelve houses of the zodiac. The third rank of angels were "of the Four Quarters." They were believed to have been "put onto the earth so that the Devil's envious will might be bridled, the determinations of God fulfilled, and his creatures kept and preserved." Conjuring them was expected to result in obtaining various semi-divine powers. They were related to the four elements and the four compass points. As James notes, this complex angelic society covered all planetary, zodiacal, and elemental operations and aimed at controlling hundreds of named and thousands of unnamed angelic creatures (in Dee 1994, 183).

Although compared with other types Dee's magic was of rather puritanical character and used very sparingly incantations, fumigations, candles, and such elaborate rituals (Clulee 1988, 206), the importance of talismans, which also were to secure the success of the actions, should not be underestimated. Dee's great wax seal, the *Sigillum Dei,* has already been mentioned; next to this, the most important talisman was based on a vision that Edward Kelly saw in Cracow, on June 20, 1584:

> Δ. It is first to be noted, that this morning (early) to E.K. lying in his bed, and awake, appeared a Vision, in manner as followeth: One standing by his beds head, who patted him on the head gently, to make him the more vigilant. He seemed to be cloathed with feathers, strangely wreathed about him all over, &c.
>
> There appeared to him [E.K.] four very fair Castles, standing in the four parts of the world: out of which he heard the sound of a Trumpet. [. . .] Out of every Gate then issued one Trumpeter, whose Trumpets were of strange form, wreathed, and growing bigger and bigger toward the end. [. . .] After the Trumpeter followed three Ensign bearers. After them six ancient men, with white beards and staves in their hands. [. . .] The four houses are the 4 Angels of the Earth, which are the 4 Overseers, and Watch-towers, that the eternal God in his providence hath placed against the usurping blasphemy, misuse, and stealth of the wicked and great enemy, the Devil. [. . .] In each of these Houses, the Chief Watchman, is a mighty Prince, a mighty Angel of the Lord: which hath under him 5 Princes. The seals and authorities of these Houses, are confirmed in the beginning of the Wold. Unto every one of them, be 4 characters, (Tokens of the presence of the Son of God: by whom all things were made in creation). (Dee 1659, 168–70)

The vision had an interesting aftermath: Kelly had another visitation, this time by a spirit which identified himself as Ave, and who helped them to interpret the vision of the four castles. For example, he called their attention to the number of creatures that passed out of the four gates: " 'The number 16 is a perfect number, consisting of 1.3.6.1 and 5.' He said furthermore, 'God the father is a standing pillar' " (168). The result of the interpretation was the creation of a complex talisman (see Figure 7.8), a golden disc version of which survives in the British Museum today.

One should not forget about the fact that the spiritual diaries are not only philosophical and mystical papers abounding in visions, prophecies, and theoretical speculations about the Enochian language, but they are also rich and vivid historical documents revealing events as well as the general way of life of wandering humanists who in great number tried to secure noble patronage for themselves, all over the courts of the continent. Since these microhistorical aspects have been explored by Wayne

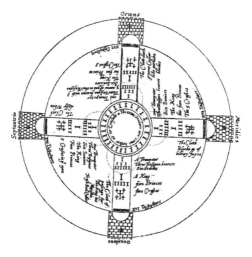

FIGURE 7.8   The "Golden Talisman." Based on Casaubon's edition of Dee 1659, *79. Author's copy.

Shumaker (1982); in two of Deborah Harkness' essays (1996 and 1997) and I have also presented a typology of the contents of the angelic conversations elsewhere (2002, 2004, and 200?), I shall now turn to examine Dee's theology and religion. Quite obviously, this is the framework in which one can attempt a general evaluation of Dee's angel magic, assessing what was realized of the Doctor's original goals during the twenty-year-long project, and paying particular attention to how the practice of scrying became integrated into Dee's ideology.

✳ DEE'S RELIGION AND THEOLOGY

The Theological Framework of His Vision

> Thus we see, that the heavenly contemplacion in this Science is no common ascending, nor for every mans pitch, neither is it to be gotten of them whiche are carried upward with one winge only, but is familier to very few, namely to them whiche have seriously reduced them selves to Unitie. [. . .] Seacret and Caelestiall is this Adepted Philosophy, wherein whosoever desireth to have true knowledge, the same must be contemplative and solitary, free from common tumult. The Spirit of GOD doth breath where it lifteth, illumineth where he wills, and whome he protecteth & shadoweth with his divine grace, he leadeth

into all knowledge of truth. Let his therefore whiche shall receive such knowledge, give thanks to the Lord GOD; & let him be answerable to that his knowledge in the deeds of Charity & in Christian lyfe, that GOD may be glorified in such Science, & the Worker of good works receive the reward of mercy, even eternall felicity in the kingdom of heaven, Amen. (Tymme 1963, 25–26)

The above passage is from Thomas Tymme's preface to his planned English translation of Dee's *Monas*, which, unfortunately, he never completed. The quotation refers to the science of alchemy and it is clear that Tymme believes it should be discussed within a theological setting. For Tymme, as for many Renaissance scholars the ultimate purpose of alchemy was to purify the soul and, by liberating it from base matter, to transmute it to higher intellectual reality. This theological interpretation was in perfect harmony with Dee's own doctrines, which, as we have seen, strived for a synthesis between the dignified ambition of man to learn all the secrets of Nature on the one hand, and on the other a concurrent and humble attitude in which he continued regarding himself as part of a divine plan and hierarchy. As Tymme asked with deep conviction: "do not all things flow from Unity through the goodness of One?" (17).

Because of this faith, it is impossible to interpret Dee's natural philosophy without taking into consideration a whole wide framework of metaphysics, theology, and occult symbolism. Furthermore, we also have to realize that in the end this theological and ideological constitution in fact wholly absorbed the scientific foundations.

Dee's ideology can be examined from two angles. One is the nature of his general doctrinal opinion. In this respect a comparison between his scholarly works and his spiritual diaries may be helpful. Second are his denominational attitudes, that is, his association with the religious struggles of the Reformation. The latter problem is particularly interesting, since some historians have emphasized his strong Protestantism, while others have spoken of his universalist, interconfessionalist religion. A peculiar case is that of Frances Yates, who in her *Astreae* (1975) presented Dee as a Protestant patriot, while in *The Rosicrucian Enlightenment* (1972) she established the image of the universalist, Rosicrucian Dee. Finally, in *The Occult Philosophy* (1979) we find both arguments amalgamated.

In relation to the present investigation of *exaltatio*, the first question is more essential. However, in respect to Dee's management of the unresolvable tensions and paradoxes of magical ambitions that inevitably seem to have accompanied the aspiration for *exaltatio*, the second aspect is equally significant, not simply for the purpose of examining the individual conscience, but because this provides a way to examine the social strategies by which the magus tried to accomplish his self-fashioning, seek patronage, and justify himself in the eyes of the other members of his community.

I believe that previous analyses of Dee's major works have already revealed the seemingly constant, hardly altering contours of Dee's theology. It centered on his deep admiration for the work of Creation and its Maker, and he never seems to have been shaken in his belief that man was privileged to become finally a partner of God, sharing his knowledge and his creative energies.

Within this constant, general theological frame, Dee's concrete programs and projects working towards the realization of *exaltatio* changed from time to time, in evolving from scientific investigations to magic and hermeticism to the practice of scrying, as I have shown above. Thinking about Dee's theology underlying the angelic conversations, one cannot fail to recall his speculations related to language philosophy and the questions of the *lingua adamica*. Thomas Tymme, in his preface to the *Monas hieroglyphica*, also referred to the angelic tongue in a theological context:

> Adam, before his fall, was by God endowed with such excellent knowledge in naturall philosophie, that is to say, with the understanding of the secrets of nature & the naturall reasons of all things, that he gave to all the Creatures of God their proper names. [. . .] And albeit the perfecion of that knowledge was much weakened by his fall, yet had he so much light thereof, that he was the first founder and inventor of Arte. (1963, 11)

The passage continues with references to Adam's posterity and the heritage of knowledge bequethed by the primordial ancestor:

> For his posterity building upon that first foundacion & by experience and advantage of his Invencion, & perfecting that which was but rude in the beginning, erected two Tables of Stone, wherein they engraved their naturall Philosophie not in letters (which were not then known) but in Hieroglyphicall characters, to the end that the presage, concerning the general Deluge to come [. . .] that if it were possible they might prevent the perill. (12)

The iconography of this pseudepigraphical myth shows parallels with that of the Bible (for example, the two stones, such as the ones containing the Laws of Moses), but as though Adam here were not the Biblical father, more like the demiurge of the *Corpus hermeticum* whose archetypal knowledge is thought to have been preserved in a hieroglyphical ur-writing. No doubt, Dee felt himself entitled to acquire this hiero-glyphical language; at the time of the *Monas* he thought that it could be generated through his magic diagram, while later on he put the stress on a more direct learning method, the angelic conversations. For him, like for Tymme, Adam was the perfect model and measure whom the magus wanted to emulate, and the key to making man the partner of God was the angelic language.

Dee's past as a humanist scholar and a bibliophile is underscored by the fact, that, even in this later mystical period, he was thinking in terms of books, texts, and writing. These traditional media remained for him equally as important as the new type of medium, the human scryer. There was a period during the time of the angelic conversations when Dee would call only one type of writing *books*, namely his own journals of the scrying séances. The most fascinating episode in this respect is the one discovered by C. H. Josten in a portion of the spiritual diaries not published by Casaubon.[33] Dee and Kelly, while staying in Prague, at a scrying session of April 10, 1586, were met by a spirit who identified himself as follows: "I am the Spirit of Wisdom. I have instructed you in the knowledge of Christ, which is the science of all things" (Dee 1965, 248). Then he commanded the Englishmen to burn all the *books* so far dictated to them by the angels, and to throw into the fireplace Kelly's small box in which he kept his *lapis philosophorum*. Here follows Dee's list of the journals to be eliminated:

> I sundered the books, or rather those folio-volumes which were either bound or decently sewn together [. . .] so they were 28 in all (namely four times seven). And they contained (as in a continued narrative) all the things which, from the first hour of our (namely EK's and JD's) conjunctions until the present hour, had been revealed and shown to us by God's faithful angels and by God Himself. And in one of those 28 volumes there were 48 individual books, most mystical and more valuable than the value of all things in the whole world might be accounted. For in them the admirable divine wisdom and power were contained which, at a time determined by God, we must use to His honour and glory. There was another volume which was ancillary to those 48 individual books; its title was '48 Claves Angelicae' and it was written entirely in the angelic language. [. . .] Another volume contained that wisdom and science, with which Enoch (by

God's will) was imbued; where there was also something agreeing with the testimony of the Apostle Judas. In that book there were contained all sacred books, full and perfect, all those books, I say, which, after and before the incarnation of Christ, had been written by the Spirit of Truth. (Dee 1965, 249–50)

Most of the books mentioned by Dee are in fact identifiable among the surviving spiritual diaries.[34] They contained either the rules, grammar, and vocabulary of the angelic language, or the magic invocations to contact the angels, or specific pieces of information provided by the angels, some of them already translated into English, some still to be deciphered. It is obvious that the Doctor had not the slightest doubt about their authenticity. More surprising is that the Englishmen were willing to obey the spiritual command and indeed burned these most valuable texts. The session was witnessed by Francesco Pucci, too, who could see how Dee cited the sacrifice of Abraham and, taking spiritual consolation from the Biblical story, threw the folios into the fire (Dee 1965, 251). The climax of the situation was Kelly's obligation to anni-hilate his magic powder and Dee gave a very dramatic account of the sufferings of his companion. The session was brought to an end by the following promise of "The Voice":

Later on make a prayer before Me, invoking the name of the Father in the name of Jesus, his Son. And be aware that, as these things were put in the fire, in the same way you will receive them again. (254)

This magic episode and the promise thereof may have reminded Dee of the wondrous rebirth of Guillaume Postel, because he noted on the magrin: "A *restitution* of the things burned and committed to the fire is promised" (ibid.).

This is where the journal fragment found by Josten ends and we cannot help but agree with the editor that from a twentieth-century viewpoint it is very difficult to judge either Dee's seeming credulity, or Kelly's possible motivations in interpreting the strict commands. On the other hand, the fragment enlightens a hitherto obscure part of the Casaubon edition, from which we learn that on April 29, Dee and Kelly became aware of a gardener-like figure in the yard of their house in Prague. The small gardener lit a fire resembling a strange pillar. They both hurried into the garden, but the mysterious character by that time was gone. The fire was also extinguished but under an almond tree they found three of the previously consumed books. The person then returned again and brought back all the perished books (Dee 1659, 418–19). The journal does not mention the restitution of Kelly's powder, but during the séance of April 18, 1587, he held it in his hand, so the black bag must have been returned, too (Dee 1659, *9).[35]

The miracle of the books, performed by God and the Spirit of Wisdom, appears to be the climax of Dee's religious experience. Next to this his explorations of the *lingua adamica* and the prophetic visions communicated by the angels should be mentioned. The most important layer of the angelic conversations consists of those pieces of information that were meant as direct instructions for learning the primordial language. These messages communicated names of angels as well as ritualistic expressions in the Enochian language, all being of cabalistic nature, each letter having numeric equivalents, too. Dee's *idée fixeé* was that the comprehension of these numerical relations would lead to the ultimate enlightenment. Interestingly, the mathematician did not entirely disappear from the obsessed enthusiast as seen when he caught the angels in an arithmetic miscalculation. Kelly was certainly a far less able mathematician than his master, but his (or the angel's) wit was more than a match for Dee's suspicion:

NALVAGE ANGEL: . . . Pray . . .

Δ. We prayed. There is an error in the last, not in the Number, but in the Letter. I will first go through the Letters, and after come to the Numbers. How many words have you received this day?

Δ. Thirteen, where of Iaida was said to be the last of the call.

NALVAGE: . . . They be more worth than the Kingdom of Poland. Be patient, for these things are wonderful.

N (The number must needs go to) the sixth, descending 309.

A The 7th ascending 360.

O The 9th ascending 1000.

O The 13th ascending 1050.

V The 17th ascending 2004. It is Vooan. It may be sounded Vaoan.

Adde those last Numbers.

Δ. Vooan *is spoken with them that fall, but Vaoan with them that are, and are glorified.* The devils have lost the dignity of their sounds.

Δ. They make 4723.

NALVAGE . . . *It is called the Mystical roote in the highest ascendent of transmutation.*

Δ. These phrases are dark; when it shall please God they may be made plain.

NALVAGE . . . *It is the square of the Philosophers work.*

Δ. You said it was a roote.

NALVAGE . . . *So it is a roote square. (Dee 1659, 80)*

After this somewhat humorous quotation it is worth returning to a passage that sums up more theoretical information about the strength of numbers and the cabalistical ur-language. At the session held in Cracow on April 21, 1584, it was Archangel Gabriel himself who joined Nalvage to deliver the teachings to Dee and his scryer:

> GABRIEL: . . . Every Letter signifieth the member of the substance whereof it speaketh. Every word signifieth the quiddity of the substance. The Letters are separated, and in confusion: and therefore, are by numbers gathered together [. . .].
>
> *E.K. Whether is this Language known in any part of the World or no? if it be, where and to whom? (Dee 1659, 92).*

This introduction is followed by what I have already quoted about Adam's privilege in his innocence as being able to speak a common language with God. The angelic diction here really reaches the poetical elevation of Pico's *De hominis dignitate*. Then we learn about the corruption of the wicked demon, Coronzon, who caused man to lose his honorific status. Being expelled from Paradise, man had to reinvent a new language that still contained fragments of the original angelic tongue: "he began to learn of necessity the Language in which he uttered and delivered to his posterity, the nearest knowledge he had of God his Creatures" (ibid.). The following linguistic explications are really amazing:

> GABRIEL: And from his own self divided his speech into three parts, twelve, three, and seven: the number whereof remaineth, but the true forms and pronounciations want; and therefore is not of that force that it was in his own dignity, much lesse to be compared with this that we deliver which Adam verily spake in innocency, and was never uttered nor disclosed to man since till now. (Dee 1659, 92)

Step by step, a complex myth unfolds concerning the history of the angelic language. After the Fall Adam spoke a degenerated form of it, which became ur-Hebrew. One of Adam's descendants, Enoch, however, was selected by the Lord to become a seer, who was given the knowledge of the old Adamic language. As Dee noted, "Let us show unto Enoch the use of the earth. And lo, Enoch was wise and full of the spirit of wisdom" (1659, 174).

The angels then told Dee about Enoch's prayer to God in which the Renaissance philosopher could recognize the archetype of his own desire for exaltation up to God:

> Oh Lord, is there any who is mortal that can measure the heavens? How, therefore can the heavens enter into man's Imagination? [. . .] Behold, Lord, how shall I ascend into the heavens? The air will not carry me, but resisteth my folly. I fall down, for I am of the earth. (1659, 196–97)

This difficulty could be overcome by the help of angel magic, which was to be performed through the holy tables, donated by God. The operation was expected to achieve even quasi-immortality:

> Behold, I offer these Tables unto thee. I require nothing but thee, through thee, and for thy honour and glory. *Yet I hope that I shall be satisfied and shall not die* (as thou hast promised) until thou gather the clouds together, and judge all things. When in a moment I shall be changed and dwell with thee for ever. (1659, 197; emphasis mine)

According to the Enochian mythology in Dee's interpretation, after fifty days of enragement "the Lord appeared unto Enoch and was mercifull unto him, opened his eyes, that he might see and judge the earth" (Dee 1659, 174). And Enoch then decided to put down his experiences in a sacred book that he titled: LET THOSE THAT FEAR GOD AND ARE WORTHY—READ.

Unfortunately Enoch's teachings became corrupted as the holy language was distorted and forged by the devil. The memory of Enoch washed away and the mystical figures and their use—the gift of God delivered unto Enoch and unto the faithful—became replaced by the signs and tokens of the devil. "These signs they call Characters [and] as the painter imitates the gestures of man, so doth the Devil imitate the substance and things created and made by God" (ibid.). As a result of Satan's machinations and the unfaithfulness of mankind, this Enochian magic was entirely forgotten and replaced by black magic. But the archangel Raphael, sent by God, now assured Dee and Kelly that they had been selected to be the recipients of this restitute knowledge:

And so Raphael descended, and he was full of the power and spirit of God. And he delivered a Doctrine, but simple, plain, full of strength and the power of the holy Ghost. [. . .] It is this self-same Art which is delivered unto you as an infallible doctrine. For now it hath pleased God to deliver this Doctrine again out of darkness and to fulfill his promise with thee for the Books of Enoch. (Dee 1659, 77)

No wonder that taking Enoch's mythology seriously as a supernatural parallel of all human sciences, Dee became obsessed by the wish to learn and practice the Enochian language, that "toungue of power." The fruits that were bestowed upon Enoch were now offered to him. At least this is what he must have understood from the promises of the Lord, transmitted to him through the angels and interpreted by his scryer, Edward Kelly. What he hoped to achieve was access to the mysteries of creation; as the angel promised, "I give you the understanding of many thousand secrets, wherein you are yet but children" and the ultimate guarantee conjured up the possibility of true *exaltatio*: "therefore you may do anything" (Dee 1994, 11).

I firmly believe that a plausible interpretation of Dee's angel magic must approach this curious phenomenon from the direction of the *lingua admica*, the search for the perfect language. Furthermore, when placing Dee's "scientific" program in a wider context, we see how Dee's visions conjure up a symbolic "world empire," consisting of knowledge (embodied by his library), wisdom (as communicated to him by the angels), and faith (represented by a reformed Christianity, a universalist and interconfessionalist religion).

The majority of visions included in the diaries appear to be verbalized versions of large scale images related to the divine cosmic order and the world of angels sustaining it. The following quotation is of particular importance because it contains a conceptual explanation about the nature of visions:

There are two kind of visions, the one by infusion of will and descending, the other by infusion by permission and ascending. The first is of the image of the Will of God descending into the body, and adjoyned to the soul of man, whose nature is to distinguish things of his own likenesse, but shut up in prison in the body, wanteth that power; and therefore being illuminated by spiritual presence, inwardly, seeth now in part, as he shall hereafter do in the whole. But note, that every vision is according to the soul of man in power: and so is received of him that seeth. (Dee 1659, 88)

The above description also connects the idea of visions to the idea of exaltation, the ultimate end of every form of magic. As I have already quoted, on June 20, 1584, they received perhaps the most elaborate vision in Cracow, the one that became the basis for the Golden Talisman. Next to this visual semiotic compound, one also finds in the diaries a verbal interpretation of this revelation where Dee offers angelological explanations:

> I expound the Vision. The 4 houses are the 4 Angels of the Earth, which are the 4 Overseers, and Watch-Towers, that the eternal God in his providence hath placed, against the usurping blasphemy, misuse, and stealth of the wicked and great enemy, the Devil. [. . .] In each of these houses the Chief Watchman is a mighty Prince, a mighty Angel of the Lord: which hath under him 5 Princes. [. . .] Ensignes, upon the Image whereof, is death: whereon the Redemption of mankind is established, and with the which he shall come to judge the Earth. (1659, 170)

In fact most of their sessions contained elements of visions, since the angels usually contacted them in the form of visual apparitions. On April 15, 1587, during their stay in Trebona, Arthur became the communicator of a notable set of visions:

> My first begotten son (namely Arthur) was assigned to the Ministry of seeing and hearing. [. . .] Whereupon, Wednesday morning I brought the Childe to the holy Table, and set before him the Stone in the frame (my first sanctified Stone) and caused him on his knees, to say the foresaid Prayer. [. . .] There appeared to him (as he judged) divers little square figures, with pricks, and divers other figures and lines, which caused him with his own hand to imitate upon a paper with pen and ink.
> ARTHUR: "Two old men with black beards, and with golden crowns upon their heads, do appear. One is now gone: this holdeth his hand before him like a Maid. Now in the place of those square marks I see two lions, the one very exactly, and gaping. About the upper brim of the Stone they appear: and the lions' feet be waxing greater and greater. . . . (Dee 1659, *4–5)

From the diaries it also becomes clear that Dee embedded the visions in a perfectly balanced rhetorical framework. He was aware that the images communicated by the spirits were to be taken as parables and enigmas and he repeatedly asked the spirits for their interpretation. For example, on April 17, 1584, in Cracow they received a very complicated vision featuring a great whale, a naked man, a cave of lions, and cedar trees. The Doctor's inquiry concerning the meanings of the vision resulted in the following allegorical explanation:

GABRIEL: The naked man is Dee, the Childe is Kelly, the Prince is the Devil, the Hill is the World, the waters are the bosom of God, the 4 beasts are the 4 Elements, the 12 Trees are the 12 parts of the Heavens, &c. The rest are not to be spoken. . . . (Dee 1659, 104)

A considerable portion of the angelic communications offers obscure historical prognostications in the Enochian style of prophecy. The predictions foretell the coming of a new age in which Dee and Kelly would have an important role since they had been chosen by God to perform certain rituals in connection with the shift to the new epoch. Dee could hardly have been more explicit than when terrifying Emperor Rudolph with God's message about the Turks: "If you will hear me and believe me, you shall triumph. If you will not hear me, the Lord, the God that made Heaven and Earth putteth his foot against your breast, and will throw you headlong down from your seat" (1659, 231). Other strange prophecies related to the fate of England as well as to the future of Christianity in Europe:

After dinner, as E.K. was alone, there appeared unto him little creatures of a cubit high: and they came to the Still where he had the spirit of Wine distilling over out of a *Retorto:* And one of them (whose name they expressed Ben) said that it was in vain so to hope for the best spirit of the Wine. [. . .] He told of England, and said, That about July or November her Majesty should from heaven be destroyed; and that about the same time the King of Spain should dye. And that this present Pope at his Mass should be deprived of life before two years come to an end. And that another Pope, who should be *Decimus quintus* of his name; And that he would begin to reform things, but that shortly he should of the Cardinals be stoned to death. . . . (April 18, 1587; 1659, *12)

Prophecies were usually combined with visions, since the information derived from angels or spirits who appeared in the stone under special circumstances. The following excerpt shows general historical prophecies mixed with personal promises directed this time to Prince Łaski:

May 22, 1585, Niepolonicze.

E.K.: "I see a great Hill of fire, a very great Mountain, and it is as if it did hang in the aire: for I see the aire under it, and I see the Sun shine on it. The Mountain fire flameth not. Now the little boy that appeared last day, standeth on the top of this Mountain."

PUER: "God hath spoken unto you, and hath gathered you together, and lo, you are become a strong sword, with the which the Nations shall be cut down, and the God of Hosts shall stretch forth his hands; And behold, you are come, and now is the time you Satan shall reap. But Satan striveth fore against you; Behold Lasky thou art become rich; But have faith: for it overcometh riches, and shall beautifie and strengthen thee. [. . .] I have brought thee unto Steven [Bathory, the Polish king] and I will give him thee into thy hands. . . . (1659, 402)

A particularly complex set of visions can be found in the *Praefatio Latina* (Dee 1965), Dee's Latin translations of some of their actions in Prague during which the Holy Spirit in sessions divided into four acts revealed a variety of forecasts as well as commandments.[36] Dee introduced the revelations with the following words: "When the three of us were seated (I ready to write, Edward Kelly sitting opposite at the same table; Francesco Pucci sitting on a bench along the wall of the oratory), there descended from on high, with some sort of spiritual sound, a voice, near to the face of E.K. [. . .] Let us now lend then our ear to the words of the Holy Spirit which are very full of the highest consolation" (Dee 1965, 241). The voice then proceeded with consolation and warnings:

Lo and behold, raise yourselves and consider: Thus speaks He who is the Comforter, Whose candle is always there to delight His people, Who has covered the sons of Sion and their garments with joy. [. . .] Behold, I am the garment of Nature and that Mother who produces the fruits of heaven and earth. And behold, Sion is shattered to pieces by the hands of disobedient sons. Yet lo and behold, o you nations and people of the earth, o you sons of sin and defenders of darkness, I am now a widow. . . . (ibid.)

Some of the advice seemed to contain astrological overtones:

Direct your eyes upwards to the stars and tell the people: Look, I understand, His letter is the end of the word which means prescience of God, in the obedience of creatures, in the fullness of time. (Dee 1965, 242)

Subsequently the attentive and the sons of peace were offered an elevated summary of the struggle between the light and darkness and how mankind recurrently had broken the covenant with God and how finally the act of salvation had been fulfilled through Christ's sacrifice. In this narrative there can be felt an interesting, populist tone that might have urged Casaubon to accuse Dee of anabaptism:

> Yet, you faithful ones and sons of peace, o you who serve your Sempiternal Father, you shall today learn from me:
> At the beginning of the Faith, a promise of God was made *from out of Heaven* as from the place and from the foundations of Him who sends out the rays, and the abundance of His truth. [. . .] When angels brought the glad tidings of peace and consolation to the face of the earth, they did not take it to Jerusalem, nor to the Temple, nor the Holy of Holies, but they took it to the fields and amongst poor shepherds. [. . .] The Saviour of the world Himself (in whom you are saved and exalted by the honour of election) was immediately subjected to tyranny of the world and to the perversity of the powers of darkness. (Dee 1965, 243)

This account is amplified into an almost revolutionary apocalypticism in the following acts of the session, when the holy spirit seems to encourage a rather individual and radical understanding of church membership, too:

> Therefore the God of heaven and earth appears to you; to you who are shepherds, placed outside the polluted city; to you who desire to find the star and seek the visitation of Him Who will be coming to you. You will return to the Temple, armed with the scourge and the power of God, and you will eject those who justify themselves. [. . .] Submit yourselves to the Church to the extent you are of the Church. 1965, 244)

The prophecy propagates such an approval of universalist toleration that the Papal Nuncio may have justly abhorred it and one can only fear what might have happened to the Englishmen had they listened to Pucci's invitations to go to Rome and test their views in front of the Holy See:

> I shall therefore not stand trial in your courts, nor shall I acknowledge that you are judges. But I shall preach penitence to you. Whosoever wishes to be wise may look neither to the right nor to the left; neither towards this man who is called catholic, nor towards that one who is called a heretic; but may he look up to the God of heaven and earth and to his Son, Jesus Christ. . . . (1965, 245)

Visions and prophecies of this kind lead historians and interpreters (especially Frances Yates) to see Dee as the propagator of a new, universalist Christian church, which aimed at a position above and beyond the rivalling denominations.

Humanism, Religion, and Denomination

If Dee's theology was stable, his denominational sympathies—as the previously quoted visions showed—had much less permanence. His ambivalence seems to be connected with his self-fashioning and his secular ambitions, too.[37] His early career was characterized by a deeply religious, but denominationally neutral, interconfessionalist attitude, a hallmark of many humanists. To understand better Dee's "scholarly religiousness," one needs to address some general questions of Renaissance heterodoxy.

If one examines the particular doctrinal beliefs of the humanists, one can see neither uniformity nor a consequent attachment to one set of religious dogmas. One reason for this flexibility may be found in their scholarly self-assuredness, according to which they were inclined to think that narrowly defined rules and beliefs were for the general populace but not for the select few of intellectuals. One should not forget, however, about the special social standing of the humanists, namely that their ideological experimentations were in close connection with their self-fashioning, secular ambitions, as they maneuvred among the unpredictable circumstances of the patronage system.

Another motivation behind their syncretism could be an effort to merge pagan philosophy with Christian theology. These two aspects resulted in a general, nondenominational religiousness, which has been called interconfessionalism by modern historians. The use of the term goes back as far as Jakob Burckhardt. He observed how Renaissance individualism led to a total aesthetization of morals and even life itself:

> These intellectual giants, these representatives of the Renaissance, show, in respect to religion, a quality which is common in youthful natures. Distinguishing keenly between good and evil, yet they are conscious of no sin. Every disturbance of their inward harmony they feel themselves able to make good out of the plastic resouces of their own nature, and therefore they feel no repentance. The need of salvation thus becomes felt more and more dimly, while the ambitions and the intellectual activity of the present either shut out altogether every thought of a world to come, or else caused it to assume a poetic instead of a dogmatic form.[38]

Burckhardt's uncompromising classification—either a pagan sceptic or a Platonist poet—was refined by Paul Oskar Kristeller's pioneering examinations of humanism. As he wrote:

The view that the humanist movement was essentially pagan or anti-Christian cannot be sustained. [...] The opposite view, namely that Renaissance humanism was in its origin a religious movement, or even a religious reaction against certain antireligious tendencies in the Middle Ages, seems to me equally wrong and exaggerated. I am convinced that humanism was in its core neither religious nor anti-religious, but a literary and scholarly orientation, that could be and, in many cases, was pursued without any explicit discourse on religious topics by individuals who otherwise might be fervent or nominal members of one of the Christian churches. (Kristeller 1961, 74–75)

In this context it becomes understandable that the keen and witty humanists preferred the philological authenticity of an ancient text to its conformity to the dogmas of one or another denomination. This is why it becomes difficult to determine the denominational affiliations of many sixteenth-century scholars; even if we know that, their writings often reflect a more general, supra- or interconfessional character. It cannot be by chance that in the time of the early Reformation it was the humanists who pioneered manufacturing bold and often fantastic plans to reunite the split Christian world; they also proposed plans for universal, and unified religions that would reconcile Christians, Jews, and Muslims. Some of these plans were fabricated on the basis of intellectual rationalism, such as Thomas More's *Utopia*; others thought of religion as a pragmatically necessary ingredient of a well-working society—like Machiavelli in the *Discorsi;* and others were dreaming of a magical religion bringing about the universal harmony of the world.

Among these enthusiasts one can mention Francesco Giorgi, a Minorite Franciscan monk (1460–1540), who wrote the *De harmonia mundi totius* in 1525 and proposed the ultimate final concordance of the various "true dogmas." In this work he brought together the biblical prophets, Hermes Trismegistus, Plato, Aristotle, Saint John, Saint Paul, and the Church Fathers in order to assemble a mystical and pantheistic world picture. His last work, *In Sacram Scripturam problemata* (1536), employed cabalistic methods in Christian exegesis.[39]

Another such enthusiast was the already discussed Guillaume Postel who in 1547 met Mother Johanna in the Venetian *Ospedaletto di Santo Giovanni e Paolo* and he identified her as the Venetian Virgin and the Angelic Pope "in whose body the spirit of God had descended and the living Christ lived within her person." From his communion with Mother Johanna, whose "little son" he became, Postel developed the doctrine of the "Restitution of All Things," supposing that "God willed that all Reasonable Creatures be united into one sheepfold; that there be a General Pardon for all with no exceptions."[40] These religious ideas became interestingly mixed with magical concepts in Postel's thought, especially those derived from Jewish cabala and Judaism.

It seems that at least in the second half of his life, Dee also became such a universalist enthusiast, a conviction which pulled him very far from the Henrician Protestantism of his early years. Interestingly, although his career as a tutor at the court of Edward VI cannot be imagined without a clear reformed standpoint, his denomination cannot be determined from the existing historical sources (Clulee 1988, 34). Nevertheless, it is improbable that in 1553 he would have received the rectory at Upton without being a faithful Protestant (Roberts and Watson 1990, 75). In spite of all this, and the fact that his patron, the Earl of Northumberland, was sent to the scaffold, he survived the shift to Catholicism under Bloody Mary. Even in 1555 when he was arrested under the charge of witchcraft, the Privy Council released him and entrusted him to the care of Bishop Bonner. Soon he addressed the bishop as his "singularis amicus," and was in the position to turn to the queen with a proposition to collect the stock of the dissolved monastic libraries and set up a new royal collection (Supplication to Queen Mary, 1556[41]). As Roberts and Watson suggested, his own ambition to establish a large private library may have been rooted in the fact that his plea to Mary was not appreciated.

The accession of Elizabeth in 1558 facilitated Dee's return to his original denomination and this began the period when he seemed to have been emotionally drawn to Protestantism. This attachment, however, had more of a patriotic character than a theological one. Frances Yates gave a detailed analysis of the protestant imperial ideology that characterized the rising empire of Elizabeth (cf. Yates's Astrea, 1975) in whose creation Dee enthusiastically cooperated. This imperial ideology was motivated not only by the drive for territorial expansion, but was also fuelled by a religious ambition to counterbalance the European Catholic powers by a Protestant league gathered under the Tudor banner. The Virgin Queen thus became a quasi-religious symbol, signifying imperial reform and a purified religion, in fact embodying a new national mythology that reached back to the legendary King Arthur.[42] The literary creators of this mythology were (among others) Philip Sidney and Edmund Spenser, while its historical documentation was fabricated by William Camden, but John Dee also contributed to the geographical and historical expansionist projects (Yates 1979, 95–109; Sherman 1995, 148–201). His outstanding work in this field was the *General and Rare Memorials Pertayning to the Perfect Art of Navigation* (1577), in which he delineated those territories which Elizabeth could claim because of her descendance from Arthur. The monumental title page of the book, designed by Dee, showed the Queen sailing on a ship called "Europa," suggesting that she could be the ideal navigator of international Protestantism (Figure 7.9; cf. Yates 1979, 85). A Greek phrase in the middle of the page—Βριτανικον Ιερογλυφικον—intertextually referred to Dee's magical opus, the *Monas hieroglyphica*, too, suggesting that his political message in this work would not be entirely different from his general, scientific-religious vision. The links between the two works are emphasized by other iconographical elements: the alchemical symbols of Sun and Moon on the *General and Rare Memorials*, as well as the inclusion of the tetragrammaton, JHVH.

While in the 1570s Dee seems to have been under the influence of Protestant ideology and nationalistic politics, at the same time, his imagination was more and more taken by a contrary intellectual trend:

FIGURE 7.9   Frontispiece of Dee's *General and Rare Memorials* ... (London, 1577). see <http://www.johndee.org/charlotte/images/title.gif>.

nondenominational interconfessionalism. As I have suggested, the rise of this permissive religious attitude can be associated with those philological investigations of the humanists which recognized the (proto)types of Christianity in some of the pagan religions. Thus they concluded that— as opposed to the denominational differences—the really important thing among the religions was their common roots, the general intuitions. Concerning the fifteenth and sixteenth centuries, of course, we cannot yet speak of tolerance in the modern sense nor an abstract Deism that would freely take off from Christianity. Nevertheless, from the time of the Florentine neoplatonists onward it became customary to mix different religious ideas in a syncretic manner. Humanist syncretism was fostered by the scholarly attitude, and its methods of using historical and literary investigations. In the following I shall look at some specific features of this humanist interconfessionalism in relation to magic, as described by Charles Zika and Paola Zambelli.[43]

In his essay "Reuchlin and Erasmus: Humanism and Occult Philosophy" (1976–1977) Zika has developed a model of intellectual evolution that helps us to understand the above demonstrated "mystical mutations" of humanist thought.[44] In order to show the different intellectual avenues along which the humanists could proceed, Zika analyzed Erasmus' ambiguous attitude toward Johannes Reuchlin.

As is well known, Reuchlin employed humanist methods to enlighten certain Old Testament loci by also studying Judaic theology. This method can be compared to Ficino's strategy of explaining Christian theology using Plato and other pagan Platonici. Neither of these methods was entirely safe: Ficino had to face the accusations of practicing pagan magic; Reuchlin was charged with practicing Judaism. From this general situation developed the notorious Reuchlin affair that lasted from 1507 almost until Reuchlin's death in 1522, concluding with a papal condemnation of Reuchlin in Rome, 1520.

In 1507, Johannes Pfefferkorn, a convert, aided by the Dominicans of Cologne, initiated a confiscation and burning of all Jewish books because they were false, written to oppose Christians, and were offensive to Jesus, Maria, and the Apostles. He also claimed that these books kept the Jews ignorant of the truth, hindering their conversion to Christianity. Prompted by complaints from influential Jewish circles, Emperor Maximilian I halted the confiscations and ordered his high chancellor, the Archbishop of Mainz, to appoint a committee to make recommendations. The two persons appointed were Jakob Hoogstraeten, grand inquisitor of Cologne, and Johannes Reuchlin, humanist, renowned

Hebraist and professor of law. Hoogstraeten reaffirmed Pfefferkorn's opinion, while Ruchlin opposed it, expessing his position in a legally and theologically brilliant essay *Recommendation whether to Confiscate, Destroy and Burn all Jewish Books*. Since Hoogstraeten's expert opinion was so different from his own,[45] Reuchlin decided to seek the support of the humanist community through publicity and developed his report into a sarcastic pamphlet.[46]

In this, now called *Augenspiegel*, Reuchlin firmly defended the valuable achievements of Hebrew culture, and as a learned humanist and jurist he pointed out the legal background that granted Jews a free practice of their religion and the use of their sacred books. He classified Jewish books in four categories out of which he condemned to fire only one, those abusing the figure of Christ. The Talmud as well as the books of the cabala were among the ones to be preserved. He suggested that cabalistic books should be translated into Latin and Hebrew exegesis should be studied by Christian theologians.[47]

Reuchlin's answer did not pacify those who sought the dawnfall of Jewish culture, and the debate continued after 1510. This "Kulturkampf" culminated in the 1517 *Epistolarum virorum obscurorum*, which is remembered by scholars as a battle between modern humanists and conservative, retrograde Dominicans.[48] Careful research, however, shows that the frontlines were not entirely between humanists and monks. It was not a unified group of humanists who sided with Reuchlin, but rather a marginalized trend of heterodox theologian-philosophers, who were following Pico della Mirandola in his enthusiasm for the Jewish cabala. Defenders of Reuchlin included Pietro Galatino, a Franciscan theologian and Hebraist, and Giorgio Bensigno, a monk from Florence, student of Ficino then Savonarola. As J. Overfield suggested, this debate was not so much about humanism as it was about anti-Semitism. This conclusion, however, is also problematic. By today, historians feel compelled to speak about anti-Judaism, the ground of which was religious-theological discrimination, not racism, as in the case of anti-Semitism.[49]

If we return to the model of Zika, we also see a more complex and complicated set of likes and dislikes.[50] Let us take Erasmus, whose opinion suffered certain alterations during the long years of the "causa Reuchlini."

It was Reuchlin who first contacted Erasmus, sending him a copy of the *Augenspiegel*, and asking for solidarity.[51] Erasmus enthusiastically answered and indeed made repeated efforts to promote the case of Reuchlin.[52] When they finally met in person, Erasmus sent the following report to Jakob Wimpfeling: "I had the chance of an affectionate meeting with Reuchlin, a man whom I not only respect as a scholar of distinction but like quite particularly for a rare kind of courtesy and personal charm."[53]

In the meantime Reuchlin became more and more absorbed in Hebrew studies and finally he published his major work on the Jewish (and Christianized) cabala. In 1517 he sent a few copies of his *De arte cabalistica* to Erasmus, authorizing him to distribute them among his English friends. While it is not clear what Erasmus personally thought of this study of the cabala, from his correspondence we can learn about an enthusiastic reception in England. It turns out that Erasmus left a copy—meant for John Fisher, Bishop of Rochester—with Thomas More, asking him to forward it. But More became so interested that first he wanted to read it. Then he passed it to John Colet, the famous humanist, who summarized his opinion in a letter to Erasmus as follows:

> My dear Erasmus, of books and knowledge there is no end. Nothing can be better, in view of this brief life of ours, than we should live a holy and pure life and use our best endeavours every day to become pure and enlightened and perfect. Those things are promised us by Reuchlin's Pythagorical and Cabalistic philosophy.[54]

Two months later Erasmus wrote an enthusiastic letter to Reuchlin, in which—although not mentioning *De arte cabalistica*—he addressed his friend with great reverence and on the other hand used rather vulgar expressions about Pfefferkorn, who still had not stopped his crusade against the Hebraist scholar.[55]

And then things suddenly started changing. Pfefferkorn continued with his attacks, fully aided by Hoogstraeten and the Dominicans. Reuchlin's case was proceeded to Rome for further inquisitorial investigation. Worst of all, the case seemed to have been contaminated with that of Luther who was just about to upset the whole Christian world. Erasmus found himself implied in both cases, especially because some letters he had written to Reuchlin (including the one mentioned above, in which he had called Pfefferkorn a ghetto criminal and an ape Christian) were printed in a pirate edition and the Rotterdam humanist had to apologize. From that time on, he started dissociating himself from Reuchlin. First he wrote to Prince Albert of Brandenburg:

> The first point I must make is this: that I have never had any connection either with Reuchlin's business or with the case of Luther. Cabbala

and Talmud, whatever they may be, have never appealed to me. The venomous conflicts between Reuchlin and the supporters of Jakob Hoogstraten I have always found extremely offensive.[56]

Then he added some wry remarks about Reuchlin in the foreword to the authorized collection of his correspondence:

> I am no 'Reuchlinist.' I belong to no man's party, and detest these factious labels. I am a Christian, and I know what 'Christian' means. I will not tolerate 'Erasmists,' and 'Reuchlinists' is not a word I know. Between me and Reuchlin nothing has passed but the civilities of ordinary friendship, and to become his champion is a thing I have never undertaken, nor does he feel the need of it.[57]

Zika argues that Erasmus showed no anti-Semitism by this opinion, rather that he saw in the cabala and the other secret sciences dangerous Judaizing tendencies that would contradict and subvert the clear, rationalist standpoint of his own humanism. He promoted a reform of Christianity that would see the religious rituals purified, freed of obscure gestures and speculations, and he saw in the hermeticist-cabalist fashion just such a muddled, murky practice and thought.[58]

The ceremoniality increasingly present in his religious attitude brought him into the company of other magical hermetists of the early 1500s, such as Lodovico Lazzarelli, Trithemius, and Agrippa. It was not only spiritual kinship, since these people also had various personal relations, forming almost a coherent group of intellectuals. Agrippa even lectured on Reuchlin's *De verbo mirifico* at the University of Dole in 1509.[59]

Zika's conclusion is that hermetic magic, although it started its career using a methodology borrowed from humanism, soon diverted from it, already in the works of Ficino. The magical renaissance of the early sixteenth century proved to be undigestable for a philologist-humanists of northern Christianity, such as Erasmus. Paola Zambelli's thorough article on early sixteenth-century humanism, theology, and magic (1970) unintentionally corroborates this view. Although Zambelli has meticulously proved the parallels and interconnectedness between the works of Erasmus and Agrippa, not mentioning here the fact that their intellectual circle of friends largely overlapped, it remains that while Agrippa openly admired Erasmus and his achievment, this admiration was not reciprocal: the name of the younger magus-hermetist does not feature in the works or correspondence of the old humanist.

Reuchlin attached a preface to his famous book on the cabala (*De arte cabalistica*, 1517), addressing Pope Leo X who was the son of Lorenzo de' Medici, il Magnifico. He praised in it the importance of the Florentine Academy and pointed out the differences between the philosophy represented by the academicians as opposed to other trends of classical humanism, represented, for example, by Petrarch:

> [Lorenzo de' Medici's] birth seems heaven-sent. Petrarch, Philelph, and Aretino brought the arts of oratory and fine speech to the "youth of Florence," so that there could be no disputing that her people wrote more lucidly and more accurately than any other nation. But it was your father who added to Florence's store of learning—wisdom that probes into the past, wisdom that lay hidden until his day in books and memorials of past times. (Reuchlin 1983, 37)

These mysteries, according to Reuchlin, had been hidden in the works of Apollonius of Tyana, Plato, Plotinus, Iamblichus, Orpheus, and, above all, Pythagoras and the Jewish cabala. Reuchlin also acknowledged the formative influence of the Florentine neoplatonist circle on his own intellectual development:

> So I set out for Italy with the first Duke of Swabia, whose private secretary I was. I spoke enthusiastically to my Duke about the Medicis . . . Your father sowed the seeds of ancient philosophy in his children. With his son they will grow to reach the roof tops; in your reign we shall reap the harvest in every language—Greek, Latin, Hebrew, Arabic, Chaldaic, and Chaldean. (ibid., 39)

This inventory makes it clear that the more he came under the influence of these works and Eastern languages, the more he defined himself less as a humanist and more as a hermetist. As Zika said, "the rhetorician-scholar gave way to a mystical philosopher, the eloquent humanist to the traditionalist representative of preclassical religion and magic" (1976–1977, 245).

—︎⁂—

A similar tendency can clearly be seen in the intellectual evolution of John Dee, too. But this pattern has to be completed by one more aspect, namely the comparison between the early modern mystical enthusiasts and the representatives of the Reformation. The common ground was

that both groups grew from the humanists with the intention of reform-
ing and revitalizing Christianity. But while the reformers from Luther
and Calvin to the radical anti-Trinitarians were attached by very strong
ties to their own communities and they always acted as their spokesmen
opposing other well-defined groups, the enthusiasts awaited the elimination of all doctrinal differences and sought a universal syncretic religion.
This project also involved plans for mystical societies but their creators
were true heirs of the humanists in that they never seriously thought of
turning their fantastic plans into practice. We may find the germs of
secret societies—such as the infamous Rosicrucians—in their works, but
we never find a mass movement nor highly organized groups associated
with them as we do with the more established trends of the Reformation.

It is interesing to notice, however, that these individualistic enthusiasts were always irritating those who were in possession of the power
technologies. This is why they could not find peace either in their own
community or among their rivals. Each large denomination produced its
own enthusiasts. Postel and Bruno among the Catholics, Weigel and
Khunrath among the Lutherans, Servet among the Unitarians—many of
them converted and reconverted several times like Francesco Pucci, and
almost as many of them finished on the stake like Servet or Bruno.

Why did they provoke so much hostility? More than one argument
can be given in explanation. The individualism radiating from the enthusiastic magical-esoteric thoughts, and especially their universalism, vio-
lated the particular interests of various groups and communities. Furthermore, the secrecy and their discourse veiled in dark allegories and mysteries evoked a danger of secret conspiracy. These people could not find
temporary shelter anywhere but in the secluded courts of aristocratic
patrons, in the circles of extravagant intellectuals or hopeful sponsors
who could be convinced of the benefits of such plans and who eventually
could finance the publication of the fantastic projects.[60]

Dee, being totally engaged in his angel magic, became one of those
enthusiasts who wandered in various parts of the Continent and preached
their mystical-occult message, never becoming exhausted in seeking the
patronage of attentive and sensitive benefactors. It should be stressed,
though, that their camp can hardly be defined as having a homogeneous
and shared ideological platform.

Interestingly, while Dee had personal contacts with many of those
contemporary enthusiasts—Postel, Bruno, Pucci, Khunrath—and in his
library accumulated heterodox works, in his own writings one finds very
few references to these intellectual challenges. A possible explanation is

that all enthusiasts thought of themselves as elect, thus they did not need either sources or proofs for illumination. The truth was revealed to them in a direct way. Dee seemingly developed such a conviction, since his spiritual diaries contain significantly fewer citations, references, and glosses than do his earlier, scholarly works. He wanted to become a prophet, an important herald of the great and general reformation in the context of which denominational differences appeared petty and insignificant. Dee's angels seemed very tolerant in this respect. A characteristic episode occurred when one of the spirits burst out against the Jesuit friars who in Prague were not willing to absolve the Protestant Kelly:

> Whosoever wishes to be wise may look neither to the right nor to the left; neither towards this man who is called a catholic, nor towards that one who is called a heretic; but may he look up to the God of heaven and earth and to his Son, Jesus Christ. Behold, the courtesan will be justified! But the hypocrite will be cast off and trodden under foot. (Dee 1965, 245)

After this apocalyptic treat (the iconography of which abounds in Enochian images such as "being trodden under foot"), the session concludes with an explicit elaboration of *exaltatio* which is drawn in a dramatic choreography by Kelly, Dee, Pucci, and The Voice:

> K[elly]: The seer may then foretell when the time is to come that will be after the harvest and the harvesters. [Dee's gloss in the margin: 'Apocalypse, chapter 14D']
> Δ: 'He who writes down and records the words of the Highest, may he in the fulness of time, show forth their strength, through the strength and support of Him Who has exalted him.'
> Fr[ancesco] P[ucci]: 'May he who has been called as a speaker abound in good works, so that he may be distinguished before his hearers and exalted in Him Who sent him.'
> [The Voice]: 'So then, whoever neglects his vocation may be ejected, and his place may be occupied by another. But to him who does the will of Him Who is teaching (which is the will of the Creator of all things) abundant grace will be granted.' (1965, 247)

A possible motivation behind interconfessionalism was the influence of the pagan-hellenistic Platonist philosophy, which the enthusiasts tried to amalgamate with the doctrines of Christianity. These neoplatonists and crypto-hermetists were often condemned by the radical reformers, such as we can see in the writings of the anti-Trinitarian Johann Sommer, who condemned Platonists as follows:

> For them the views of Plato seemed similar to that of Christians; so it is no wonder that deceived by the likeness of notions they did so many horrible things, although originally they did not want more than to grasp everything in rational categories and to describe the way of incarnation, the birth of Christ, his genealogy from the Father, etc. (*Refutatio scripti Petri Carolii*, 18, quoted by Szczucki 1980, 101)

This quotation clearly shows how far a professional theologian—even if belonging to the most radical branch of the Reformation—and a universalist enthusiast for whom the denominationally codified dogmas were of little importance could be from each other. But even this ideological division was not clear and stable in the Renaissance. Let us think of John Dee, who, when returning to England, sent Sommer's work to the Archbishop of Canterbury for refutation, because he found its anti-Trinitarianism a wicked and harmful doctrine:

> I exhibited to the Archbishop of Canterb. two books of blasphemy against Christ and the Holy Ghost &c., desiring him to cause them to be confuted. One was Christian Franken, printed anno 1585, in Poland. The other was of one Somerus against one Carolius printed in Ingolstadt anno 1582 in octavo. (October 13, 1592; cf. Dee 1998, 257)[61]

From this we can conclude that the tolerance of the humanists and the radical reformers were manifest in rather divergent areas and the patience for each other could be seen only in exceptional cases among the early modern intellectuals (such as Servet, Sebastian Franck, or Valentin Weigel).

The role of interconfessionalism and its relation to humanism on the one hand and to the Reformation on the other was an interesting chapter in the history of early modern culture, but one should also remember that by the seventeenth century this situation had changed. The revolutionarized information exchange through the general use of inexpensively printed books, changes in the university curricula, and such projects as Alsted's monumental *Encyclopaedia* made possible at least a temporary coexistence of nonaristocratic, middle-class, patrician communities or even church officials on the one hand and universalist enthusiasts on the other. Some of them could well coordinate their esoteric interests with sober activities such as church administration or regular teaching. Good examples are the Protestant Johann Valentin Andreae, occult adviser of the Princes of Wolfenbüttel and respected leader of the local Lutheran community, or the Catholic Athanasius Kircher, who was a Jesuit, taught all over Europe, and organized schools and museums, while living in his own fantastic transcendental dreamworld.

It is a fascinating story through which alternative humanism unfolds from the time of Ficino to the late seventeenth century, the world of van Helmonts, Kirchers, Jerome Drexels, Thomas Vaughans. And somewhere in the middle of this process we find Dee, emerging in the camp of Renaissance enthusiasts, wholly occupied with his angelic conversations. It seems that his chiliasm and his Enochian prophecy and magic tied him to those visionaries who, growing out from the humanist tradition, did not join the official camps of the Reformation but rather started preaching a more mystical, alternative reform. The eastern fringes of Central Europe—Poland, Silesia, Hungary, and Transylvania—played an important role in these projects. Many of the enthusiasts found temporary shelter in the courts far away from the centers of the European great powers. At the same time, these states—in a constant political and ideological flux—seemed to be stimulating missionary targets. Robert Evans has called attention to the missionary character of Dee's Central European journeys and he has pointed out the similarities between Elizabeth and Rudolf II, which—in Dee's eyes—predestined both of them to be the recipients of his mystical message:

> An important item on the agenda was provided by the mystical and occult aspects of sovereignity. The apotheosis of the ruling families was accomplished in verse and image, ceremonial masque and heroic portrait. [. . .] The seriousness of the preoccupation can be seen not only in Rudolfine Prague, but in Elizabethan England, where the queen was surrounded by a similar mass of allegorical apostrophizing from scholars like Dee and poets like Spenser. Both the unmarried Emperor and the Virgin Queen were widely regarded as figures prophetic of significant change in their own day, as symbols of a lost equilibrium when they were dead. (1973, 275)

It is this lure of East-Central Europe that leads us to the question of the social context of Dee's intellectual activities, that is, the examination of the interpretive community of his messages. In my last chapter I shall investigate this aspect through the filter of Dee's Central European experience, then through the editorial strategy Meric Casaubon exercised when sixty years later he decided to publish the Doctor's spiritual diaries conceived mostly in those faraway parts of the Continent.

8

Dee and the Interpretive Community

The previous chapter approached Dee's intellectual output as an individual effort seeking the unattainable, as a lifelong series of recurrent attempts to reach out from the mundane and material world and penetrate the sphere of the mysterious Other. As we have seen, his last initiative was to the world of angels.

This whole enterprise, however, has a hitherto largely unexplored social aspect. Namely, that those who strived for intimacy with the Other were not confining their activity to individual philosophical-theological-scientific speculations and experiments; on the contrary, they inevitably fell into the focus of public attention. Partly because they themselves had missionary messages that they wanted to share with their community and this public role became a corner stone of their self-fashioning strategy, and partly because they became increasingly alien and irritating to those who were less able to reach out for bridges between this and the transcendental world. Thus the seeker of the Other *became* the threatening Other for the community whose members and especially whose ideological leaders felt compelled to handle the problem by working out power technologies to contain the alien elements in their social microcosms.

While I will examine these power technologies in the second subchapter, in the first subchapter I shall look at Dee's career in Central Europe, which became for him a region of inspiration as well as a possible testing ground in which to pour out the mystical lesson gained through his intimation with angels.

"Eastward Ho!" Dee, Patronage, and Central Europe

The Lure of East-Central Europe

As we have seen, among Dee's readings one of his first strongly decisive mystical inspirations, Trithemius' *Steganographia*, is associated with Central Europe. A young Hungarian nobleman helped the penniless Doctor copy the work, and what is more, he even invited Dee to Hungary to instruct him in the occult arts: "Now I stand at the curtesye of a noble man of Hungarie who hath promised me leave thereto, after he shall perceyve that I may remayne by him longer (with the leave of my Prince) to pleasure him also with such pointes of science, as at my handes he requireth."[1] Who this Hungarian nobleman was, extending the first invitation for Dee to visit East-Central Europe, we do not know for sure. But it is interesting to speculate on a plausible identity, especially since although the Doctor apparently did not accept his offer, it would become a longstanding inspiration. It might have propelled him to visit Maximilian's coronation in Pozsony (Pressburg, today's Bratislava in Slovakia) in the fall of 1563, and he may have remembered this encounter twenty years later when he decided to follow the Count Albert Laski to his Polish estates, thus choosing East-Central Europe as the principal setting of his angelic conversations.

One of the possible candidates would be Johannes Sambucus (János Zsámboky), the famous Hungarian humanist, bibliophile, and emblematist who had an impressive international network of acquaintances and—just like Dee—possessed an outstandingly large and valuable private library.[2] In 1563 he visited his publisher, Plantin, in Antwerp and there or somewhere else coinciding with Dee's continental journey in 1562 and 1563 they could have met. He was also present at the coronation in Pozsony, which occasion may have offered a chance for reunion. In spite of the possibilities, we have no evidence that the two scholars ever met, although Dee possessed some of Sambucus' books in his collection (R&W 720, 793, 964, 1170). Sambucus' candidacy for Dee's "Hungarian nobleman" is nevertheless weak for the following obvious reason: Sambucus was a renowned scholar but not a nobleman. Dee, sensitive to social hierarchy, would probably not have made such a mistake in his correspondence to Cecil; furthermore, it is unlikely that Sambucus would have wanted to study the occult arts from anyone.

Another more likely candidate might be Boldizsár Batthyány (Balthasar Batthyany), whom Robert Evans rediscovered for English readers (1973, 120; 1975, 35–37). A brief introduction to his career provides an interesting Central European parallel to the activities of Dee or that of some noblemen of alternative thinking such as the "Wizard" Earl of Northumberland in England.

Batthyány (1530–1590) developed one of the most brilliant noble courts in the vicinity of the Hungarian capital, Pozsony, in West Hungary. His career started in the Habsburg court of Vienna, then, in the 1560s, he spent a few years in Italy and France, finally becoming a page to King Francis and Mary Stuart. From a letter written to his parents we know that in 1560 he witnessed the outbreak of the first Huguenot war in Amboise.[3] According to historical sources he spent over two years in France and he seems to have made acquaintances among local Protestant families as well as refugees from the Low Countries. Among those one can mention the printer-publisher family, the Wechels, and the famous botanist Carolus Clusius (Charles de l'Ecluse) who escaped from Flanders in 1561. Wechel's son-in-law, Jean Aubri, became Batthyány's bookseller for many subsequent years and Clusius spent an important period of his career at Batthyány's Hungarian court working on his opus on the flora of Hungary.[4]

Although there is no historical proof, it is not impossible that in 1562 and 1563 the Hungarian magnate made a journey from Paris to the Netherlands and in the circle of Willem Silvius he could have easily come across the English Doctor. His later patronage of Clusius makes it plausible that he would also have invited Dee to Hungary. This possibility is even more plausible if we think of Batthyány's notable interest in alchemy and the occult arts.

Batthyány's humanist circle at his court in Németújvár (today's Güssing in Eastern Austria) developed in the 1570s and was centered around his significant library. Unfortunately this collection has dispersed, and unlike Dee's library, we do not have even its catalogue. The only documentation concerning Batthyány's books are the valuable set of receipts issued by the magnate's bookseller, Jean Aubri, which also contain detailed lists of the purchased items. From these it becomes clear that Batthyány's interest was not of the usual humanist-theological sort but, similar to Dee's, was more centered on natural philosophy, the esoteric lore, history, and literature. Next to Hermes Trismegistus, Raymundus Lullus, and Paracelsus we find contemporary editions of Rabelais, Machiavelli, Castiglione, and Jean Bodin.[5]

Batthyány also patronized a number of humanists, Hungarians and foreigners alike. One of his main advisors was Elias Corvinus, a humanist from Pozsony and Vienna whose sixty-one letters to his patron survive from the years between 1557 and 1587. It is obvious that Corvinus acted as a go-between connecting the court of Németújvár with the humanists of Pozsony, as well as the Imperial Court in Vienna. From this correspondence the following names attract the attention of the Dee scholar: Hugo Blotius, the chief librarian of the Habsburgs; Paul Fabritius, royal astronomer in Vienna; Crato von Kraftheim, imperial physician; and a number of local and wandering alchemists. From Corvinus' letters we learn that in the 1570s Batthyány ordered more and more books on alchemy and occult philosophy. Representative titles include "Theatrum diabolorum," "Coelum philosophorum," "Dialogi de alchimia," and Gerhard Dorn's *Lapis metaphysicae, Chimicum artificiae.* The most expensive book commissioned by the Hungarian was Paracelsus' *Disputatio de medicina nova.* In 1574 Batthyány entrusted Corvinus with finding some more Paracelsica. In 1577 he bought the hermetic *Pimander* and Tomás Jordán's book on the plague. Interestingly, Jordán of Transylvania, a Hungarian wandering humanist and medical doctor, had met Conrad Gessner, the Swiss polymath, just a few months before Dee visited the professor in Zurich. Their inscriptions in Gessner's *album amicorum* almost follow each other.[6] Other occult items in Batthyány's book orders are Martin Ruland's alchemical lexicon, Porta's *Magia naturalis,* and Chasseneux's *Catalogus gloriae mundi,* the same work that Albert Laski exchanged with Dee for a Bible in Poland (R&W 226).

We also learn from the correspondence that from 1572 there was an alchemical laboratory in Németújvár. While at that time Corvinus lived in Vienna, the magnate was experimenting by himself and regularly reported his progress to his advisor (Barlay 1986, 209–11). This happened at the same time as another Englishman, and what is more, Dee's own disciple, turned up in Pozsony. The famous visitor was young Philip Sidney who, together with Edward Dyer, had studied chemistry with Dee around 1570.[7]

The promising nineteen-year-old aristocrat and poet came to Hungary in 1573 as part of a three-year-long grand tour sponsored by his patron, Sir Francis Walsingham. Since Walsingham was the father of the British secret service, he also entrusted Sidney to write reports to him on what he experienced in the various European countries. As historians have verified, Sidney indeed was to observe the Turkish wars and the state of the Hungarian fortifications.[8] However, we should not forget the poet's memorable remark about Hungarian heroic poetry in his *Defence of Poesy:*

In Hungary I have seen in the manner at all feasts, and other such meetings, to have songs of their ancestors' valour, which that right soldierlike nation think one of the chiefest kindlers of brave courage. (quoted from Abrams 1986, 516)

This is yet another mysterious reference to Hungary and the Hungarians, but again there is no exact proof as to where Sidney might have seen such feasts and meetings embellished with the performance of heroic songs. One strong possibility is Batthyány's court in Németújvár, which was just a short ride from either Vienna or from Pozsony. Sidney's host in Pozsony was the town physician, Georg Purkircher, a prominent member of Batthyány's humanist circle.[9] In Vienna a number of humanists could call the Englishman's attention to Batthyány, but we should not forget that earlier in Frankfurt Sidney had lodged in the house of Andreas Wechel, a close acquaintance of the Hungarian nobleman. And, finally, we cannot exclude the possibility that Batthyány's name turned up in the conversations between Sidney and Dee when the young traveler was being prepared by his older tutor for the continental grand tour.

It is interesting to follow the story of Sidney's European journeys since several of his meetings and episodes look forward to John Dee's later mission. After having traveled in Italy for almost a year, the poet turned up in Vienna again in August 1574 and stayed in the house of Michael Lingelsheim, imperial councillor. During the fall, from there he took a journey to Cracow, wanting to visit the Valois king, Henry, but by the time he got there, Henry had already resigned and returned to Paris. Sidney left the Polish capital disappointed by the political anarchy. On the other hand, he spent a few pleasant days in Silesian Wrocław (Breslau) where he visited Andreas Dudith, the Hungarian-born humanist and politician who in a few years time would sceptically comment on Dee's performances at the Polish and imperial courts. In Dudith's house Sidney met another protagonist of Dee's future stay in Prague: Crato von Kraftheim, the imperial physician (Gömöri 1991, 30). On his way back to Vienna Sidney also stopped in Brno where he enjoyed the hospitality of Tomás Jordán, the doctor who had visited Conrad Gessner in Zurich a few months before Dee and who later became imperial physician to Rudolf II.

Three years later Sidney came to Central Europe for the second time. In March 1577, Queen Elizabeth sent him to the Palatinate and to Prague, officially to express her sympathies in regard to the deaths of the Elector Palatine and Emperor Maximilian, but he also had a clandestine assignment: to tap the opinion of Central European princes concerning a Protestant league.[10] Traveling via Brussels, Heidelberg, and Nurnberg, Sidney and his escort arrived in Prague for Easter Week and during his stay he had two audiences with Rudolf II. Beside political activities he also had time to visit the ancient city and its surroundings: the star-shaped hunting lodge, the Hvezda, even found its way into the *New Arcadia*.[11]

Perhaps the most interesting episode was Sidney's meeting with the English Catholic exile, Edmund Campion, who at that time had a residence in the Prague convent of the Jesuits. Campion had been Sidney's instructor in rhetoric during his studies at Oxford, but in the meantime had become an arch-enemy in the eyes of Puritan English politicians. Now the Protestant youth decided to visit his old master secretly. Sidney had to be cautious in undertaking such a visit, since several members of his delegation were spying on him. Thus we learn about the meeting only from Campion's correspondence. This suggests that Sidney was seriously tempted to convert to Catholicism. Although the English poet is remembered as an ardent Protestant and a patriot, in the tolerant and cosmopolitan atmosphere of Rudolphine Prague he may have come into the lure of the old religion. His crypto-Catholic attitude becomes the more interesting if we recall John Dee—another Protestant-patriot—and his similar enchantment a decade later, when, in spite of his Protestantism, he attended confession and took the holy communion both in Cracow and Prague.[12]

The last episode of Sidney's East-Central European travels relating to Dee's upcoming mission is his probable meeting with Count Albert Laski. According to Anthony Wood's *Athenae Oxoniensis*, in 1577 while staying in Frankfurt, Sidney received two letters from Poland containing invitations for him to take the Polish throne. Zantuan (1968, 6–7) suggests that the only person in the position to put forward such a fantastic plan was Albert Laski. Whether this story is true or not, it is a fact that in the fall of 1573 Sidney had met Laski in Venice and when the Polish Palatine came to London in May 1583, he was not only well received at the court of Elizabeth, but Sidney was nominated to be his personal escort.

There is no doubt that young Philip Sidney consulted John Dee on the circumstances of Vienna and Pozsony before his first trip to Central-Europe in 1572 and 1573. Later on, it was Sidney who had a lot to tell his old master about his experiences there and it is also most probable that Sidney was the mastermind behind Laski's getting acquainted with Dee. They first met on the thirteenth day of Laski's stay in England, in Leicester's house in Greenwich (May 13, 1583; Dee 1842, 20). Five days later Laski visited Dee's Mortlake home and, as we know, he soon became a participant of the angelic conversations.

In what way was their meeting a congenial affiliation? Each of them represented for the other an aspect of the mysterious Other, an embodiment of their secret desires. For Dee, Laski meant a piece of East-Central Europe, a kind of Promised Land from where Hungarian noblemen popped up to help him learn the arcane teaching of the *Steganographia* and where splendid royal courts, such as that at the coronation of Maximilian II, might have guaranteed secure patronage, fame, high social status, as well as attentive ears to his most sacred angelic messages. For Laski, Dee was the embodiment of the hermetic magus, somebody who could personally experience and testify about the magical *exaltatio*, a scientifically-based *unio mystica* with the deity, the Platonic Other where the souls crave to return from the material world. Nor should one forget that Dee and Kelly were practicing alchemists whose experiments might eventually yield the amount of gold frighteningly absent from Laski's bankrupt treasury.

Who was this extravagant Pole, whom the monographs on Dee describe as a fairy-tale personality rather than a real historical character and whom even Robert Evans' book treats rather passingly? Laski (sometimes called Alasco but his original Polish name was Olbracht Łaski, 1530–1605) came from a leading aristocratic family; one of his uncles was Cardinal Jan Łaski, an outstanding politician and patron in the time of the Polish Renaissance. His father, Hieronim Łaski, Palatine of Sieradz, visited England in 1527 as a Polish envoy and made a very good impression on Henry VIII and on Cardinal Wolsey (Zins 1974, 55). Yet another Jan Łaski (1499–1560), younger brother of Hieronim, became one of the instrumental supporters of the Reformation in England, previously having started his career as a humanist and a personal acquaintance and follower of Erasmus. This Jan had met several Englishmen during his studies in Italy and followed the invitation of Leonard Coxe to the British Isles, soon claiming that his family's descent was in fact from the English nobility. From 1548 he lived permanently in England and earned the appreciation of the leaders of the English Reformation, such as Archbishop Thomas Cranmer.[13]

Albert Laski recalled the stature of his father, Hieronim, and was one of the most colorful specimens of Polish Renaissance personalities: a magnate, a mercenary, a learned humanist, a patron of writers, and a publisher of books, at the same time a ruthless politician. In many ways he can be compared to Dee's possible "Hungarian nobleman," Boldizsár Batthyány, or to the Doctor's later Czech patron, Vilém Rožmberk.[14] Laski was in fact born in Upper Hungary, in the city of Késmárk, which

at that time was a family dominion. This town is several time mentioned
in Dee's Central-European diaries, and this is where Laski was running
an alchemical laboratory and where one of his alchemists, the Silesian-
German Adam Schröter, translated Paracelsus' *Archidoxae magica*. The
work was published in Cracow in 1569 and was dedicated "Illustri ac
Magnifico Domino Alberto a Lasko, Palatino Siradiensi etc." The lengthy
introductory essay by Schröter not only paid tribute to Laski as patron
(also eloquently praising his father, Hieronimus), it further testified to
the magnate's genuine interest in the occult arts.

It would be interesting to know if Dee ever received a copy of this
Cracow *Archidoxae* edition, but since he lived in Laski's household, one
can hardly imagine he did not at least see it. Although the English
Doctor had known the text from the editions he had possessed since the
1570s, he must have been pleased to read Schröter's introduction in
which Hermes Trismegistus was mentioned as someone who had learned
medicine directly from the angels and Enoch was remembered for his
particularly long life gifted by God. Schröter called Paracelsus a direct
descendant of Trismegistus and Enoch, and finally directly referred to
magical *exaltatio*: "The essence of the whole work is to teach in general
how it is possible to prepare an appropriate medicine against any kind of
illness and finally to reach *exaltatio*; by the help of which the human
body miraculously and from all illnesses and future accidents for a long
time can be liberated and immunely preserved."[15]

The exact nature of Laski's mission is not known. Polish historians
suggest that as a notorious "king-maker," he might have had in mind the
establishment of an alliance against the Catholic king, Stephen Bathory.[16]
As we know, nothing significant came out of this obscure political com-
mission; on the other hand, he witnessed in Oxford the debate of Giordano
Bruno with the local professors and had many other interesting cultural
encounters. Finally, he returned to Poland with two Englishmen in his
retinue, both parties having exalted hopes about the alchemical and magical
experiments to come.

The Lure of Dee and Kelly for Eastern Europe

Among intellectuals traveling in the late-Renaissance in East-Central
Europe—such as Carolus Clusius, Francesco Pucci, Jacobus Palaeologus,
Christian Francken, and others—John Dee and Edward Kelly have al-
ways aroused a great deal of interest in the eyes of Eastern European

historians of humanism and science. There is more than one reason for this. First of all, one should think of the high prestige of Dee in English science historical scholarship.[17] Furthermore, one should remember the amazingly voluminous autobiographical documents, especially the intriguing spiritual diaries of Dee, that document his Eastern European sojourns. Until the early 1980s Eastern European scholars interpreted Dee's visits as a major impetus from the West facilitating the development of natural science in the east-central part of the continent[18] and they found confirmation for this in the works of their western colleagues.[19] As I have described earlier, since the 1980s John Dee's image as an Elizabethan intellectual has undergone several phases of metamorphosis. Debates concerning the Yates thesis have also eroded his reputation as an outstanding natural scientist and the previously established link between hermeticism, magic, and the advancement of learning. In this context, when we reevaluate Dee's Eastern European mission, we have to put the following questions for consideration: What brought the English travelers to such remote places of Europe? What message or mission did they convey to their hosts? In what way did this influence Eastern European intellectual life? Did they get anything in return from Eastern Europe?

There are three groups of sources relating to Dee's eventful East-Central European journeys. First, there are external references (hearsay, humanist correspondence, and reports of agents) that are quite scarce. Secondly, we have Dee's "public" private diaries that show a busy humanist with a tight itinerary, traveling constantly and meeting a great number of people; however, little is revealed about the exact nature of his contacts and the contents of his conversations. (No doubt, he was fully occupied with continual efforts to secure patronage for himself and his family.) Third, most exhaustive are his spiritual diaries, the journals of the angelic conferences, which, of course, are the most intimate of all the documents and deal not only with the séances and Dee's prophetic visions but also provide complex insights into the everyday life of the two wandering prophets and their relatives.

Since recent biographical writings[20] throw ample light on these domestic aspects, I shall only briefly refer to some characteristic features and episodes which are specifically connected to the questions I have posed above.

I think in the previous subchapter I have given a detailed enough assessment of Dee's possible motivations in accepting Count Laski's invitation and trying his fortunes at the courts of East-Central Europe. He clearly felt dissatisfied in regard to his advancement in England; he clearly had an urge to share his angelic messages with attentive and at the same time powerful persons; he clearly had idealistic hopes about the status and prestige of the occult arts at the Central European courts; and he must have had enough self-confidence to think that a scholar-prophet like himself would be warmly welcomed in those courts.

In spite of the contrary opinion of some historians, I shall argue that he was not entirely mistaken in his expectations and that his five years spent in Central Europe should not be considered a complete failure. At first sight, though, the diaries seem to prove that the adventures on the far side of the Continent again failed to yield the desired results. On the debit side can be mentioned that Laski's support soon dried up and Dee was no more successful in Prague. Rudolf did not take to him and he was not the least inclined to give Dee the title of "Royal Mathematicien." Back in Cracow, Dee met King Bathory three times, but the ruler remained suspicious of his mission. The worst events followed only after that: as a result of the machinations of the papal nuncio, Dee was temporarily expelled from the Habsburg lands, but fortunately the Czech magnate, Count Rožmberk, provided shelter for him and his kin.

On the credit side one should take into consideration that in spite of all their eccentricity the Englishmen were nowhere kicked out or simply chased away. On the contrary, they enjoyed royal and aristocratic patronage and most of their expenses were covered for half a decade. When Dee returned to England, he traveled like a prince. He had three coaches with twelve Hungarian horses. In the Habsburg territories twenty-four soldiers escorted him with the passport of the Emperor, and in German lands they also had three or four bodyguards. It is true that most of these expenses were covered by loans, but back in England, Dee duly cashed them with his queen. According to the *Compendious Rehearsal* (Dee 1851, 34), the Doctor requested Elizabeth to compensate him for expenses and losses to the value of 2306 pound sterlings!

During their continental sojourn, the Englishmen enjoyed the two quietest years in Trebona (Třeboň), on the Rožmberk estate. However, neither financial success nor an intellectual environment comparable to Dee's former private academy in Mortlake, England, can be documented there. Was the little cultivated Eastern European society too unsophisticated to sympathize with Dee's mission or were the Englishmen simply too eccentric? If we look at the independent documents on the intellectual atmosphere of Rudolfine Prague, or even the local aristocratic center of Trebona, we cannot help feeling that the second explanation is more likely.

It also appears that Dee's strategy to attract his potential patrons misfired. What is more, his apocalyptic and highly idiosyncratic message was frightening. On introducing himself he promised to reveal, on the basis of the angelic conversations, the greatest secrets of the world but the contents of his séances did not in fact radically differ from the prophecies of widespread contemporary apocalyptic literature. No doubt, he knew well about the Book of Enoch and he had an effective choreography to perform the updated version of the prophecies. However, a pathetic as well as ironic feature of his argument was that while he communicated the angelic messages to king and emperor, he bluntly threatened them in the name of the celestial powers unless they followed his directions. Because of this, each audition involved high dramatic suspense, combined with the atmosphere of tragicomedy. Nevertheless, their detailed descriptions in Dee's spiritual journals reveal important information to the psychoanalyst as well as to the historian of mentalities, revealing not only Dee's excentric personality, but also the characteristics of the interpretive community to whom the messages were directed.

The English Doctor had his first important royal audience in Central Europe at the Prague court of Rudolf II. He appeared before the Emperor on September 3, 1584, after elaborate preparations, and the audition lasted a full hour (Dee 1659, 230–31). At the beginning of the conversation Dee reviewed his major work, the *Monas hieroglyphica*, and pointed out that it had been dedicated to Rudolf's father, Maximilian II. After Dee's introductory remarks the emperor admitted that he had difficulties in following the Doctor's train of thought. Changing the topic, Dee then explained how he had became disappointed in earthly sciences and how he had turned to angelic metaphysics. The openly magical program, already quoted above (Dee 1659, 321), definitely horrified the emperor. On top of this, Dee poured out to him his missionary program:

> It pleased God to send me his Light; and his holy Angels, for these two years and a half, have used to inform me: yea, they have brought me a Stone of that value that no earthly Kingdom is of that worthinesse as to be compared to the vertue and dignity thereof, etc.
>
> The Angel of the Lord hath appeared to me, and rebuketh you for your sins. If you will hear me, and believe me, you shall Triumph: if you will not hear me, The Lord, the God that made Heaven and Earth, putteth his foot against your breast, and will throw you headlong down from your seat.
>
> Moreover, the Lord hath made his Covenant with me:[. . .] If you will forsake your wickednesse, and turn unto him, your Seat shall be the greatest that ever was: and the Devil shall become your prisoner:

Which Devil, I did conjecture, to be the Great Turk. This my Com-
mission, is from God. (Dee 1659, 231)

Hearing these prophecies Rudolf could hardly maintain his quietness. He
assured Dee that he would consider his message carefully and dismissed
the Doctor. Dee, in spite of all his efforts, could never again obtain an
audience with the emperor, which fact contributed to his decision to
move to Cracow and try his fortune with King Stephen Bathory.

Albert Laski introduced him to the king on April 17, 1585, Wednesday. The first meeting was short and formal; Bathory postponed the
detailed discussion until after Easter (Dee 1659, 397). From this time on,
the spirits inserted pronouncements concerning Bathory in their messages. For example on April 24: "Stephen, lift up thy head amongst the
stars of Heaven; for the spirit of God is with thee, [. . .] but the Lord will
reprehend thee for thy sins" (Dee 1659, 398). Then, on May 20,

> I greatly thirst after Steven, for the course of things are at hand,
> Behold, I will bless him, that he may leave blessing unto thee,
> Behold, I will place thee unto him, as his right leg, and he shall
>   stand.[. . .]
> Therefore and with speed go before Steven. (401)

A curious episode took place on May 22. Kelly was conversing with a
spirit called Puer, and the demon asked in what language to scold Bathory.
Laski, present at the séance, requested Hungarian. Puer/Kelly, however,
skilfully avoided the task:

> Hungarian is hateful unto me; For it is full of iniquity; Neither will I
> speak unto him my self that he shall (yet) hear me. I will open my
> mouth in Latin for thy sake: and if he become obedient, I will also
> appear unto him my self and unto you all, [. . .] but to overcome him
> by Miracles it needeth not, for by him the people are not edified, but
> by my words he shall understand, that I touch him, although Satan
> stand by him.
>
>   But go thou [Albert Laski] unto him, and speak unto him liberally,
> when he hath heard me, if he receive me, my blessing is upon him of
> necessity. (402)[21]

A day later (May 23) Bathory sent for Dee and Laski. He received
them in the dining hall; he was sitting next to the southern window
opening to the new garden, and addressed them in Latin:

Egit mecum Dominus Palatinus, ut vos audirem de rebus istis magnis
& raris loquente . . . — The Palatine has told me that I should listen
[to] what you have to say about great and rare things. (402)[22]

Dee answered with a lengthy theological explication in which he argued
that prophecies did not become invalid in the time of the New Testament
and quoted the Scriptures to prove the validity of divine revelation. At the
end of his speech he repeated to Stephen the offer he had made to Rudolf:

Et paeteritarum nostrorum Actionum libros 24, paratus sum videndos
exhibere—I am ready to exhibit at your Majesty's request the 24 books
of our former actions; some of those have been written in Latin and
Greek, the others in English. (Dee 1659, 404)

The king's answer is not incorporated in the diary; instead, Dee's thanks-
giving is included for having been led to the Polish court. A few days
later, on May 27, another audience was granted in the king's private
chamber. During this the Englishmen set up a session of angelic conference and a spirit through Kelly's mouth spoke to the king as follows:

Listen carefully, Stephen. Who nurtured you from the cradle? Is it not
that King of Glory. By whose grace all power is subjected in heaven and
earth? Did he not raise you with his powerful arm, from an ordinary
soldier to a greater one, and so to the greatest kingdom? Why, then, did
you introduce such a dark cloud, full of so much fog and ingratitude,
between your God and your soul? (Dee 1659, 405; Dee 1998, 181)

It is interesting to ponder how the king felt at such speeches. As a devout
Catholic he probably deeply believed in the existence of spirits and must
have appreciated that he was chosen as a recipient of a sacred message.
On the other hand, he must have also been perplexed at how little
informed the supernatural being was in calling him an ordinary soldier.
It is true that he did not inherit the Polish throne but was elected to it;
however, prior to that he had been the Prince of Transylvania and had
came from one of the most distinguished Hungarian aristocratic families.
    A day later, at a private session a "Green Man," called Ilimese, strictly
commanded Dee to scold the king severely at their upcoming meeting:

Thus saith the Lord: thou must answer Stephen according to the hard-
ness of his hart: Answer him thus, "Lo, King, the God of Heaven and
Earth hath placed me before thee, and hath shewed unto thee his will.

[. . .] Behold (O King), I can make the Philosophers Stone. Bear thou therefore the charge, and give me a name within thy court that I may have access unto thee! and yearly maintainance of thee for us both. (Dee 1659, 407)

Whether the spirits were indeed worrying about Dee's material needs or whether that Kelly just wanted to make sure that patronage would not be forgotten is hard to tell. But it is even more puzzling as to why Dee avoided these formulas referring to their possible settlement in Cracow at their next—and last—audition with King Stephen. That happened on June 4, and the diary-entry relating the meeting is extremely short. We learn only that the king, Laski, and Dee participated in it, there was no spiritual conference, and the Doctor plainly reconfirmed his honesty in delivering the divine message to Bathory:

Ecce (O Rex) Deus Coeli & Terrae, me ante oculos Vestros posuit: the King of Heaven & Earth has led me in front of your eyes and has revealed his will. As for me, [God] has brought me up from my youth in his fear and led me to desire true Wisdom. By the help of which I have arrived at the comprehension of the secrets of Nature, (ecce) in nomine Dei. (Dee 1659, 408)

In fact, Dee repeated nothing of the message of Ilimese, the Green Man. Needless to say, the outcome of the final audience was similar to that of the Prague scenario, and since Bathory offered no position to the Englishmen, Dee and Kelly returned to Prague.

Two more episodes in the spiritual diaries describe Dee's search for patronage. One is an interlude in Prague when Dee learned that at the imperial court he had been exposed to wicked gossips, even plotting, which aimed at driving him out of the capital. The charge at the table of the apostolic Nuncio *inter alia* was that Dee did not hesitate

to offer to the Emperor [. . .] an apparition of blessed spirits (which they, however, call and believe to be evil ones) with the aid of certain magical characters. [. . .] Also [it was said] that the Imperial Majesty had purposely recoiled from that [offer] lest he should burden his conscience with scruples or cause some danger to his soul. [. . .] They believe in fact that the dealings [of Mr. Dee] with the Emperor might rather have originated from another, more important matter. I am indeed of the opinion [comments the secretary who prepared this memo for the Emperor] that they prefer one philosophers' stone to ten visions of angels.[23]

This quotation may explain why at other times Dee desperately tried to convince both Rudolf and King Bathory that he was able to produce the philosophers' stone (Dee 1659, 243, and also as quoted from 407). There was evidently a fatal discrepancy between the Doctor's intention and his clients' expectations. In spite of all this, the continental mission cannot be considered altogether a failure.

From this time on Dee and his scryer did not have access to royal circles. On the other hand, they developed a strong association with Francesco Pucci, the heretic and apostate who also took part in many of their séances.[24] It is noteworthy that after their first meeting in Cracow, Pucci seems to have followed Dee to Prague; later on they met in Erfurt during Dee's temporary exile, and, finally, the Italian forced himself on them as company in Trebona. His presence is associated with the most mystically significant episode of Dee's years on the Continent: the miracle of the books in Prague (see above, pp. 219–20).

In Dee's opinion Pucci was a mean character whose intrigues contributed to the expulsion of Dee and his associates from the territory of the Habsburg empire in May 1586 (cf. Dee 1569, 428). The Italian nevertheless must have been a very strong character because the Doctor could not easily free himself from his influence. As is well known, Pucci converted several times to and from Catholicism and tried various Reformed denominations, including a brief encounter with anti-Trinitarianism. At the time of his meeting with Dee and Kelly, he was taking one of his swings back to the Popish religion and was seeking protection from the papal nuncios. The new administrator, Bishop Filippo Sega, who arrived in Prague in April 1586, probably through Pucci's information, soon became alarmed by the obscure revelations of the Englishmen and thought that their content should be examined by the Catholic authorities in Rome. Although Pucci recommended the journey to Italy, Dee in time realized that no success and appreciation would be waiting for him at the seat of the Holy Inquisition. His position worsened enough in Prague since he had to leave the Habsburg lands at short notice.

The Doctor then temporarily moved to Germany until his new patron, Count Rožmberk, secured for him permission to return and stay in Trebona. The company spent two years there and the last Eastern European chapters of the spiritual diary contain magical sessions held in the Rožmberk castle. During the Trebona period the angels suggested important corrections to the system of evocations (cf. Dee 1994, Appendices A–C), and it was there that the Englishmen got supernatural instruction to carry out the infamous wife-swapping project (Dee 1659, *19–21 [new numbering]).

After a few years of break, Dee continued writing his private diary. These entries show the Doctor increasingly socializing from 1586 on. Traveling envoys, merchants, and scholars; English, French, and German visitors; and a few local characters are mentioned.

When contrasting the spiritual and the private diaries, we see two sides of Dee emerging. The latter was an active, versatile, prestigious humanist on the move while the former was an isolated monomaniac who had lost contact with reality and turned toward some obscure, inner dreamworld. This double nature, in fact, can be detected in the spiritual diaries themselves. It is surprising to see how few characters are mentioned on the several hundred pages of the angelic records: Dee, Kelly, Laski, and the two rulers; next to them a few royal administrators (like Dr. Jacob Kurtz), Ambassador de San Clemente, and the heretic Pucci are named; in addition, Dee meticulously registered the names of their landlords and pages. This illustrates that even these obscure and emotional journals can be occasionally used as enlightening social documents.

We learn, for example, that their journey from England to Poland lasted several months, beginning on September 21, 1583 and ending only on February 3, 1584, in Lasko Town where they were lodged "in the Provost his fair house by the Church" (Dee 1659, 62).

The description of their quarters in Prague, in the house of Tadeáš Hájek, the famous astronomer and alchemist, is even more dramatic:

August 1–9, 1584. On Wednesday the first day of August, at afternoon (hora 3) we entered on our journey toward Prague, in the Kingdom of Beame [sic!], whither we came on Thursday seven-night after, by 3 of the clock, that is exactly in eight days. We came by coach. I, E.K. and his brother, and Edmond Hilton, so that we came to Prague Augusti 9 by the new calendar.

   August 15. Wednesday. We began on the day of the Assumption of the blessed Virgin Mary: in the excellent little stove or study of Dr. Hageck his house lent me, by Bethlehem in old Prague: which study seemed in times past (anno 1518) to have been the study of some student or skilful of the Holy Stone. A name was in divers places of the study, noted in letters of gold and silver, *Simon Baccalaureus Pragensis*. And among other things manifold written very fairly in the study (and very many hieroglyphical notes philosophical, in birds, fishes, fruits, leaves and six vessels, as for the philosopher's works), these verses were over the door:

Immortal honour, and equal glory, are owed to the one
By whose wit this wall is adorned with colour.

And of the philosopher's work (on the south side of the study) in three
lines uppermost was this written:

This art is precious, delicate and rare.
Our learning is a boy's game and the toil of women.
All you sons of this art, understand that none may reap the fruits
of our elixir except by the introduction of the elementall stone,
and if he seeks another path he will never find the way
nor attain the goal.
(Dee 1659, 212; Dee 1998, 134–35)

From many of the entries one can reconstruct the structure of
households, even learn the names of some of the servants (cf. Harkness
1997). This is how a certain Emericus, probably a Hungarian, became
eternalized, having came from Laski's estate of Késmárk (then Hungary, today in Slovakia) with some errands (Dee 1659, 91). The following lively account reveals the semiotics of the display of power in early
modern Poland:

Remember that on Saturday, after noon, the Chancelour came to Cracow,
with 60 coaches in his company and train: he bringing in a close Coach
(covered with red) the Lord Samuel S. Boroskie Prisoner, whom he
took Friday night before, at his sisters house, being separated from his
Souldiers and servants, &c. (May 7, 1584; Dee 1659, 118)

We also learn that, in spite of his Protestant denomination, Dee
attended Catholic services in Cracow and even took communion at Easter.
Preceding this, he was convinced by the angels that "The Bread that was
ministered by Christ unto his Disciples, was not a figure of his body, but
his true body. So the Minister using the office and person of Christ in
office, pronouncing the words, doth also give unto the people not Bread,
but the true body" (Dee 1659, 372). It led him to accept, at least temporarily, the Catholic doctrine and he decided on admitting his sins
before a confessor who was none other than the famous neoplatonic
philosopher and commentator of the hermetic texts Hannibal Rosselli:[25]

April 19, 1585. I took ghostly counsel of Dr. Hannibal, the great
divine, that had now set out some of his commentaries upon Pymander,
Hermetis Trismegisti.

April 20, 1585. Saturday. I received the Communion at the
Bernardines, where that Doctor is a Professor. (Dee 1659, 397; Dee
1998, 178)

The mention of Doctor Rosselli reminds us that he is practically the
only humanist scholar who is named in the spiritual diaries, and the
Italian's commentaries on Hermes Trismegistus' *Pymander* is almost
the only book that Dee mentions by title beyond his own wiritings.[26] All
this is surprising from a man who possessed the largest private library in
contemporary England and who was carrying an impressive five-hundred-
volume traveling library with him. To this Roberts and Watson ironically
remark: "there is little reference to books in the conversations with angels—no doubt because one does not question angels about matters which
are already dealt with in print" (1990, 54).

Roberts and Watson (1990, 53–54) have clarified that in the hastily
selected but still huge traveling library Dee had unevenly selected works
from his comprehensive collection. He preferred his hermetic books and
beloved Paracelsica, and works on alchemy (perhaps at Kelly's suggestion), and he also took a sizable part of his Hebrew collection, which
might indicate his growing or ongoing interest in the cabala.[27]

Compared with his previous continental journeys the Doctor indeed
seems to have bothered much less with acquiring books and manuscripts.
It is still notable, however, that even in the most difficult moments of his
life he could never be entirely dispassionate about precious textual pieces.
For example, during his travels in Central Europe he often asked his
spirits whether to take his books or not on a certain leg of the journey
(e.g., Dee 1659, 243).

The bibliophile Dee is shown by his generous present of a fifteenth-
century Greek manuscript of Boëtius' *De consolatione philosophiae* in which
he inscribed a laborious dedication addressing the rector of the Jagellonian
University, Martin of Silesia.[28] Sometime in Poland he also presented
Kelly with an 1555 Estienne Bible (R&W 1099) and in exchange received from Laski a 1564 Venice folio of "Catalogus gloriae mundi
Chassenei" (R&W 226).

Dee also bought two manuscripts. He acquired a medieval library list
in Erfurt, during his most desperate weeks of exile—he probably planned
to identify his own manuscripts at home by the help of this manual (R&W
DM24). On his way back to England, he bought another manuscript in
Lübeck. This is a connoisseur's piece: George Ripley's magnificently illustrated alchemical scroll.[29]

Dee also recorded his most important moves to gain or enhance patronage. He included in the spiritual diaries his letters to Emperor Rudolf as well as his writings to his queen:

> May 11, 1586. Sunday. I came to Leipzig, and was at Peter Hans Swartz his house lodged. I found Laurence Overton, an English merchant. [. . .] There I also found a corteous gentleman called Mr. Francis Evers, the Lord Evers his son of the north. [. . .] I cannot omit to pass without memory the copy of one letter which I wrote to the Queen of England, her Secretary, the Right Honourable Sir Francis Walsingham, as followeth: "Right Honourable Sir, I am forced to be brief. That which England suspected was also here, for these two years, almost (secretly) in doubt, in question, in consultation Imperial and Royal, by honourable espies, fawning about me, and by other discoursed upon, pried and peered into. The Apostolic Nuncio, after his year's suit unto me to be acquainted with me [. . .] is gone to Rome with a flea in his ear, that disquieteth him, and terrifieth the whole state Romish and Jesuitical. Secretly they threaten us violent death . . . Sir, I trust I shall have justice for my house, library, goods and revenues, &c. [. . .] No human reason can limit or determine God his marvellous means of proceeding with us. He hath made of Saul (E.K.) a Paul. The Almighty bless her Majesty, both in this world and eternally: John Dee." (Dee 1998, 196)

The excited and not too coherent diction of his letter can be explained by his desperation: his trip to Leipzig was during a time of exile when his and his family's fate was most uncertain. Obviously, the Doctor mobilized all his energy to consolidate their state, political and financial alike. But the above letter also indicates that as opposed to Deacon's suspicion (1968), it was not he who was spying, but rather he who became the prey of the spies of Rome.

Two years prior to this letter Dee had given a totally different account of his audience with Rudolf. At that time he had still been optimistic about his future career as "Imperial Mathematicien" and gave a very vivid description of the choreography of auditions in the Emperor's private chamber:

> September 3, 1584. Hereupon I went straight up to the Castle: and in the Ritter-Stove or guard-chamber I stayed a little. In the mean space I sent Emericus to see what was of the clock: and the Chamberlain (Octavius Spinola) spied him out of the Emperor's chamber window,

and called him, who came up to me, and by that time was the Chamberlain come out to me; and by Emericus he understood that I was the man the Emperor waited for.

He came to me very courteously, hora tertia exacte a meridie, told me of the Emperor's desire to see me and to speak with me. So he returned to the Emperor into the privy chamber, and came out again for me, and led me by the skirt of the gown through the dining-chamber, into the privy-chamber, where the Emperor sat at a table, with a great chest and standish of silver before him, my Monas and letters by him, &c. I came toward him with due reverence of three cursies, who showed me a gracious and cheerful countenance. (Dee 1998, 142)

As we know, the audience brought rather bleak results; however, the lack of imperial grace was not enough to curb the Doctor's ambitions.

These, almost randomly selected examples corroborate my feeling that Dee lived an almost schizophrenic double life in East-Central Europe. The psychotic and visionary loner on the one hand can be contrasted with the vivid and exuberant scholar-magus who maintained his contacts and sought new acquaintances. One must be careful then when trying to answer the previously posed questions: did East-Central Europe gain anything from the Dee mission and did Dee and Kelly get anything in return?

The balance is actually more even that it looks at first sight. While at home Dee collected books, organized a private academy, managed geographical expeditions, and suggested a reform of the calendar, he did little of this sort in Eastern Europe. He did not even practice the occult art in that complex, esoteric-humanist form as he had previously at home. His message for Eastern Europe was a mystical, religious lesson, but without the innovative dogmatics of the radical reformers who temporarily camped in Poland or in Hungary (the Sozzinis, Palaeologus, or Francken). In fact, Dee was abhorred by the vistas of sceptical anti-Trinitarianism.

The Eastern European historian becomes most intrigued by learning about Dee's contacts with Christian Francken, the infamous heretic who, probably for the first time in European intellectual history, reached as far as systematic philosophical atheism.[30] In July 1587, probably in Trebona, Dee received two books from Francken. He took them back to England (being probably one of the first intellectuals to import anti-Trinitarianism to Britain), but as we have seen, he sent them to the archbishop of Canterbury to be theologically refuted (see above, p. 239).

One might say that Dee's religious eclecticism converged with the denomination of his patrons: at the Elizabethan court he appeared as a nationalist Anglican, near the Catholic Stephen Bathory he confessed and took the holy communion, in Habsburg Prague he also professed Catholicism, writing that "Luther, Calvin wilfully, obstinately erring; the Pope is not Antichrist; and *Ecclesia nostra Mater*" (Dee 1659, 411–12). On top of this interconfessionalist heterodoxy he developed a strong chiliasm, an inclination for Enochian prophecy with an apocalyptic imagery. While John Dee of England had been a follower of Roger Bacon and Trithemius, the wandering prophet of Eastern Europe is more an intellectual relative of the late Guillaume Postel, the similarly universalist Francesco Pucci, or Bruno and Campanella, the enthusiasts. All this, however, had relatively little effect on the Polish or Hungarian intelligentsia who had more affinity for religious controversies than for philosophical mysticism.

This ambiguous, slightly disappointing picture emerges from the external sources as well. Dee's name is not an important issue either in secret service reports or in the correspondence of the papal nuncios; he is not mentioned in the royal annals of the Polish court after his audiences with King Stephen, and he received only passing mentions in the correspondence of the outstanding scientist-humanists of the Prague imperial court, such as Crato von Kraftheim or Tadeáš Hájek (Hagecius) whose house sheltered the Doctor in the Bohemian capital (Dee 1659, 212).

It seems that Dee received the most extensive treatment in the letters exchanged between Hájek and his Silesian friend in Breslau (Wrocław), the Hungarian-born humanist Andreas Dudith. Unfortunately Hájek's letters are not extant, but we have Dudith's answers whose two mentions are of great interest. Dudith, who had hosted Philip Sidney in his Wrocław home in 1574 and otherwise had various contacts with English politicians and scholars, wrote rather lengthily about the English Doctor on December 20, 1585, not long after he had relocated from Poland to Prague. In this letter Dudith mentioned Dee with great reverence and asked Hájek to inquire from the Doctor if he could recommend to him a resident mathematician to whom he was willing to offer a respectable salary. Dudith also wrote to Pucci, the "Florentine patrician and nobleman" whom he seems also to have esteemed highly, and asked him the same, that is, to suggest a mathematician to satisfy his personal needs.[31]

There is no record whether along their several journeys between Prague and Cracow the Englishmen ever stopped in Wrocław to meet Dudith, whose esteem seems to have waned by 1587 when on January

3 he again mentioned Dee in his letter to Hájek. The reference reflects a great deal of uncertainty and ends with a sarcastic remark: "I have heard a lot about the English all which seem perplexing and little credible to me. Since some people ascertain that he speaks with the angels, I do not know whom to believe."[32] Then he mentions that apparently the spirits returned mere coal in lieu of the treasures Dee had collected for them, and even this coal burned into ashes.[33]

The above quotations corroborate Shumaker's wry remark: "Few of the persons admitted to the séances were deeply impressed, and some were frankly sceptical" (1982, 48). On the contrary, a more than enthusiastic remark can be found about Dee in the materials deriving from Václav Budovec, noted Lutheran leader in Prague, also an intellectual quite sensitive to certain kinds of mysticism. As we know from Robert Evans, he knew Dee personally and in a later recollection remembered as follows:

> A learned and renowned Englishman whose name was Doctor Dee came to Prague to see the Emperor Rudolf II and was at first well received by him; he predicted that a miraculous reformation would presently come about in the Christian world and would prove the ruin not only of the city of Constantinople but of Rome also. These predictions he did not cease to spread among the populace.[34]

Recently Deborah Harkness commented on this passage, suggesting that "Dee was not only intent merely on contacting angels, nor in keeping detailed diaries of those conversations. He was determined to communicate and discuss his concerns about the natural world and its future with the angels, his associates in the conversations, and, as Budovec reminds us, with a broad popular audience" (1999, 11). There is no reason to have doubts about Dee's ambition to spread his message to the largest possible audience; however, Harkness neglects the fact that Budovec's account dates from 1616, a time when the Rosicrucian excitement and an upsurge of magical interest aggravated the Lutheran community all over Central Europe. His recollection of Dee and the Doctor's impact on Prague twenty years earlier must be seen from this special vantage point.

By 1616 Dee was long dead and his fame as a scholar started transsubstantiating into a legendary lore, the clear signs of which we find in seventeenth and eighteenth-century Central Europe. Let us start from the late 1580s, when Dee was staying in Trebona on the Rožmberk estate. According to his private diary he lead a most active social life, regularly meeting with the Count Rožmberk as well as numerous local and international intellectuals, including an amazingly large number of Englishmen.[35]

As we know, the Rožmberks, Vilém and Peter Vok, had splendid courts and residences in Southern Bohemia, which were not only centers of significant local power, but also places of learning and pilgrimage destinations for wandering humanists and scientists. In their castle of Krumlov they accumulated a ten-thousand-volume library, one of the largest collections in contemporary Central Europe. In neighboring Trebona an alchemical laboratory was functioning for many years, and Vilém Rožmberk was as interested in Paracelsus and his work as was Laski the Pole and the Hungarian Batthyány. Vilém even employed humanist-alchemists to translate Paracelsica into Czech, as several ornate manuscripts still testify in the State Archives of Třeboň Castle and elsewhere (Evans 1973, 212–13).[36]

The archives in Trebona have preserved a large body of complex correspondence between Vilém Rožmberk, his managers, and many passersby who were seeking patronage and/or refuge on his estates and in his laboratory.[37] In this heap of material there is surprisingly little to be found about the activities of Dee and Kelly. Apart from a two-page manuscript, which seems to be a copy of some fragments of Dee's diary from 1583 through 1587,[38] there is only one letter (from Doctor Carl Wideman to Vilém Rožmberk) that explicitly refers to Kelly's alchemical experiments,[283] and there is no mention of Dee at all. As it turns out, Vilém—in cooperation with Emperor Rudolf—had large-scale projects for not only laboratory alchemy but also for metallurgy and mining. Hence a great number of experts were busy with various undertakings (Adam of Hradec, Václav Vřesovic, Peter Hlavsa, Daniel Prandtner, the above mentioned Carl Wideman, Melchior Horning, and others—see Evans 1973, 216), but Dee must have had only a marginal share in this work, if any. Although he visited Kaiser Rudolf Stadt (Rudolfov), the center of the new metallurgical experiments, in December 1588 (Dee 1998, 238), his only purpose there was to oversee the making of his coaches, being prepared for the return journey to England that started on March 11, 1589.

My suggestion is that while Dee and Kelly seem to have had little impact on their Eastern European contemporaries, they left behind an image that soon grew into inflated legends. Evans mentions many households from the Czech lands where manuscripts of their works have been preserved, and there is also one seventeenth-century example from Hungary.[40] Furthermore, I have already mentioned Budovec's story that depicts Dee as an important prophet-philosopher of the late Renaissance, almost as somebody who was preparing the way for the Rosicrucians.

This Rosicrucian image may have been grounded when Dee stayed in Bremen on his return journey and met the mystical adept of Hamburg, Heinrich Khunrath. Perhaps the English Doctor suggested that his colleague visit Vilém Rožmberk because in 1591 he was Vilém's court physician and by 1598 he received Rudolf's special copyright privileges for his works (Evans 1973, 214; Szulakowska 2000, 79). From Bremen Dee also corresponded with his old patron and friend, Moritz, the Landgrave of Hesse-Kassel, one of the chief patrons of the occult arts in contemporary Germany.

I argue that the transformation of natural philosophy and science during the late Renaissance also produced an epistemological vacuum that temporarily was filled by various magical applications. This explains the great popularity, even prestige, of magic during the sixteenth and the first half of the seventeenth centuries, and also the readiness of patrons to support such experiments. The development of such complex and intellectually ambitious alchemical patronage was most characteristic of the German *kulturkreis* of Central Europe, as seen in Emperor Rudolf's Prague or in some of the German princely courts which all had strong connections with their local universities and always had a supply of learned enthusiasts (Heidelberg, Kassel, Weikersheim, Wolfenbüttel, Helmstedt).[41] Dee evidently wanted to capitalize on this trend and market his own mysticism in such a cultural milieu. Alternatively, his dignified stature, when remembered a decade or so later, could be associated with the aims of the Rosicrucians.

The Dee type of intellectuals with their occult and chiliastic visions were primarily loners; however, their attitude logically culminated in the emergence of secret societies, working for the reformation of the world. Although according to the historical sources Dee never had any direct link with any organized secret society, let alone the Rosicrucians, he has been associated with them both in modern scholarship as well as by writers in the early modern period. Frances Yates argued that his *Monas* and his activities in Central Europe fostered the genesis of the Rosicrucian manifestos published in and around 1616.[42] As is known, these documents—growing out of a distinctively Lutheran-Pietist ideological foundation—promised the general reformation of the world through the aid of a secret society, the members of which would pursue politics, science, and religion for the purpose of saving mankind.

Some researchers of Rosicrucianism have found the archetype of this program in the *Naometria* of a certain Simon Studion, which was a prophetic-apocalyptic work, propagating the alliance of the Lily (France), the Lion (England), and the Nymph (the Palatinate of Württenberg) on common religious grounds (Lutheran Evangelicalism).[43] According to Yates the tone of the work is similar to that of Dee's prophecies in the East-Central European angelic conferences, and she suggested that Studion and Dee's patrons in this region formed a homogeneous intellectual circle.[44] The forging of a homogeneous intellectual society was undoubtedly a gross simplification by Yates, and Urszula Szulakowska's recent book offers very good evidence concerning just how divided even the closest Lutheran mystical circles were if one scrutinizes such previously undistinguished Pietists as Andreae, Arndt, Khunrath, or their enthusiast idol, Valentin Weigel (2000, 82–86; 145–52).

It is also true, on the other hand, that Dee indeed had personal contacts with a number of the patrons and scholars associated with the genesis of Rosicrucianism, and the following facts perhaps corroborate what I have just suggested, namely that in the 1610s Dee's image may have been used in a symbolic sense when the intellectual pedigree of Rosicrucianism had to be assembled.

1. It is a fact that Dee indeed dreamed of a general religious and political reform of a unified Europe—which he of course imagined to be united under a British banner just as Postel had earlier propagated a French-coordinated continental integration. It is also noteworthy that Dee in his *Monas hieroglyphica* offered a mystical-scientific method for the enhancement of the human intellect by which the reforms could be accomplished.

2. Undoubtedly, the *Monas* excercised quite a strong impact on certain trends of seventeenth-century intellectual history. It was republished in Lazarus Zetzner's famous compendium, the *Theatrum chemicum* (1602 and subsequent editions), which was used in all corners of the Continent. Even Carlos Gilly, a scholar definitely sceptical about Dee's direct influence on the Rosicrucians, admits that Dee's diagram of the hieroglyphic monad could be one of the archetypes of Adam Haslmayr's "character cabalisticus" included in the German Rosicrucian's *Consideratio Figurae Ergon et Parergon Fratrum RC* (unpublished manuscript of 1626; cf. Gilly 1995, 35). Gilly also sees a possible cross-influence between Dee's monad and Philippus à Gabella's alchemistical treatise on vitriol, published in his *Secretoris philosophiae consideratio brevis, nunc primum una cum Confessione Fraternitatis RC in lucem*

edita (Kassel, 1615; cf. Gilly 1995, 73). Finally, Gilly concludes as follows: "Dee, with many others, belonged to that alchemist-hermeticist tradition from which the alchemists and theosophists of the seventeenth century learnt a lot" (1995, 74).

3. According to the above, we should reconsider the fact that—although Rosicrucianism cannot be equated with Christian cabala (as Yates 1972, 89, superficially suggested)—a mystical natural philosophy based on number symbolism, such as that of Dee, strongly featured in the thinking of the Rosicrucians, too. As we know, also from Gilly, in 1619 an eccentric enthusiast Philip Ziegler, turned up in Nurnberg and called himself the king of the Rosicrucians ("Origines Philippus von Gottes Gnaden erwählter und gekrönter König von Jerusalem, Siloh, Joseph und David, der Brüder des Rosenkreutzes Oberster und unüberwindlichster Zepter des Königs in Sion"). This Ziegler in a later, strongly numerological work mentioned Dee and called him—as a member of the Rosicrucians—his spiritual brother ("Joh. Dee Londinensis Anglus de Fratribus RC;" cf. Gilly 1988, 83).

Dee's impact on the seventeenth-century German courts was recently reassessed by Bruce T. Moran (1991, 92–100), who introduced his chapter on "The Rosicrucian Connection" as follows:

> There existed a natural language which linked the books of nature, man, and Scripture. Attempts at its reconstruction marked the efforts of Renaissance Neoplatonists like Pico, Ficino, Reuchlin and Agrippa, and defined many parts of Paracelsian literature as well. Among them all, however, it was John Dee's *Monas hieroglyphica* which became the best known exercise in pursuing the real meaning of nature by means of a natural creative language—in this case a language reduced to a universal symbol reflecting the unity of the world. Dee's influence, may, in fact, have been partially responsible for one of the most interesting episodes in the search for a natural language. In this instance, the idea of a language of nature filtered through traditions of Christian cabalism and Paracelsian prophetic mysticism to appear finally in the early seventeenth century in treatises describing the brotherhood of the Rosy Cross. (1991, 92–93)

4. Finally, one should recall how easily Rosicrucianism found its way back to England. In part it was due to the works of another

loner, Robert Fludd, which nevertheless had their influence in Germany as well as on the early scientific societies of England. Fludd's views promoted the English translations of the Rosicrucian manifestos in the mid-seventeenth century by Thomas Vaughan.[45]

The most recent data concerning Dee's "Rosicrucianism" derive from the research of Roberts and Watson and Urszula Szulakowska. According to these, in 1618 "ex bibliopolio Frobenio" in Hamburg Roger Bacon's *Epistolae de secretis operibus et naturae et de nullitate magiae* was published in John Dee's edition. The editorial work had of course been done decades earlier, as I have hinted above (cf. p. 194). The German publisher must have acquired Dee's old manuscript and was careful enough to print the text together with the English Doctor's notes and marginalia. The title page straightforwardly identifies Dee as the editor of the text: "Opera Johannis Dee Londinensis e pluribus castigata [. . .] cum notis quibusdam partim ipsius Johannis Dee, partim edentis" (Roberts and Watson 1990, 62). The preface is dedicated to the Rosicrucian Brothers and sums up the complicated textual history: the edition is based on the 1594 Oxford edition that they could obtain only by borrowing the private copy of an acquaintance.

But who could be the editor(s) and whose copy were they using? According to Roberts and Watson, the editors must have been the assistants of Dee's last years, John Pontois and Patrick Saunders. The former many times visited Germany and Silesia and had contacts with the Paracelsist Johannes Montanus in Strigau whose name is mentioned in the preface. Saunders, in 1619 wrote an inscription in the *album amicorum* of a Rosicrucian from Lübeck, Joachim Morsius. That year Morsius traveled in England and his album also preserves the inscriptions of Ben Jonson and William Camden, together with Cornelius Drebbel, chief mechanician of James I, and János Bánfihunyadi who under the name of Johannes Banfi Hunyades was a researcher in London's Gresham College.[46] According to the hypothesis put forward by Roberts and Watson, Morsius visited Saunders while he was in London because he wanted to get acquainted with the disciple of the famous Doctor Dee.[47]

William Sherman continued to trace this line; he observed that in the Hamburg edition (for the title page see Figure 8.1) not only were Dee's marginalia carefully printed, but these were acknowledged by the Doctor's monogram. According to Sherman "the reproduction of his reading notes implies that Dee was also valued as an interpreter" (Sherman 1995, 43). Interestingly, although Frances Yates does not seem to have

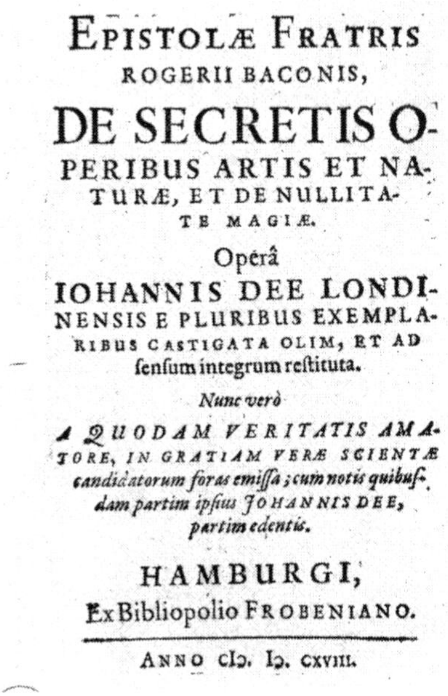

EPISTOLÆ FRATRIS
ROGERII BACONIS,
DE SECRETIS O-
PERIBUS ARTIS ET NA-
TURÆ, ET DE NULLITA-
TE MAGIÆ.

Operâ
IOHANNIS DEE LONDI-
NENSIS E PLURIBUS EXEMPLA-
RIBUS CASTIGATA OLIM, ET AD
senfum integrum reſtituta.

Nunc verò
A QUODAM VERITATIS AMA-
TORE, IN GRATIAM VERÆ SCIENTÆ
candidatorum foras emiſſa; cum notis quibuſ-
dam partim ipſius JOHANNIS DEE,
partim edentis.

HAMBURGI,
ExBibliopolio FROBENIANO.

ANNO CIɔ. Iɔ. CXVIII.

FIGURE 8.1   *Epistolae Fratris Rogerii Baconis, De secretis [. . .] naturae [. . .] Ioanni Dee ad sensum integrum restituta* (Hamburg: Frobenius, 1618), title page. Herzog August Bibliothek, Wolfenbüttel [107 Phys. /4/].

noticed this Hamburg edition, she was aware of Gabriel Naudé's reference to Dee's Bacon. According to the French mathematician and Rosicrucian writer,

> If we had the book which John Dee, citizen of London and a very learned philosopher and mathematician, says that he composed in defence of Roger Bacon in which he shows that all that is said about his marvellous works should be ascribed to nature and mathematics, rather than to a commerce with demons, which he never had, I protest that I would speak no more about him. . . . (Yates 1972, 110)[48]

Another interesting reference to Dee from the time of rising Rosicrucianism was unearthed by Urszula Szulakowska. While reading Khunrath, that ambiguous and mysterious Pietist-enthusiast, she noticed that the German alchemical theologian considered Dee one of his principal mentors. In the dedication of his *Quaestiones Tres Per-Utiles* (Leipzig, 1607), he referred to Dee as "Londinensem [. . .] hoc est, Sapientiae Sincerioris Gazophylacem magnum; Angliae Hermetem" (Szulakowska

2000, 79). The same terms are repeated in Khunrath's *Amphitheatrum Aeternae Sapientiae*—an esoteric work that Evans called "the most grandiose even of that magniloquent age" (1973, 214).

Tracing the changing reputation of Dee, Sherman's remark seems to be a good interim conclusion: "Less than twenty years after his death, Dee's textual remains were generating competing portraits—the cabalist magician and the Baconian mathematician—in relation to a group whose own affiliations to occult philosophy and mainstream science were being contested" (1995, 43).

Although Dee's image was greatly damaged in England by Casaubon's 1659 publication of the *True and Faithful Relations...*, this book in English had no major effect on the Continent where, especially in Central Europe, Dee's mythical reputation continued to grow (sometimes through curious mutations) well into the eighteenth century. A good example is Hungary, where in 1774 the first systematic chronicler of Hungarian science, István Weszprémi, remembered a grandiose program related to Dee's visit in 1563. As he wrote,

> [In 1584] Laski invited Kelly and Dee to Hungary, who were pleased to accept the offer, especially Dee who had had practised his craft of alchemy in Hungary already earlier in 1563 for a long time and to the great admiration of a number of people. [...] The chemical college was opened in Laski's castle in 1584 where the landlord received a thorough instruction in the chemical arts and he tortured the mineral world day and night with fire, however, at the end flunked as it usually happens. . . . [49]

The quality of this unfounded hearsay can be compared to the seventeenth-century English rumors about Dee's raising the dead and other such nonsense;[50] its contents are somewhat surprisingly different. While it was not uncommon in contemporary Hungary that decent scholars and humanists were accused of sorcery and the black arts,[51] it is surprising that Dee, whose angel magic in fact had some kinship with those charges, did not inspire any Faustian legends in this part of Europe. It seems that here the image associated with the writer of the *Monas hieroglyphica* continued to be more appealing and this may be the reason why in eighteenth-century Vienna a hermetic treatise on *exaltatio* could be published under his name.

In 1794 the following curious work appeared in the Habsburg capital: *Das Büchlein der Venus*, which was included in a larger work offering old magical literature for the lovers of secret sciences (*Handschriften für Freunde geheimer Wissenschaften*, Wien: Blumauer). The "Book of Venus," a manual of invocations for calling forth various spirits, listed John Dee as author. Its Latin original was relatively widespread in Germany: there are three surviving manuscripts, one in Erlangen, one in Munich, and one in the Warburg Library in London.[52] The origin of this text is obscure, but there is no likelihood of Dee's authorship. Rather it seems to be a German work, reaching back to the tradition of ceremonial magic described by Kieckheffer (1997). As Jörg Martin (1989) suggests, it may have happened that the text became associated with the name of Dee in the seventeenth century, due to the reputation established during his East-Central European travels.

It is equally interesting to ask why this work was translated into German in the Vienna of the Enlightenment, and why it was important for the editor to emphasize Dee's authorship. Perhaps it was because the antiquarian works of Weszprémi and others revived the interest in the English Doctor, or perhaps because the intellectual atmosphere that produced Mozart's *The Magic Flute* was ripe for such publications. Regardless, it is clear that the interpretive community never ceased to be interested in Dee, partly because his obscure, admirable, and disquieting figure continued to have an attracting, frightening appeal of the Other for the populace, partly because his desire for the unattainable *exaltatio* was all too well-known to most people, even centuries after his death.

These seventeenth- and eighteenth-century examples of Dee's reception provide the missing links that connect the mystical truths behind his hieroglyphic diagram and the burning anxieties of the angelic conferences with the romantic revival of the nineteenth century and with those modern novels, paintings, films, and operas that I mentioned in the introduction.

Meric Casaubon and the Politics of Interpretation

Magician, Heretic, and Witch

John Dee's intentions in his magical operations and the angelic conversations were entirely pious: he was striving toward a mystical union with God. Looking at Dee's reception, however, we see that neither his contemporaries nor following generations were unanimous in appreciating such piety. On the contrary, in his life and later, he was recurrently labeled a conjuror, a witch, or an arch-heretic. He wrote several apologies in which he compared himself to such victims, as Socrates, Apuleius of Megara, Giovanni Pico della Mirandola, or Johannes Trithemius.[53] In fact these charges crop up paradigmatically in the intellectual and social atmosphere of the early modern period and the representatives of the magical-hermetic tradition received them almost without exception. To understand the nature of these charges and the mechanism of power politics behind them, one has to look at the relationship between pious, white magic as opposed to wicked, diabolical or black sorcery, and their connections to witchcraft and heresy.

It is interesting to note that the actual proofs and documents of black magic are extremely scarce. The philosophers interested in magic always emphasized their devout aspirations, which were primarily to praise the Creator by demonstrating a human dignity that would corroborate the notion of man having been created after the true image of God. The most eminent way to prove this was to accomplish *exaltatio*, the magus elevating himself into the divine spheres, to the side of the Supreme Being.

Significantly, most of the information about black magic, such as harmful operations, devil worship, or pacts with the infernal forces, derives either from—more or rather less well-founded—denunciations, from public or legal accusations, or from literary works. Most notable of the latter type is the Faust legend and the various theatrical and narrative fictions based on it. I have never come across an authentic first-person account (let alone in the most private diary form) from the early modern period admitting the intentional practice of black magical operations. On the other hand, none of the great magi who did their best to manifest their most pious aims with magic could escape charges of sorcery, heresy, even witchcraft.

Cornelius Agrippa, for example, was often accused of black magic—and a famous black magical handbook was even written under his name ("The Fourth Book" of Agrippa's *De Occulta Philosophia*, which was also attributed to Pietro d' Abano).[54] He was not able to waive the suspicions, in spite of his repeated efforts to prove that his magic was totally dependent on religion. For example, in Chapter 3:36, titled "De homine, quomodo creatus ad imaginem Dei," Agrippa explicated the doctrine of the magic dignity of man in a strictly Christian context: "Notwithstanding the true image of God is his Word. The wisdom, life, light and truth existing by himself, of which image man's soul is the image . . ." (Agrippa 1997, 579).

Paracelsus, one of Dee's important models, received similar charges from even such a learned man as Conrad Gessner, the encyclopedist:

"Once a pupil of Theophrastus and his private assistant reported strange tales concerning the latter's intercourse with demons . . ." (quoted by Jung 1983, 119). One wonders what the motivation was for those often extreme charges and if they showed any characteristic pattern at all. My answer to the latter question is "yes," and I suggest that the overall problem can and should be researched with the help of historical anthropology and historical social psychology.

As it may have become clear by now, magic, even in its most pious, Christian form, represented a sort of heterodoxy that posed a challenge, the threat of subversion against the existing ideological system. The defensive nature of orthodoxy is excellently described by J. Neusner: "a convention, well-established in a variety of studies, is that one group's holy man is another group's magician: 'what I do is a miracle, but what you do is magic' " (1989, 4–5).

As I see it, the orthodox defense system included the following steps. First, the threatening challenge had to be clearly and unhesitantly labeled as something very dangerous in order that it could be separated and isolated from the healthy body of the community. The labels had to be reminiscent of a most contagious epidemic so that no one would even think of experimenting with it. As such, the most severely regarded threats were *heresy* on the one hand (usually identified with Arianism or Anabaptism), and *witchcraft* on the other. Since witchcraft was usually treated as a subgenre of black magic, the circle was closed; the feedback to magic provided that the white magician could be labeled as a black sorcerer.

Second, the isolated phenomenon had to be either radically expurgated or radically understood and so familiarized. After this could follow its neutralization and, if necessary, appropriation. During this process the labels and charges were used symbolically rather than literally. This technology was to assure the community that no wicked diabolism could be ultimately effective against God's merciful providence. So if the people were careful and watchful enough, the danger, after all, was not that great.

In the following subchapter I shall trace the social and ideological mechanisms through which the interpretive community—represented by Dee's posthumous publisher, the *Späthumanist* Meric Casaubon— tried to understand (and thus familiarize and neutralize) Dee's encounter with the Other. His strategy led to the identification of the English Doctor as someone who had become possessed. That is, he came to represent the Other as something to be frightened of, something that had to be separated and isolated from the community. This was accomplished by labeling him a "heretic" and a "witch"; however, the follow-

ing step was to demystify his magic by explaining his angelic conferences as delusion and madness.

To understand the procedure I shall refer to the mechanisms of
"inventing" madness in order to contain and appropriate transgression—
as they have been described by Michel Foucault (*Madness and Civilization*) and Stephen Greenblatt (*Renaissance Self-Fashioning*). Especially
pertinent to my argument is the way the latter demonstrates the handling
of the Other through self-fashioning within the contexts of early modern
societies. His inventory of these "handling mechanisms" offers a good
introduction to this topic:

> —Self-fashioning involves submission to an absolute power or author-
> ity situated at least partially outside the self—God, a sacred book, an
> institution such as church, court, colonial or military administration.
>
> —Self-fashioning is achieved in relation to something perceived as alien,
> strange, or hostile. This threatening Other—heretic, savage, witch,
> adulteress, traitor, Antichrist—must be discovered or invented in order
> to be attacked and destroyed.
>
> —The alien is percieved by the authority either as that which is un-
> formed or chaotic (the absence of order) or that which is false or
> negative (the demonic parody of order). Since accounts of the former
> tend inevitably to organize and thematize it, the chaotic constantly
> slides into the demonic, and consequently the alien is always con-
> structed as a distorted image of the authority.
>
> —One man's authority is another man's alien.
>
> —When one authority or alien is destroyed, another takes its place.
>
> —There is always more than one authority and more than one alien in
> existence at a given time.
>
> —Self-fashioning is always, though not exclusively, in language.
>
> —The power generated to attack the alien in the name of the authority
> is produced in excess and threatens the authority it sets out to defend.
> Hence [this process] always involves some experience of threat, some
> undermining, some loss of self. (Greenblatt 1980, 9)

Meric Casaubon's lengthy Preface clearly illustrates the above postulated phases of isolation, familiarization, and neutralization of the danger;
represented by Dee.

Casaubon (1599–1671), son of Isaac Casaubon one of Renaissance
Europe's great scholars, was himself an erudite scholar whose criticisms of

the new science inspired Thomas Sprat's *History of the Royal Society.* One of his most famous works is *Of Credulity and Incredulity in Things Natural, Civil, and Divine* (1668), in which he examines arguments for and against a belief in witches and other occult phenomena, sharing the view that Christians must believe in them or else depart with all beliefs in the supernatural. His views must have been formed by his encounter with the diaries of John Dee.

Casaubon's Politics

Casaubon says in the Preface that his patron invited him to publish Doctor Dee's newly recovered magical journals with the intention of saving Christian souls from such delusions and since "it is very possible that every Reader will not at the first be so well able of himself to make that good use of this sad Story as is aimed at, my chiefest aim in this Preface is to help such" (Dee 1659, Preface, *2[55]).

Casaubon, above all, posed two questions in connection with the angelic conversations: 1. if spirits existed at all; and 2. if yes, what sort of spirits were Dee's instructors. After having given a humanist-like survey of classical and contemporary literature on apparitions and spirits, Casaubon concluded that it was undoubtedly demons that appeared before the Doctor and his medium, Kelly. His rhetoric is remarkable: in the initial passages he writes in a sceptical-ironical tone, but later he leads the reader step-by-step in the belief concerning the existence of spirits: "I cannot satisfie my self how any Learned man, sober and rational, can entertain such an opinion that there be no *Divels* nor *Spirits*, &c." (*18). At the same time—citing Luther and William Perkins—he elaborately asserts that the spirits having appeared to Dee could not be but wicked ones, in fact devils. And his judgment is that the person who associated himself with devils of necessity becomes a witch. He describes this act as "pawning his Soul [to Satan], such is the power of this kind of Spiritual delusion" (*34).

From the theme of witchcraft he turns to the question of heresy and identifies Dee's delusion with Anabaptism. In the Preface he several times mentions that Dee's personal characteristics, such as his enthusiasm and philosophical independence, facilitated the swelling of heresy in his mind:

> Some men come into the world with *Cabalistical Brains;* their heads are
> full of mysteries; they see nothing, they read nothing, but their brain

is on work to pick somewhat out of it that is not ordinary. [. . .] Reason and Sense that other men go by, they think the acorns that the old world fed upon; fools and children may be content with them but they see into things by another *Light*. They commonly give good respect unto the *Scriptures* (till they come to profest *Anabaptists*) because they believe them the Word of God and not of men; but they reserve unto themselves the Interpretation. . . . (*23–24)

So far goes the identification and isolation of the alien Other. The case, having now been identified with the most dangerous supernatural transgressions, seems frightening enough to discourage imitation. But what is hyperbolically inflated on the one hand has to be familiarized and demystified on the other in order to corroborate the feeling in the community that the threat is controllable. It can be contained. Casaubon reaches this aim by rationalizing and explaining Dee's case on theological as well as on psychological grounds and in this respect his argumentation is no less remarkable.

He definitely rules out that the spiritual diaries could be produced by imposture or fraud:

We intended thereby to justifie what is here printed against any suspition of forgery. [. . .] By *Truth and Sincerity*, intending not only Dr. Dee's fidelity in relating what he himself believed, but also the *reality* of those things that he speaks of, according to his relation: his only (but great and dreadful) error being, that he mistook false lying Spirits for Angels of Light, the Divel of Hell for the God of Heaven. (*26)

On the contrary, Casaubon attributed the Doctor's enthusiasm to a colossal epistemological misinterpretation, a mistake resulting from the deficiency of his character, but by no means being simple fantasy:

We will easily grant that a distempered brain may see, yea, and hear strange things, and entertain them with all possible confidence, as real things, and yet all but fancy, without any real sound or Apparition. But these sights and Apparitions that Dr. Dee gives here an account, are quite another nature; [. . .] I say, and not without the intervention and operation of Spirits, as will easily appear to any man by the particulars. [. . .] These things could not be the operation of a distempered Fancy, will be a sufficient evidence to any rational man. (*26)

After having confirmed the reality of the spiritual conversations, Casaubon applies a rather flat, demystifying, and certainly firmly orthodox critique of Dee's attitude toward his apparitions. First, he discredits the reality of the program of Renaissance neoplatonist magi concerning the *exaltatio* of man: "it is against all Reason as well as Religion to believe that a creature so much inferior to God, by nature as man is, should see every thing as He seeth and think as He thinks" (*32). Second, he identifies the desire for *exaltatio* with simple pride, *hybris*: "his own deceitful heart it may be suggested unto him, *that he might glorify God*; but certainly, that himself might become a *glorious man* in the world, and be admired" (*32). Third, he treats this hubris as a very natural thing, not to be surprised at: "if *Pride* and *Curiosity* were enough to undoe our first Parent [. . .] should we wonder if it had the same event in Dr. Dee, though otherwise, as he doth appear to us, innocent, and well qualified" (*32).

This argumentation was perfectly in line with Casaubon's wider philosophical outlook, which represented learned but orthodox conservativism identifying sadducism (the denial of spirits) and atheism as the main threatening drives against the church, traditional values, and "good learning." In his other works, such as the *Treatise Concerning Enthusiasme* (1655) and *Of Credulity and Incredulity* (1670), he always clearly pinpointed the enemies: atheism and scepticism on the one hand and enthusiasm and pride on the other.[56] Dee obviously fell in the latter category, together with his compatriot, the also "enthusiastic" Robert Fludd, of whom Casaubon wrote as follows:

> Robert Fludd, with whom such professions of zeal for the glory of God are very frequent and ordinary: and to that end to set out his glory in its greatest lustre, doth propose unto us the consideration of the Philosophers Stone, applying all or most mysteries of the Scripture to it; so that in very truth, his zeal was more for the Philosophers Stone, then God; or the Philosophers Stone, a God of his own making, for which he was so zealous.[57]

It is characteristic that Casaubon never questioned either Dee's high intellectual abilities or his good intentions; however, he also argued that Dee's mistakes were comparable to the faults of witches, magicians, and heretics, especially the Anabaptist enthusiasts. Through their example, he demonstrates that a strong trust in prayer is "of much more danger and delusion, than many do believe" (*53). Casaubon's motivations in judging Dee became obvious from the Preface: from within an orthodox community—let it be the community of humanists, university scholars, or believers of a set of religious dogmas—noncomformist behavior and dissenting ways of thinking cannot be classified positively. His argumentation is a fine blend of correct psychological observations, sound philological analyses, and a clearly ideologically motivated appropriation of the unorthodox Other. All this becomes crystal clear when he rounds out his Preface by giving the reasons why he decided to publish these documents and explains the moral teaching of John Dee's example:

> Several good uses that may be made of this book:
> The first is against Atheists, and such as do not believe that there be any Divels or Spirits. [. . .] I do not know what can be more convincing than this sad story. This is a great point and a great ground of Religion: for if there be Spirits indeed, so wicked and malicious, so studious and so industrious, to delude men, and to do mischief, which is their end, all which is so fully represented in this Relation, then certainly must it follow, that there is a great overruling Power, that takes care of the Earth and of the Inhabitants of it. [. . .] England might have been over-run with Anabaptism long before this: God be thanked that it was not then, and God keep it from still. . . . (*50)
> In the last place all men may take warning by this example, how they put themselves out of the protection of the Almighty God, either by presumptuous unlawful wishes, or by seeking not unto Divels only, directly (which Dr. Dee certainly never did, but abhorred the thought of it in his heart) but unto them that was next relation unto Divels, as Witches, Wizzardes, Conjurers, Astrologers, Fortune-tellers, and the like, yea, all books of that subject, which I doubt [= fear], were a great occasion of Dr. Dee's delusion. (*54)

Interestingly enough, Casaubon did not deal in depth with the role of Kelly in the angelic conferences and this has long intrigued scholars. The first historian who offered a serious analysis of *The True & Faithful Relations* was Wayne Shumaker and he came to the conclusion that "Kelly was evidently not a man worthy of reliance" (1982, 26). In spite of the refined argumentation of his study, Shumaker treated Kelly all along as a simple fraud and interpreted his relationship with Dee as a ruthless manipulator to his victim.[58] His analysis overlooked the possibility of that psychological and micro-social situation that Geoffrey James expounded: "Kelly was forced to stay with Dee because the money that the doctor gave him supported Kelly's wife and brother. It was Dee, not Kelly, who was gaining the benefit from the magical ceremonies, for it sated his lust for 'radical truths.' "[59] Biographical data, indeed, suggest nothing venerable about the character of Kelly; however, the fraud theory is weakened by numerous episodes when he seems to have worked against his own interests in cooperation with his master. On several occasions it was he who tried to convince Dee of the wicked and unfaithful nature of the spiritual beings who appeared in the crystal. He also pointed out mistakes the supernatural informants were making. One of the most often quoted episodes is when after a session devoted to some geographical questions, Kelly

> came speedily out of his study, and brought in his hand one volume of Cornelius Agrippa his works, and in one chapter of that book he read the names of countries and provinces collected out of Ptolemaeus. Whereupon he inferred that our spiritual instructors were coseners to give us a description of the world, taken out of other books: and therefore he would have no more to do with them. (May 24, 1584; Dee 1998, 127)

Dee's faith in the spirits, just as on other occasions, remained unshakable:

> I am very glad that you have a book of your own wherein these geographical names are expressed. Whereby you may perceive how your reason is marvellously confounded by your wilful fantasy: for so much as, wherein you would find fault in our spiritual instructors' doings, therein they have done that which I requested them, as appeareth: and that to the intent of known countries we might understand which angels had the government. [. . .] This is too gross your error. (ibid.)

Again, it is rather difficult to understand Kelly's motivations with the proposal of the infamous matrimonial cross-matching on the basis of dishonest cheating (cf. Dee 1659, *20–21. [new numbering]). Eventually he caused more trouble for himself than whatever he gained from the action.

I believe that the extraordinary and strained psychotic symbiosis in which the two men and their families spent their days invites a complex combination of arguments. We cannot help feeling that Kelly either must have believed, at least to some extent, in the prophecies he was communicating, or, if he pretended and invented, he successfully deceived himself as well. In an atmosphere in which, as Shumaker characterizes, "images and phrases stored up from the Bible, the often overheated pulpit oratory of the period, occultist reading, and dream imagery" (1982, 31) constituted the sources of every day as well as scholarly discourse, Dee's naive logic and Kelly's behavior are equally perplexing, but at the same time understandable.

To comprehend this milieu, it is enough to remember the extraordinary situation when Edward Alleyn, leading actor of the Elizabethan age, once so perfectly identified himself with Doctor Faustus that at the appearance of the stage devils he stopped the performance and together with the whole audience spent the rest of the evening in fervent prayers.[60]

—⚉—

At this point I would like to draw some conclusions from what I have so far said concerning the hermeneutical practices of the interpretive community in relation to Dee's magic. To begin with, it seems that against all the efforts of Renaissance magi and/or modern historians, we still do not possess any guaranteed means to distinguish clearly between high and low/popular magic, or between white and black practices. Because of the theological implications, even the most pious magic can be interpreted as heresy and hubris inspired by Satan. Dee's angel magic is a good example of how complex and ambiguous is this phenomenon of intellectual history.

Dee was often unjustly accused of sorcery and Anabaptist dissent. At the same time, he indeed was an interconfessionalist, and the fact that sometimes even Kelly thought the angels to be malevolent and deceiving shows that certain principles, intentions, and practices are indistinguishable. In the previous chapters, I have repeatedly arrived at the recognition that magic is in itself contradictory and paradoxical in nature—consider the tensions behind Pico's relation to astrology, Agrippa's recognition of Simon Magus, Paracelsus' Faustian rebellion, or Dee's realization of the ambiguity of catoptrics: from "optical science" to scrying.

The greatest merit of Casaubon's Preface is that while he tried to describe in an exact, scholarly way the possible motivations and psychological conditions of Dee, quite intuitively he discovered that mechanism that made occultism one of the important catalyzers of Western culture. His characterization of Dee's "enthusiasm" (quoted above) highlighted the drive for seeking "The Light" and the ambition "to reserve unto themselves the *Interpretation . . .*" (emphasis mine, Preface, *24). Seeking the light and practicing freedom of interpretation are those things that produce the most elevating and at the same time the most dangerous things. Because

that for divers years he had been earnest unto God in prayer for Wisdom; that is as he interprets himself, That he might understand the secrets of Nature that had not been revealed unto men hitherto; to the end, as he professeth, and his own deceitful heart it may be suggested unto him, That he might glorify God; but certainly, that himself might become a glorious man in the world. . . . (Preface, *32)

Casaubon's words reveal that double perspective through which we cannot help seeing the shadows of some dark forces behind even the purest ambitions of the white magus. On the other hand, as in the case of Marlowe's Faustus, even in the worst manifestations of hubris and fatal decisions, we can behold the charisma of heroic individualism and tragic greatness.

In looking at Dee's thought, works, ideology, and symbolic expression, I argue that those historians who offer their interpretation in relation to other systems of culture and civilization (such as science or religion), no matter how many useful details they discover and explain, still miss the ultimate target. These efforts unavoidably end up with setting up typologies, separating white and black magic, identifying them with period styles, and finally forging grand narratives. And on the way they fail to address the fascinating question: what provides that inner dynamism of magic that it could be invariably compelling, independent of epoch, even after the great Scientific Revolution of the seventeenth century?

I have been trying to approach magic by always concentrating on its paradoxical character, the vehicle of which has been the program of *exaltatio*, which balanced ambition, power politics, and self-fashioning against an openness of mind and yearning for the highest and the infinite. Such an approach to magic leads us to our present age where it has influenced fields from cultural anthropology (parapsychology, modern mysticism, New Age and Enochian magic), through philosophy (Rudolf Steiner, René Guénon, Manly P. Hall), to great modern artists who have sought inspiration from magic in a variety of ways (W. B. Yeats, Marcel Duchamps, Vassily Kandinsky, Leonora Carrington, Derek Jarman, Umberto Eco) and whose works invite ever new interpretations.

9

Conclusion:
Dee and Renaissance Symbolism

Until now I have been trying to inquire into the ideology of John Dee through the works that he absorbed ("input") and through the texts in which he gave a symbolic expression to the "radicall truthes" he was seeking ("output"). I have also looked at his reception by examining the reactions of the interpretive community. In the last passages of the previous chapter I mentioned the long and complex tradition of magic, which is still lively and productive in our own age, inspiring new works as well as interpretations. As I hinted in the introduction, Dee's works and his symbolically elaborated figure has been present in all cultural epochs since the seventeenth century, and his image continues to be an intellectual inspiration as well as a literary and artistic theme. He may be recognized in such classical theatrical heroes as Shakespeare's Prospero or Ben Jonson's Subtle, and he returns in twentieth-century novels (Meyrink's *The Angel of the West Window*, Eco's *Foucault's Pendulum*, and Ackroyd's *The House of Doctor Dee*), plays, paintings, even operas. To discuss all this would require another book, and I am sure somebody is already working on it.

As an epilogue to this monograph, I would like to look at a single stanza of a sixteenth-century poetical work, the literary symbolism of which shows a crucial parallel to that program Dee tried to express in his mystical-natural philosophy. I am thinking of a microcosmic unit of Edmund Spenser's *The Faerie Queene*, a particular poetical vision that I see as an image twinned with the hieroglyphic monad. If I interpreted Dee's cosmogram as a condensed mandalaic symbol of all transcendental experience, so I could call Spenser's "House of Alma" an artistic experiment attempting to speak the *lingua adamica*.

It is interesting to notice that while in the time of the great Renaissance epistemological paradigm shift the natural scientist still spoke a language heavily mixed with rhetorical elements and allegorical narration, poetry, the natural medium of myths, fables, and allegories in turn developed an ambition to include scientific theses, and cosmic schemes. This is what happens in Spenser's much disputed cryptic stanza describing the House of Alma. As is well known, Spenser's epic poem is an allegorical work, meaning that each and all of its elements have to be translated from picture language to a plane of abstract meanings. Alma herself is the soul, and her house is the body, a place of harmony and temperance. (The episode takes place in Book Two, which is devoted to the virtue of Temperance.) This allegorical castle is described by Spenser as follows:

> The frame thereof seemd partly circulare,
> And part triangulare, O worke diuine;
> The two the first and last proportions are,
> The one imperfect, mortall, foeminine;
> Th' other immortall, perfect, masculine,
> And twixt them both a quadrate was the base,
> Proportioned equally by seven and nine;
> Nine was the circle set in heauens place,
> All which compacted made a goodly diapase.
>
> (FQ II.ix.22; quoted from Spenser 1980, 251)

This stanza is surrounded by a fairly transparent allegorical narration concerning Goddess Alma's harmonious and self-controlled nature. However, the design of the very house has perplexed readers since it was first written. Some suggest that the description refers simply to the basic proportions and dimensions of the human body; others argue that what we have here is a revelatory word-emblem that refers to the dualism of the macro- and microcosms, the correspondences of the Great Chain of Being, and that, similarly to Dee's monad, it contains mystical number symbolism based on the neoplatonic philosophy. In both cases this symbolism can be boiled down to the contrast of One and Two, referring to this existence and the Other, in terms of a threatening abyss that these mystical cosmograms can bridge in a revelatory way.

The mystical, neoplatonic interpretation was established by Sir Kenelm Digby (1603–1665), probably the best of Spenser's early critics. In 1628 he wrote a letter to Sir Edward Stradling (published in 1643) in which he tried to document what he had stated in another of his treatises:

> [Spenser] had a solide and deepe insight in Theologie, Philosophy (especially the Platonike) and the Mathematicall sciences, and in what others depend of these three. [. . .] Tis evident that the Authors intention in this Canto is to describe the bodie of a man inform'd with a rationall soul, and in prosecution of that designe he sets down particularly the severall parts of the one and of the other—as they make one perfect compound.[1]

In his detailed analysis Digby spoke about the four elements, the three Paracelsian qualities, the nine angelic hierarchies, the seven planets, concluding that of all God's works Man is the noblest and the most perfect—he is a little world, and himself a god ("O worke diuine!"). Thus Spenser can be found as "a constant disciple of Platoes School" as he speaks about the perfect harmony of the created universe (cf. the phrase "diapase" referring to the eight-scale musical system, the *diapaison*), demonstrating this harmony in the human microcosm, for "in Nature there is not to be found a more compleat and more exact Concordance of all parts, than that which is betweene the compaction and conjunction of the Body and Soul of Man" (Spenser 1971, 157).

If we compare the two hermeneutical traditions, that is, the one which identifies Alma's House simply with the physical dimensions of the human body and the one which associates it with the Platonic universalism, we see that they are not exclusive to each other. The common denominator between the two concepts is the recognition of certain dialectical opposites in this created world (body/soul, man/cosmos, mutability/eternity); however, they still claim the unity of the whole system. This unity is provided by the unifying plan of the Creator and can be comprehended through the overall present analogies, and correspondences of the universe. As Spenser's contemporary Sir Richard Barckley put into words in his *A Discourse of the Felicitie of Man* (1598),

> The great God of Nature hath tyed together all his creations with some meane things that agree and participate with the extremities, and hath composed the intelligible, ethereall, and elementarie world, by indissoluble meanes and boundes [. . .] between brute beastes, and those of a spirituall essence and understanding, which are the Angels, he hath placed man, which combineth heauen and this elementarie world. (quoted by Patrides 1973, 435)

The above description as well as Spenser's stanza naturally call to mind the much discussed concept of the premodern world model about the macro- and microcosms which have been often explained by the metaphors "the scale of nature" or "the Great Chain of Being" (see the introduction of this book).

This metaphorical-allegorical world picture was well known in Elizabethan England and could serve various ideological standpoints. The macrocosm-microcosm analogy could function as a didactic allegory trying to explain the structure of the universe in a simplified model. One should read Henry Peachem's emblem in his *Minerva Brittana* (1610) this way:

> Heare what's the reason why a man we call
> A little world? and what the wisest ment
> By this new name? two lights Celestiall
> Are in his head, as in the Element:
> Eke as the wearied Sunne at night is spent,
>   So seemeth but the life of man a day,
>   At morn hee's borne, at night he flits away.
> [. . .]
> Of Earth, Fire, Water, Man thus framed is,
> Of Elements the threefold Qualities.
>   (Quoted from Hollander and Kermode 1973;
>   cf. Figure 2.6)

In a more complicated approach Sir Walter Raleigh in his *The History of the World* (1614) used a fairly conventional biblical framework when discussing the relationship between man and cosmos:

> Man, thus compounded and formed by God, was an abstract or model, or brief story of the universal, in whom God concluded the creation and work of the world, and whom he made the last and most excellent of his creatures, being internally endued with a divine understanding. [. . .] And whereas God created three sorts of living natures, to wit, angelical, rational, and brutal; giving to angels an intellectual, and to beasts a sensual nature, he vouchsafed unto man both the intellectual of angels, the sensitive of beasts, and the proper rational belonging unto man, and therefore saith Gregory Nazianzen: 'Man is the bond and chain which tieth together both natures.' And because in the little frame of man's body there is a representation of the universal, and (by allusion) a kind of participation of all the parts thereof, therefore was man called microcosmos, or the little world. (1.2.5; quoted from Hollander and Kermode 1973, 324–25)

Although Raleigh's text is basically orthodox, we can feel in it a touch of mysticism, reminding us of the Platonic doctrine of *exaltatio*, namely the notion that man can leave his place in the Chain of Being and can try to elevate himself to the supernatural spheres. As I have mentioned above, Ernst Cassirer (1963) considered this notion the greatest intellectual innovation of the Renaissance as opposed to the Middle Ages. I have already analyzed Ficino's views and Pico's oration on this theme, but even in such a popular version of neoplatonism like Castiglione's *The Courtier* (1528), the thesis is clear. Sir Thomas Hoby's translation appeared in 1561 and exercised considerable influence on the poetry of Spenser. A quotation from Book Four:

> Think now of the shape of man, which may be called a little world, in whom every parcel of his body is seen to be necessarily framed by art and not by hap, and then the form altogether most beautiful. (Abrams 1986, 1011)

> [. . .] Man of nature endowed with reason, placed, as it were, in the middle between these two extremities, may, through his choice inclining to sense or reaching to understanding, come nigh to the coveting, sometime of the one,sometime of the other part. (1007)

One of the more learned exponents of this view among Spenser's contemporaries was John Dee. As we have seen, he accepted the neoplatonic view of man's special faculties and flexible nature and also incorporated into his system the possibility of magical operations. In the *Mathematical Preface* Dee described "anthropographie," the study of man's microcosm as one of the highest degrees among the "artes mathematicall":

> [Anthropographie] is an Art restored, and of my preferment to your Seruice. I pray you, thinke of it, as of one of the chief pointes, of Human knowledge. Although it be, but now, first confirmed, with this new name: yet the matter, hath from the beginning, ben in consideration of all perfect Philosophers. Anthropographie is the desception of the Number, Measure, Waight, Figure, Situation, and colour of euery diuerse thing, contayned in the perfect body of MAN. [. . .] If the description of the heuenly part of the world, had a peculiar Art, called *Astronomie:* if the description of the earthly Globe hath his peculiar arte, called *Geographie,* if the matching of both hath his peculiar Arte, called *Cosmographie:* which is the description of the whole and universall frame of the world: Why should not the description of Him who is the Lesse World: and from the beginning, called *Microcosmus,* [. . .] who also participateth with Spirites, and Angels: and is made to the Image

and similitude of God: haue his peculiar Art and be called the *Arte of Artes*. (Dee 1975, c.iii)

To strengthen his standpoint, Dee referred to Pythagoras, to Durer's *De symmetriae humani corporis*, to Vitruvius's anthropomorphic theory of architecture, and, last but not least, to Agrippa's *De occulta philosophia*. From his argumentation it is quite clear that he understood the macrocosm-microcosm analogy not merely as a metaphor which explains certain correspondences in nature, but rather as a mystical symbol which in itself contains something of the ultimate essence of the world and its creator.

As we have also seen, to grasp this metaphysical essence, Dee himself constructed his magical-mystical emblem, the hieroglyphic monad. By the early seventeenth-century such magical emblems and diagrams became fairly common in hermetic and alchemical literature throughout the process which—due to the development of printing and book publishing—can be termed as the period of the popularization of secret sciences. The large visual dictionaries of late Renaissance magic, such as the works of Robert Fludd and Athanasius Kircher, could rely on Dee's monad as an important forerunner of their hermetic semiotics.

The previously reviewed examples demonstrate three ways of interpretation of the macrocosm-microcosm analogy: the didactic-conventional, the religious-mystical, and the philosophical-metaphysical. Spenser's description of the House of Alma, no doubt, belongs to the last category. The question, however, remains: how deeply philosophical was it, and how essential was this emblematic image in the context of the poet's art and world picture? To answer this question let me digress to what E. H. Gombrich wrote about the complementary classes of symbolic images, with a special reference to the ontological and epistemological questions of Renaissance iconography.

According to his crucial study (Gombrich 1972, 123–99), there are three sources of images, namely: *experience* (representation of an object), *convention* (representation of an idea—allegory), and *expression* (private symbolism—the artist's conscious or unconscious mind). The first case is simple and unambiguous: the representation is imitation, the copy of something already physically existing—it is nothing other than primary reception, or sensation. The second two classes contain images which are the products of the intellect; they are transformed or transmitted representations of physical and/or mental sensations.

According to their function, these mental images can be ascribed to three traditions. As Gombrich says, "Our attitude toward the image is bound up with our whole idea about the universe" (125). The three traditions are the following: *didactic* (metaphor, the Aristotelian tradition), *revelative* (symbolic-intuitive, the Platonic tradition), *magical* (powerful esoteric signs, the hermetic tradition).

The didactic metaphor is the *expression* of an idea, the product of intellectual activity. Its function is decorative and entertaining, it has to improve the poverty of the language, and it possesses a certain explanatory, illustrative power in order to make discursive speech clearer. The Platonic tradition, however, attributed a different power to the symbolic image. For the neoplatonist the image was a *revelation* of something higher, that is, a metaphysical truth which could not be expressed by discursive speech. Consequently the image was not considered the product of rational thinking, but of a momentary intuition which all of a sudden could enlighten the observer.

This process is not unlike the technique of the gnostic philosopher who tried to capture Divine Wisdom in visual revelations. Of the gnostic's knowledge Plotinus said, "It must be not thought that in the Intelligible World the gods and the blessed see propositions: everything expressed there is a beautiful image" (*Enneads* 5.8, quoted by Gombrich 1972, 158).[2]

Spenser himself tried to create such a Platonic-revelatory imagery in his *Fowre Hymnes*, when describing earthly and heavenly beauty and love. His allegory of Wisdom-Sophia runs as follows:

> There in his bosome Sapience doth sit,
> The soueraine dearling of the Deity,
> Clad like a Queene in royall robes, most fit
> For so great powre and peerelesse maiesty.
> ("An Hymne of Heavenly Beavtie";
> *Fowre Hymnes*, IV. 183–86;
> quoted from Spenser 1970, 598)

An extreme case of the revelatory image is the esoteric sign which has magic power. It does not only symbolize the intuitively perceptible truth but it is a *representation* of the idea (deity or demon) itself. This is how the medals of zodiacal decans have healing power in Ficino's *De vita coelitus comparanda*, this is how Faustus can compel Mephistophilis to appear in his magic circle, and this is how Dee and Kelly could call angels by the help of their "great seal." Or as the seventeenth-century popular imagination suggested, they could even raise the dead practicing their abominable art in cemeteries (Figures 9.1 and 9.2).[3]

FIGURE 9.1   Conjuring the Devil. Frontispiece of Marlowe's *Doctor Faustus* (London, 1620); see <http://www.perseus.tufts.edu/Texts/faustus.html>.

FIGURE 9.2   Dee and Kelly conjuring the dead (17th-century broadsheet). Reproduced from Seligmann 1971, 204.

Spenser's description of Alma's House is undoubtedly a symbolic image, in fact a word-emblem, as defined by Peter Daly (1998, 83–113), but the question remains whether it is the expression, the revelation, or the representation of its idea. In my opinion this problem cannot be solved by trying to assume the author's perspective, as neither Spenser's actual readings not his intellectual preoccupations, even less his authorial intention, can be reconstructed in its entire authenticity from our present-day situation. Gombrich classified symbolic images according to the intention of their creators. But we can approach the problem from the other direction, from the reader's viewpoint. And then we shall ask if Alma's Castle *can be interpreted* as a didactic or rather as a revelatory image; to be more precise, we can ask if the wider context of Spenser's art allows this or that type of interpretation.

I am inclined to say that Alma's Castle is a revelatory word-emblem, under the influence of the hermetic way of thinking and, what is more, is inspired perhaps directly by Dee's monad. Before the actual interpretation, I intend to argue that Spenser's artistic world and what we know about the author's intellectual horizon *do not exclude* the possibility of such a reading. And this is the border not to be crossed, the boundary limiting the ambition of the literary critic. Because every great work of art has such a paradoxical nature that it needs commentary, still no commentary can fully exhaust the work's meaning.

It is a commonplace in English literary history to label Spenser as a neoplatonist,[4] but scholars also have found more specific and more radical occult elements in his works. Fowler (1964) demonstrated the presence of an esoteric number symbolism throughout *The Faerie Queene*, and Røstvig (1969) used Francesco Giorgi's *De harmonia mundi totius* to interpret the eclogues of *The Shepheards Calender*. Spenser's biography also contains elements which hint at the sources through which he could have developed an interest in the occult arts. His acquaintance with Dee is only indirectly corroborated from the correspondence of Gabriel Harvey,[5] but his friendship with Sidney is well known, as is known Sidney's various contacts with the Doctor. It has also been suggested that behind the philosophy of the *Areopagus*—among others—the ideas of Dee might be detected (French 1972, 135–59).

Hopper (1940, 966) and Fowler (1964, 265–84) suggested that Alma's House should be read in relation to Dee's hieroglyphic monad. I am ready to join this view, adding that although no direct formal correspondences can be found between the monad and Alma's House, the idea of the anthropomorphic castle can easily be seen as a verbally constructed, concise esoterical image.

Fowler's analysis of Spenser's number symbolism is too complicated, requiring such complex mathematical apparatus that the literary critic becomes sceptical about whether even a *poeta doctus* could afford to handle them while in the process of constructing a large, several thousand line poem. I believe that when interpreting poetry, it is more convenient to look for the framework or reminiscences of certain philosophical ideas than the scientific tenets themselves. I agree with Fowler (and Kenelm Digby) who claim that Spenser was a poet interested in and influenced by the hermetic philosophy, but I also think that one should differentiate between the doctrines of a system of thought and the product of artistic creation.

I have found it very instructive that Frances Yates established an intellectual link between the threefold structure of Alma's emblematic house and the threefold world model of Giorgi and Agrippa (1979, 97–98). However, unlike in her usually imaginative cross-interpretations of texts and illustrations, in this case she said: "The actual figure which Spenser is here describing is difficult to determine." Following her path I am going to add to the existing interpretations a few illuminating iconographical parallels (for a more detailed version of this reading, see Szőnyi 1984).

In the 1578 French edition of Giorgi's *Harmonia mundi* one finds an explanatory diagram, showing the three spheres of the world—angelical, celestial, elemental—arranged into three circles. The large circles accommodate smaller circles, of which each further three are separated from each other by altogether four horizontal lines. Thus each world-sphere is associated with the numbers 1, 3 (and 9), and 4—corresponding to the geometric figures of circle, triangle, and square.[6] One finds similar numerological-geometrical speculations in Charles de Bouelles' already cited work (see, for example, Figure 2.2), an imaginatively illustrated book that was available to English intellectuals and was in Dee's library (R&W 311).

If we try to arrange geometrically Spenser's description—"partly circular, part triangular, twixt them both a quadrat was the base"—the greatest problem is caused by the word *twixt* which, according to *The Oxford Dictionary of English Etymology*, has a double meaning: "between" or "in the midst of two," "in the center of the two." When saying "partly circular, part triangular," Spenser also does not specify which is inside and which is outside. Taking all this into consideration, we can construct at least three different arrangements:

The frame thereof seemed patly circulare,
And part triangulare, O worke diuine;
And twixt them both a quadraqte was the base . . .

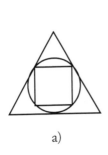

a)

b)

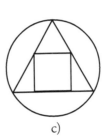

c)

All three figures can be associated with some features of the organic world model (correspondences, analogies, number symbolism) and all three have numerous representations in early modern occult iconography. According to the (a) version the divine mind (triangle = Holy Trinity) embraces the whole of the world which consists of celestial (circle = planets and the Zodiac) and elemental (square = the four elements and qualities) spheres. Their proportions are seven and nine, the former meaning the sum of heavenly and earthly things (3 + 4), the latter the multiplication of the Holy Ternary. The House of Temperance thus includes equally the whole universe and the human microcosm because man's body consists of the four elements and the four body liquids (humors). The compound of these constitutes his nature and psychology.

One should also remember the notion that the human organism is neither independent of the workings of nature nor of the cosmos. It depends on the influences of the stars and the planets which transmit the heavenly energies. The human organs are the receptors of those celestial influences and thus can be symbolized by a circle. The triangle may stand for the human intellect, as an image of God. As Augustinus wrote, "Numerus ternarius ad animam pertinet, quaternarius ad corpus." According to Plato there are three souls, the vegetative, the sensitive, and the rational—the same as three persons in the Trinity.

A seventeenth-century engraving from Tobias Schütz's *Harmonia macrocosmi cum microcosmi* enlightens the above. The human figure (microcosm) is standing in a circle of the universe. He is chained to a female figure above him who represents Nature but another chain leads up to the Will of God. The picture is bordered by the portraits of Trismegistus and Paracelsus, associated with the geometrical shapes of quadrat and triangle, also referring to Paracelsus' revolution in changing the four elements for the three essentials.[7] The four elements and the Paracelsian qualities are represented by a square and a triangle on the title page of a 1582 Basel edition of Paracelsus. These elements are, however encircled by the celestial sphere, thus illustrating arrangement (c) for which we shall see further examples below (see Figure 9.3). The ideology of this diagram is encapsuled in the aphorism: "Omnia ab uno—ad unam omnia."

The (b) reading is a variant of the previous interpretation, except that here the geometrical shapes are not inside each other, rather on top of one another. Thus this arrangement is more analogous to the Great Chain of Being or Giorgi's diagram. Another esoteric visual illustration to this arrangement can be found in a late seventeenth-century edition of Jakob

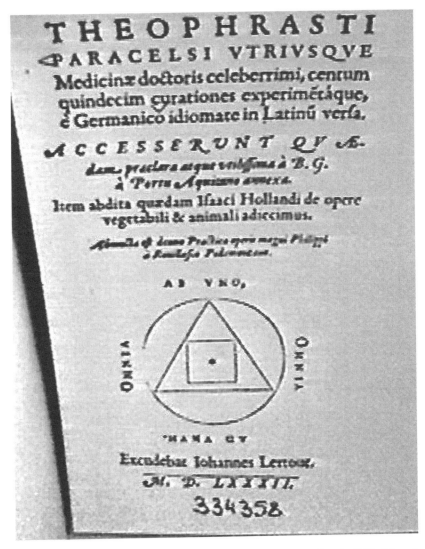

FIGURE 9.3   The four elements and the Paracelsian qualities in a celestial circle. Philippi Aureoli Theophrasti Paracelsi Utriusque Medicinae doctoris celeberrimi, centum quindecim curationes experimentamque . . . (Basel: Johannes Lertout, 1582). Wroclaw University Library, "Na Piasku" [334.358].

Boehme (Figure 9.4). This esoteric emblem is abstract, clear, and compact. Its first level of meaning refers to the alchemical transmutation: Luna and Mercury unite in order to meet in Sol. The basis of the transmutation is the elemental world (quadrat at the bottom of the picture).

FIGURE 9.4 Jakob Boehme, *Signatura rerum*, title page (Amsterdam, 1682). Herzog August Bibliothek, Wolfenbüttel [K3 Helmst. 8o].

The middle is the sphere of Mercury (a circle divided into eight slices, representing balanced harmony). As Spenser wrote, "all which compacted made a goodly diapase." The goal of the transmutation is signified by a triangle. Boehme's diagram at the same time is more than a simple al-chemical emblem. The transmutation is taking place in a cosmic frame-work—instead of the alembic we see the circle of the Zodiac—and there is also a hint of a religious-spiritual layer of meaning. Similar to Dee, Boehme's illustrator also combined the signs of the cross, of Luna and Sol, deriving "the philosophers' Mercury" (☿). At the bottom of the picture we see the shape of the heavenly Jerusalem—its shape is a square with twelve gates on its walls, and with the Lamb in the middle. This, and the inscription in the left hand corner—*Signatura rerum*—remind the interpreter that here we deal not only with a natural phenomenon but an occult program in which the purification of nature is identical with the transmutation of the human soul. To put it simply, the goal is the *exaltatio*.[8]

While Boehme's pictorial vision is fusing naturalistic and abstract elements into a symbolic whole, an interesting diagram of Charles de

Bouelles offers a pure and curious geometric scheme to relate square, circle, and triangle to the human intellect. In his *De intellectu* one finds a small figure in which a square embraces two symmetrical semicircles, while the diagonals of the quadrat also constitute four triangles. The inscriptions in the two halves designated by the semicircles point to "Mundus" and "Intellectus," suggesting the unity of the two, in harmony with the sense of Spenser's poem (Figure 9.5).[9]

The (c) interpretation is suggested by Kenelm Digby's reading. According to him,

> Mans soul is a circle, whose circumference is limited by the true center of it, which is onely God. [. . .] By the Triangular Figure he very aptly designes the body: as for the Circle is of all other figures the most perfect and most capatious: so the Triangle is the most imperfect, and includes least space. It is the first and lowest of all figures. [. . .] Mans Body hath all the properties of imperfect matter. And—as the feminine sex is imperfect and receives perfection from the masculine: so doth the Body from the Soul, which to it is in lieu of a male. (quoted in Spenser 1971, 152–55)

Here Digby alludes to the lines "The one imperfect, mortall, foeminine; / Th' other immortall, perfect, masculine," and according to his interpretation the perfect soul contains the imperfect body which consists of the four elements. In the occult-esoterical tradition we can easily find iconographical representations of this arrangement, too. While the former two

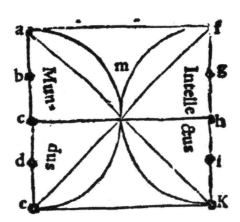

FIGURE 9.5   Mundus and Intellectus in Charles de Bouelles' symbolic geometry. *Liber de intellectu* (Paris, 1510), 86ʳ. Herzog August Bibliothek, Wolfenbüttel [E 391 Helmst 2o].

have a kinship primarily with hermetic cosmologies, the last is related to alchemical discourse.

According to this, the geometrical bodies placed in each other represent a development from chaos to perfection (square—triangle—circle). Such a diagram can be found in Samuel Norton's *Mercurius redivivus* (first edition 1630; cf. Figure 9.6). The drawing shows the Tree of Life with a venomous toad among the roots while at the top of the tree, among red and white roses, there is a crown, a symbol of unity. Alongside the circles and triangles we find triples significant for both alchemy and spiritual transmutation: white—black—red, Jupiter—Mars—Venus, water—earth—fire, spirit—soul—body, heaven—sun—male, earth—moon—female. In the square there are Mercury and Anthropos—both of them are seeking purification, and transmutation by the help of Christ.

One of the most interesting variants of arrangement (c) can be found in Michael Maier's *Atalanta fugiens*. This most famous alchemical emblem book was designed by such a German scholar-mystic who at one time had also been Rudolf II's physician and later on became instrumental

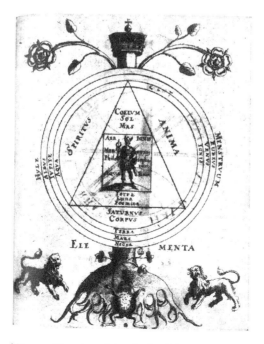

FIGURE 9.6   Samuel Norton, *Mercurius redivivus*. In *Dreyfaches Hermetisches Kleeblatt, vigilantem de Monte Cubiti* (Nürnberg, 1667), 354. Herzog August Bibliothek, Wolfenbüttel [Xfilm 1:568].

in the development of Rosicrucian literature (Figure 9.7). On the picture
an alchemist is shown in the posture of a *geometer* who is constructing
a diagram of transmutation in accordance with the motto:

> Make a circle from a man and a woman, out of this a square, out of
> this a triangle.
> Make a circle, and you will have the Philosophers' Stone.
> (Emblem 21; translated by H. M. E. de Jong; from de Jong 1969, 166)

As it can be seen, the adept is already completing the final, outer
circle. The last line of the attached epigram underlines the significance of
the project: "If such a great thing is not immediately clear in your mind
/ Then know, that you will understand everything, if you understand the
theory of Geometry" (de Jong 1969, 167). One cannot help immediately
recalling Dee's *Mathematicall Praeface*:

> There is (gentle Reader) nothing (the word of God onely set apart)
> which so much beautifieth and adorneth the soule and minde of man,
> as doth the knowledge of good artes and sciences: as the knowledge of
> naturall and moral Philosophie. [. . .] Many other artes also there are

FIGURE 9.7   Alchemy and geometry. Michael Maier, *Atalanta fugiens* (Oppenheim, 1618), 93. Herzog
August Bibliothek, Wolfenbüttel [196 Quod (1)].

which beautifie the minde of man: but of all other none do more
garnishe & beautifie it, then those artes which are called Mathematicall.
Unto the knowledge of which no man can attaine, without the perfecte
knowledge and instruction of the principles, groundes, and Elementes
of Geometrie. . . . (Dee 1570, ☞.ii)

Maier's emblem has been interpreted by many. Jung primarily analyzed its alchemical contents (1980, 126), while Heninger pointed out its
cosmic significance (1977, 189–90). According to the latter the geometric transmutation reflects the harmony as well as the tension between idea
and realization. The same dichotomy was expressed by Robert Fludd,
too. On his esoteric diagram the two circles and the inserted triangle
between them represents on the one hand how God contains the idea of
the world and on the other the perfect, harmonious relationship between
God and the world (Figure 9.8).

The basis of all these concepts and, furthermore, that of the whole
occult world picture, was a Platonic dualism postulating a divide between
the perfect, eternal ideas and the changing, mutable material realm. According to the platonists, humans live in a world which is always in the
process of becoming something; still it has no absolute existence. In this
constant change the program of *exaltatio* could provide some fair prospect.
I cannot describe this perspective better than Heninger has already done:

> Nevertheless, this constant change can itself be a source of hope. Per-
> haps it conceals a pattern, a cosmic scheme, a sacred plan, and the
> constant change is the efficient means whereby the divine will is real-
> ized. Perhaps the objects of this world are arranged hierarchically and

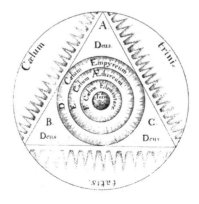

FIGURE 9.8   The idea of the world in God. Robert Fludd, *Utriusque cosmi . . . historia* (Oppenheim,
1617–1619), 1:20. Somogyi Library, Szeged [E.d. 1049].

aspire to the perfection of the ideas from which they receive their
forms, so that by change the lower transmute toward the higher. There
is even the optimistic hope that man, placed midway on the *scala
intellectualis*, will ascend to consort with superior creatures, with saints
and angels, rather than descending to grovel with beasts, and he will
fulfill the claim of Genesis that he is created in the image of the deity."
(1977, 190–91)

This hope nurtured the idea of the Great Chain of Being and the
sacred narrative of the Genesis gave a goal to humankind, which had
always been among the thoughts of mystical philosophers and which
became openly searched for from the time of the Renaissance. This was
the program that inspired Spenser to compose the poetical Alma's House
and this urged Doctor Dee to fashion the hieroglyphic monad.

From this perspective it becomes negligible if we read Alma's House
according to the (a), (b), or (c) variants. More important will be, however, to realize that the poet was bound neither by the disciplinary rigor
of philosophers nor by the logic of rational and discursive thinking. In
his artistic freedom he could most efficiently express the paradox nature
of dualism, the dichotomy in unity which is most manifest in the nature
of man. Let us remember that the Canto describing Alma's House begins
with the following lines:

> Of all Gods workes, which do this world adorne,
> There is no one more faire and excellent,
> Then mans body both for powre and forme,
> Whiles it is kept in sober gouernment;
> But none then it, more fowle and indecent,
> Distempered through misrule and passions bace:
> It growes a Monster, and incontinent
> Doth loose his dignitie and natiue grace.
> Behold, who list, both one and other in this place.
>   (FQ II.ix.1)

This recognition drives the monumental engine of *The Faerie Queene*,
from the first lines to the *Mutability Cantoes*. I would argue that this
poetical strength and insight keeps the poem among the greatly appealing
treasures of our culture even today. We still value and *use* this poem in
spite of the fact that its ideological basis has been eroded while the
pedant or "enthusiastic" exponents of this ideology—the doctors and
philosophers—have also been forgotten or, at best, reduced to the subject
matter of doctoral dissertations written on "strangely neglected topics."[10]

John Dee seems to be a spectacular exception. Although his works, one by one, have been disproved of being cornerstones of early modern science or intellectual history, his personality, his thought, and his visions continue to invite scholarly interpretations and artistic deliberations. It seems that his meticulous and painstaking self-fashioning has been so successful that it has much outlived the person whose advancement it was to serve.

—∿—

I hope to have convincingly shown that cultural symbolization inextricably intertwined with the occult philosophy not only until the time of the Scientific Revolution but that it still keeps on to being active. I also hope that John Dee has well served to demonstrate the workings of intellectual syncretism so characteristic for the epistemological techniques of many early modern Europeans. Since these techniques have not disappeared even after the Cartesian turn, we ought to examine the history of esoterism with the best scholarly means at our disposal.

At the conclusion of this book, I remind my reader once again that while until recently, magically-minded intellectuals like John Dee were examined from the perspective of science history, today we should rather be inclined to assess them in their own right, as representatives of an integral and alternative system of thought. Such an approach to Renaissance magic (and also to modern occultism) may hopefully yield an ever more refined understanding.

Notes

1. PRINCIPLES AND DEMARCATIONS

1.David Fenton was kind enough to supply me with the following list of contemporary works featuring John Dee the Magus: Simon Rees's *The Devil's Looking Glass* (1985); Ian Sinclair's parapsychological guidebook to London *Lights Out for Territory: Nine Excursions in the Secret History of London* (1997); Stephen Lowe's play *The Alchemical Wedding*; the opera by John Harle and David Pountney *Angel Magick*; Hana Maria Pravda's filmscript and Derek Jarman's films (*Angelic Conversations, Jubilee*) as well as many of Jarman's paintings.

2. Cf. the historiographical summary in Malcolm B. Hamilton, *The Sociology of Religion: Theoretical and Comparative Perspectives* (London: Routledge, 1994), chapter 2.

3. Among the various trends of postmodern critique against historicism in cultural and literary theory, I have been influenced by the early Foucault, primarily *The Order of Things: An Archeology of the Human Sciences* (New York: Vintage, 1973); Clifford Geertz's interpretive anthropology in *The Interpretation of Cultures* (New York: Basic Books, 1973) and *Local Knowledge* (New York: Basic Books, 1983); and Hayden White's highly challenging approach to the literary-rhetorical engines of historical discourse in *Metahistory: The Historical Imagination in Nineteenth-Century Europe* (Baltimore: Johns Hopkins University Press, 1973), *Tropics of Discourse: Essays in Cultural Criticism* (Baltimore: Johns Hopkins, 1978), and *The Content of the Form* (Baltimore: Johns Hopkins, 1987). Beyond these works, a few influential contributions in literary criticism should be mentioned, such as Frank Lentricchia's *After the New Criticism* and Stephen Greenblatt's *Renaissance Self-Fashioning* (both by the University of Chicago Press, 1980). These works sharpened my attention to follow the debate about new historicism over the past fifteen years, and what I found problematic in this "subjective materialist" approach (as I call it) to the theory of interpretation, I tried to correct from the works of the new hermeneuticists (Gadamer, Ricoeur, Jauss, Iser). No matter how deeply influenced I have become by poststructuralism, I am still deeply indebted to the great generation of intellectual and art historians who belonged to the Warburg school, such as Gombrich, Kristeller, Panofsky, Walker, Wind, and Frances Yates. Works representing different approaches in the history of science will be referred to at appropriate points of my discussion.

4. Here I cannot resist the temptation—following the footsteps of Clulee (1988) and Sherman (1995)—to summarize the historiography of Dee studies, as I see it. As for

the Doctor's biography, see the concise and accurate "Annals" in Roberts and Watson 1990, 77–78. Recently Edward Fenton (in Dee 1998) has offered an ordered selection of Dee's diaries with comments which also provide a full account of Dee's life, though only from 1577. Less comprehensive but detailed surveys about the various parts of his career can be found in the significant body of scholarly literature dealing with diverse aspects of his work.

5. See the so-called hermeticism debate. Pro Yates: Burke 1974; Copenhaver 1978; Debus 1978; Metaxopulos 1982; Tannier 1984. Against Yates: Garin 1977; McGurie 1977; Rosen 1970; Rossi 1975; Schmitt 1978; Trinkaus 1970; Vickers 1979; Vickers 1984 [Introduction]; Westman 1977. Particularly balanced later views: Clulee 1988, 128–29; Copenhaver 1990; Curry 1985; and, most recently, Hanegraaff 2001.

6. The medieval contexts have recently been explored by Stephen Clucas in his articles mapping Dee's interest in the manuscript literature of the Solomonic art (1998; 200?).

7. A typical example of this sort or argumentation can be found in J. L. Heilbronn's introductory essay to the *Propaedeumata Aphoristica* (Dee 1978, 12). Lynn Thorndike's opinion is exceptional for the period of its composition: "[Dee's] attempted experiments with angels were in accord with his attributing greater operations to soul than body and with his semi-spiritual view of nature" (1924–1958, 6: 392).

8. Cf. the essays in the following recent collections: Bergier 1988; Buck 1992; Lindberg and Westman 1990; Merkel and Debus 1988; Neusner 1989; Porter and Teich 1992.

9. Raman Selden, *A Reader's Guide to Contemporary Literary Theory* (Lexington: The University Press of Kentucky, 1985), 4–5.

10. I must add that many colleagues were in fact sympathetic to my personal dilemmas concerning methodology and doctrines. For example, Richard Helgerson and Michael O'Connell at the Huntington Library greatly helped me to reorientate myself among the changing issues of American cultural and literary theory.

11. Norman Rabkin, *Shakespeare and the Problem of Meaning* (Chicago: University of Chicago Press, 1981), 1.

2. Mysticism, Occultism, Magic Exaltation

1. Cf. Hankiss 1998. As is well known, it was Ernst Cassirer who first launched an extensive study of these symbolic systems (*The Philosophy of Symbolic Forms*, 1996 [1953]).

2. An interesting, inspired account of the loss of Eden and man's ambition for self-deification is *Das verlorene Paradies* by Edgar Dacqué (München and Berlin: Oldenbourg, 1940). Among the more scholarly books I have used with profit for understanding this mytho-psychic phenomenon and its cultural sublimation, I should mention here Frick 1973; Trinkaus 1970; and Wind 1968.

3. *Phaedo* 69d. I am quoting Wind's wording here (1968, 4) as opposed to Hugh Tredennick's translation in Plato 1963, 52.

4. Porphyry, *Life of Plotinus*, 10 (quoted in Wind 1968, 5).

5. Cf. Jurii Lotman, *Universe of the Mind: A Semiotic Theory of Culture* (London: Tauris, 1990). A post-structuralist reception of Lotman has been offered by Attila Kiss in *The Semiotics of Revenge. Subjectivity and Abjection in English Renaissance Tragedy* (Szeged: JATEPress, 1995, Papers in English and American Studies 5).

6. *Comment. in Somnium Scipionis*, I, 14, 15. See a detailed analysis in Lovejoy 1960, 63. An English publication of the text is found in Macrobius, *Commentary on the Dream of Scipio,* tr. and intr. William Harris Stahl (New York: Columbia University Press, 1966, 1990, Records of Civilization 48).

7. Cf. *Enneads* 3.2–3, 4.8, 5.2, 6.6, and Aristotle's *Metaphysics*, esp. Books 7 and 12 on matter, essence, and cosmos.

8. Heninger's anthology *The Cosmographical Glass* (1977) is a beautifully illustrated, useful primer to monitor this evolution of visual imagination.

9. References to Roberts and Watson's catalogue (1990) will appear in the following format throughout this volume: R&W 311, 583, 689, 871, 2031, B227, B302. Dee's copy of the 1510 edition of *De intellectu* is R&W 311. On Bouelles see Thorndike 1923–1958, 6:38–43.

10. Ficino, *De christiana religione*, chapter 14 (in Ficino 1576, 19). I am quoting Yates's translation (1964, 119). See also Sears Jayne's commentary on Ficino's sources, pointing out the roots of his argumentation in Aquinas and other medieval authorities (Jayne 1985, 5–7).

11. Vickers (1984) is a useful anthology of essays treating these developments. It should be noted, however, that the editor's own study in this volume—"Analogy Versus Identity: The Rejection of Occult Symbolism, 1580–1680"—argues for an oversimplified typology and has been criticised by post-structuralist intellectual historians.

12. A classical critical edition of the *Tabula smaragdina* is Ruska 1926. I am quoting the text from its sixteenth century English translation: Bacon 1992, 16.

13. *De mundi sphaera, sive cosmographia* (Paris: Vascosanus, 1555), 2r. Dee in fact had three copies of this book: R&W 66, 326, B305a.

14. Detailed analyses of this diagram can be found in Godwin 1979a, 46, and Heninger 1977, 152. For further readings on the micro/macrocosm theory, see Corvin-Krasinski 1960; Garin 1983, 49–56; Hall 1972, 55–69; Müller-Jahncke 1985, 135–44; Schipperges 1962.

15. *Thesaurus linguae latinae. Editus iussu et auctoritate consilii ab academiis societatibusque diversarum nationum electi.* Leipzig: Teubner, 1931–1953 (9 Vols.), 5: col. 1156–57 (*"exaltatio, -onis ab exaltare"*).

16. I am citing the following Bible editions: Vulgata 1983 and KJV 1994.

17. As appears in English in British Library MS Sloane 3641, fol. 8. Edited for the web by Adam Maclean, <www.levity.com/alcemy/maryprof.html>. Latin and German versions can be found in the *Auriferae artis* (1572); Arnaldus de Villa Nova's *Opus aureum* (1604); and in the sixth volume of the *Theatrum chemicum* (1661).

18. "Ripley's Treatise of Mercury and the Philosopher's Stone" in *Aurifontina Chymica: or, a collection of fourteen small treatises concerning the first matter of philosophers . . .* (London, 1680), edited by Adam Maclean <www.levity.com/alchemy/ripmerc.html>.

3. THE SOURCES OF RENAISSANCE MAGIC

1. Cambridge, Trinity College, MS 0.4.20; Oxford, Bodleian, MS Ashmole 1142 fols. 1–74. See the List of References for Dee 1583 and 1990.

2. See, for example, Yates 1969, 11: "If the catalogue were published with a good subject index, scholars would be able to know at a glance what Dee had on subjects which interested him." This wish was fulfilled by Roberts and Watson (cf. Dee 1990) with not only a good subject index but also a straightforward numbering of the inventory which makes references to Dee's library plain and easy.

3. One of the most accurate descriptions of this cultural evolution was offered by Paul Oskar Kristeller (1956; 1961). See also, among other works, Gilmore 1952; Vasoli 1968; 1976; 1996; Rabil (ed.) 1988; Klaniczay, Kushner, and Stegmann (eds.) 1988.

4. Arnaldo Della Torre, *Storia dell'Accademia Platonica di Firenze* (Firenze, 1902); P. O. Kristeller, "Lay Religious Traditions and Florentine Neoplatonism," in Kristeller 1956, 99-122; August Buck, "Die humanistischen Akademien in Italien" in Fritz Hartmann and Rudolf Vierhaus (eds.), *Der Akademiegedanke im 17. und 18. Jahrhundert* (Brehmen-Wolfenbüttel: Jacobi Verlag, 1977); Michele Maylender, *Storia delle Accademie d'Italia,* 5 vols., 1926–1930 (Bologna: Arnaldo Forni, 1977); Cesare Vasoli, "Cultura e 'mitologia' nel principato (considerazioni sulla 'Accademia fiorentina')" in Vasoli 1980.

5. Ficino 1576, 1537; quoted among others by Yates 1964, 13.

6. Although the Yates thesis was grounded in the Bruno book, she summarized her views in a condensed and programmatic essay in which she openly established the causal relationship between magic and the Scientific Revolution ("The Hermetic Tradition in Renaissance Science," 1968). She planned to document this relationship in her book on the Rosicrucian Enlightenment (1972), while in her last book she once again restated her concepts in relation to some specific motifs of English Renaissance cultural history (*The Occult Philosophy in the Elizabethan Age,* 1979).

7. Lactantius, *Div. inst.* (I.vi, II.xv, IV.iv, IV.ix); Augustinus, *De civ. Dei* (VIII.xxiii, XVIII.xxix); Yates 1964, who in chapter 1 reviews the various opinions of early Christian writers on the hermetic texts; cf. also Copenhaver 1992 (xliii–xlvii).

8. Cf. James M. Robinson (ed.), *The Nag Hammadi Library in English* (San Francisco: Harper and Row, 1988); Jean-Pierre Mahé, *Hermès en haute-Egypte,* Vol. 1: *Les Textes Hermétiques de Nag Hammadi et leurs parallèles Grecs et Latins;* Vol. 2: *Le Fragment du Discours parfait et les Définitions Hermétiques Arméniennes* (Québec: Presses de l' Université Laval, 1978–1982, Bibliothèque Copte de Nag Hammadi 3, 7). The Hungarian Egyptologist, László Kákosy has also contributed important clues to the relation of hermeticism and Egypt, as testfied by the Nag Hammadi lore. See Kákosy, "Gnosis und ägyptische Religion," in *Le origini dell' gnosticismo* (Leiden: Brill, 1967), 238–47, and his monograph: *Fény és káosz. A kopt gnósztikus kódexek* (Budapest: Gondolat, 1984).

9. Cf. Thorndike 1923–1958, 2:214–29.

10. Cf. Copenhaver 1992, lxvii. See also Thorndike 1923–1958, 219, 221; Emma J. and Ludwig Edelstein, *Asclepius: A Collection and Interpretation of the Testimonies* (Baltimore: Johns Hopkins University Press, 1945); Loris Sturlese, "Saints et magiciens: Albert le Grand en face d'Hermès Trismégiste," *Archives de philosophie* 43 (1980): 615–34; and various chapters in Peter Dronke, ed., *A History of Twelfth-Century Philosophy* (Cambridge: Cambridge University Press, 1988).

11. Scott 1924–1936, 1:51–81; see also Nock 1945–1954, 2:275–95; Festugière 1950–1954, 2:18–27; Copenhaver 1992, 213–14.

12. On the magic of the *Asclepius*, and especially sections 23–24 and 37–38, see Grese 1988, 48 ff. and Josef Kroll, *Die Lehren des Hermes Trismegistus* (Münster: Universitätsverlag, 1913; 1928).

13. On the Renaissance myths of the Golden Age and their relationship with the culture of early modern England, see Levin 1969 and Mebane 1989.

14. *Isaaci Casauboni . . . Exercitationes XVI. Ad Cardinalis Baronii Prolegomena in Annales*, London, 1614. The sections referring to the *Hermetica* are *Exercit.* I.10 (pp. 70 ff.). Of Casaubon's opinion on Hermes, see Grafton 1983.

15. He had Ficino's "Anthologia esoterica" in an 1516 Venice edition (R&W, 256) which contained the *Asclepius* and the first fourteen treatises of the *Corpus hermeticum* under the collective title, *Poemander*. He also had a Greek manuscript of the *Corpus hermeticum* (R&W, DM20) which is now in the Landesbibliothek Kassel (2° MS Chem. I.), bearing Dee's signature from 1567 and his extensive marginalias. Furthermore, he possessed an 1500 Paris edition (B&W, 1282), a hitherto unidentified edition, possibly the 1505 Estienne edition with Lazzarelli's *Crater hermetis* (see Roberts and Watson 1990, 99) and the 1554 Greco-Latin Turnebus editio (R&W, 388).

16. Cf. Allen 1984, and 1994; Copenhaver 1988, and 1990.

17. One has to begin again with Ficino's *Anthologia esoterica* which offered a selection of Plotinus, Porphyry, Iamblichus, Proclus, Psellus, and Synesius. Apart from this valuable collection, Dee had Ficino's edition of Plotinus in a 1540 publication (R&W, 108). He also had Iamblichus (R&W, 410, B177) and many volumes with the works of Porphyry and Proclus (cf. the index in Roberts and Watson 1990, 224).

18. Cf., for example, Plato, *Republic* 365a, 366a, 378a; *Meno* 99c–d; *Timaeus* 71c–72d; and Plotinus, *Enneads*, II.9.14.

19. On Ficino's self-declared and actual indebtedness to Plotinus in *De vita* see Kaske's "Introduction" in Ficino 1989, 25 ff. See also Copenhaver 1988, 80–84.

20. On Plotinus' relation to magic see Armstrong 1995, 207–10; also Dodds 1951, Appendix 2; P. Merlan, "Plotinus and Magic," *Isis* 44 (1953): 341–38; and A. H. Armstrong, "Was Plotinus a Magician?" *Phronesis* 1.1 (1955): 73–79. On Porphyry's *Life*, see R. Harder, "Zur Biographie Plotins," in Harder, *Kleine Schriften* (Munich: Beck, 1960), 275–95.

21. A. C. Lloyd quotes Bidez's *La vie de l'Emperor Julien* (Paris, 1930), p.2., in Armstrong 1995, 277.

22. Thomas Taylor's translation in Ronan's edition (Iamblichus 1989), 62.

23. Brussels: Maurice Lambertin, 1928, 139–51 [text: 148–51].

24. Copenhaver collated two printed editions (Ficino, *Index eorum* . . . Venice, 1497, and the 1576 Basel *Opera*) and two manuscripts (Laurentianus Plut. 82.15, and Laurentianus Strozz. 97). See Copenhaver 1988, 103.

25. In Iamblichus 1989, 150. The text is based on É. des Places' edition, *Oracles Chaldaiques* (Paris: Les Belles Lettres, 1971), 219.14–220.32.

26. Ficino's attachement to this theme will be discussed later. For the relationship between Ficino and Proclus' locus, see Copenhaver 1988, 95 n. 8–9.

27. One should note that Iamblichus' other English translator, Alexander Wilder, renders the phrase "Hermaic opinions" as "Hermetic doctrines."

28. A recent exhibition in Florence, *Marsilio Ficino e il ritorno di Ermete Trismegisto* has once again reconfirmed the great effect of Hermes Trismegistus on Ficino's thought. See the scholarly publication of the catalogue, Gentile and Gilly (eds.) 2001.

29. Originally published as *Index eorum quae hoc in libro habentur. Iamblichus de mysteriis* . . . (Venice, 1497, and subsequent editions), cf. Kristeller 1937–1945, cxxxiv–v.

30. Chronologically listing some of those authors: Dee possessed Isidore of Seville's *De natura rerum* (R&W M94a) and *Etymologiae* (R&W 1375); Rabanus Maurus' *De natura* and *De mystica* (R&W 231); John of Salisbury (R&W 1269); William of Auvergne, *Opera* (R&W 219); a long list of works by Albertus Magnus, e.g. *De divinatione* (R&W M117e), *Summa naturalium* (R&W 183, B193, M155) and the pseudo-Albertian *Magia naturalis et vera*; many works by Thomas Aquinas (R&W 92, 1272, 1421, B279, M6, etc.) and Roger Bacon (see note 31 below); the *Conciliator controversiarum* by Pietro d'Abano (R&W 81); Robert Holcot's *Questiones* . . . (R&W M78); *De imagine mundi* by Pierre d'Ailly (R&W 272); and, last but not least, Jean Gerson's *De probationes spirituum*, including his famous treatise "De artibus magicis ac magorum maleficiis" (R&W 1553, B162).

31. Since up to the late sixteenth century there were few printed editions of Bacon, Dee mostly possessed manuscripts. Among others were his *Annotationes super Aristotelem de secretis secretorum* (R&W M56), *De commendacione utilitatis astronomiae* (R&W CM36w), *Breve breviarium & De pincipiis naturae* (R&W DM166), *Opus maius* (R&W M149), and *De speculis comburentibus* (R&W BM31), but he had in print Bacon's *De secretis operibus artis et naturae* (Paris, 1542; R&W 616) and the pseudo-Baconian *Speculum alchimiae* (Nurnberg, 1541; R&W 1433).

32. On Joachim and the Reformation, see Reeves 1976 and Williams 1980.

33. I primarily mean Kieckhefer's own books, *Magic in the Middle Ages* (1989) and *Forbidden Rites* (1997). Cf. furthermore the recent collection of essays on medieval divinatory literature (*Conjuring Spirits. Texts and Traditions of Medieval Ritual Magic*, ed. Claire Fanger, 1998) which also features an essay by Kieckhefer. Here I would like to mention some PhD theses by a new generation of young scholars who have devoted themselves to various aspects and classifications of medieval magic and most probably will rewrite its history quite radically: Frank Klaassen has completed an extensive study on English magical manuscripts between 1300 and 1600; Sophie Page has studied magic at St. Augustine's Canterbury in the late Middle Ages and Benedek Láng has surveyed the

diffusion of magical literature in East-Central Europe. A common and notable feature of these investigations is that they turn their attention toward the pragmatics of magic, that is the use and readership of magical texts in the Middle Ages.

34. Clucas 200?, n. 164. The manuscript is Sloane 313, a fourteenth-century copy of the *Liber Juratus*, here attributed to Honorius Magister Thebarum (R&W DM70). Roberts and Watson have identified Dee's handwriting in the manuscript and they have also found an inscription, stating that the text had been in the possession of Ben Jonson, too.

35. There has been a continuous scholarly debate about the use of the term *popular*. By employing the term *underground*, I refer to a mixed register of culture which was practiced by intellectuals, often *déclassée*, expelled clerics, and rebel scholars who were not content with dealing only with canonical materials and often became attracted to ideas and practices of spurious origin. Cf. Kieckheffer's expression, "clerical underground" (1989, 151ff.), or William Eamon who speaks about an "intellectual proletariat" in his *Science and the Secrets of Nature: Books of Secrets in Medieval and Early Modern Culture* (Princeton: Princeton University Press, 1994), 69.

36. Thorndike 1923–1958, 2:220f. The greatest recent project to trace the survival of Hermes in the Middle Ages is Polo Lucentini and Vittoria Perrone Compagni's *I testi e i codici di Ermete nel Medievo* (Florence: Polistampa, 2001). See also Lucentini, "L'Ermetismo magico nel sec. XIII," in *Sic itur ad astra: Studien zur mittelalterlichen, insbesondere arabischen, Wissenschaftgeschichte. Festschrift für Paul Kunitzsch zum 70. Geburtstag* (eds. Menso Folkerts and Richard Lorch, Wiesbaden: Harrassowitz Verlag, 2000), 409-450; and Antonella Sannio, "Ermete, mago e alchimista nelle bibliothece di Guilelmo d'Alvernia e Ruggero Bacone," *Studi medievali* 4.1 (2000): 151–209. On William of Auvergne's distinctions see also Steven P. Marrone, "William of Auvergne on Magic in Natural Philosophy and Theology," in Jan A. Aertsen, Andreas Speer (eds.), *Was ist Philosophie im Mittelalter?* (Berlin, New York: de Gruyter, 1998, Miscellanea mediaeval 26), 741–8; and on the *Speculum astronomiae* (attributed to Albertus Magnus) see the critical edition of Paola Zambelli: *The Speculum Astronomiae and Its Enigma: Astrology, Theology, and Science in Albertus Magnus and his Contemporaries* (Boston: Kluwer, 1992). This whole complex intellectual historical development (and its historiography) is usefully summarized in Benedek Láng's Ph.D. dissertation: *Readers of Magic Texts and Handbooks in Central Europe (15th Century)* (Budapest: Central European University, 2003), Chapter One.

37. Sloane 313, late fourteenth century, quoted by Thorndike 1923–1958, 2: 281, 285.

38. See David Pingree's suggestions about the composite nature of magic in the *Picatrix* (1980, 1–15; also 1981 and 1986) and Nicholas Clulee's discussion (1988, 130–32).

39. The most important codices are as follows: CORPUS HERMETICUM: Laurentianus 71, 33 (14th c.); Parisinus Graec. 1220 (mid-14th c.); Vaticanus Graec. 237 (14th c.); Bodley 3388 (15th c.); ASCLEPIUS: Bruxellensis 10054 (early 11th c.); Monacensis 621 (12th c.); Vaticanus 3385 (12th c.). A full list and description can be found in Scott 1924, 1:20–22, 49–50.

40. The original Arabic text with a German translation was published by Ritter and Plessner 1962; the Latin by Compagni 1975, then by Pingree 1986. Surviving manuscripts

are: Paris, Bibliothèque Nationale (MS Par.lat. 10272, 15th C.); Biblioteca Nazionale, Firenze (Magl. XX, 20, dated 1536); British Museum (Sloane 1305, 17th C.). The manuscripts are described by Thorndike 1924–1958, 2:822–24. Some important studies on the *Picatrix*: include Pingree 1980, 1981 and 1986; Clulee 1988, 130–32; Garin 1983, 46–55; Müller-Jahncke 1985, 31, 51; Yates 1964, 49–57, 70–82.

41. Cf. Ritter and Plessner's edition (1962). The cited passage is my translation.

42. Quoted by Yates 1964, 52–53 (from the British Library manuscript [Sloane 1305, 52rff.]).

43. In the Arabic text the name of the city is al-Ašmūnain (Ritter and Plessner 1962, 254–55). For commentaries on this passage, see Garin 1983, 52; Yates 1964, 54.

4. FLORENTINE NEOPLATONISM AND CHRISTIAN MAGIC

1. On Ficino's neoplatonism, cf. the following basic works: Ficino 1985 (introduction by Searse Jayne); Ficino 1989 (introduction by Carol V. Kaske and John R. Clark.); Allen 1984; Copenhaver 1988a, 274–85; Dress 1929; Garin 1961; Kristeller 1943; Kuczynska 1970; Marcel 1958 and 1964–1970; Saitta 1954; Schmidt-Biggemann 1998, 408–16.

2. Cf. Ficino 1576, 530–73. The best authoritative edition is Ficino 1989. On the history of the publication and reception of *De vita*, see Kristeller 1937, 1:ixiv–ixvi. Discussions of Ficino's astral magic can be found in Bullard 1990; Copenhaver 1988a, 274–85; Kaske 1982; Moore 1982; Tarabochia-Canavero 1977 and 1997; Zambelli 1972; Zanier 1977; and, of course, in the introduction and notes of Ficino 1989.

3. Cf. Ficino 1944, chapter 7.4.

4. Cf. *Asclepius* 24a and 37–38, as well as Plotius, *Enneád* 4.3.11. On Ficino's indebtedness to Hermes Trismegistus, see the catalogue of the recent exhibition in Firenze, Gentile and Gilly (eds.) 2001.

5. *The Individual and the Cosmos . . .* , 1963 (1927).

6. On Ficino's commentary of the Platonic charioter, see Allen 1981 and 1984.

7. *In convivium Platonis de amore*, 1475. Ficino himself translated it into Italian, too (*Sopra lo Amore di Platone*), but it was published only in an posthumous edition in 1544. Beside Ficino's 1576 *Opera*, I used Sears Jayne's Latin-English critical edition (Ficino 1944), which was republished in a revised edition in 1985.

8. Cf. Copenhaver 1986 and 1988a; Allen 1994; and the documents of the hermeticism debate mentioned in my introduction.

9. For general introductions to magic, see "Magic" in *The Encyclopedia of Religion*, ed. Mircea Eliade (New York: Macmillan, 1987), 9: 81–112; "Occultism" in *Encyclopedia Britannica* (Chicago: The University of Chicago Press, 1991), Macropedia, 15th edition, 25: 76–98; "Magie" in *Encyclopaedia Universalis* (Paris: Editeur à Paris, 1992), 14: 255–62. See also Butler 1980; Flint 1991; Seligmann 1971; Spence 1960.

10. In outlining the cabala, I have used the following works: Blau 1944; Goetschel 1985; Halevi 1979; MacGregor Mathers 1991; Scholem 1974 and 1980; Secret 1985.

11. On Christian cabala, see the detailed introductions in Scholem 1974 and Goetschel 1985; also recently Schmidt-Biggemann 1998, 188–205.

12. Scholem 1974, 213–14. The transliteration of Hebrew words greatly varies in English reference books. No matter from where the information is taken, throughout my book I follow Scholem's transliteration conventions.

13. Ricius was a Jewish convert who became professor of Greek and Hebrew at the University of Pavia in 1521. "The Gate of Light" is a shortened translation of Abraham Gikatilia's treatise on the names of God and the sefirah. On his system see Heninger (1977, 88 including a reproduction of the elaborate title page of Ricius' work) and Schmidt-Biggemann 1998, 175–79, 272–85; also his "Christian Kabbala" (in Coudert 1999, 99–102).

14. Cesare d' Evoli, *De divinis attributis, quae sephirot ab hebraeis nuncupata* (Venice: Franciscus Zilettus, 1573), 8ᵛ. Cf. R&W 489.

15. On the nature of this esoterism and on warnings explaining the dangers of becoming exposed to the secret teachings, see Goetschel 1985, chapter 3.

16. On the magical power of words, see Tambiah 1968; on the language philosophy of the cabala, cf. Idel 1989.

17. As Pico writes, he with great pains acquired the translated Hebrew books and in them he could find not only the testimonies of the Jewish faith but also great Christian truths: "Pope Sixtus the Fourth took the greatest pains and interest in seeing that these books should be translated into the Latin tongue for a public service to our faith. [. . .] When I had purchased these books at no small cost to myself, when I had read them through with the greatest diligence, I saw in them not so much as Mosaic as the Christian religion" (sections 35–36; Pico 1948, 252).

18. On the rise of Christian cabala, cf. Blau 1944; Gundersheimer 1963; Secret 1985; Spitz 1963; and Yates 1979. About Pico's interest in the cabala, see Garin 1961 and Yates 1964. Some further characteristics of Christian cabala, for example, its relation to hermeticism, have been treated in Charles Zika's articles on Reuchlin (1976 and 1976–1977).

19. The critical edition of the *Theses* is Pico 1973. See also Bohdan Kieszkowski's thorough introduction to this publication.

20. Critical edition by Eugenio Garin (Pico 1942). In the following discussion I am quoting the English edition of Cassirer and Kristeller (Pico 1948). On the *Oratio* see the recent evaluation of Schmidt-Biggemann 1998, 269–72.

21. Critical edition by Garin (Pico 1946); commentary in Garin 1983, 83–113.

5. OCCULT PHILOSOPHY, SYMBOLISM, AND SCIENCE

1. London, Public Record Office, SP Domestic XXVII.63. Dated from Antwerp, 16 February 1563. Published by R. W. Grey in Dee 1854, 1–16. While the original publication is indecisive for the year of writing, Clulee mentions 1562 (1988, 303) but Roberts and Watson checked the manuscript and list it under 1563 in their "Annals of Dee's Life" (1990, 76 and 190).

2. Frances Yates (1964, 140–46) and the Warburg scholars (cf. Secret 1985, 157–58) of course emphasized the Neoplatonic infuence on his work. Recent Dee scholars, such as Clulee (1988, 123, 127) put the stress on the medieval heritage. A new monograph that aims at balancing the two extremes is Brann 1999. After decades of studying Trithemius, the author offers an analysis of the controversy over occult studies in the monastic culture of early modern Europe.

3. See Shumaker 1982, 91–132; also Baron 1978, 23–39; Brann 1977; Glidden 1987; and Müller-Jahncke 1985, 61 ff.

4. Trithemius to Arnold Bostius, quoted by Brann, 1999, 85. The letter was published in several Renaissance works, such as in Trithemius' own *Poligraphiae Libri VI* (Basel: Furter, 1518), 100 ff.; furthermore in Johann Weyer's *De praestigiis daemonum* (Basel: Oporinus, 1566), 150 ff.; in J. Boissard's *De divinatione et magicis praestigiis* (Paris, 1616); and in Athanasius Kircher's *Polygraphia nova* (Roma: Varesi, 1663), "Appendix apologetica," 1–2. Cited by Thorndike 1923–1958, 4: 524, and Brann 1999, 274.

5. Cf. Brann 1999, 89; Heninger 1977, 84–86, 103–04, 170–71; Thorndike 1923–1958, 5: 535, 837; 6:438–43; and Joseph M. Victor, *Charles de Bouelles, 1479–1533: An Intellectual Biography* (Geneva: Droz, 1978).

6. Bovillus to Ganay, 8 March, 1509 (?), published in Bovillus, *Liber de intellectu* . . . (Paris: de Hallewin, 1510), 172ʳ, facsimile (Stuttgart: Friedrich Frommann, 1970). I am summarizing this letter from the quotations of Brann and Thorndike.

7. *De verbo mirifico* (1494) and *De arte cabalistica* (1500, 1517).

8. The great-grandfather of Maximilian II to whom Dee dedicated the *Monas hieroglyphica* in 1564.

9. *De septem secundeis, id est, intelligentiis, sive spiritibus orbes post Deum moventibus libellus sive Chronologia mystica.* The first reliable Latin edition was published in 1567 (Cologne: Birckmann), subsequently in the 1600 edition of Trithemius' *Poligraphia.* Thorndike (6: 441) mentions a 1522 Latin edition from Nurnberg; however Brann does not know about it. On the other hand the latter cites two German adaptations: Nurnberg 1522, and Speyer 1529 (1999, 325).

10. On the intellectual kinship of Trithemius and Agrippa, see Brann 1999, 152–61; Müller-Jahncke 1991, 29–39; and Zambelli 1976, 88–103.

11. I have consulted the following editions of *De occulta philosophia*: Agrippa 1550, 1967, and 1970. For the English quotations I am using the new edition of James Freake's 1651 translation, edited and annotated by Donald Tyson (Agrippa 1997).

12. "The Brahmin" is mentioned by Philostratos and Hieronymus and might have lived in the first century A.D. His activities are otherwise unknown (cf. Magyar 1990, 172).

13. Cf. Boethius, *Consolation of Philosophy*, 3.9; also Plato, *Timaeus*, 31e, as elements of order 53b.

14. Cf. my chapters on the *Corpus hermeticum* and the *Picatrix*, above.

15. According to Donald Tyson this man may have been Abbot Trithemius, whom the young Agrippa visited and consulted on matters of magic (Agrippa 1997, 534).

16. Geber (perhaps the Arab Abu abdullah Jaber ben Hayyam), was supposed to be an eighth- or nineth-century alchemist. His most famous work in Latin translation, *Summa perfectionis magisterii*, was very popular throughout the Middle Ages and the Renaissance (cf. Berthelot 1893; Stillmann 1960, 176–81, 276–86).

17. This "Fourth Book" was published in English in the seventeenth century. Its contents are discussed with extensive quotations in Waite 1961, 77–89, 324–25.

18. Dee in fact possessed several different copies of *De occulta philosophia*: beside the authoritative 1550 Basel edition (R&W 742), he had the very rare *editio princeps* of 1531 (R&W 1271) and the 1559 Marburg edition that also contained the Fourth Book (R&W 743).

19. See, for example, Webster's fine differentiation between the natural philosophy of Agrippa and Paracelsus in his *From Paracelsus to Newton* (1982).

20. "Henrici Cor. Agrippae censura, sive Retractatio de Magia, ex sua declamatione de Vanitate scientiarum, & excellentia verbi Dei," see Agrippa 1550, 505.

21. The idea of Mannerism as an independent stylistic period was put forward by the art historian Max Dvorak ("Greco and Mannerism," 1920). One of the important inspirations for studying Mannerism came from the Hungarian-born cultural historian Arnold Hauser; see his *The Social History of Art* (1951; Book One, Chapters 5–7; in Hauser 1985, 97–172) and his monumental *The Origins of Modern Art and Literature: The Development of Mannerism since the Crisis of the Renaissance* (1964, English edition, Hauser 1986). The critical appraisal of the debate can be found in Klaniczay 1977; see also E. Battisti *L'antirinascimento* (1962, Milano: Garzanti, 1989); Claude-Gilbert Dubois, *Le Manierisme* (Paris: Presses universitaires de France, 1979); Gerard Gillespie, "Renaissance, Mannerism, Baroque," in G. Hofmeister, ed., *German Baroque Literature, The European Perspective* (New York: Frederick Ungar, 1983), 3–24; Hiram Haydn, *The Counter Renaissance* (New York: Scribner, 1950); James V. Mirollo, *Mannerism and Renaissance Poetry* (New Haven and London: Yale, 1984); Caroline Patey, *Manierismo* (Milano: Editrice Bibliografica, 1996).

22. I have used the 1530 Antwerp edition of *De incertitudine . . .* and its 1575 English translation. As for the comparison between *De occulta philosophia* and *De incertitudine*, my reading has been greatly influenced by Keefer 1988.

23. The modernized quotation is from Keefer 1988, 634. Here Keefer notes on the relationship between Agrippa's "intellectus passibilis" and Ficino's terminology when he states that gods are immortal and active, men mortal and passive, while demons are immortal but passive (cf. *In convivium platonis de amore*, 6.3; Ficino 1944, 80, 185).

24. "But blessed are your eyes, for they see: and your ears, for they hear" (Matthew 13:16) and "Nevertheless when it shall turn to the Lord, the veil shall be taken away" (2 Corinthians 3:16).

25. Cf. Wisdom 7:17–21, as quoted in my introductory chapter.

26. See also Yates 1964, 131. As opposed to this hypothesis, Nauert 1965, 106–11, pointed out that official church authorities and the theologians of the Sorbonne immediately condemned *De incertitudine . . .* , a fact which leads Keefer (1988, 618) to rule out the possibility that Agrippa wrote his work with the intention to provide a safety valve for the tensions around him.

27. For a comparison between Agrippa and Marlowe's Faustus, see Keefer 1991, 182.

28. Cf. *The Praise of Folly*, sections 66–67 and the notes to these passages in Erasmus 1971, 204–08. On Erasmus and Agrippa, see again Yates 1979, 44. Agrippa's satire is analyzed by Bowen 1972 and Korkowski 1976.

29. Nauert 1965, 110. Cf. *Opus epistolarum Erasmi*, ed. P. S. Allen and H. W. Garrod (Oxford, 1906–1911), 10: 203, 209–11. On the personal relationship of Agrippa and Erasmus, see also Zambelli 1969.

30. On Erasmus and magic, see also below, p. 232–36.

31. On Simon Magus and gnosticism, see Beyschlag 1975; Grant 1966; Kákosy 1984, 18–21; Keefer 1988; Thorndike 1923–1958, 1:17. Sources: the apocryphal *Acts of Peter* (*Actus Petri cum Simone* 28–32, in R. A. Lipsius and M. Bonnet, eds., *Acta apostolorum apocrypha* [3 vols.], 1891–1903 [reprint Hildesheim, 1959]), and some Patristic authors (Irenaeus, *Adversus haereses* I. 23.2–4; Pseudo-Clementine, *Recognitiones* II. 6.7.12; Eusebius, *Historia ecclesiastica* II. 1.13–4; Hippolytus, *Refutationes* VI. 20.3). See also Karl Pieper, *Die Simon Magus Perikope (Apg 8, 5–24): Eine Beitrag zur Quellenfrage in der Apostelgeschichte* (Munster: Aschendorff, 1911, Neutestamentliche Abhandlungen 3.5).

32. According to Trithemius, who personally met the historical Faustus, this charlatan wrote the name of Simon on his visiting card (Brann 1999, 64–65). Frank Baron, writing about the historical Faustus, also mentions Melanchton, and how he associated Faustus with Simon Magus (1978, 75, 86).

33. For an extensive treatment of this phenomenon, see Fehér 1995.

34. Examples and interpretations abound in most standard handbooks of science history. The full-value inclusion of magic in the history of science took place in the 1960s and 1970s, and details were discussed in the so-called hermeticism debate referred to above.

35. For the influence of Paracelsus on Western intellectual thought, see Debus 1965 and 1977; Pagel 1958; Webster 1976 and 1982.

36. In order to orientate in the huge and complex literature on Paracelsus, cf. the bibliographies of Sudhoff 1958 [1527–1893]; Weimann 1963 [1932–1960] and Dilg-Frank 1984 [1961–1982], and Peter Dilg and Hartmut Rudolph's recent collection of essays on the new directions of Paracelsus research (1993). The collected works of Paracelsus were first time published by Johannes Huser in ten volumes (Paracelsus 1589–1591); the definitive twenty-volume critical edition was prepared by Karl Sudhoff, Wilhelm Matthiessen, and Kurt Goldammer (Paracelsus 1922–1925; 1923; 1928–1933; 1955–1973). Throughout this chapter, wherever possible, I shall quote the following English translations of Paracelsus: 1894, 1951, and 1975. Among the voluminous literature on Paracelsus I have profited from the fundamental studies of Jung (1942), Walter Pagel (1958; 1985) and Will-Erich Peuckert (1976); also from Ambrose 1992; Boas 1962; Goldammer 1953, 1967, and 1979; Kämmerer 1971; Koyré 1971, Ch. 3; Müller-Jahncke 1985; Webster 1982; and Weeks 1997. See also the recent collections of essays: Dilg and Rudolph (eds.) 1995; and Zimmermann (ed.) 1995.

37. *Die Neun Bücher der Archidoxen*, Paracelsus 1589–1591, 6:1-98; Paracelsus 1894, 2:3–81; Paracelsus 1928–1933, 3:91–200. Dee had the following German editions: R&W 1475, 1494, 2263 (all from 1570); R&W 1474 (from 1572); R&W 1492 (from 1574).

He also had the following Latin versions: R&W 1502 (from 1570) and R&W 2221 (from 1575).

38. *Archidoxis magica*, Paracelsus 1589–1591, 10A: 67–138; Paracelsus 1928–1933, 14: 437–99. Turner's English translation has been republished in a facsimile edition: Paracelsus 1975.

39. German editions are R&W 1463 (from 1571); R&W 1474 and 2267 (from 1572). Latin editions are R&W 2233 (from 1570) and R&W 2221 (from 1575).

40. *Astronomia Magna*, Paracelsus 1589–1591, 10: 1–397; Paracelsus 1928–1933, 12: 1–144. Recent studies on the *Astronomia magna* are John D. North, "Macrocosm and Microcosm in Paracelsus" (in Dilg and Rudolph 1995, 41-58); Ute Gause's "Aspekte der theologischen Anthropologie des Paracelsus" (in Dilg and Rudolph 1995, 59–70); Wolf-Dieter Müller-Jahncke, "Makrokosmos und Mikrokosmos bei Paracelsus" (in Zimmermann 1995, 59–66); and Hartmut Rudolph, "Prädestination und 'seliges Leben.' Ein Beitrag zur Verhältnisbestimmung von Weltbild und Theologie bei Paracelsus" (in Zimmermann 1995, 85–98).

41. It would be profitable to compare Paracelsus' theology to the spiritual wing of the early Reformation. He admittedly was for a while under the influence of the reformed mystic, Sebastian Franck, but the idea of mystical rebirth was not alien from Caspar Schwenckfeld and Valentin Weigel, either. The necessity of further research in this direction has been pointed out to me by Bálint Keserű. To my knowledge the only extensive comparative study among the mentioned mystics is Koyré 1971. See also the recent article of Horst Pfefferl, "Die Rezeption des paracelsischen Schrifttums bei Valentin Weigel" (in Dilg and Rudolph 1995, 151–68).

42. I am employing here the standard notation referring to Paracelsus' *Sämtliche Werke*. The Roman numerals indicate the section (I=*Medizinische, naturwissenschaftliche und philosophische Schriften*; II=*Die theologischen und religionsphilosophischen Schriften*), the Arabic numerals refer to the volume and page number in that section (cf. Paracelsus 1922–1925, 1923, 1928–1933, 1955–1973).

43. In his seventeenth-century portraits, Paracelsus is usually shown holding a sword, on the handle of which the word Azoth is inscribed. According to some broadsheets, Azoth was an *elixir vitae*, a secret medicine Paracelsus had discovered and kept in the handle of his sword. The term appears already in early alchemistical literature (Zozimos, Olympiadorus) and is called by the name of Hermes, or *spiritus animatus*, the philosophers's stone. Others think it refers to the beginning and the end: Zeus and Theos (Jacobi in Paracelsus 1951, 248).

44. "Of Characters" (Paracelsus 1975, 43–44).

45. In the terminology of Paracelsus the sidereal body (or ethereal body, *astrum*) is the refined upper layer of the physical body which consists of air and fire and receives the occult influences of the stars. The sidereal body provides man with sidereal knowledge, that is, the knowledge of occult sympathies (cf. Jacobi in Paracelsus 1951, 262; and Müller-Jahncke 1985, 76–77).

46. Cf. Jung [1942] 1983, 130; Walker 1958a, 119, and 1972. On Adam Kadmon see Schmidt-Biggemann 1998, 217–25; on the *prisca theologia*, see Schmidt-Biggemann 1998, 91 ff.

47. *Astronomia magna*, I,12:292; quoted by Müller-Jahncke 1985, 69. In respect of the *prisca theologia* one should think again of the spiritualistic trends of the German Reformation. I have already mentioned Sebastian Franck who had some influence on Paracelsus (Dee also had several works by Franck—R&W 1175, 2180–82), while both of them contributed to the mystical philosophy of Valentin Weigel (1533–88) who interestingly fused Reformation theology and esoteric Neoplatonism. In his *Der gülden Griff* (printed only in 1613) he claimed that for the microcosmic man, the church would be unnecessary because he himself was the temple. "Every man can be a deified Christ if he leaves the old Adam behind," he added. Cf. Koyré 1971, Ch. 4.1–2; Zeller 1979, 105–24; Szulakowska 2000, 80–101; also Wilhelm Kühlmann, "Paracelsismus und Häresie. Zwei Briefe der Söhne Valentin Weigels aus dem Jahre 1596," *Wolfenbüttler Barocknachrichten* 18 (1991): 24–33; Horst Pfefferl, "Valentin Weigel und Paracelsus," in *Paracelsus und sein dämonenglaubiges Jahrhundert* (Wien: Verband der Wissenschaftlichen Gesellschaften Osterreichs, 1988, Salzburger Beitrage zur Paracelsusforschung, 26), 77–95.

48. ". . . das gestirn in der eusseren welt und das gestirn in der kleinen welt haben ir constellation oder confluenz mit einander, und ist ein lauf und ein wirkung nach ort irer conjunction" (I:12, 48).

49. These three phases naturally correspond with the main stages of the alchemical transmutation: *solutio (prima materia)—separatio—conjunctio (exaltatio)*. Cf. Nicholl 1980, 38–40; and the chapter "Paracelsus' dreifaches Mensch" in Schmidt-Biggemann 1998, 286–96.

50. On his views on women see Ambrose 1992, and Jacobi in Paracelsus 1951, 23–27.

51. Cf. *De fundamento scientiarum sapientiae* (I, 13:287–335).

52. *De religione perpetua*, II, 1:100–01. Quoted in Paracelsus 1951, 134, and in a slightly different translation in Jung 1983, 130.

53. Cited by Jung 1983, 117. I did not find this statement in Agrippa's preface to *De incertitudine . . .* , but it can be found in the translators' prefaces of both early modern English editions. The quoted text is from the 1651 English publication of *De occulta . . .* where it concludes the paratext "The Life of Henry Cornelius Agrippa, Knight" (Agrippa 1997, xlix).

54. Biblical scholarship defines the *apocrypha* as sacred books whose belonging to the canon is uncertain or has been finally denied by the authorities; *pseudepigrapha* denotes the body of works which were falsely attributed to ideal figures featured in the Old and New Testaments. Modern scholarship states that by now the terms do not imply anything spurious; the use of the term is simply inherited from earlier scholars, that is, traditional (cf. Charlesworth 1983, xxiv–vi).

55. An English translation of *1Enoch*, edited by E. Isaac with critical apparatus, has been published in Charlesworth 1983, 5–12. Here one finds full bibliographical details of the surviving manuscripts, too.

56. Agrippa in one of his writings called Hermes Trismegistus the incarnation of Enoch. Cf. Agrippa's *In praelectione Hermetis Trismegisti*, published in Garin 1955, 122–23.

57. Quoted by Brann 1999, 65. On Mercurio see P. O. Kristeller, "Marsilio Ficino e Lodovico Lazzarelli," *Annali della R. Scuola Normale Superiore di Pisa* 2.7 (1938): 237–62; also Kristeller 1956, 228, 249.

58. Thorndike 5:438. Lazzarelli's treatise has been published by E. Garin (cf. Lazzarelli 1955). On Lazzarelli see Kristeller 1956, 221–57; Secret 1985, 74–77; and Walker 1958, 64–72.

59. In Chapter 3.36 Agrippa extensively quoted Lazzarelli's *Crater hermetis* to prove the possibility of deification: "God gave man reason that like deities / He might bring forth gods with capacity..." (Agrippa 1997, 582). As Keefer notes: "Some Renaissance humanists did find a principle of coherence in the *Hermetica*, and that this principle was a religious one, is suggested by Lodovico Lazzarelli: 'Christianus ego sum [...] et hermeticum simul esse non pudet' " (1988, 625).

60. Surprisingly, Postel has been discussed in Dee scholarship as little as Paracelsus. Peter French briefly mentioned him; Yates and Heilbronn (1978) neglected him entirely. Clulee did not pay much attention to him either although, as we shall soon observe, he did highlight a few crucial connections. Harkness (1999) often mentions Postel in passing but this is only the beginning of the full recognition of his influence on Dee's thought.

61. My following summary is based on Niceron, Johan Peter, *Nachrichten von den Begebenheiten und Schriften berümter Gelehrten mit einige Zusätzen* (Halle: Chr. Peter Francken, 1753); Bouwsma 1957; Kuntz 1981 and Secret 1985, 151–218.

62. Niceron, 348.

6. The Ideology and Occult Symbolism of Dee's Natural Philosophy

1. These trends appeared no earlier than the late sixteenth century, as an offspring of the cross-fertilization of neoaristotelism and some versions of the radical Reformation, for example, anti-Trinitarianism.

2. "Her Majestie very gratiously took me to her service, at Whitehall before her Coronation..." (Dee 1851, 12). "Before her Majesties coronation I wrote at large [...] what in my judgement the ancient astrologers would determine of the election day of such a tyme, as was appointed for her Majestie to be crowned, A. 1558" (21).

3. For the intellectual horizon of these people, see de Smet 1970, 13–29; also Dee's remarks in the Preface of the *Propaedeumata* and in 1851, 5, 58–59; 1570, biiiijr.

4. The *Propaedeumata* and the *Monas* are series of aphorisms, prefixed by longer prefaces. The *Mathematicall Praeface* is sui generis an introduction, while his last printed work, the *General and Rare Memorials...*, is a chapter from a larger unpublished manuscript.

5. The original Latin uses the word *Gamaea* for the stone. This characteristic terminology, meaning "talisman," refers to Paracelsus.

6. On his Paracelsica see p. 133; on his getting acquainted with Trithemius' Steganographia, see p. 105–06.

7. For the annals of Dee's life, see Roberts and Watson 1990, 75–79.

8. London, BL, Cotton Vitellius C.VII, art. 1. f 7v. Quoted by C. H. Josten in Dee 1964, 89.

9. Dee's work was republished in Lazarus Zetzner's *Theatrum chemicum* (Ursel, 1602, and several subsequent editions), and Carlos Gilly, the well-known historian of the Rosicrucians—otherwise rather sceptical about Dee's influence on the movement—admits that Dee's diagram could have inspired Adam Haslmayr's "character Cabalisticus" in his unpublished *Consideration Figurae Ergon et Parergon Fratrum RC* (1626) as well as Philippus à Gabella's studies on vitriol (published in his *Secretoris Philosophiae Consideration Brevis, nunc primum una cum Confessione Fraternitatis RC in lucem edita*, Kassel, 1615). Cf. Gilly 1995, 35, 73. Later, Dee's monad also turned up in Athanasius Kircher's works and in some of the illustrated editions of Boehme.

10. Basel 1556, 102. See also the comments of Harkness on Valeriano and hieroglyphics, 1999, 84–85. On the Renaissance interest in hieroglyphics, see for example Wittkower's "Hieroglyphics in the Renaissance," in Wittkower 1977, 113–28, and other pertinent studies on Horapollo. On the early modern symbolic interpretations of Horapollo and hieroglyphics, see the classic studies of Giehlow 1915 and Volkmann 1962. On the relationship of literary emblematics and hieroglyphics, see Daly 1998, 1727, and Daniel Russel 1988, 227–43.

11. "The Preface," p. 38 [unnumbered] of Dee 1659; quoted by Walton 1976, 116.

12. Clulee 1988, 127. Dee's library catalogue lists (among others) the following books on pythagorean and cabalistical topics: "Hierocles in pythagorica," Basel, 1543 (R&W 1022, B148); "Sphaera pithagorica" (R&W CM36h); "Georgio Veneti harmonia mundi totius," Paris, 1545 (R&W 221); "Archangelus Burgonovetus in cabalistarum dogmata ex Joh. Picus Mirandola collecta expositio," Venice, 1559 (R&W 997); "Johannes Reuchlin De verbo mirifico," Cologne, 1532 (R&W 1043); "Raymundi Lulli opusculum de auditu cabalistico," Venice, 1518 (R&W 2104). On Pythagorean number symbolism, see Heninger 1974 and 1977; and Koenigsberger 1979; on the symbolism of the cabala, see Blau 1944; Halevi 1979: Scholem 1974 and 1980.

13. On Ficino's "Anthologia esoterica" see above, pp. 66–7, 81.

14. This linguistic interpretation of the monad was first suggested by Walton 1975 and Clulee 1988, recently further developed by Eco 1995, 185–90; myself (Szőnyi 1997 and 2001); and Harkness 1999, 82 ff.

15. Håkansson's book was published just when I completed my manuscript. Thus, apart from two pieces of valuable information, I have not been able to use his study in depth. Cf. Håkansson 2001, 213, where he refers to Dee's marginalia in Synesius' *De insomiis*, pointing out the connection between his concept of the adept and the hermetic man: "Mens adepta. Vide Hermetis Pimander cap. 4. de Monade" (*Index eorum*, fol. 45v).

16. Since I had no chance to study the *Index eorum* in the Folger Library, for this information I thank Håkan Håkansson who recently examined the volume (cf. Håkansson 2001, 285).

17. 3.21; Ficino 1989, 355–57 (emphasis mine). See also Allen's analysis of the same topic in Ficino's *De numero fatali* (Allen 1994, 91–97, and 109).

18. Baldassare Castiglione—Sir Thomas Hoby, *The Courtier* (1561), Book IV: Love. Quoted from Abrams 1986, 1: 1006.

19. See also his *Erklärung der Gantzen Astronomey* (Paracelsus 1589–1591, 10:398–434 = 1928–1933, I, 12:447–77; also translated into English by Waite in Paracelsus 1894, 2:282–317). Dee had an 1567 German edition (R&W 1461) in which he could read: "The magus can transfer the powers of a whole celestial field into a small stone, which is called gamaheus" (Paracelsus 1894, 2:300). On Paracelsus' influence on Dee's chemical experiments, cf. Szulakowska 1999.

20. Eco 1995, 187. Some important works relating to the early modern quest for the universal language are Alessandro Bausani, *Geheim und Universalsprachen: Entwicklung und Typologie* (Stuttgart: Kohlhammer, 1970); Arno Borst, *Der Turmbau von Babel. Geschichte der Meinungen über Ursprung und Vielfalt der Sprachen und Völker*, 4 vols (Stuttgart: Hiersemann, 1957–1963); Joscelyn Godwin, *Athanasius Kircher. A Renaissance Man and the Quest for Lost Knowledge* (1979b); James Knowlson, *Universal Language Schemes in England and France 1600–1800* (Toronto: University of Toronto Press, 1975); Wilhelm Schmidt-Biggemann, *Topica universalis: Eine Modellgeschichte humanistischer und barocker Wissenschaft* (1983); Gerhard F. Strasser, *Lingua universalis. Kryptographie und Theorie der Universalsprachen im 16. und 17. Jahrhundert* (Wiesbaden: Harrassowitz, 1988, Wolfenbütteler Forschungen 38); Marina Yaguello, *Les Fous du langage: Des langues imaginaires et de leurs inventeurs* (Paris: Éditions du Seuil, 1984). As far as I am informed, the latest publication on the *lingua adamica* is the collection of essays edited by Alison Coudert (*The Language of Adam / Die Sprache Adams*, 1999) which has a useful paper by Wilhelm Schmidt-Biggemann on the "Christian Kabbala: Joseph Gikatilia, Johannes Reuchlin, Paulus Ricius, and Jakob Böhme" (Coudert 1999, 81–122) and one by Marion Leathers Kuntz on Guillaume Postel's combining the idea of the Original Language with his program of *restitutio omnium* (123–50). It is surprising, though, that there is only one passing mention of John Dee in the whole volume.

21. R&W 868. See the editors note: "Dee's copy is RCP Library; it is heavily annotated by Dee, throughout" (Roberts and Watson 1990, 94).

22. "Neque spectare solum, sed etiam animo reputare" (3.19; Ficino 1989, 346–477).

23. Quoted by Nicholl 1980, 48, from Roger Bacon [attrib.], *The Mirror of Alchimy*, London, 1597, 16. Dee, not surprisingly, possessed four copies of the Latin version of this tract: R&W 1433, DM2, DM6, DM81.

24. Facsimile edition: Dee 1975 with Allen Debus' critical introduction. See also Kenneth J. Knoespel's new historicist approach (1987) and the appropriate chapters in Clulee 1988 (143–77). Shorter interpretations can be found in the cited works of French 1972; Harkness 1999; Heilbron 1987; Rowse 1972; Webster 1982; Yates 1972, 1979.

25. This shift is examined in the essays collected in Vickers 1984, including the editor's lengthy introduction: "Analogy Versus Identity: The Rejection of Occult Symbolism." The consequences of this paradigm shift in mathematics have been analyzed in Fehér 1995, 1–26.

26. *Von der französischen Krankenheit 3 Bücher* (Paracelsus 1922–1925, 7:202; Paracelsus 1951, 55–56). Dee had this treatise in an 1553 Frankfurt edition (R&W 1473).

7. ILLUMINATION AND ANGEL MAGIC

1. It is a great pity that Whitby's Ph.D. dissertation of 1981 (reprinted by Garland in 1988) is practically unattainable. His article of 1985 laid the foundations for a unified view of early modern sience, medieval ceremonial magic, and Renaissance angelology.

2. London, BL, MS Sloane 3188, fol. 5; Dee 1988, 6; Dee 1996, 1.2. Since I had access to Whitby's 1988 publication of the early spiritual diaries (Dee 1988) only for a limited time and I had little time to spend with the original manuscript in London, I am citing these texts from the selections of Geoffrey Jones (Dee 1994) and Edward Fenton (1998), and, wherever I can, from Clay Holden's transliterated internet edition (1996). Here Holden has rendered Dee's text into three PDF files. I am referring to the internet loci by a double number: the first refers to the file corresponding to Dee's *Mysteriorum Liber* Primus, Secundus, and Tertius; the second indicates the screen/page number in Acrobat Reader.

3. Cf. Dee 1851, 53, 69–84; interpretations of Dee's apologies include Pickering 1986; Szőnyi 1991.

4. Cf. Genesis 1:26–27, 2:19.

5. On the medieval and Renaissance reception of Enoch and Dee's awareness of this literature, see above p. 147 ff.

6. Dee 1659, 170; I thank Giulio Gelibter who called my attention to this textual parallel.

7. Cf. studies on medieval optics such as Lindberg 1976; Szulakowska 1995 and 2000; and on Dee's interest in optics, see Clulee 1988, 46–59; Harkness 1999, 63–78; Szulakowska 2000, 29–30, 35–40.

8. On spiritual alchemy see Jung 1980 and 1983; Merkur 1990; Roob 1997; Waite 1888; Zadrobílek 1997.

9. Secret (1990, 50) quotes the 1546 Paris edition from pages 90–91.

10. Hamburg, 1618, then republished in the fifth volume of Lazarus Zetzner's *Theatrum Chemicum* (Strassburg, 1602–1661). The second volume of this collection also reprinted Dee's *Monas hieroglyphica*. Although this volume was first published in 1602, the Doctor did not seem to have taken notice of the continuation of his fame.

11. Cf. Bacon 1659. This publication was listed in Cooper's *Catalogue of Chymicall Books* (Cooper 1987, 9; No. 18).

12. London: T. Walkey (cf. under "Sources," Cooper 1987, 42; No. 145).

13. See the chapters on them, above, and also on the *Monas*, in relation to Ficino.

14. Exodus 28:15–31; cf. Evans 1976, 29, 36, 72–73; Wallis Budge 1961, 215, 270, 327–28; Whitby 1985, 27; 1988, 1:63–75.

15. For description of catoptromantic practices, see Martino Delrio's *Disquisitionum magicarum libri sex* (Lyons, 1608), 283; Jules Boulenger, *Opusculorum systema* (Lyons, 1621), 2:199–200; for comments, see Pierre Janet, *Sur la divination par les miroirs et les hallucinations subconscientes* (Bulletin de l'Université de Lyon, 1987 July).

16. On Dee's various shew-stones and some doubts concerning Dee's obsidian mirror, cf. Harkness 1999, 29–31; Whitby 1988, 1:137–41. The "Walpole-story" unfolds from the correspondence of the eccentric earl (see *The Letters of Horace Walpole,* ed. Paget Toynbee, Oxford: Clarendon, 1904, 8:22–23); see also Hugh Tait, " 'The Devil's Looking-Glass'; the Magical Speculum of Doctor Dee." In Warren Hunting Smith (ed.), *Horace Walpole. Writer, Politician and Connoisseur* (New Haven, Ct.: Yale University Press, 1967), 195–212.

17. John of Salisbury in Migne, *Patrologia Latina* CIXC, 408; Reisch, *Margarita philosophica nova* (Strassburg, 1512), 23; cited by Gansiniec 1954, 8. As we have seen, Dee had Reisch's 1504 Strassbourg edition (R&W 1385).

18. In Cardano, *De rerum varietate,* Lyon, 1663, cited by Gansiniec 1954, 12. For other anecdotes see also Johann Wier, *De praestigiis daemonum* (Cologne, 1566), 139; Joachim Camerarius, *Praefatio super Plutarchi* (Basel, 1566), 323; Thomas Naogeorgius (=Kirchmeyer), *Regnum papisticum* (Basel, 1559), 166.

19. Examples by Gansiniec 1954, 11 ff. In my native city of Szeged, even as late as in 1730, witchcraft prosecutors would ask: "Wie hast du aus Kristall, aus Glas, Spiegeln den Menschen gewahrsagt?" Cf. János Reizner, *Szeged története* (Szeged, 1900), 4:390.

20. Some of the notable manuscript collections of ceremonial magic from Renaissance England are London, BL, MS Bodley 951 (Ars notoria, fifteenthth century); London, BL, MS Harleian 181 (Ars notoria, sixteenth/seventeenth century; Solomon's *Book of Vertues*); London, BL, MS Royal 17.A.XLII (*Liber Sacer* and *Cephar Raziel*—in English, fifteenth/sixteenth century); London, BL, MS Sloane 313 (Honorius Magister Thebarum's *Liber juratus*); London, BL, MS Sloane 384 (*Liber Salomonis Raziel,* sixteenth/seventeenth century); and Oxford, Bodleian, MS Ashmole 1515 (*Ars notoria,* Latin and English, sixteenth century).

Collections related to Dee's contemporaries include London, BL, MS Additional 36674 ("The Book of Dr. Cajus": scrying experiments of Humphrey Gilbert and John Davies, glossed by Gabriel Harvey—also contains Dee's *De heptarchia mystica,* Forman's "An excellent booke of the arte of Magicke," and some standard texts of magic, for example, Pietro d'Abano and Agrippa's "Fourth Book"); and London, BL, MS Sloane 3851 (magical tracts collected by Arthur Gauntlet and Anonymous "Invocations to call a spirit into a chrystall Stone"). References to these collections can be found in Clucas 200?; Clulee 1988, Whitby 1985 and 1988; 1:75–94.

21. Clucas 200?; Fanger 1998; Kieckhefer 1989, 1997.

22. Clucas 200?, n. 164 (the MS is Sloane 313).

23. In n. 166 Clucas quotes Dee 1581–1583 [*Lib. Myst.*], fol. 12 verso: "De Sigillo Emeth vide Reuchlini Cabalisticae Lib 3 et Agrippa[m] Lib. 3 cap.11." Further glosses of Dee mention Agrippa (1.11); the *Elementis magicis* of Pietro d'Abano (1.25, 2.29); the *Arbatel* (1.26); and again Agrippa ("which was in my oratorie almost under my wyndow," 1.26).

24. See Abano's seal in Agrippa 1550, 568, on Dee's Golden Talisman below, 214–5.

25. Besterman 1965, 19. See also Whitby 1988, 1: 137–41; and Harkness 1999, 29–31.

26. Once again, for Paracelsus on shining coal and beryls, see the *Erklärung der gantzen Astronomey*, I, 12:463–66, 478–79, 506. See also Gerhard Dorn, *Dictionarium Theophrasti Paracelsi* (Frankfurt, 1583), 24 ("Beryllus est speculum ex crystallo superstitiose consecratum ab auguristis") and Martin Ruland's *Lexicon alchemiae* (Prague, 1612, 101), which followed the above definition: "BERILLUS is a Crystal Mirror superstitiously consecrated to auguries"; "BERILLISTICA is the art of perceiving visions in the Berillus" (Ruland 1984, 70).

27. See Laycock 1994, 28–29. On Pantheus and Dee see Clulee 1988, 97, 127, 235; Håkansson 2001, 227–28; and Harkness 1999, 88–99; 167, 171, 181, 204.

28. Recent works on angelology and angel magic include Bussagli 1995; James 1995; Rosa 1992; and Scazzoso 1967.

29. Cf. Harkness' analysis of Dee's use of Pompilius Azalus (*De omnibus rebus naturalibus*). Dee's annotated copy is the Venice edition of 1544 (R&W 134; Harkness 1999).

30. R&W 678, 969, 1884. The first survives in the Cambridge University Library with his annotations. He seems to have bought it in 1563, at the same time he became acquainted with a manuscript of the *Steganographia* (Roberts and Watson 1990, 92).

31. Cf. Clucas 2003; Kieckhefer 1997; Waite 1961. On Dee's angels see Harkness 1999, 46–51; Jones 1995, 82–101; Whitby 1988, 1:117–18.

32. See above, p. 200, and also below, p. 274.

33. See Dee 1586, "Praefatio Latina in Actionem Primum ex 7 . . ." (Oxford, Bodleian, MS Ashmole 1790, art. 1. fols. 1–9), published by C. H. Josten in Dee 1965.

34. Cf. Dee 1583a, 1583–1587, 1584, 1585.

35. One should note that the numbering of the volume restarts after p. 448. Page numbers from this section at the end of the volume are marked by an asterisk (*).

36. This is the same journal from which I previously summarized the "miracle of the books."

37. These aspects have been highlighted in recent monographs on Dee, especially Clulee's chapter titled "The Vagaries of Patronage," and Sherman 1995. Dee's example is by no means unique among sixteenth-century intellectuals. About his spiritual relative, Guillaume Postel, the biographer Bouwsma had to remark more than once: "The relationship between Postel and the [left-wing Protestant] Basel group provides a nice illustration of the complexity of religious alliances in the sixteenth century" (1957, 10 and passim).

38. Burckhardt 1995, 323.

39. Cf. Kraye 1988, 310–6; Secret 1985, 126–40; Vasoli 1976, 131–403; Walker 1958, 112–19; Yates 1979, 29–36, 127–33.

40. Paris, BN, MS fonds franç. 2115, fol 105^v, quoted by Marion Kuntz 1981, 78.

41. The full text was published in Dee 1851, then in Roberts and Watson 1990, 194–95. For information on Dee's early career, see French 1972, 34–35, 41–42; Clulee 1988, 32–34; Sherman 1995, 36–38.

42. An important analysis of the social-religious context behind the cult of the Virgin Queen was developed by Keith Thomas (1971). See also the recent works of Hackett 1996, especially the chapters "The Meanings of Virginity" (pp. 72–94) and

"Patronage, Prayers and Pilgrimages" (128–63); and Levin 1994, 10–39 ("Elizabeth as a Sacred Monarch").

43. Zambelli 1970, 1976; Zika 1976–1977.

44. Zika's much more detailed Ph.D. dissertation (University of Melburn, 1974) has recently been published in German: *Reuchlin und die okkulte Tradition der Renaissance* (Sigmaringen: Thorbecke, 1998, Pforzheimer Reuchlinschriften 6).

45. *Consultatio venerandi ac benedocti Iacobi Hochstraten haereticae pravitatis magistri contra immundos libros Iudaeorum.* The piece was published only in 1516 in Johannes Pfefferkorn's *Defensio Joannis Pepericorni contra famosas et criminales Obscurorum virorum epistolas* (Cologne: Quentel); cf. Peterse 1995, 152.

46. *Doctor Johannes Reuchlins Augenspiegel* (Tübingen: Thomas Anshelm, 1511). Cf. the new English edition of his *Recommendations*, Reuchlin 2000.

47. On the Reuchlin affair, see Max Brod, *Johannes Reuchlin und sein Kampf* (1965, Wiesbaden: Fourier, 1989); Frank Geerk, *Die Geburt der Zukunft : Reuchlin, Erasmus und Paracelsus als wegweisende Humanisten* (Karlsruhe: von Loeper Literaturverlag, Ariadne Buchdienst, 1996); Hajo Holborn (ed.), *On the Eve of the Reformation: Letters of Obscure Men* (New York: Harper and Row, 1964); J. Overfield, "A New Look at the Reuchlin Affair," *Studies in Medieval and Renaissance History* 8 (1971): 167–207; Peterse 1995; and the introduction in Reuchlin 2000.

48. Zika 1976–1977, 223–24. As I am going to show, the case is not so simple. Recently Hans Peterse has also argued and called for a historiographical revaluation (1995, 5–7).

49. Peterse clearly makes this differentiation (1995, 2n. 3) and Elisheva Carlebach— as opposed to earlier historians—also uses the term *anti-Judaism* (in Reuchlin 2000, 20).

50. These were also neglected by another, much quoted article by Gundersheimer 1963. He, too, decided that Erasmus was simply an anti-Semite.

51. Reuchlin to Erasmus, Frankfurt, 1514 April Fair (Ep290, in Erasmus 1974–1994, 2:285–86).

52. For example, in letters to Cardinal Raffaele Riario (London, May 15, 1515, Ep333 in Erasmus 1974–1994, 3:90–91) and to Cardinal Domenico Grimaldi (London, May 1515, Ep335, *op. cit.*, 3:98).

53. Frankfurt, April 1515 (Ep326B, Erasmus 1974–1994, 3:76–77).

54. John Colet to Erasmus (London, June 1517, Ep593, Erasmus 1974–1994, 4:398).

55. Erasmus to Reuchlin (Louvain, November 15, 1517, Ep713, *op. cit.*, 4:203–04).

56. Erasmus to Albert of Brandenburg (Louvain, October 19, 1519, Ep1033, *op. cit.*, 7:110).

57. Erasmus to the Reader (Louvain, October/November 1519, Ep1041, *op. cit.*, 7:129); originally published in Erasmus' *Familiarum quolloquiorum formulae* (Louvain: Martens, 1519).

58. Cf. my further and more detailed investigation of Erasmus' attitude to Reuchlin, "Erasmus, Reuchlin, and the Magical Renaissance," in Marcell Sebők (ed.), *The Republic of Letters* (Budapest: Collegium Budapest publications, forthcoming).

59. Tyson in Agrippa 1997, xviii. The story is told by Henry Morley who wrote a life of Agrippa in the nineteenth century, parts of which were republished in Agrippa 1898. The section concerning Agrippa and Reuchlin is pp. 228–55, especially 252–55. See also Zambelli 1970, 38.

60. For the intellectual atmosphere of these Mannerist courts see Evans 1973; Fučiková 1997; Hauser 1986; Klaniczay 1977; Trevor-Roper 1976; etc.

61. See also Dee 1842, 42; Dee 1998, 257. The books were identified by a Hungarian scholar, Róbert Dán (1979, 225–30): Christian Francken, *Praecipuarum enumeratio causarum* (Cracow: Aleksy Rodecki, 1584) and Johannes Sommer, *Refutatio scripti Petri Carolii editi Wittenbergae* (Cracow: Aleksy Rodecki, 1582). The latter has been found in the Library of Lambeth Palace where, next to the preface dated 1572, Dee remarked: "Quo anno apparuit illa admirabilis stella . . . ." Cf. Roberts and Watson 1990, 157 (R&W D20 and D9).

8. DEE AND THE INTERPRETIVE COMMUNITY

1. Dee 1854, 10–11.

2. On Sambucus, cf. Hans Gerstinger, *Aus dem Tagebuch des kaiserlichen Hofhistoriographen Johannes Sambucus 1531–1584 : Cod. Vind. Lat. 9039* (Graz: Böhlau, 1965); Holger Homann, *Studien zur Emblematik des 16. Jahrhunderts Sebastian Brant, Andrea Alciati, Johannes Sambucus, Mathias Holtzwart, Nicolaus Taurellus* (Utrecht: Haentjens Dekker and Gumbert, 1971); István Monok (ed.), *Die Bibliothek Sambucus: Katalog; nach der Abschrift von Pál Gulyás* (Szeged: Scriptum, 1992).

3. A summary of his career—based on various Hungarian scholarly and archival sources—can be found in my book, Szőnyi 1998, 66–69.

4. Caroli Clusii *Atrebatis Rariorum aliquot stirpium, per Pannoniam, Austriam, & vicinas quasdam prouincias obseruatarum historia: quatuor libris expressa*. Antuerpiae: Ex officina Christophori Plantini, 1583.

5. A full and analytical list of the receipts is given by Béla Iványi, *A magyar könyvkultúra múltjából*. Ed. Bálint Keserű (Szeged: JATE, 1983, Adattár XVI-XVII. századi szellemi mozgalmaink történetéhez 11), 389–437. See also the works of Evans cited above and Barlay 1979 and 1986.

6. Jordán's inscription is dated October 1, 1562, as visitor 163 while Dee's name appears as visitor 175 on April 23, 1563 (see Durling 1965, 139–41). On Jordán see also Evans 1973, 207–08.

7. See Thomas Moffet's contemporary biography of Sidney (1940, 75). Also French 1972, 126–58, and Yewbrey 1981.

8. See Gál 1969; Gömöri 1991; Osborn 1972.

9. On Purkircher, see Birnbaum 1985, 306–07, and Osborn 1972, 103.

10. For the details of Sidney's diplomatic mission, see Duncan-Jones 1991, 120–31.

11. The house in the forest where after the threatening prophecy Basilius and his daughters take refuge is modeled on the Hvezda: it is star-shaped and is painted yellow

while inside is filled with mythological-emblematic paintings. Cf. Katona 1998, 178 ff.; and Martin Stejskal, "The Hvezda Summer residence," in Zadrobílek 1997, 271–74.

12. Cf. Dee 1659, 397; Dee 1965, 237–38.

13. English sources and reference works to John à Lasco are cited by Zins 1974, 118–26.

14. On Laski, cf. Żelewski 1973, 18.2: 246-50; on his contacts with English and European humanists, cf. Evans 1973, 212–29; Szőnyi 1998, 49 ff.; and Zantuan 1968.

15. "ARGUMENTUM autem totius operis est, docere in genere, quomodo quaelibet cuiusquae morbi appropriata medicina, debeat et possit praeparari, et ad summum *exaltari*: ita ut corpus humanum per eam quasi miraculosè, certò tamen ab omni morbo, futurisque accidentibus, ad longissimam usque aetatem liberetur, et immune conservetur" (Paracelsus 1569, "Argumentum").

16. Żelewski 1973, 18.2: 248; Zins 1974, 177; on the general English-Polish relations in the later sixteenth century, see also J. Jasnowski, "England and Poland in the XVIth and XVIIth Centuries," *Polish Science and Learning* 48.7 (1948): 15–19.

17. See F. R. Johnson (1937); E. G. R. Taylor (1930); and emphatically Frances Yates (1964, 1969, 1972) and Peter French (1972).

18. Apart from the already mentioned Zantuan 1968 and Zins 1974, from Hungarian scholarship, see Dán 1979; Klaniczay 1973, 254, 268–69; Schultheiss and Tardy 1972; Szőnyi 1980.

19. Particularly Evans 1973; French 1972; and Yates 1972. See, however, the much less enthusiastic opinion of Firpo 1952.

20. Cf. Deborah Harkness (1996, 1997, 1999); Michael Wilding (1999a, 1999b); and Benjamin Woolley 2001.

21. Shumaker ironically comments on Kelly's being alert to avoid the request of Laski (1982, 49).

22. The Latin quotations of Casaubon's edition have been partly given in English translation by Fenton (Dee 1998, 181 ff.)

23. *Prefatio Latina*, Dee 1965, 228–29. Bracketed insertions are both by Josten and me.

24. On Pucci, see Evans 1973, 102–05; Harkness 1999, 58-9. Also Elie Barnavi, *La périple de Francesco Pucci. Utopie, hérésie et verité religieuse dans la Renaissance tardive* (Paris: Hachette, 1988); Mario Biagioni, "Prospettive di ricerca su Francesco Pucci," *Rivista Storica Italiana* 107.1 (1995): 133–53; Miriam Eliav-Feldon, "Secret Societies, Utopias, and Peace Plans: The Case of Francesco Pucci," *Journal of Medieval and Renaissance Studies* 14 (1984): 139–58; L. Firpo and R. Piattoli (eds.), *Francesco Pucci, Lettere* (Florence, 1955); Lech Szczucki, *W kręgu myślicieli heretyckich* (Warsaw, 1972), 256–65.

25. On Rosselli, see Czerkawski 1967.

26. Except for the discussion on Trithemius which had still happened at one of the early séances back in England (Dee 1659, 13).

27. Harkness 1999, 190–04, pinpoints the close relationship of Dee's chiliastic visions to contemporary Jewish and cabalistic literature.

28. Cracow, Jagiellonian Library, MS 620. Cf. Zins 1974, 274. The Latin dedication is partially quoted by Roberts and Watson 1990, 117. According to them, in this dedication Dee used his most elaborate and self-conscious presentation italic hand (26).

29. R&W DM91. On the Ripley scrolls, see Stanton J. Linden, "Reading the Ripley Scrolls: Iconographic Patterns in Renaissance Alchemy," in György E. Szőnyi (ed.), *Iconography East & West* (Leiden: Brill, 1996, Eymbola & Emblemata 7), 236–50; also Linden 1996, 193–224.

30. In his treatise, entitled *Disputatio inter theologum et philosophum de incertitudine religionis Christianæ* (cc. 1591). Cf. Firpo 1952; Szczucki 197; and Bálint Keserű's unpublished Ph.D. thesis.

31. On Dee: "Est ni fallor, adhuc isthic D. Dee, Anglus, Mathematicus insignis; et ut audio, hospes videtur est. Illius consuetudo et familiaria colloquia multum iuvare, et promonere istas veras cognitiones et studia potuerunt. Aiunt eum visiones, nescio quas, h[. . .] observo te; libere et candide (ut tenus est mos) significes mihi quid tu de his rebus sentias; qui sanar[. . .] har[. . .] cognitione, prudentia, iudicio, et rerum usu magno praeditus, unus olim optime de his rebus iudicare potes. Est in eorum contubernio; aut certo ipsis notus Anglis, qui cum Dee versam[. . .]; Franciscus Puccius nobilis et patricius Florentinus: ad eum scribo. Rogo, ut ei inclusas hic litteras certo reddi cures, et responsum expectas. Iam a multis annis, ne[. . .] meminisse credo, diligenter, per amicos, aliquem Mathematicum quaeso; non elementarium, sed qui maiores progressus servi[. . .]; nec tamen adhuc reperire quenq[. . .] potui. [. . .] Quoniam frustru id spero; observo te, ne evitato cum ipso Dee consilio, aliquem mihi reperiatis, qui mecum vivere velit. Tractabo eum humaniter, et salarium annuum de vera voluntate illi constituam." Prague /Ostrejov Astronomical Library, MS Akc. 1949/594, fol. 130. The Prague manuscript is the photocopy of the Wroclaw University Library MS R 247, an eighteenth-century copy by Samuel Benjamin Klose, which was annihilated during World War II. The original Dudith manuscript had been taken to Germany where it was lost. I thank this information to the librarians of the "Na Piasku" Library in Wrocław, and to Michal Pober for obtaining me a photocopy of the Dudith-Hájek correspondence from Prague.

32. "De Anglis multa audivi; illud unum mihi et stupendum videtur et parum credibile: quod aliqui certo affirment eos colloquia cum angelis nescio quibus miscere" (MS cit., fol. 136). Through other channels, Stephen Clucas (in 200?, n. 258) also quotes this passage, which was first referred to by the Polish Renaissance historian Henryk Barycz. See his "W poszukiwaniu kamienia filozo-ficznego, czyli traktat o Michale Sędziwoju," in Barycz, *Z epoki renesansu, reformacji i baroku* (Warsaw: PIW, 1971), 600 ff.

33. "Sed si chrysopoenam adamantem ut scribis, puto atros esse, illos genios, qui pro thesauris carbones illis dabunt: quin etiam carbones ipsos absument, et cineres relinquent" (MS cit., fol. 136).

34. Evans' translation (1973, 224) from Budovec's *Circulus horologi Lunaris et Solaris* (Hanau, 1616), 245.

35. Only from 1588 alone the *Private Diary* mentions the following British visitors in Trebona: Edmond Cooper, Edward Dyer, Francis Garland, John Hammond, Edward Rowles, Thomas Southwell, Mr. Swift and Mr. Stale, and Mr. Yong (Dee 1998, 232–38).

36. Apart from Evans' groundbreaking study, see also the recent Czech literature on the subject, for example, the following articles in Fučiková 1997: Paula Findlen, "Cabinets, Collecting and Natural Philosophy," 209–20; György E. Szőnyi, "Scientific and Magical Humanism at the Court of Rudolf II," 223–31; the English summaries in Zadrobílek 1997: Vladimír Kuncitr, "Alchemy in the Czech Lands," 276–79; Luboš Antonín, "Magia Naturalis and the Aristocratic Society of Bohemia and Moravia in the Seventeenth and Eighteenth Centuries," 310–13; and the papers in Konečný 1998: Václav Bužek, "Zwischen dem rudolfinischen Prag und den Höfen der Magnaten mit dem Wappen der fünfblättigen Rose," 75–81; Jürgen Müller, "Arcana Imperii," 184–92. See also Jan Sviták's 1980–89 trilogy; Petr Vágner, *Theatrum Chemicum: Kapitoly z dějin alchymie* (Prague: Paseka, 1995); Václav Bužek (ed.), *Dvory velmožu s erbem ruže* (Prague: Mladá Fronta); etc.

37. The correspondence is collected in State Archive Třeboň, MS Rosenberka 25.I–II.

38. Třeboň, MS Rosenberka 25.I.38; cf. Cotton, Appendix LXVI, which was Casaubon's source for Dee 1659.

39. Třeboň, MS Rosenberka 25.I.28.

40. See Evans 1979, 354–58; the Hungarian manuscript can be found in Budapest, Széchenyi Library (OSZK), 239 quart. Germ., 48 (cf. Evans 1973, 226).

41. On the magical contexts of some German courts, cf. Yates 1972; Evans 1973; and recently Moran 1991; Jost Weyer, *Graf Wolfgang II von Hohenlohe und die Alchemie. Alchemistische Studien in Sloß Weikersheim, 1587–1610* (Sigmaringen: Jan Thorbecke, 1992); and Debra L. Stoudt, " 'Proba tum est per me': The Heidelberg Electors as Practicioners and Patrons of the Medical and Magical Arts," *Cauda Pavonis* 14.1 (1995): 12–18.

42. Yates 1972, 46–7 argued for textual interrelatedness between the *Monas hieroglyphica* and the *Confessio fraternitatis*. On the Rosicrucian literature, see Arnold 1955; Bugaj 1991; Frick 1973; Gilly 1988 and 1995; Gorceix 1970; Hocke 1959; Janssen 1988; Montgomery 1973; Peuckert 1956; Schick 1980.

43. The manuscript of *Naometria* can be found in Stuttgart, Württemberg Landesbibliothek, Cod. theol. 4.23.34. It is reviewed by Yates 1972, 33–34; its relation to the Rosicrucians had been asserted by A. E. Waite, *Brotherhood of the Rosy Cross* (London, 1924), 639 ff. The idea goes back to an eighteenth-century theologian of Württemberg, Ludwig Melchior Fischlin (cf. Gilly 1995, 21). Gilly himself considers Studion's *Naometria* not a direct source of the Rosicrucian manifestos, rather as a typologically related work belonging to the literature of late sixteenth-century chiliasmus (Gilly 1988, 70 ff.).

44. Yates mentioned the following persons who, in some way, could indeed be associated with each other: Christian of Anhalt, the mastermind of the Elector Palatine Frederick; the elector himself; Moritz, Landgrave of Hesse-Kassel; Vilém Rožmberk; and a number of humanists-scholars already mentioned: Andreae, Bruno, Croll, Dee, and Khunrath (1972, 30–40). Since the publication of *The Rosicrucian Enlightenment*, most of Dame Frances' propositions have been rejected by historians as artificially forged links; however, my analysis will suggest that the supposition of certain intellectual influences perhaps is not so fantastic and unfounded.

45. Cf. F. N. Pryce's facsimile edition (1923) and Yates modern edition of the text (1972, 235–60). On the impact of the manifestos in England, see also Maclean 1988.

46. The Dutch-born inventor Drebbel was James I's alchemist before he took employment with Rudolf II in Prague in 1610; cf. Evans 1973, 189–90; Szőnyi 1995, 116; Robert Grudin, "Rudolf II of Prague and Cornelius Drebbel: Shakespearean Archetype?" *The Huntington Library Quarterly* 54 (1991): 181–205; and Roy Strong, *Henry, Prince of Wales, and England's Lost Renaissance* (London: Thames and Hudson, 1986), 216. On Banfi Hunyades, see George Gömöri, "New Information on János Bánfihunyadi's Life," *Ambix* 24 (1977): 170–74; and John H. Appleby, "Arthur Dee and Johannes Banfi Hunyades: Further Information on their Alchemical and Professional Activities," *Ambix* 24 (1977): 96–109.

47. They cite a German book on Morsius where this traveller is called "an Idealbild eines Rosenkreutzers" (Heinrich Schneider, *Joachim Morsius und sein Kreis*, Lübeck, 1929, 101—cf. Roberts and Watson 1990, 63).

48. Naudé obviously refers to Dee's lost work *Speculum unitatis, sive Apologia pro Fratre Rogerio Bacchone Anglo* (cf. the preface to the *Propaedeumata Aphoristica*, Dee 1978, 116).

49. Johannes Dee potissimum, qui ante iam anno 1563 in Hungaria artem transmutandi metalla, non sine multorum admiratione diu multumque agitavit, immo Maximiliano quoque Imp. et Reg. Hungariæ Monadem suam, hieroglyphice, mathematice, magice, cabbalistice, anagogice explicatam, Antverpiæ anno 1564 impressam, inscripsit et Posonii obtulit. Anno 1584 in Castello Laszkyano Collegium alchemisticum asperitur in aurea hac arte Laszkyus fidelissime insituitur, regnum minerale vario igne diu satis torquetur, et tandem miser novissime omnium turpiter, ut fieri adsolet, delutidur (Weszprémi 1960, 186–87).

50. Cf. Johnson's the *Alchemist* (2.6.20 and 4.1.85–91); Samuel Butler's *Hudibras* (2.3.235–38); and John Weever's *Ancient Funerall Monuments*, which has a horrifying story about Kelly's violating sepulchres (London: Thomas Harper, 1631, 45–46). Comments on these are in Szőnyi 1991.

51. Among others, subject to such accusations were Albert Molnár Szenci, famous humanist, dictionary writer, translator of the Psalmody, and Bible aditor; also Johann Heinrich Bisterfeld, German humanist and diplomat, who for some time taught and served in Transylvania (cf. Szőnyi 1991, n. 21–23).

52. London, Warburg MS FBH 510; Erlangen MS 854; Munich, Bayerische Staatsbibliothek, Cod. Lat. 27005. See Jörg Martin, *Johannes Dee: 'De tuba Veneris.' Eine magische Handschrift des 16. Jahrhunderts. Edition, Übersetzung und Kommentar*, M.A. thesis, University of Bonn, 1989 (copy in the Bodleian Library, Oxford). French 1972, 84, also mentions the Warburg manuscript; however, he does not seem to be aware of the fact that Dee could not be its author.

53. Cf. his apologies in the *Mathematicall Praeface* (Dee 1975, A2ᵛ); in his *A Letter Containing a Most Briefe Discourse Apologeticall* (1592); or the *A Letter Nine yeeres Since*; *To the Kings most excellent maiestie* which he even published as a broadside in 1604. His posthumous editor, Meric Casaubon, also felt compelled to reproduce some parts of these apologies (Dee 1659,*56–64). Evaluation of the charges against Dee can be found in Pickering 1986 and Szőnyi 1991.

54. Cf. Dee 1998, 35n. 9; and Waite 1961, 77–89.

55. The Preface has no printed page numbers. Following it, with the table of contents, the numbering starts with p. 1. Page references to the Preface, marked by asterisks, are my calculations.

56. A detailed analysis of the *Treatise Concerning Enthusiasme* is offered by Heyd, *"Be Sober and Reasonable"* (1995), in the chapter "Meric Casaubon and Henry Moore" (72–92). It is surprising, though, that Heyd makes no mention of Casaubon's programmatic Preface to Dee's diary.

57. Casaubon 1669, 21, reprinted in Casaubon 1976. On his philosophical views and cultural policy, see Paul J. Korshin's introduction in Casaubon 1970, and David G. Lougee's introduction in Casaubon 1976.

58. It may be noted that Clucas 200? severely criticizes Shumaker's study, primarily condemning its patronizing tone: "he allows his impatience with the 'unreliable prophecies' to interefere with his historical account of Dee's thought" (text corresponding to n. 37).

59. Dee 1994, xxv; see also Bassnett 1990 for a corroboration of this view.

60. Several versions of this anecdote survive, for example, in William Prynne's *Histriomastix* (1633) and in a book published by Vautrollier, an Huguenot bookseller of Blackfriars. Cf. Philip Henderson, *Christopher Marlowe* (New York: Harper and Row, 1974), 135; and Anthony Burgess, *Shakespeare* (Hammondsworth: Penguin, 1970), 103.

9. CONCLUSION: DEE AND RENAISSANCE SYMBOLISM

1. *A Discourse Concerning Edmund Spencer*, MS about 1628, quoted from Spenser 1971, 150–52.

2. I have further developed Gombrich's typology in order to turn it into a semiotics of occult symbolism in my following studies: "Semiotics and Hermeneutics of Iconographical Systems," in Jeff Bernard, Gloria Withalm, and Karl Müller (eds.), *Bildsprache, Visualisierung, Diagrammatik* (Akten zweier internationaler Symposien 1) *Semiotische Berichte* 19.1–4 (1995 [1996]): 283–313; and "The Powerful Image: Towards a Typology of Occult Symbolism," in Gy. E. Szőnyi (ed.), *Iconography East & West* (Leiden: J. Brill, 1996, Symbola & Emblemata 7), 250–63. See also Szulakowska 2000, 1–12.

3. For the background of the necromantic legend spread about Kelly (and Dee) by John Weever, see my article, Szőnyi 1991 (and Casaubon's Preface, in Dee 1659, *55).

4. Cf. Robert Ellrodt, *Neoplatonism in the Poetry of Spenser* (Geneva, 1960); A. Fowler, "Emanations of Glory: Neoplatonic Order in Spenser's *The Faerie Queene*," in Kennedy and Reither (eds.), *A Theatre for Spenserians* (Toronto, 1973); E. Bieman, "Neoplatonism: The Ghost of Spenser's Fiction," in David A. Richardson (ed.), *Spenser: Classical, Medieval, Renaissance, and Modern* (Cleveland, 1977); and D. Burchmore, "Neoplatonic Cosmology in Spenser's Legend of Friendship," in *Spenser at Kalamazoo* (Cleveland, 1981). See also the article "Neoplatonism" in *The Spenser Encyclopedia* (Toronto, 1990).

5. "Would to God in Heaven I had awhile [. . .] the mystical and supermetaphysical philosophy of Doctor Dee"—Harvey to Spenser, in Harvey, *Letter Book 1573–1580*,

(London, 1884), 71. See my article on Dee and hermeticism in *The Spenser Encyclopedia* (1990, 211, 358–59), and for a detailed analysis, see Szőnyi 1984, 369–84.

6. Francesco Giorgi, *L' Harmonie du monde* (Paris, 1578). The diagram is reproduced in Yates 1979, Fig. 4.

7. Tobias Schütz's illustration is reproduced and commented in Debus 1978, 28.

8. On the historiography and development of the seventeenth-century illustrations to Boehme's works, see Christoph Greissmar, *Das Auge Gottes: Bilder zu Jakob Böhme* (Wiesbaden: Harrassowitz, 1993, Wolfenbütteler Arbeiten zur Barockforschung 23).

9. The corresponding text reads: "Humanus anunus & mundus: unum & orbem complet & quadratum. Huius quadrati centrum & punctum intersectionis dyametrorum est intellectus. Unde sit ut iterum intellectus: deprehendat esse utriusque nature oppositio" (Bouelles 1510, 86v).

10. It cannot be by chance that Wayne Shumaker entitled his work dealing with Dee's angelic conferences and similar early modern topics *Renaissance Curiosa* (1982).

Bibliographies

Including abbreviations.
Manuscripts of Dee's works are listed in the first section of the
bibliography, other cited manuscripts are listed in the
Index under the heading "MSS, cited.

JOHN DEE'S WORKS

1) In the Order He Wrote Them

1556. "A Supplication to Queen Mary . . . for the Recovery and Preservation of Ancient
Writers and Monuments." London, BL, MS Cotton Vitellius C. VII. fol. 310 [pub-
lished in Dee 1851, 46–47; Dee 1990, 194–95].

1558. *Propaedeumata Aphoristica . . . de praestantioribus quibusdam naturae virtutibus.*
London: Henry Sutton [second edition, London: Reginald Wolfe, 1568; modern edition by Wayne Shumaker in Dee 1978].

1564. *Monas hieroglyphica.* Antwerp: Willem Sylvius [further editions: Frankfurt, 1591;
in Lazarus Zetzner's *Theatrum chemicum*, Strassburg, 1622, 2:191–230; modern edition by C. H. Josten in Dee 1964].

1570. *Mathematicall Praeface* [to *The Elements of Geometry of Euclid of Megara*, tr. Henry
Billingsley]. London: John Daye [facsimile edition and introduction by Allen G. Debus,
New York: Science History Publications, 1975].

1570–1590s. *Private diaries.* Inscriptions in Joannes Stadius' *Ephemerides novae* (Cologne,
1570) and in Antonius Maginus' *Ephemerides coelestium motuum* (Venice, 1582); cop-
ied by Ashmole (Oxford, Bodleian, MSS Ashmole 423, 487, 488) and published in
Dee 1842 and 1998.

1573. *Parallaticae commentationis praxeosque nucleus quidam.* London: John Daye.

1577. *General and Rare Memorials Pertayning to the Perfect Art of Navigation.* London:
John Daye [facsimile: "The English Experience" 62, Amsterdam and New York:
Theatrum Orbis Terrarum, 1968].

1578. *Her Majesties title Royall* (in 12 Velam skins of parchment, faire written for her Majestis use . . . —cf. Dee 1851, 25, No. 3).

1581–1583. "Mysteriorum libri" [angelic conversations in Mortlake]. London, BL, MSS Sloane 3188, 3677.

1582. "A Playne Discourse . . . concerning y needful reformation of y vulgar kallender." Oxford, Bodleian, MS Ashmole 1789, fols. 1–40 [and several other copies].

1583. "Catalogus librorum bibliothecae (externae) Mortlacensis. . . ." Cambridge; Trinity College, MS 0.4.20; Oxford, Bodleian, MS Ashmole 1142, fols. 1–74 [facsimile reprint in Dee 1990].

1583a. "Liber mysteriorum, sextus et sanctus" [Book of Enoch]. London, BL, MSS Sloane 3189, 2599.

1583–1587. "Mysteriorum libri" [angelic conversations from Mortlake, Poland, and Bohemia]. London, BL, MS Cotton Appendix XLVI [published by Meric Casaubon in Dee 1659].

1584. "48 claves angelicae." London, BL, MSS Sloane 3191, art. 1.; 3678, art 1 [extracts published by Geoffrey James in Dee 1984 and 1994].

1585. "Liber scientia auxilii, & victoriae." London, BL, MSS Sloane 3191, art .; 3678, art 2 [extracts published by Geoffrey James in Dee 1984 and 1994].

1586. "Praefatio Latina in Actionem Primum ex 7. . . ." Oxford, Bodleian, MS Ashmole 1790, art. 1, fols. 1–9 [published by C. H. Josten in Dee 1965].

1588. "De heptarchia mystica; Tabula bonorum angelorum; Fundamenta invocationum." London, BL, MS Sloane 3191 arts. 3–5, 3678 arts. 3–5 [published by Robert Turner in Dee 1983 and extracts in Dee 1994].

1592. "The Compendious Rehearsall of John Dee . . . made unto the two Honorable Commissioners. . . ." London, BL, MS Cotton Vitellius C. VII, fols. 7-13; Oxford, Bodleian, MS Ashmole 1788, fols. 7–34 [published in Dee 1851, 1–45].

1595–1601. Diary. See Dee 1880.

1597. "ΘΑΛΑΤΤΟΚΡΑΤΙΑ ΒΡΕΤΤΑΝΙΚΗ, sive de imperii brytannici Jurisdictione in mari. . . ." London, BL, MS Harley 249, fols. 95–105; MS Royal 7 C. XVI, fols. 158–65.

1599. *A Letter Containing a Most Briefe Discourse Apologeticall . . . 1592.* London: Peter Short [rpt. London, 1603; facsimile in *The English Experience*, 502, Amsterdam and New York, 1973].

1604. *A Letter Nine yeeres Since, Containing a Most Briefe Discourse Apologeticall . . . ; To the Kings most excellent maiestie; To the Honorable Assemblie of the Commons in the Present Parliament.* Broadside, London: Peter Short.

1607–1608. "Alchemical notes." Oxford, Bodleian, MS Ashmole 1486, art. 5.

2) Editions After Dee's Death

1659. *A True and Faithful Relation of What Passed between Dr. John Dee [. . .] and Some Spirits. . . .* Ed. Meric Casaubon. London: T. Garthwait (rpt. Glasgow: Golden Dragon Press / Antonin Publishing Co., 1974].

1841. "Letter to Lord Burghley, October 3, 1574"; "Directions to Arthur Pitt and Charles Jackman for a voyage to Cathay, May 15–17, 1580." In James O. Halliwell-Philips, ed. *A Collection of Letters Illustrative of the Progress of Science in England.* London.

1842. *The Private Diary and Catalogue of His Library of Manuscripts of Dr. John Dee* [Diary 1540s–1590s]. Ed. James O. Halliwell. Manchester: Camden Society, vol 19 [rpt. New York, 1968].

1843. "Letter to Elizabeth I, November 10, 1588." In Henry Ellis, ed. *Original Letters of Eminent Literary Men of the Sixteenth, Seventeenth, and Eighteenth Centuries.* London: Camden Society Publications, 23, 33–39.

1851. *Autobiographical Tracts* [The Compendious Rehearsal . . . (1592); "A Supplication to Queen Mary . . . for the Recovery and Preservation of Ancient Writers and Monuments" (January 15, 1556); "A Necessary Advertisement" (from the *General and Rare Memorials*, 1577); "A Letter Containing a most briefe discourse apologeticall" (1592)]. Ed. James Crossley. Manchester: Chetham Society Publications, vol. 24.

1854. "Letter to Sir William Cecil, February 16, 1563." Ed. R. W. Grey. Philobiblon Society. *Bibliographical and Historical Miscellanies* 1.12: 1–16.

1880. *Diary, for the Years 1595–1601, of Dr. John Dee, Warden of Manchester from 1595–1608.* Ed. John E. Bailey. Privately printed.

1921. *A List of Manuscripts Formerly Owned by Dr. John Dee.* Ed. M. R. James. Oxford: OUP.

1964. "A Translation of John Dee's *Monas hieroglyphica*, with an Introduction and Annotations." Tr. and ed. C.H. Josten [with facsimile of the original], *Ambix* 12: 112–221.

1965. C. H. Josten, "An Unknown Chapter in the Life of John Dee ['Praefatio Latina in Actionem Primum ex 7 . . .]." *Journal of the Warburg and Courtauld Institutes* 28: 233–57.

1975. *The Mathemathicall Preface to the Elements of Geometry of Euclid of Megara.* Ed. Allen G. Debus. New York: Science History Publications.

1978. *John Dee on Astronomy. "Propaedeumata Aphoristica" (1558 and 1568). Latin and English.* Ed. and tr. Wayne Shumaker. Intro. J. L. Heilbron. Berkeley: University of California Press.

1983. *The Heptarchia Mystica of John Dee* ["De heptarchia mystica," "Tabula bonorum angelorum," "Fundamenta invocationum," 1588]. Ed. Robert Turner. Tr. Christopher Upton. Edinburgh: Magnum Opus Hermetic Sourceworks 17 [second enlarged edition: Wellingborough, 1986].

1988. *Misteriorum libri,* 22 December 1581–23 May 1583. In Christopher Whitby, *John Dee's Actions with Spirits.* New York: Garland, 2:1–408.

1990. *John Dee's Library Catalogues* [with facsimiles]. Eds. Julian Roberts and G. Watson. London: The Bibliographical Society.

1994. *The Enochian Magick of Dr. John Dee* [extracts: "Mysteriorum libri," 1583–1607; "48 claves angelicae," 1584; "Liber scientia auxilii & victoriae," 1585]. Ed. and tr. Geoffrey James. St. Paul, Min.: Llewellyn Publications [first edition 1984].

1996. *Mysteriorum libri, 1581–1583.* In Clay Holden, ed. *The John Dee Publication Project.* 20 August 2002. <www.dnai.com/~cholden/>.

1998. *The Diaries of John Dee.* Ed. Edward Fenton. Charlbury, Oxfordshire: Day Books.

SOURCES AND THEIR MODERN EDITIONS

Abrams, M. H. (general editor). 1986. *The Norton Anthology of English Literature.* Fifth Edition. New York: Norton.

Agrippa, H. C.[von Nettesheim]. 1530. *De incertitudine & vanitate omnium scientiarum.* Antwerp; ❑ 1550. *De occulta philosophia Lib. III, Item, Spurius Liber de Caeremoniis Magicis qui Quartus Agrippae habetur. Quibus accesserunt, Heptameron Petri de Abano, etc.* Basel: Godefroy et Beringen; ❑ 1575. *Of the Vanitie and vncertaintie of Artes and Sciences.* Tr. James Sanford. London: Henry Bynnemann; ❑ 1651. *Three Books of Occult Philosophy.* Tr. James Freake. London: Gregory Moule; ❑ 1898. *Three Books of Occult Philosophy.* Ed. Willis F. Whitehead, including some parts of Henry Morley's *Life of Agrippa.* Chicago: Hahn and Whitehead; ❑ 1955. *In praelectione Hermetis Trismegisti.* In Garin, Brini, Vasoli, and Zambelli (eds.) 1955, 120–35; ❑ 1967. *De occulta philosophia* (Köln, 1533). Ed. Karl Anton Nowotny. Graz: Akademia Druck und Verlag; ❑ 1970. *Opera* (Lyon, 1550, 2 vols). Ed. Richard H. Popkin. Hildesheim and New York: Olms; ❑ 1997. *Three Books of Occult Philosophy.* Tr. James Freake (London, 1651), completely annotated with modern commentary by Donald Tyson. St. Paul: Llewellyn Publications.

Al-Baghdadi, Muhammad. 1570. *Libro del modo di dividere le superficie Mondato in luce la prime volta da M. Giovanni Dee da Londra e da M. Frederico Commandius da Urbino.* Ed. John Dee Tr. F. Commandius. Urbino: G. Concordia.

Artephius. 1999. *The Secret Book of Artephius.* Ed. Adam Maclean. 23 June 1999. <www.levity.com/alchemy>.

Bacon, Roger. 1618. *Epistolae de secretis operibus et natura et de nullitate magiae.* Ed. John Dee. Hamburg: Frobenius; ❑ 1659. *Discovery of the Miracles of Art, Nature, and Magick. Faithfully translated out of Dr. Dees own copy, by T. M. and never before in English.* London: Simon Miller; ❑ 1923. *Roger Bacon's Letter Concerning the Marvelous Power of Art and of Nature and Concerning the Nullity of Magic.* Ed. Tenney L. Davis. Easton, Penn.: Chemical Publishing; ❑ 1992. *The Mirror of Alchimy. Composed by the Thrice-Famous and Learned Fryer, Roger Bachon* (1597). Ed. Stanton J. Linden. New York: Garland (English Renaissance Hermeticism 4).

Bibles: KJV 1994 = *The Bible, King James Version* (London, 1603). Network Version, 1994. 14 June 1999. <http://diderot.uchicago.edu/Bibles/KJV.form.html>; ❑ Vulgata 1983 = *Biblia Sacra iuxta Vulgatam versionem.* Editio tertia emendata. Stuttgart: Deutsche Bibelgesellschaft, 1983.

Bouelles, Charles de. 1510. *Liber de intellectu. . . .* Paris: Henri Estienne (facsimile: Stuttgart–Bad Cannstatt: Friedrich Frommann Verlag, 1970.)

Casaubon, Meric. 1970. *A Treatise Concerning Enthusiasme* (1655). A facsimile reproduction of the second edition of 1656. Ed. Paul J. Korshin. Gainesville, Fla.: Scholars' Facsimiles and Reprints; ❑ 1976. *A Letter to Peter du Moulin Concerning Natural*

Experimental Philosophie (1669) and *Of Credulity and Incredulity* (1668, 1670). Ed. David G. Lougee. Delmar, N.Y.: Scholars' Facsimiles and Reprints.

CH = *Corpus hermeticum.* Cf. Scott 1924–1936; Nock 1945–1954; Copenhaver 1992; Reitzenstein 1904 [*Poimandrés*].

Charlesworth, James H. ed. 1983. *The Old Testament Pseudepigrapha. Volume 1: Apocalyptic Literature and Testaments.* New York: Doubleday.

Cicero, Marus Tullius and Ambrosius Aurelius Macrobius. 1952. *Commentary on the Dream of Scipio.* Transl. and intr. William Harris Stahl. New York: Columbia University Press, 1952 (Records of Civilization 48).

Compagni, Vittoria Perrone. 1975. "Picatrix Latinus. Concesioni filosofico-religiose e prassi magica," *Medioevo* 1: 237–337.

Cooper, William. 1987. *A Catalogue of Chymicall Books, 1673–1688.* A verified edition by Stanton J. Linden. New York and London: Garland.

Copenhaver, Brian P. (ed.). 1992. *Hermetica. The Greek Corpus Hermeticum and the Latin Asclepius in a new English translation with notes and introduction.* Cambridge: Cambridge University Press.

Enoch = Charlesworth 1983.

Erasmus of Rotterdam. 1971. *Praise of Folly and Letter to Martin Dorp, 1515.* Intro. A. H. T. Levi. Tr. Betty Radice. Harmondsworth: Penguin; ❑ 1974–1994. *The Correspondence.* 11 vols. Co-ordinating editor Beatrice Corrigan. Toronto: University of Toronto Press (part of the Collected Works of Erasmus).

Ficino, Marsilio. 1497, 1516. *Index eorum, quae hoc in libro habentur. Iamblichus, de mysteriis Aegyptiorum.* . . . Venice: Aldus; ❑ 1576. *Opera* (2 vols). Basel: Henric Petri; ❑ 1944. *Commentary on Plato's "Symposium" on Love* (1475). Tr. Sears Jayne. Columbia: University of Missouri; ❑ 1985. *Commentary on Plato's "Symposium" on Love* (1475). Ed. and tr. Sears Jayne. Dallas: Spring Publications; ❑ 1989. *Three Books on Life. A Critical Edition and Translation with Introduction and Notes.* Ed. Carol V. Kaske and John R. Clark. Binghamton, N.Y.: State University of New York Press (Medieval and Renaissance Texts and Studies 57).

Forman, Simon. 1849. *The Autobiography and Personal Diary of Dr Simon Forman.* Ed. James O. Halliwell. London.

Garin, E., M. Brini, C. Vasoli, and P. Zambelli (eds.) 1955. *Testi umanistici sull'ermetismo.* Roma: Archivio di Filosofia.

Hollander, John, Frank Kermode (eds.). 1973. *The Literature of Renaissance England.* London and New York: Oxford University Press (The Oxford Anthology of English Literature).

Iamblichus of Chalcis. 1989. *On the Mysteries—De mysteriis Aegyptiorum* [with two extracts from the lost works of Proclus *On the Sacred Art* and *On the Signs of Divine Possession.*] Ed. Stephen Ronan. Tr. Thomas Taylor and Alexander Wilder. London: Chthonios Books.

Kelley, Edward. 1893. *The Alchemical Writings of Edward Kelly.* Ed. A. E. Waite. New York: Samuel Weiser (rpt. 1976) ❑ 1999. *The Theatre of Terrestrial Alchemy.* Ed. Adam

Maclean from *Tractatus duo egregii, de Lapide Philosophorum, una cum Theatro astronomiae terrestri cum Figuris . . . , curante J.L.M.C.* [Johann Lange Medicin Candidato] (Hamburg, 1676). 24 June 1999. <www.levity.com/alchemy/terrastr.html>.

Lazzarelli, Lodovico. 1955. *Crater hermetis.* In Garin, Brini, Vasoli, and Zolmbelli; (eds.) 1955, 50–75.

MacGregor Mathers, S. L. 1991. *The Kabbalah Unveiled. Containing Books of the Zohar* (1926). London: Arkana (The Penguin Group).

Marlowe, Christopher. 1991. *Doctor Faustus. A 1604 version edition.* Ed. Michael Keefer. Peterborough, Ont.: Broadview Press.

Mary, the Prophetess. 1999 = *The Practise of Mary the Prophetess in the Alchemicall Art.* Ed. by Adam Maclean from British Library MS Sloane 3641, fols. 1–8. 24 June 1999. <www.levity.com/alchemy/maryprof.html>.

Moffet, Thomas. 1940. *Nobilis, or a View of the Life and Death of a Sidney; and Lessus Lugubris* (1593). Ed. Virgil B. Heltzel and Hoyt H. Hudson. San Marino, Cal.: Huntington Library.

Nock, A. D. and A.-J. Festugière (eds.). 1945–1954. *Corpus hermeticum* (Vol I: *Corpus hermeticum I–XII*; Vol. II: *Corpus hermeticum XII–XVIII, Asclepius*; Vol. III: *Fragments extraits de Stobèe I–XXII*; Vol. IV: *Fragments extraits de Stobèe, Fragments divers*). Paris.

Paracelsus, Philippus Theophrastus Aureolus Bombastus von Hohenheim. 1569. *Archidoxiae Philippi Theophrasti Paracelsi Magni . . . Libri X. Nunc primum studio et diligentia Adami Schröteri. Marginalibus annotationibus, & Indice copiosissimo, per Ioannem Gregorium Macrum.* Cracoviae: Matthiae Wirzbietae; ❑ 1589–1591. *Erster Theil der Bücher und Schriften . . . Philippi Paracelsi genannt* (10 Vols.). Ed. Johann Huser. Basel: Conrad Waldkirch; ❑ 1894. *The Hermetic and Alchemical Writings of Aureolus Philippus Theophrastus Bombast, called Paracelsus the Great* (2 Vols.). Ed. A. E. Waite. London: James Elliot (rpt. Berkeley: Shambala, 1976); ❑ 1922–1925. *Sämtliche Werke.* Abteilung I: *Medizinische, naturwissenschaftliche und philosophische Schriften.* Vols. 6–9. Eds. Karl Sudhoff and Wilhelm Matthiessen. München: O.W. Barth; ❑ 1923. *Sämtliche Werke.* Abteilung II: *Die theologischen und religionsphilosophischen Schriften.* Vol. 1. Eds. Karl Sudhoff and Wilhelm Matthiessen. München: O.W. Barth; ❑ 1928–1933. *Sämtliche Werke.* Abteilung I: *Medizinische, naturwissenschaftliche und philosophische Schriften.* Vols. 1–5; 10–14. Eds. Karl Sudhoff and Wilhelm Matthiessen. Berlin: R. Oldenbourg; ❑ 1951. *Selected Writings.* Ed. Jolande (Shékács) Jacobi. Princeton: Princeton University Press (Bollingen Series 28); ❑ 1955–1973. *Sämtliche Werke.* Abteilung II: *Die theologischen und religionsphilosophischen Schriften.* Vol. 2, 4–7. Ed. Kurt Goldammer. Wiesbaden: Franz Steiner; ❑ 1975. *The Archidoxes of Magic.* Tr. Robert Turner (1656). Ed. Stephen Skinner. London: Askins / New York: Samuel Weiser.

Picatrix. See Ritter and Plessner 1962; Compagni 1975.

Pico della Mirandola, Giovanni. 1942. *De hominis dignitate; Heptaplus; De ente et uno, e scritti vari.* Ed. Eugenio Garin. Firenze: Vallecchi; ❑ 1946. *Disputationes adversus astrologiam divinatricem libri I–XII.* Ed. Eugenio Garin. Firenze: Vallecchi; ❑ 1948. "Oration on the Dignity of Man" (1485). In E. Cassirer, P. O. Kristeller, and J. H. Randall (eds.). *The Renaissance Philosophy of Man.* Chicago: University of Chicago

Press, 223–54; ❏ 1973. *Conclusiones sive Theses DCCCC. Romae anno 1486 publice disputandae, sed non admissae.* Ed. and intro. Bohdan Kieszlowski. Geneva: Droz.

Plato. 1963. *The Collected Dialogues, Including the Letters.* Ed. Edith Hamilton and Huntington Cairns. Princeton: Princeton University Press (Bollingen Series 71).

Plotinus. 1984. *The Essential Plotinus. Representative Treatises from the Enneads* (1963). Ed. and tr. Elmer O'Brien. Indianapolis: Hackett; ❏ 1991. *The Enneads.* Tr. Stephen MacKenna. Intro. John Dillon. Harmondsworth: Penguin.

Porphyry. 1989. *Letter to Anebo.* Tr. Thomas Taylor and Alexander Wilder. In Iamblichus 1989, 14–21. ❏ 1991. *On the Life of Plotinus and the Arrangement of His Work.* In Plotinus 1991, cii–cxxvi.

Postel, Guillaume. 1544. *De orbis terrae concordia.* Basel: Oporinus; ❏ 1553. *De originibus.* Basel: Oporinus.

Reitzenstein, R. 1904. *Poimandres. Studien zur griechisch-aegyptischen und früh-christlichen Literatur.* Leipzig.

Reuchlin, Johann. 1517. *De arte cabalistica.* Hagenau: apud Thomam Anshelmum; ❏ 1983. *On the Art of the Kabbalah* [De arte cabalistica] (1517). Ed. and tr. Martin and Sarah Goodman. New York: Abaris Books; ❏ 2000. *Recommendation whether to confiscate, destroy, and burn all Jewish books: a classic treatise against anti-semitism* [Gutachten über das Jüdische Schrifttum, 1511]. Ed., tr., and foreword by Peter Wortsman; intro. Elisheva Carlebach. New York: Paulist Press (A Stimulus Book).

Proclus. 1988. "Proclus on the Priestly Art According to the Greeks" [ed. and tr. Brian Copenhaver]; "Proculi Opusculum de sacrificio interprete Marsilio Ficino Florentino." In Ingrid Merkel and Allen G. Debus (eds.). *Hermeticism and the Renaissance.* Washington: Folger Shakespeare Library, 102–10. ❏ 1989. "On the Sacred Art" and "On the Signs of Divine Possession." Tr. Stephen Ronan. See Iamblichus 1989, 146–150.

Pseudo-Dionysius, the Areopagite. 1987. *The Complete Works.* Ed. Colm Luibheid, Paul Rorem, and Rene Rogues. New York: Paulist Press.

Ritter, Gerhard, and Martin Plessner (eds.). 1962. *"Picatrix." Das Ziel des Weisen von Pseudo-Magriti.* London: Warburg Institute (Studies of the Warburg Institute 27).

Ripley, George [attrib.]. 1999. "A Treatise of Mercury and the Philosophers Stone." In *Aurifontina Chymica: or, a Collection of Fourteen Small Treatises Concerning the First Matter of Philosophers, for the Discovery of their Mercury.*.. (London, 1680). Ed. Adam Maclean. 23 June 1999. <www.levity.com/alchemy/ripmerc.html>.

Ruland, Martin. 1984. *A Lexicon of Alchemy* (1612, tr. A.E. Waite, 1893). York Beach, Maine: Samuel Weiser.

Ruska, J. F. 1926. *Tabula smaragdina* (1896). Heidelberg: Winter.

R&W = Roberts and Watson 1990. This abbreviation refers to items in Dee's catalogues, as they are numbered in Roberts and Watson's edition.

Scott, Walter. 1924–1936. *Hermetica* (Vol. I: *Introduction, Texts and Translation*; Vol. II and III: *Commentary*; Vol. IV: *Testimonia, Appendices and Indices*). Oxford: Clarendon.

Spenser, Edmund. 1970. *Poetical Works.* Ed. J. C. Smith and E. de Selincourt. Oxford: Oxford University Press; ❏ 1971. *Spenser—The Critical Heritage.* Ed. R. M. Cummings.

New York: Barnes and Noble; ❏ 1980. *The Faerie Queene*. Ed. A. C. Hamilton. London: Longman.

Theatrum Chemicum, praecipuos selectorum auctorum tractatus [. . .] continens. 1602–1661. (Vols. 1–3: 1602; 4: 1613; 5: 1622; 6: 1661). Ursel and Stuttgart: Lazarus Zetzner.

Tymme, Thomas. 1963. *A Light in Darknesse, Which illumineth for all the Monas Hieroglyphica of the famous and profound Dr. John Dee, Discovering Natures closet and revealing the true Christian secrets of Alchimy* (c. 1610). Oxford: New Bodleian Library.

Weever, John. 1631. *Ancient Funeral Monuments*. London (facsimile: Amsterdam and New York: Theatrum Orbis Terrarum, 1979, The English Experience 961).

Whetstone, George. 1586. *The English Myrror. A Regard Wherein al estates may behold the Conquests of Enuy*. London: I. Winders for G. Seton.

Weszprémi, István. 1960. *Succinta medicorum Hungariæ et Transylvaniæ Biographia* (1774). Centuria prima (new edition). Budapest: Medicina.

Zohar = MacGregor Mathers, S. L. 1991.

REFERENCE WORKS PARENTHETICALLY CITED

(This list contains only those reference works which I found directly related to my research topic. Other books, mentioned in connection with theoretical or philological issues, are given full description in the notes.)

Adamik, Tamás. 1997. "Introduction." In Adamik (ed.). *Apokrif iratok—apokalipszisek*. Budapest: Telosz.

Allen, Michael J. B. 1981. *Marsilio Ficino and the Phadrean Charioter*. Berkeley: University of California Press (UCLA Center for Medieval and Renaissance Studies 14); ❏ 1984. *The Platonism of Marsilio Ficino. A study of his "Phaedrus" Commentary, its sources and genesis*. Berkeley: University of California Press (UCLA Center for Medieval and Renaissance Studies 21); ❏ 1994. *Nuptial arithmethic. Marsilio Ficino's Commentary on the Fatal Number in Book VIII of Plato's Republic*. Berkeley: University of California Press.

Ambrose, Elizabeth Ann. 1992. "Cosmos, Anthropos and Theos: Dimensions of the Paracelsian Universe," *Cauda Pavonis* 11.1: 1–7.

Armstrong, A. H., et. al. 1995. *The Cambridge History of Later Greek and Early Medieval Philosophy* (1967). Cambridge: Cambridge University Press.

Arnold, P. 1955. *Histoire des Rose-Croix et les origines de la Franc-Maçonnerie*. Paris: Mercure de France.

Atwood, Mary Anne. 1918. *A Suggestive Inquiry Into the Hermetic Mystery with a Dissertation on the More Celebrated of the Alchemical Philosophers Being an Attempt towards the Recovery of the Ancient Experiment of Nature* (1850). New edition Walter L. Wilmhurst. Belfast: William Tait (facsimile: New York: AMS, 1984).

Barlay, Ö. Szabolcs. 1979. "Boldizsár Batthyány und sein Humanisten-Kreis," *Magyar Könyvszemle*: 231–51; ❏ 1986. *Romon virág. Fejezetek a Mohács utáni magyar reneszánsz történetéből*. Budapest: Gondolat.

Baron, Frank. 1978. *Doctor Faustus. From History to Legend*. München: Wilhelm Fink; ❏ 1982. *Faustus. Geschichte, Sage, Dichtung*. München: Wilhelm Fink; ❏ 1986. "A Faust-monda és magyar változatai," *Irodalomtörténeti Közlemények*: 22–36; ❏ 1992. *Faustus on Trial. The Origins of Johann Spies's "Historia" in an Age of Witch Hunting*. Tübingen: Niemeyer.

Barr, James. 1992. *The Garden of Eden and the Hope of Immortality*. London: SCM Press.

Bassnett, Susan E. 1990. "Revising a Biography: A New Interpretation of the Life of Elizabeth Jane Weston (Westonia), based on her autobiographical poem on the occasion of the death of her mother," *Cahiers Elisabéthains* 37: 1–8.

Bergier, Jean-Francois (ed.). 1988. *Zwischen Wahn, Glaube und Wissenschaft: Magie, Astrologie, Alchemie und Wissenschaftgeschichte*. Zurich: Fachvereine.

Berthelot, M.P.E. 1893. *Chimie au Moyen Age* . Paris: Imprimerie nationale.

Beyschlag, K. 1975. *Simon Magus und die christliche Gnosis*. Göttingen.

Birnbaum, Marianna D. 1985. *Humanists in a Shattered World. Croatian and Hungarian Latinity in the Sixteenth Century* (UCLA Slavic Studies 15). Colombus, Ohio: Slavica Publishers.

Blau, Joseph. 1944. *The Christian Interpretation of the Cabala in the Renaissance*. New York: Columbia University Press.

Boas, Marie. 1962. *The Scientific Renaissance, 1450–1630*. New York: Harper and Row.

Boorstin, Daniel J. 1983. *The Discoverers. A History of Man's Search to Know His World and Himself*. New York: Random House.

Bouwsma, William J. 1957. *Concordia mundi: The Career and Thought of Guillaume Postel (1510–1581)*. Cambridge: Harvard University Press.

Bowen, Barbara C. 1972. "Cornelius Agrippa's *De vanitate*: Polemic or Paradox?" *Bibliothèque d'humanisme et renaissance* 34: 249–56.

Brann, Noel L. 1977. "The Shift from Mystical to Magical Theology in the Abbot Trithemius." In Western Michigan University Medieval Institute, *Studies in Medieval Culture* 11: 147–59; ❏ 1999. *Thritemius and Magical Theology. A Chapter in the Controversy over Occult Studies in Early Modern Europe*. Albany: State University of New York Press (SUNY Series in Western Esoteric Traditions).

Buck, August (ed.). 1992. *Die okkulten Wissenschaften in der Renaissance*. Wiesbaden: Harrassowitz (Wolfenbütteler Abhandlungen zur Renaissanceforschung 12).

Bugaj, Roman. 1976. *Nauki tajemne w Polsce w dobie Odrodzenia*. Wrocław: Ossolineum; ❏ 1991. *Hermetyzm*. Wrocław: Ossolineum.

Bullard, Melissa Meriam. 1990. "The Inward Zodiac: A Development in Ficino's Thought on Astrology," *Renaissance Quarterly* 43.4: 687–709.

Burckhardt, Jakob. 1995. *The Civilization of the Renaissance in Italy*. Ed. L. Goldscheider, including Middlemore's 1878 translation. London: Phaidon.

Burke, John G. 1974. "Hermetism as Renaissance World View." In Robert S. Kinsman (ed.), *The Darker Vision of the Renaissance. Beyond the Fields of Reason.* Berkeley: University of California Press.

Bussagli, Marco. 1995. *Storia degli angeli. Racconto di immagini e di idee.* Milano: Rusconi.

Butler, E. M. 1980. *The Myth of the Magus* (1948). Cambridge: Cambridge University Press.

Calder, I. R. F. 1952. *John Dee Studied as an English Neo-Platonist.* 2 vols. Unpublished Ph.D. Thesis. University of London.

Cassirer, Ernst. 1963. *The Individual and the Cosmos in the Renaissance.* New York: Barnes and Noble. (= Cassirer 1927. *Individuum und Kosmos in der Philosophie der Renaissance.* Leipzig and Berlin [Studien der Bibliothek Warburg 24]); ❑ 1996. *The Philosophy of Symbolic Forms* (1953). New Haven: Yale University Press.

Clucas, Stephen. 1998. " 'Non est legendum sed inspiciendum solum': Inspectival Knowledge and the Visual Logic of John Dee's *Liber mysteriorum*." In Alison Adams and Stanton J. Linden (eds.). *Emblems and Alchemy.* Glasgow: Glasgow University Press (Glasgow Emblem Studies 3), 109–133. ❑ 200?. "John Dee's angelic conversations and the *ars notoria*: Renaissance magic and mediaeval theurgy." In Clucas (ed.), *John Dee: Interdisciplinary Approacheas.* Dordrecht: Kluwer—forthcoming.

Clulee, Nicholas H. 1971. "John Dee's Mathematics and the Grading of Compound Qualities," *Ambix* 18: 178–211. ❑ 1973. *The Glas of Creation. Renaissance Mathematicism and Natural Philosophy in the Work of John Dee* (unpublished Ph.D. thesis). University of Chicago; ❑ 1988. *John Dee's Natural Philosophy. Between Science and Religion.* London: RKP.

Copenhaver, Brian P. 1978. "Hermeticism and the Scientific Revolution." *Annals of Science* 35: 527–31; ❑ 1986. "Renaissance Magic and Neoplatonic Philosophy: *Ennead* 4.3–5 in Ficino's *De vita coelitus comparanda*." In Giancarlo Garfagnini (ed.), *Marsilio Ficino e il ritorno di Platone.* 2 vols. Firenze; ❑ 1988. "Hermes Trismegistus, Proclus, and the Question of a Philosophy of Magic in the Renaissance." In Merkel and Debus 1988, 79–110; ❑ 1988a. "Astrology and Magic." In Schmitt and Skinner 1988, 264–300; ❑ 1990. "Natural Magic, Hermeticism and Occultism in Early Modern Science." In Lindberg and Westman 1990, 261–301; ❑ 1992. "Introduction." See Copenhaver (ed.) 1992, under "Sources."

Corvin-Krasinski, C. von. 1960. *Mikrokosmos und Makrokosmos in religionsgeschichtlicher Sicht.* Düsseldorf: Patmos Verlag.

Coudert, Alison (ed.). 1999. *The Language of Adam / Die Sprache Adams.* Wiesbaden: Harrassowitz (Wolfenbütteler Forschungen 84).

Curry, Patrick. 1985. "Revisions of Science and Magic." *History of Science* 23: 299–325.

Czerkawski, J. 1967. "Hannibal Rosseli jako przedstawiciel hermetyzmu filozoficznego w Polsce," *Roczniki Filozoficzne* 15.1: 119–140.

Daly, Peter M. 1998. *Literature in the Light of the Emblem* (1979). Toronto: University of Toronto Press.

Dán, Róbert. 1979. "Erdélyi könyvek és John Dee," *Magyar Könyvszemle*: 223–30.

de Jong, H. M. E. 1969. *Michael Maier's "Atalanta" Fugiens': Sources of an Alchemical Book of Emblems.* Leiden: Brill.

Deacon, Richard. 1968. *John Dee: Scientist, Geographer, Astrologer, and Secret Agent to Elizabeth I.* London.

Debus, Allen G. 1965. *The English Paracelsians.* London: Oldburne; ❏ 1977. *The Chemical Philosophy. Paracelsian Science and Medicine in the Sixteenth and Seventeenth Centuries.* 2 vols. New York: Science History Publications; ❏ 1978. *Man and Nature in the Renaissance.* Cambridge: Cambridge University Press.

Delumeau, Jean. 1995. *History of Paradise: the Garden of Eden in Myth and Tradition.* New York: Continuum.

Dilg, Peter–Hartmut Rudolph (eds.). 1993. *Resultate und Desiderate der Paracelsus-Forschung.* Stuttgart: Franz Steiner; ❏ 1995. *Neue Beiträge zur Paracelsus-Forschung.* Stuttgart: Akademie der Diözese Rottenburg.

Dilg-Frank, Rosemarie. 1984. *Paracelsus-Bibliographie. Internationales Schrifttum-Verzeichnis: 1961–1982* (Kosmographie 5). Wiesbaden: F. Steiner.

Dodds, E. R. 1951. *The Greeks and the Irrational.* Berkeley: University of California Press.

Dress, Walter. 1929. *Die Mystik des Marsilio Ficino.* Berlin and Leipzig.

Duncan-Jones, Katherine. 1991. *Sir Philip Sidney. Courtier Poet.* New Haven and London: Yale University Press.

Durling, Richard J. 1965. "Conrad Gesner's *Liber amicorum* 1555–1565." *Gesnerus* 22: 134–159.

Eco, Umberto. 1995. *The Search for the Perfect Language.* Oxford: Blackwell (The Making of Europe).

Eliade, Mircea. 1968. *Myths, Dreams, and Mysteries. The Encounter Between Contemporary Faiths and Archaic Reality.* London: Collins; ❏ 1992. *Essential Sacred Writings From Around the World.* San Francisco: Harper and Row.

Evans, Joan. 1976. *Magical Jewels of the Middle Ages and the Renaissance* (1922). New York: Dover.

Evans, R. J. W. 1973. *Rudolf II and His World. A Study in Intellectual History 1576–1612.* Oxford: Clarendon (corrected paperback edition: London: Thames and Hudson, 1997); ❏ 1975. *The Wechel Presses: Humanism and Calvinism in Central Europe 1572–1627.* Oxford: The Past and Present Society (Supplement 2); ❏ 1979. *The Making of the Habsburg Monarchy 1550–1700. An Interpretation.* Oxford: Clarendon.

Faivre, Antoine, and Rolf Christian Zimmermann (eds). 1979. *Epochen der Naturmystik.* Berlin: Erich Schmidt.

Fanger, Claire (ed.). 1998. *Conjuring Spirits. Texts and Traditions of Medieval Ritual Magic.* Phoenix Mill, U.K.: Sutton Publishing; ❏ 1998a. "Plundering the Egyptian Treasure: John the Monk's *Book of Visions* and its Relation to the Ars Notoria of Solomon." In Fanger 1998, 216–50.

Fehér, Márta. 1995. "The 17th Century Crossroads of the Mathematization of Nature." In Márta Fehér, *Changing Tools. Case Studies in the History of Scientific Methodology.* Budapest: Akadémiai, 1–26.

Festugière, A.-J. 1932. *L'idéal religieux des Grecs et l'Évangile*. Paris: J. Gabalda; ❑ 1950–1954. *La Révélation d'Hermès Trismégiste*. 4 vols. Paris: Lecoffre; ❑ 1954. *Personal Religion Among the Greeks*. Berkeley: University of California Press ❑ 1967. *Hermétisme et Mystique païenne*. Paris: Aubier-Montaigne; ❑ 1972. *Etudes de religion grecque et hellénistique*. Paris: J. Vrin.

Firpo, Luigi. 1952. "John Dee, scienziato, negromante e avventuriero." *Rinascimento* 3: 25–84.

Flint, Valerie I. J. 1991. *The Rise of Magic in Early Medieval Europe*. Princeton: Princeton University Press.

Fowden, Garth. 1986. *The Egyptian Hermes: A Historical Approach to the Late Pagan Mind*. Cambridge: Cambridge University Press.

Fowler, Alastair. 1964. *Spenser and the Numbers of Time*. London: RKP.

French, Peter J. 1972. *John Dee: The World of an Elizabethan Magus*. London: RKP.

Frick, Karl R. H. 1973. *Die Erleuchteten. Gnostisch-theosophische und alchemistisch-rosenkreuzerische Geheimgesellschaften bis zum Ende des 18. Jahrhunderts—ein Beitrag zur Geistesgeschichte der Neuzeit*. Graz: Akademische Verlag.

Fučiková, Elizka, et al. (eds.). 1997. *Rudolf II and Prague. The Court and the City*. London and Prague: Thames & Hudson and Skira.

Gansiniec, Ryszard. 1954. "Krystalomancja." *Lud* [Poland] 41: 1–83.

Garin, Eugenio. 1961. *La cultura filosofica del Rinascimento italiano: Richerche e documenti*. Firenze; ❑ 1977. "Ancora sull'ermetismo," *Revista critica di storia della filosophia* 32: 342–47; ❑ 1983. *Astrology in the Renaissance. The Zodiac of Life* (1976). London: RKP; ❑ 1988. *Ermetismo del Rinascimento*. Roma: Riuniti.

Gál, István. 1969. "Philip Sidney's Guidebook to Hungary." *Hungarian Studies in English* [Debrecen] 4: 53–64.

Gentile, Sebastiano, and Carlos Gilly (eds.). 2001. *Marsilio Ficino e il ritorno di Ermete Trismegisto*. Firenze: Bibliotheca Medicea Laurenziana and Amsterdam: Bibliotheca Philosophica Hermetica.

Giehlow, Karl. 1915. *Die Hieroglyphenkunde des Humanismus in der Allegorie der Renaissance*. Leipzig: Jahrbuch der Kunsthistorischen Sammlungen des allerhöchsten Kaiserhauses, Vol. 22.1.

Gilly, Carlos. 1988. "Iter Rosicrucianum. Auf der Suche nach unbekannten Quellen der frühen Rosenkreuzer." In Janssen (ed.) 1988, 63–90; ❑ 1995. *Cimelia Rhodostaurotica. Die Rosenkreuzer im Spiegel der zwischen 1610 und 1660 entstandenen Handschriften und Drucke*. Ed. Carlos Gilly. Amsterdam: In de Pelikaan (Bibliotheca Philosophica Hermetica).

Gilmore, Myron Piper. 1952. *The World of Humanism 1453–1517*. 2 vols. New York: Harper.

Glidden, Hope H. 1987. "Polygraphia and the Renaissance Sign: The Case of Trithemius." *Neophilologus* [Groningen] 71.2: 183–95.

Godwin, Joscelyn. 1979a. *Robert Fludd. Hermetic Philosopher and Surveyor of Two Worlds*. London: Thames and Hudson; ❑ 1979b. *Athanasius Kircher. A Renaissance Man and the Quest for Lost Knowledge*. London: Thames and Hudson.

Godwin, William. 1834. *Lives of the Necromancers: or an account of the most eminent persons in successive ages, who have claimed for themselves, or to whom has been imputed by others, the excercise of magical power.* London: Frederick J. Mason.

Goetschel, Roland. 1985. *La Kabbale.* Paris: Presses Universitaires de France.

Goldammer, Kurt. 1953. *Paracelsus. Natur und Offenbarung. (Heilkunde und Geisteswelt* V., ed. Johannes Steudel). Hannover: Oppermann; ❏ 1967. "Das Menschbild des Paracelsus zwischen theologischer Tradition, Mythologie und Naturwissenschaft." In Robert Mühlher and Johann Fischl (eds.). *Gestalt und Wirklichkeit. Festgabe für Ferdinand Weinhandl.* Berlin, 375–95; ❏ 1979. "Magie bei Paracelsus. Mit besonderer Berücksichtigung des Begriffs einer 'natürlichen Magie,' " *Studia Leibniziana.* Sonderheft 7: 30–51.

Gombrich, E. H. 1972. " 'Icones Symbolicæ': Philosophies of Symbolism and their Bearing on Art." In Gombrich. *Symbolic Images* (Studies on Renaissance Iconology, 1948–1972). London: Phaidon. 123–99.

Gorceix, B. 1970. *La Bible des Rose-Croix.* Paris: Presses Universitaires de France.

Gömöri, George. 1991. "Sir Philip Sidney's Hungarian and Polish Connections." *Oxford Slavonic Papers* 24: 23–33.

Grafton, Anthony. 1983. "Protestant Versus Prophet: Isaac Casaubon on Hermes Trismegistus." *Journal of the Warburg and Courtauld Insitutes* 46: 78–93.

Grant, R. M. 1966. *Gnosticism and Early Christianity.* New York: Columbia University Press.

Greenblatt, Stephen. 1980. *Renaissance Self-Fashining.* Chicago: University of Chicago Press.

Grese, William C. 1988. "Magic in Hellenistic Hermeticism." In Merkel and Debus 1988, 45–59.

Gundersheimer, Werner. 1963. "Erasmus, Humanism and the Christian Cabala." *Journal of the Warburg and Courtauld Institutes* 26: 40–51.

Hackett, Helen. 1996. *Virgin Mother, Maiden Queen. Elizabeth I and the Cult of the Virgin Mary.* London: Macmillan.

Håkansson, Håkan. 2001. *Seeing the Word. John Dee and Renaissance Occultism.* Lund: Lund Universitet (Ugglan, Minervaserien 2).

Halevi, Z'ev ben Shimon. 1979. *Kabbalah.* London: Thames and Hudson.

Hall, Manly P. 1972. *Man. The Grand Symbol of the Mysteries. Essays in Occult Anatomy.* Los Angeles: Philosophical Research Society.

Hanegraaff, Wouter J. 2001. "Beyond the Yates Paradigm: The Study of Western Esotericism between Counterculture and New Complexity." *Aries* 1.1: 5–38.

Hankiss Elemér. 1998. *Az emberi kaland.* Budapest: Helikon; ❏ 2001. *The Human Adventure: Understanding the Role of Fear in Western Civilization.* Budapest: Central European University Press.

Harkness, Deborah. 1996. "Shows in the Shewstone: A Theater of Alchemy and Apocalypse in the Angel Conversations of John Dee." *Renaissance Quarterly* 49: 707–37; ❏ 1997. "Managing an Experimental Household: the Dees of Mortlake." *Isis* 88: 242–62; ❏ 1999. *John Dee's Conversations with Angels. Cabala, Alchemy, and the End of Nature.* Cambridge: Cambridge University Press.

Hartman, Franz. 1891. *The Life and the Doctrines of Paracelsus.* New York: John W. Lovell.

Hauser, Arnold. 1985. *The Social History of Art* (1951). New York: Vintage Books; ❏ 1986. *Mannerism: The Crisis of the Renaissance and the Origin of Modern Art* (1964). Cambridge and London: Belknap Press of Harvard University Press.

Heilbron, J. L. 1978. "Introductory Essay to John Dee's *Propaedeumata Aphoristica* (1558 and 1568)." In Dee 1978, 1–105.

Heninger, S. K., Jr. 1974. *Touches of Sweet Harmony. Pythagorean Cosmology and Renaissance Poetics.* San Marino, Cal.: Huntington Library; ❏ 1977. *The Cosmographycal Glass. Renaissance Diagrams of the Universe.* San Marino, Cal.: Huntington Library.

Heyd, Michael. 1995. *"Be Sober and Reasonable." The Critique of Enthusiasm in the Seventeenth and Early Eighteenth Centuries.* Leiden: Brill.

Hocke, Gustav René. 1959. *Manierizmus in der Literatur. Sprach-Alchemie und esoterische Kombinazionskunst.* Hamburg: Rowohlts.

Hopper, Vincent F. 1940. "Spenser's House of Temperance." *PMLA* 55: 958–67.

Idel, Moshe. 1989. *Language, Torah, and Hermeneutics in Abraham Abulafia.* Albany: State University of New York Press (SUNY Series in Judaica).

James, Geoffrey. 1995. *Angel Magic. The Ancient Art of Summoning and Communicating with Angelic Beings.* St. Paul: Llewellyn Publications (World Religion and Magic Series).

Janssen, F. A. (ed.). 1988. *Das Erbe des Christian Rosenkreuz. Vorträge gehalten anläßlich des Amsterdamer Symposiums 18–20 November 1986.* Amsterdam: In de Pelikaan (Bibliotheca Philosophica Hermetica).

Jayne, Sears. 1985. "Introduction to Ficino's Commentary on Plato's *Symposium.*" Dallas: Spring Publications [see also Ficino 1985 among "Sources"].

Johnson, F. R. 1937. *Astronomical Thought in Renaissance England.* Baltimore: Johns Hopkins University Press.

Josten, C. H. 1965. "An Unknown Chapter in the Life of John Dee ['Praefatio Latina in Actionem Primum ex 7 . . . , 1586']." *Journal of the Warburg and Courtauld Institutes* 28: 233–57.

Jung, Carl Gustav. 1942. "Paracelsus as a Spiritual Phenomenon" In Jung 1983, 109–91. (Original publication: *Paracelsica: Zwei Vorlesungen über den Arzt und Philosophen Theophrastus.* Zürich: Rascher); ❏ 1980. *Psychology and Alchemy.* London: RKP; ❏ 1983. *Alchemical Studies.* London: RKP.

Katona, Gábor. 1998. *Vallás, szerelem, diplomácia: Sir Philip Sidney élete és művészete* [Religion, love, diplomacy: the life and art of Sir Philip Sidney]. Debrecen: Kossuth Egyetemi Kiadó (Orbis Litterarum 4).

Kaske, Carol V. 1982. "Marsilio Ficino and the Twelve Gods of the Zodiac." *Journal of the Warburg and Courtauld Institutes* 45: 195–202.

Kämmerer, E. W. 1971. *Das Lieb-Sele-Geist-Problem bei Paracelsus und einigen Autoren des 17. Jahrhunderts* (Kosmographie 3.). Wiesbaden: Steiner.

Kákosy, László. 1984. *Fény és káosz. A kopt gnósztikus kódexek* [Light and Chaos. The Coptic gnostic codici]. Budapest: Gondolat.

Keefer, Michael. 1988. "Agrippa's Dilemma: Hermetic 'Rebirth' and the Ambivalences of *De vanitate* and *De occulta philosophia.*" *Renaissance Quarterly* 41.4: 614–53; ❏ 1991. "Introduction and Notes." In Marlowe's *Doctor Faustus.* Peterborough, Ont.: Broadview Press, xi–xcii.

Kieckhefer, Richard. 1989. *Magic in the Middle Ages.* Cambridge: Cambridge University Press; ❏ 1997. *Forbidden Rites. A Necromancer's Manual of the Fifteenth Century.* Phoenix Mill, U.K.: Sutton Publishing; ❏ 1998. "The Devil's Contemplatives: The *Liber iuratus*, the *Liber visionum* and the Christian Appropriation of Jewish Occultism." In Fanger 1998, 250–66.

Klaniczay, Tibor. 1973. "A reneszánsz válsága és a manierizmus" [The crisis of the Renaissance and Mannerism]. In *A múlt nagy korszakai.* Budapest: Szépirodalmi, 226–85; ❏ 1975. *A manierizmus.* Budapest: Gondolat; ❏ 1977. *Renaissance und Manierismus. Zum Verhältnis von Gesellschafts-struktur, Poetik und Stil.* Berlin: Akademische Verlag.

Klaniczay, Tibor, Eva Kushner, and André Stegman (eds.). 1988. *L'Époque de la renaissance.* Vol. 1: *L'Avènement de l'esprit nouveau (1400–1480).* Budapest: Akadémiai (Histoire Comparée des Littératures de Langues Européennes).

Klibansky, Raymond. 1939. *The Continuity of the Platonic Tradition during the Middle Ages.* London: Warburg Institute (new edition: München, 1981).

Knoespel, Kenneth J. 1987. "The Narrative Matter of Mathematics: John Dee's Preface to the *Elements* of Euclid of Megara (1570)." *Philological Quarterly* 66: 27–46.

Koenigsberger, Dorothy. 1979. *Renaissance Man and Creative Thinking. A History of Concepts of Harmony 1400–1700.* Hassocks, Sussex: Harvester.

Konečný, Lubomír. 1998. *Rudolf II, Prague, and the World.* Prague: Artefactum.

Korkowski, Eugene. 1976. "Agrippa as Ironist." *Neophilologus* 60: 594–607.

Koyré, Alexandre. 1971. *Mystiques, Spirituels, Alchemistes du XVIe siècle allemand.* Paris: Gallimard (Collection idées 233) [= *Mistycy, spirytualiści, alchemicy niemieccy XVI wieku. K. Schwenckfeld, S. Franck, Paracelsus, W. Weigel.* Gdansk: Slowo/Obraz, 1995].

Kraye, Jill. 1988. "Moral Philosophy." In Schmitt and Skinner 1988, 301–87.

Kristeller, Paul O. 1937–1945. *Supplementum Ficinianum Marsilii Ficini Florentini philosophi Platonici opuscula inedita et dispersa.* 2 vols. Firenze: Olschki (rpt. 1973); ❏ 1943. *The Philosophy of Marsilio Ficino.* New York: Columbia University Press (rpt. Glouscester, Mass.: Smith, 1964); ❏ 1956. *Studies in Renaissance Thought and Letters.* Rome: Ed. di Storia e di Letteratura (rpt. 1969); ❏ 1961. *Renaissance Thought. The Classic, Scholastic, and Humanist Strains.* New York: Harper and Row.

Kuczyńska, Alicja. 1970. *Filozofia i teoria piękna Marsilia Ficina.* Warszawa: Wiedza Powszechna.

Kuntz, Marion. 1981. *Guillaume Postel. Prophet of the Restitution of All Things. His Life and Thought.* The Hague: Martinus Nijhoff (International Archives of the History of Ideas, 98).

Laycock, Donald. 1994. [1978]. *The Complete Enochian Dictionary. A Dictionary of the Angelic Language as Revealed to Dr. John Dee and Edward Kelly.* York Beach, Maine: Samuel Weiser.

Levin, Carole. 1994. *"The Heart and Stomach of a King": Elizabeth I and the Politics of Sex and Power.* Philadelphia: University of Pennsylvania Press.

Levin, Harry. 1969. *The Myth of the Golden Age in the Renaissance.* Bloomington: Indiana University Press.

Lindberg, David C. 1976. *Theories of Vision from Al-Kindi to Kepler.* Chicago: University of Chicago Press.

Lindberg, David C., and Robert S. Westman (eds.). 1990. *Reappraisals of the Scientific Revolution.* Cambridge: Cambridge University Press.

Linden, Stanton J. 1996. *Dark Hieroglyphics: Alchemy in English Literature from Chaucer to the Restoration.* Lexington: University Press of Kentucky.

Lloyd Jones, G. 1983. Introduction to Johannes Reuchlin's *On the Art of the Kabbalah [De arte cabalistica]* (1517). New York: Abaris Books.

Lloyd, A. C. 1995. "The Later Neoplatonists." In Armstrong 1995, 272–330.

Lovejoy, Arthur O. 1960. *The Great Chain of Being* (1936). New York: Harper and Row.

MacGregor Mathers, S. L. 1991. *The Kabbalah Unveiled. Containing Books of the Zohar* (1926). London: Arkana (The Penguin Group).

Mahé, J.-P. 1978–82. *Hermès en Haute-Egypte.* 2 vols. Quebec Presses l'Université Laval.

Magyar, László András. 1990. Introduction and notes to a selection of Agrippa's *De occulta philosophia* in Hungarian translation. Budapest: Vízöntő.

Marcel, Raymond. 1958. *Marsile Ficin.* Paris: Les belles lettres (Classiques de la humanisme 6); ❏ 1964–1970. *Marsile Ficin: théologie platonicienne de l'immortalité des âmes.* 3 vols. Tr. and ed. Raymond Marcel. Paris: Les belles lettres.

Maróth, Miklós. 1995. "Filozófia és szerelem az arab gondolkodásban" [Philosophy and love in Arab thought]. In Pál–Szőnyi–Tar (eds.). *Hermetika, mágia. Ezoterikus látásmód és művészi megismerés.* Szeged: JATEPress (Ikonológia és műértelmezés 5), 23–4.

Martin, Jörg. 1989. *Johannes Dee: 'De tuba Veneris.' Eine magische Handschrift des 16. Jahrhunderts. Edition, Übersetzung und Kommentar.* M.A. thesis. University of Bonn.

McGuire, J.E. 1977. "Neoplatonism and Active Principles: Newton and the *Corpus Hermeticum.*" In Lynn White (ed.). *Hermeticism and the Scientific Revolution.* (Papers read at the Clark Library Seminar, March, 1974). Los Angeles: UCLA, W.A. Clark Memorial Library, 93–142.

Maclean, Adam. 1988. "The Impact of the Rosicrucian Manifestos in Britain." In Janssen (ed.). 1988, 170–80.

Mebane, John S. 1989. *Renaissance Magic and the Return of the Golden Age. The Occult Tradition and Marlowe, Jonson, and Shakespeare.* Lincoln: University of Nebraska Press.

Merkel, Ingrid, and Allen G. Debus (eds.). 1988. *Hermeticism and the Renaissance. Intellectual History and the Occult in Early Modern Europe.* Washington, D.C. and London: Folger Shakespeare Library and Associated University Presses.

Merkur, Daniel. 1990. "The Study of Spiritual Alchemy: Mysticism, Goldmaking, and Esoteric Hermeneutics." *Ambix* 37: 35–45.

Metaxopoulos, Emile. 1982. "A la suite de F. A. Yates. Débats sur le role de la tradition hermétiste dans la révolution scientifique des XVIᵉ et XVIIᵉ siècles." *Revue de Synthèse* 103: 53–65.

Montgomery, John Warwick. 1973. *Cross and Crucible. Johann Valentin Andreae.* 2 vols. The Hague: Nijhoff.

Moore, Thomas. 1982. *The Planets Within. Marsilio Ficino's Astrological Psychology.* Lewisburg: Bucknell University Press.

Moran, Bruce T. 1991. *The Alchemical World of the German Court. Occult Philosophy and Chemical Medicine in the Circle of Moritz of Hessen (1572–1632).* Stuttgart: Franz Steiner Verlag.

Müller-Jahncke, Wolf-Dieter. 1979. "Von Ficino zu Agrippa. Der Magie-Begriff des Renaissance-Humanismus im Überblick." In Antoine Faivre and Rolf Christian Zimmermann (eds.) 1979, 24–51; ❏ 1985. *Astrologisch-magische Theorie und Praxis in der Heilkunde der frühen Neuzeit.* Wiesbaden and Stuttgart: Franz Steiner (Sudhoffs Archiv, Beiheft 25); ❏ 1991. "Johannes Trithemius und Heinrich Cornelius Agrippa." In Richard Auernheimer and Frank Baron, (eds.) *Johannes Trithemius. Humanismus und Magie im vorreformatorischen Deutschland.* München: Profil, 29–39.

Nauert, Charles. 1965. *Agrippa and the Crisis of Renaissance Thought.* Illinois Studies in the Social Sciences 55. Urbana: University of Illinois Press.

Neusner, Jacob, E. S. Frerichs, and P.V. McCracken Flesher (eds.). 1989. *Religion, Science, and Magic.* New York and Oxford: Oxford University Press.

Nicholl, Charles. 1980. *The Chemical Theatre.* London: RKP.

Osborn, James M. 1972. *Young Philip Sidney, 1572–1577.* New Haven: Yale University Press.

Pagel, Walter. 1958. *Paracelsus. An Introduction to Philosophical Medicine in the Era of Renaissance.* Basel and New York: S.W. Karger (2nd. rev. ed. 1982); ❏ 1985. *Religion and Neoplatonism in Renaissance Medicine.* Ed. Marianne Winder. London: Variorum Reprints.

Patrides, C. A. 1973. "Hierarchy and Order." In Philip E. Wiener (ed.). *Dictionary of the History of Ideas.* New York: Scribner's Son, 2: 434–49.

Peterse, Hans. 1995. *Jacobus Hoogstraeten gegen Johannes Reuchlin: ein Beitrag zur Geschichte des Antijudaismus im 16. Jahrhundert.* Mainz: Zabern.

Peuckert, Will-Erich. 1956. *Pansophie. Ein Versuch zur Geschichte der weissen und schwarzen Magie* (1936). Berlin: Schmidt; ❏ 1976. *Paracelsus* (1944). Hildesheim and New York: Olms.

Pickering, Chris. 1986. "The Conjuror John Dee: The Myth 1555–1608" *The Hermetic Journal* 33: 5–16.

Pingree, David. 1980. "Some Sources of the GHAYAT AL-HAKIM." *Journal of the Warburg and Courtauld Institutes* 43: 1–15. ❏ 1981. "Between *Ghaya* and *Picatrix* I: The Spanish Version." *Journal of the Warburg and Courtauld Institutes* 44: 27–56; ❏ 1986. *Picatrix: the Latin Version of the "Ghayat Al-Hakim."* Studies of the Warburg Institute 39. London: Warburg Institute.

PMLA = *Publications of the Modern Language Association.*

Porter, Roy, and Mikulas Teich (eds.). 1992. *The Sientific Revolution in National Context.* Cambridge: Cambridge University Press.

R&W = Roberts and Watson 1990.

Rabil, Albert, Jr. (ed.). 1988. *Renaissance Humanism. Foundations, Forms, and Legacy. Vol. 2: Humanism Beyond Italy.* Philadelphia: University of Pennsylvania Press.

Rabkin, Norman. 1981. *Shakespeare and the Problem of Meanings.* Chicago, University of Chicago Press.

Reeves, Marjorie. 1976. *Joachim of Fiore and the Prophetic Future.* London: SPCK.

Roberts, Julian, and Andrew G. Watson. 1990. *John Dee's Library Catalogues* (with facsimiles). London: Bibliographical Society.

Roob, Alexander. 1997. *The Hermetic Museum: Alchemy and Mysticism.* Köln and London: Taschen.

Rosa, F. ed. 1992. *L'angelo dell' immaginazione. Atti del seminario di antropologia letteraria.* Trento: Dipartimento di Scienze Filologiche e Storiche (Collana Labirinti 1).

Rosen, Edward 1970. "Was Copernicus a Hermeticist?" In Stuewer (ed.) 1970, 163–71.

Rossi, Paolo. 1975. "Hermeticism, Rationality, and the Scientific Revolution." In M. L. Righini-Bonelli and William R. Shea (eds.). *Reason, Experiment, and Mysticism in the Scientific Revolution.* New York: Science History Publications.

Røstvig, Maren-Sofie. 1969. "The Shepheards Calendar—A Structural Analysis." *Renaissance and Modern Studies* 13: 49–75.

Rowse, A. L. 1972. *The Elizabethan Renaissance. Vol. 1: The Life of the Society. Vol. 2: The Cultural Achievement.* London: Macmillan.

Russell, Daniel. 1988. "Emblems and Hieroglyphics: Some Observations on the Beginnings and Nature of Emblematic Forms." *Emblematica* 1: 227–43.

Saitta, Giuseppe. 1943. *Marsilio Ficino e la filosofia dell'umanesimo.* Firenze: Le Monnier.

Scazzoso, Piero. 1967. *Ricerche sulla struttura del linguaggio dello Pseudo-Dionigi. Introduzzione alla lettura delle opere pseudo-dionisiane.* Milano: Soc. Ed. Vita e Pensiero.

Schick, Hans. 1980. *Die geheime Geschichte der Rosenkreuzer* (1942). Schwarzenburg: Ansata Verlag (Documenta Rosicruciana 1).

Schipperges, H. 1962. "Einflüsse arabischer Medizin auf die Mikrokosmosliteratur des 12. Jahrhunderts." *Miscellaneae Mediaevalia* 1962.1: 139–42.

Schmidt-Biggemann, Wilhelm. 1983. *Topica universalis: Eine Modellgeschichte humanistischer und barocker Wissenschaft.* Hamburg: Meiner (Paradeigmata 1); ❏ 1998. *Philosophica perennis. Historische Umrisse abendlandischer Spiritualität in Antike, Mittelalter und Früher Neuzeit.* Frankfurt: Suhrkamp.

Schmitt, Charles B. 1978. "Reappraisals in Renaissance Science," *History of Science* 16: 200-14.

Schmitt, Charles B., et al (eds.). 1988. *The Cambridge History of Renaissance Philosophy.* Cambridge: Cambridge University Press.

Scholem, Gershom G. 1974. *Major Trends in Jewish Mysticism* (1941, 1946). New York: Schocken Books; ❏ 1980. *La Kabbala et sa symbolique.* Paris: Payot.

Schultheisz, Emil, and Tardy Lajos. 1972. "The Contacts of the Two Dees and Sir Philip Sidney with Hungarian Physicians." *Orvostörténeti Közlemények,* O Suppl. 6: 97–111.

Secret, François. 1979. "Palingenesis, Alchemy and Metempsychosis in Renaissance Medicine." *Ambix* 26: 81–92; ❏ 1985. *Les Kabbalistes chrétiens de la renaissance* (1964). Milan: Arché (Bibliotheque de l'unicorne, ser. fr. 30); ❏ 1990. "Alchimie, palingénésie et metempsychose chez Guillaume Postel." *Chrysopoeia* 3: 3–62.

Seligmann, Kurt. 1971. *Magic, Supernaturalism and Religion* (1948). New York: Pantheon Books.

Sherman, William H. 1995. *The Politics of Reading and Writing in the English Renaissance.* Amherst: University of Massachusetts Press.

Shumaker, Wayne. 1982. *Renaissance Curiosa.* New York: State University of New York, Center for Medieval and Early Renaissance Studies (Medieval and Renaissance Texts & Studies 8).

Smith, Charlotte Fell. 1909. *John Dee: 1527-1608.* London: Constable.

Spence, Lewis. 1960. *An Encyclopedia of Occultism.* New York: University Books.

Spitz, Lewis W. 1963. *The Religious Renaissance of the German Humanists.* Cambridge: Harvard University Press.

Stillman, John M. 1960. *The Story of Alchemy and Early Chemistry* (1924). New York: Dover.

Stuewer, R. H. (ed.). 1970. *Historical and Philosophical Perspectives of Science.* Minneapolis: University of Minnesota Press.

Sudhoff, Karl. 1958. *Bibliographia Paracelsica [1527–1893].* Graz: Akademische Druck und Verlagsanstalt.

Sviták, Jan. 1980–1989. *Hermetic Philosophy in Renaissance Prague: 1. John Dee in Bohemia, 2. Sir Edward Kelley, 3. Elizabeth Johanna Weston.* Chico, Cal.: Author's Edition (translated into Czech and published in Prague, 1990–1993).

Szabó, Árpád, and Zoltán Kádár. 1984. *Antik természettudomány* [Natural Science in the Antiquity]. Budapest: Gondolat.

Szathmáry, László. 1986. *Magyar alkémisták* [Hungarian alchemists] (1928) Ed. Gazda István. Intro. Iván Fónagy and Móra László. Budapest: Könyvértékesítő Vállalat (Tudománytár reprintek).

Szczucki, Lech. 1980. *Két XVI. századi eretnek gondolkodó (Jacobus Palaeologus és Christian Francken)* [Two sixteenth-century heretics: Palaeologus and Francken]. Budapest: Akadémiai (Humanizmus és reformáció 9).

Szőnyi, György Endre. 1978. *Titkos tudományok és babonák. A 15–17. század művelődéstörténetének kérdéseihez* [Secret sciences and superstitions in the fifteenth through seventeenth centuries]. Budapest: Magvető (Gyorsuló idő); ❏ 1980. "John Dee an Elizabethan Magus and his Links with Central Europe." *Hungarian Studies in English* [Debrecen] 13: 71–85; ❏ 1984. " 'O worke diuine': The Iconography and Intellectual

Background of Almas's House in Spenser's *The Faerie Queene*." In Tibor Fabiny (ed.). *Shakespeare and the Emblem*. Szeged: JATE (Papers in English and American Studies 3), 353–94; ❏ 1990. "John Dee," "Hermeticism." In A. C. Hamilton, general editor, *The Spenser Encyclopedia*. Toronto: University of Toronto Press, 211, 358–59; ❏ 1991. "Traditions of Magic: Faust and John Dee at European Courts and Universities." *Cauda Pavonis* 10.3: 1–8; ❏ 1995. "The Social and Ideological Context of the Magician in Jacobean Drama." In James Hogg (ed.). *Jacobean Drama as Social Criticism*. New York and Salzburg: The Edwin Mellen Press, 107–25; ❏ 1997. "A matematika vagy a költészet tanít az angyalok nyelvére? John Dee és a *lingua universalis*" [Is it mathematics or poetry that teaches the language of the angles? John Dee and the *lingua universalis*]. In Balázs Mihály (ed.). *Művelődési törekvések a korai újkorban. Tanulmányok Keserű Bálint tiszteletére*. Szeged, 1997 (Adattár XVI-XVIII. századi szellemi mozgalmaink történetéhez 35), 575–91; ❏ 1998. *'Exaltatio' és hatalom. Keresztény mágia és okkult szimbolizmus egy angol mágus műveiben* [*Exaltatio* and Power: Christian magic and occult symbolism in the works of an English magus]. Szeged: JATEPress (Ikonológia és műértelmezés 7); ❏ 2001. "Ficino's Talismanic Magic and John Dee's Hieroglyphic Monad." *Cauda Pavonis* 20.1: 1–11; ❏ 2002. "The Language of the Other: John Dee's Experiments with Angelic Conversations." In Ina Schabert (ed.), *Imaginationen des Anderen im 16. Und 17. Jahrhundert*. Wolfenbüttel: Herzog August Bibliothek (Wolfenbüttler Forschungen 97), 73–98; ❏ 2004. *Gli angeli di John Dee*. Roma: Tre Editori; ❏ 200?. "Ars Sintrillia, Scrying, and the Universal Language. Paracelsian and Other Contexts for John Dee's Angel Magic." In Stephen Clucas (ed.). *John Dee: Interdisciplinary Approaches*. Dordrecht: Kluwer Academic Publishers [forthcoming].

Szulakowska, Urszula. 1995. "Geometry and Optics in Renaissance Alchemical Illustration: John Dee, Robert Fludd, and Michael Maier." *Cauda Pavonis* 14.1: 1–12; ❏ 1999. "Paracelsian Medicine in John Dee's Alchemical Diaries." *Cauda Pavonis* 18.1–2: 26–31; ❏ 2000. *The Alchemy of Light. Geometry and Optics in Late Renaissance Alchemical Illustration*. Leiden: Brill (Symbola et Emblemata 10).

Tambiah, S. J. 1968. "The Magical Power of Words." *Man* 3: 175–208.

Tannier, Bernard. 1984. "Une nouvelle interprétation de la 'philosophie occulte' à la Renaissance: L'oeuvre de Frances A. Yates," *Aries* 2: 15–33.

Tarabochia-Canavero, Alessandra. 1977. "Il 'De triplici vita' di Marsilio Ficino," *Rivista di filosofia neo-scolastica* 69.4: 697–717; ❏ 1997. "Tra ermetismo e neoplatonismo: l'immagina della *natura magia* in Marsilio Ficino." In Linos G. Benakis (ed.). *Néoplatonisme et philosophie médiévale*. Brepols: Société Internationale pour l'Étude de la Philosophie Médiévale. 273–90.

Taylor, E.G.R. 1930. *Tudor Geography*. London: Methuen.

Thomas, Keith. 1971. *Religion and the Decline of Magic. Studies in Popular Beliefs in sixteenth and seventeenth-century England*. London: Weidenfeld and Nicholson (rpt. London: Penguin University Paperbacks, 1973).

Thorndike, Lynn. 1923–1958. *History of Magic and Experimental Science*. 8 vols. New York: Columbia University Press.

Tillyard, E. M. W. 1946. *The Elizabethan World Picture*. London: Macmillan.

Trevor-Roper, Hugh. 1976. *Princes and Artists. Patronage and Ideology at Four Habsburg Courts, 1517–1633*. London: Thames and Hudson.

Trinkaus, Charles. 1970. *In Our Image and Likeness. Humanity and Divinity in Italian Renaissance Thought* (2 vols.). Chicago and London: University of Chicago Press.

Vasoli, Cesare. 1974. *Profezia e ragiona: studi sulla cultura del Cinquecento e del Seicento.* Napoli: Morano; ❏ 1976. *Umanesimo e rinascimento.* Palermo: Palumbo.

Vasoli, Cesare (ed.). 1968. *Studi sulla cultura del Rinascimento.* Manduria: Lacaita; ❏ 1976. *Magia e scienza nella civilta umanistica.* Bologna: Il Mulino; ❏ 1980. *La cultura delle corti.* Bologna: Cappelli; ❏ 1994. *Italia e Ungheria all'epoca dell'umanesimo corviniano.* Firenze: Olschki; ❏ 1996. *Civitas mundi: studi sulla cultura del Cinquecento.* Roma: Edizioni di storia e letteratura.

Vickers, Brian. 1979. "Frances Yates and the Writing of History," *Journal of Modern History* 51: 287–316; ❏ 1984. "Analogy Versus Identity: the Rejection of Occult Symbolism, 1580–1680." In Brian Vickers (ed.) 1984, 95–165.

Vickers, Brian (ed.). 1984. *Occult and Scientific Mentalities in the Renaissance.* Cambridge: Cambridge University Press.

Volkmann, Ludwig. 1962. *Bilderschriften der Renaissance, Hieroglyphik und Emblematik in ihren Beziehungen und Fortwirkungen* (1923). Nieuwkoop: De Graaf.

Völker, Walther. 1958. *Kontemplazion und Ekstase bei Pseudo-Dionysius Areopagita.* Wiesbaden: Steiner.

Vurm, Robert B. 1997. *Rudolf II and His Prague: Mysteries and Curiosities of Rudolfine Prague between 1550–1650.* Prague: Author's Publication.

Waite, A. E. 1888. *Lives of Alchemistical Philosophers . . . and some account of the spiritual chemistry.* London: Redway; ❏ 1961. *The Book of Ceremonial Magic. The secret tradition of Goetia, including the rites and mysteries of goetic theurgy, sorcery and infernal necromancy* (1911). Secaucus, N.J.: Citadel Press.

Walker, D. P. 1958. *Spiritual and Demonic Magic from Ficino to Campanella.* London: Warburg Institute; ❏ 1958a. "The Astral Body in Renaissance Medicine." *Journal of the Warburg and Courtauld Institutes* 21: 119–33; ❏ 1972. *The Ancient Theology. Studies in Christian Platonism from the Fifteenth to the Eighteenth Centuries.* London: Duckworth.

Wallis Budge, E. A. 1961. *Amulets and Talismans.* New York: University Books.

Walton, Michael T. 1976. "John Dee's *Monas Hieroglyphica*: Geometrical Cabala." *Ambix* 23: 116–23.

Webster, Charles. 1976. *The Great Instauration. Science, Medicine and Reform 1626–1660.* London; ❏ 1982. *From Paracelsus to Newton. Magic and the Making of Modern Science.* Cambridge: Cambridge University Press.

Weeks, Andrew. 1997. *Paracelsus: Speculative Theory and the Crisis of the Early Reformation.* Albany: State University of New York Press (SUNY Series in Western Esoteric Traditions).

Weimann, Karl-Heinz. 1963. *Paracelsus Bibliographie 1932–1960* (Kosmographie 2). Wiesbaden.

Westman, Robert S. 1977. "Magical Reform and Astronomical Reform: The Yates Thesis Reconsidered." In Lynn White (ed.). *Hermeticism and the Scientific Revolution* (Papers read at the Clark Library Seminar, March, 1974). Los Angeles: UCLA, W. A. Clark Memorial Library.

Whitby, C. L. 1985. "John Dee and Renaissance Scrying." *Bulletin of the Society for Renaissance Studies* 3.2: 25–36; ❏ 1988. *John Dee's Actions with Spirits.* 2 vols. New York: Garland (reprint of University of Birmingham, Ph.D. Dissertation, 1981).

Wilding, Michael. 1999a. "Edward Kelly: A Life." *Cauda Pavonis* 18.1–2: 1–26; ❏ 1999b. *Raising Spirits, Making Gold and Swapping Wives: The Adventures of Dr John Dee and Sir Edward Kelly.* Sidney: Abbott Bentley (Nottingham: Shoestring Press).

Williams, Ann (ed.). 1980. *Prophecy and Millenarianism. Essays in Honour of Marjorie Reeves.* London: Longman.

Wind, Edgar. 1968. *Pagan Mysteries in the Renaissance.* London: Faber and Faber.

Wittkower, Rudolf. 1977. *Allegory and the Migration of Symbols.* London: Thames and Hudson.

Woolley, Benjamin. 2001. *The Queen's Conjurer. The Science and Magic of Dr. John Dee, Advison to Queen Elizabeth I.* New York: Henry Holt.

Yates, Frances A. 1964. *Giordano Bruno and the Hermetic Tradition.* London and Chicago: RKP / University of Chicago Press; ❏ 1968. "The Hermetic Tradition in Renaissance Science." In Charles S. Singleton (ed.). *Art, Science, and History in the Renaissance.* Baltimore: Johns Hopkins University Press; ❏ 1969. *The Theatre of the World.* London: RKP; ❏ 1972. *The Rosicrucian Enlightenment.* London: RKP; ❏ 1975. *Astraea. The Imperial Theme in the Sixteenth Century.* London: RKP; ❏ 1978. *Majesty and Magic in Shakespeare's Last Plays.* Boulder: Shambala (originally published as *Shakespeare's Last Plays: A New Approach.* London: Routledge, 1975); ❏ 1979. *The Occult Philosophy in the Elizabethan Age.* London: RKP.

Yewbrey, Graham. 1981. *John Dee and the "Sidney Group": Cosmopolitics and Protestant "Activism" in the 1570's.* University of Hull, unpublished Ph.D. thesis.

Zadrobílek, Vladislav. 1997. *Opus magnum. The Book of Sacred Geometry, Alchemy, Magic, Astrology, the Kabbala, and Secret Societies in Bohemia.* Prague: Trigon.

Zambelli, Paola. 1970. "Cornelio Agrippa, Erasmo e la teologia umanistica." *Rinascimento* [2nd Series] 10: 29–88; ❏ 1972. "Le problème de la magie naturelle à la Renaissance." In *Magia, astrologia e religione nel Rinascimento*, Convegno polacco-italiano, Varsavia 1972. Warsaw: Ossolineum, 48–82; ❏ 1976. "Magic and Radical Reformation in Agrippa of Nettesheim." *Journal of the Warburg and Courtauld Institutes* 39: 88–103.

Zanier, Giancarlo. 1977. *La medicina astrologica e sua teoria: Marsilio Ficino e i suoi critici contemporanei.* Roma: Edizioni dell'Ateneo.

Zantuan, Konstanty. 1968. "Olbracht Łaski in Elizabethan England," *The Polish Review* (Spring): 3–22.

Żelewski, R. 1973. "Olbracht Łaski." In *Polski Słownik Biograficzny.* Warszawa: PIW, 18: 246–50.

Zeller, W. 1979. "Naturmystik und spiritualistische Theologie bei Valentin Weigel." In Faivre and Zimmermann 1979, 105–24.

Zika, Charles. 1976. "Reuchlin's *De verbo mirifico* and the Magic Debate of the Late Fifteenth Century." *Journal of the Warburg and Courtauld Institutes* 39; ❏ 1976–1977. "Reuchlin and Erasmus: Humanism and Occult Philosophy." *The Journal of Religious History* 9: 242–43.

Zimmermann, Volker (ed.). 1995. *Paracelsus. Das Werk—Die Rezeption*. Stuttgart: Franz Steiner.

Zins, Henryk. 1970. "English Trade with Russia and the Problem of Narva in the Mid-Sixteenth Century." *Laurentian University Review* 2.3: 3–22; ❏ 1974. *Polska w oczach anglików XIV–XVI w.* Warszawa: PIW.

Index

353

Made in the USA
Lexington, KY
02 December 2013